C#

fast&easy.
web development

C#

fast&easy
web development

Aneesha Bakharia

Premier
Press

Premier
Press

Publisher: Stacy L. Hiquet

Marketing Manager: Heather Buzzingham

Managing Editor: Sandy Doell

Senior Acquisitions Editor: Emi Smith

Project Editor: Heather Talbot

Editorial Assistant: Margaret Bauer

Technical Reviewer: Greg Perry

Copy Editor: Kris Simmons

Interior Layout: Shawn Morningstar

Cover Design: Phil Velikan

Indexer: Kelly Talbot

Proofreader: Jenny Davidson

ISBN: 1-931841-05-5

Library of Congress Catalog Card Number: 2001096213

Printed in the United States of America

02 03 04 05 06 RI 10 9 8 7 6 5 4 3 2

This book is dedicated to my family.

Without their support and encouragement this book would not have been completed.

Acknowledgments

I would like to thank:

- My Grandmother, Rada, for inspiring me to achieve the impossible.

- My parents, Abdulah and Juleka, for funding my early computing ventures.

- Emi Smith (Senior Acquisitions Editor), for letting me write a book on cutting-edge Web technology. I would not have been able to complete this book without her patience, dedication, and encouragement every step of the way.

- Heather Talbot (Project Editor), for guiding this book through production over a lengthy period of time. Heather's dedication, experience, and insightful suggestions have immensely improved the final product.

- Kris Simmons (Copy Editor) for fine-tuning the words of a programmer.

- Greg Perry (Technical Editor) for his thorough review, high-level direction, and advice. This book is much more useful to C# programmers as a result.

- Jenny Davidson (Proofreader) for her close attention to detail.

- My family (Kulsum, Hajira, Shaida, Julie, Ebrahem, Rashid, Cassim, Anne, and Judy) for their continuous support.

- My cousins, Zaeem, Celine, and Tess for making life so much fun.

- Heather Buzzingham (Marketing Manager), Kelly Talbot (Indexer), and Shawn Morningstar (Layout Technician) for magically transforming my words and pictures into a book.

- Scott Guthrie for always being approachable and sending beta versions of .NET to an Australian-based author.

- Tracy Williams for starting my writing career.

- Peter Fitzsimon from Microsoft Australia for sending me the copy of the Release Candidate that I used to complete this book.

- Microsoft for making Web development much easier.

- Madonna for making excellent music.

- You for purchasing this book.

About the Author

Aneesha Bakharia is a Web Developer and author. She is fluent in C++, Java, JavaScript, ASP, JSP, HTML, XML, and Visual Basic. Aneesha specializes in creating dynamic database-driven Web sites. She has a Bachelor of Engineering degree in Microelectronic Engineering and has various postgraduate qualifications in multimedia, online course development, and Web design. In her spare time, she is a keen Madonna fan. She can be reached via e-mail at bakharia@squirrel.com.au.

Contents at a Glance

Contents

Introduction

Welcome to C# Fast & Easy Web Development!

It has been a pleasure to be the author of this visual introduction to building dynamic Web sites with ASP.NET and C#. ASP.NET has totally revolutionized Web development and made everything easier to do. This has allowed me to cover topics that I never would have thought possible at a beginner level. Advanced database integration, input field validation, data caching, file uploading, Web Services, sending email messages, handling exceptions and designing complex user interfaces are just a few topics that I was able to cover in a visual beginner level book. It certainly is a good time to be a beginner. I hope you have as much fun learning ASP.NET and C# as I did writing this book.

Who Should Read This Book?

This book is designed to rapidly bring a beginner up to speed with C# and ASP.NET. The visual step-by-step approach of this book will be appreciated by readers with no prior programming experience. C# and ASP.NET are both taught from first principles in an easy and intuitive manner. A basic understanding of HTML is all you need.

Even if you are an experienced C++, Java, Visual Basic, PHP, JSP, ColdFusion, or ASP developer you will find the practical examples and simple explanations the fastest way to learn about exciting new technologies including C#, ASP.NET, ADO.NET, and Web Services.

What You Need to Get Started

The source code for this book is available for download from http://www.premierpressbooks.com/downloads.asp.

To run the code samples in this book you need:

- Windows 2000 or Windows XP Professional

- Internet Information Services (IIS)

- ASP.NET (http://www.asp.net/download.aspx)

- SQL Server 2000 or Access 2000/XP

- Visual Studio.NET (optional)

All the examples in this book have been tested in ASP.NET Version 1. If errors are, however, found, errata will be posted on the Web site.

Web Development will never be the same. Let the fun begin...

Conventions Used in This Book

You will find several special elements that will make using this book easier.

TIP
Tips tell you about new and faster ways to accomplish a goal.

NOTE
Notes delve into background information regarding a given topic.

CAUTION
Cautions warn about pitfalls and glitches in an application or procedure.

1

.NET, C#, and ASP.NET

.NET is the future of application development. It not only facilitates the creation of Windows, Web, and component-based applications but also provides the architecture for software to be delivered as a service. At the heart of .NET is a new object-oriented programming language called C#. C# has the power and flexibility required to build the next generation of applications. In this chapter, you'll discover:

- The .NET framework
- The Common Language Runtime (CLR)
- C#
- ASP.NET

What Is .NET?

.NET improves the way applications are built today. It simplifies the manner in which you develop and deploy both Web and Windows-based applications. .NET is also ambitious because it provides a blueprint for the seamless integration of distributed applications running on disparate platforms.

.NET has the following advantages:

- .NET treats all languages equally. You can program the .NET application in VB.NET, JScript.NET, and C#.NET. Many other languages, such as Eiffel, Haskell, Cobol, and Perl, are available through third-party vendors. These languages can easily inherit classes from other languages. An application built in VB.NET, for example, can inherit from a C# class. The Common Language Runtime (CLR), which is responsible for program execution, defines a common typing system that all languages must adhere to. You can select the language that meets your development requirements.

- .NET provides a rich set of base classes. You can access these classes from any language.

- .NET incorporates key technologies such as ASP.NET (Web), Windows forms (Windows GUI), and ADO.NET (data access).

- .NET bridges the gap between developing Windows and Web applications. You can now develop Web applications as you do Windows GUI applications.

- .NET introduces Web services. This technology exposes application logic over the Internet and allows other applications to easily reuse the exposed functionality. Web services are based upon industry standards such as XML, HTTP, and Simple Object Access Protocol (SOAP).

- .NET simplifies application deployment. There is no longer a need to register components. Application deployment simply involves copying the files to a new computer. You can even run different versions of the same component. Applications that use older versions of components won't break—the end of DLL hell.

The Common Language Runtime

The Common Language Runtime manages program execution. .NET programs compile not into machine language for a specific machine, but into a special pseudo-code called *Microsoft Intermediate Language* (*MSIL*). Any type of computer that has CLR installed can run programs compiled into MSIL because CLR converts the pseudo-code to the specific machine's language. The upshot is that vendors only have to write one compiler per language: a compiler that translates the language to MSIL. Any .NET-based computer will then be able to run it. This removes the burden from compiler vendors who in the past had to write a different version of each language's compiler for each kind of computer that would run it. The CLR is responsible for converting the MSIL into native code using a Just-In-Time (JIT) compiler. The CLR simplifies development by taking care of memory management and exception handling. The CLR also provides debugging and profiling services to all .NET languages.

NOTE

Code executed by the CLR is known as managed code.

Introducing C#

C# is a language specifically designed to build .NET applications. In many respects, Microsoft has created the perfect programming language. C# incorporates the best features of other popular programming languages, such as C, C++, Java, and Visual Basic. The result is a super language that can create any type of application. C# has an elegant syntax just like Java. It offers programming power that was previously only available in C++. You can use Rapid Application Development (RAD) tools to build C# applications. In fact, it is just as easy to develop a GUI-based Windows application in C# as it is in Visual Basic.

- C# is simple. C, C++, and Java programmers will feel comfortable with the C# language syntax.

- C# is object-oriented. C# supports encapsulation, inheritance, and polymorphism. These concepts make it easier to structure and modify an application. Chapter 7, "Object-Oriented Programming," will introduce these concepts.

- C# is modern. C# was designed from scratch by Microsoft to include built-in support for authoring software components. C# supports exception handling and garbage collection (automatic memory management), and it is type safe.

Introducing ASP.NET

Building and deploying Web applications have never been easier. ASP.NET brings the following key innovations to Web development:

- ASP.NET simplifies application development. ASP.NET uses an event-driven programming model that is similar to the way Visual Basic currently works. Basically, code that resides on the server can respond to events that occur with a Web browser.

- ASP.NET lets you separate code and content. This enables you to change programming logic without affecting the layout of a site, and vice versa.

- You can use RAD tools such as VisualStudio.NET to develop Web applications.

- You can program ASP.NET in any .NET language. You can use VB.NET, JScript.NET, and C#. This book focuses on using C# to program ASP.NET, but you can easily obtain the functionality using any of the other .NET languages. C# does have the advantage of being a full-blown object-oriented language that helps you model robust applications.

- ASP.NET simplifies application configuration. A centralized XML file is responsible for the storage of Web application settings.

- ASP.NET simplifies application deployment. You just need to copy your files to another server to install your Web application. You no longer have to install components and reboot the server.

- ASP.NET supports multiple devices. ASP.NET delivers a rich user interface to Internet Explorer clients. Other browsers that do not support the level of interactivity Internet Explorer implements will just receive HTML 3.2-compliant pages. ASP handles this automatically. It is also possible to target mobile devices.

- ASP.NET offers improved application tolerance. Processes that fail are automatically restarted.

- ASP.NET offers improved scalability. You can cache ASP.NET applications to improve performance. You can also store session state in either a special state server or an SQL database.

- ASP.NET has enhanced functionality. It is possible to send email, upload files, generate images, and password-protect your Web site using built-in functionality.

Getting Started

I bet that you are eager to get started building ASP.NET applications in C# after reading about all those great advantages. The following sections will help you set up all the software that the examples in this book require. You will even get to build a simple page in C# that displays the current date and time.

Installing Internet Information Server

Internet Information Server (IIS) is the required Web server for running ASP.NET applications. IIS comes with Windows 2000 and Windows XP Professional, but is not always installed by default. The instructions that follow will guide you through the process of finding out whether IIS is installed and installing it if it is not already installed.

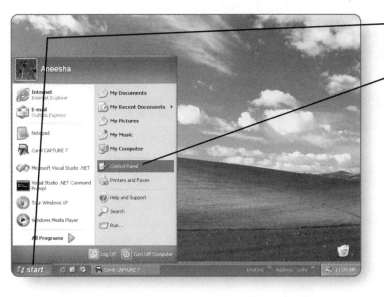

1. Click on Start. The Start menu will appear.

2. Click on Control Panel. The Control Panel window will open.

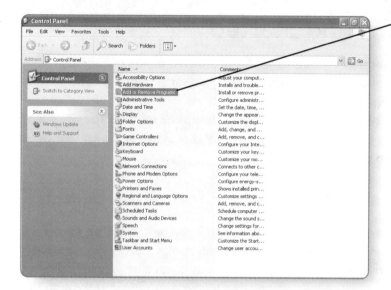

3. Double-click on Add or Remove Programs. The Add or Remove Programs window will open.

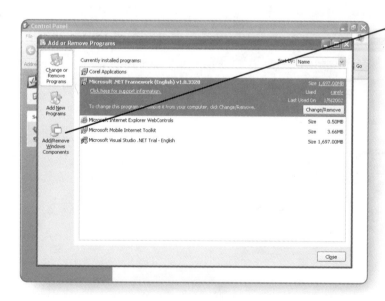

4. Click on Add/Remove Windows Components. The Windows Components Wizard window will open.

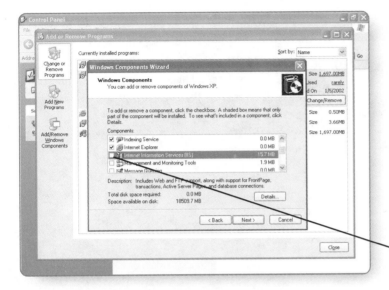

NOTE

If the checkbox next to Internet Information Server is not checked, IIS is not installed. Follow steps 5 through 20 to install IIS. If the checkbox is checked, IIS is already installed and you can skip steps 5 through 10.

5. Click inside the checkbox next to Internet Information Services. The box will be checked.

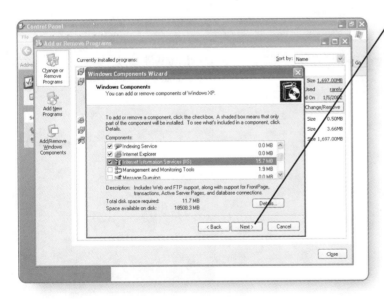

6. Click on Next. The installation of IIS will begin. You will be asked to insert the Windows XP CD into your CD-ROM drive.

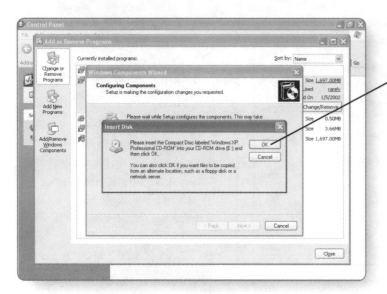

7. Insert the Windows XP CD into your CD drive.

8. Click on OK. The installation of IIS will continue.

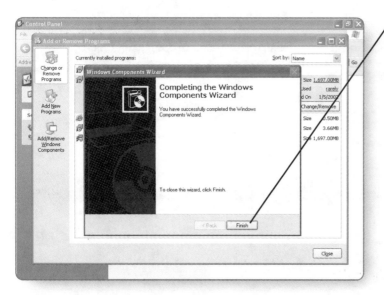

9. Click on Finish. The Windows Component Wizard window will close.

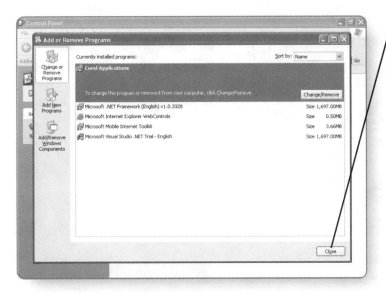

10. Click on Close. The Add or Remove Program window will close.

We will now determine the name of your computer, which will be required when you access your local IIS Web server through a Web browser.

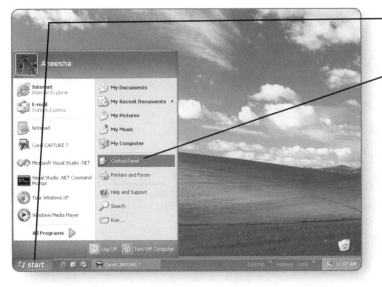

11. Click on Start. The Start menu will appear.

12. Click on Control Panel. The Control Panel window will open.

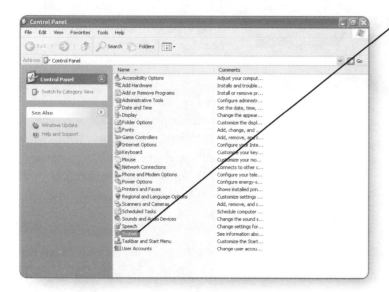

13. Double-click on System. The System Properties window will open.

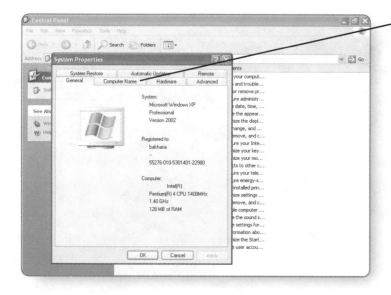

14. Click on the Computer Name tab. The contents of the tab will be displayed.

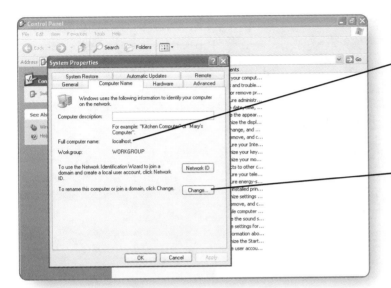

NOTE

The name of your computer will be displayed. Write down the name for future reference.

15. Click on Change if you would like to change the name of your computer. The computer Name Change window will open.

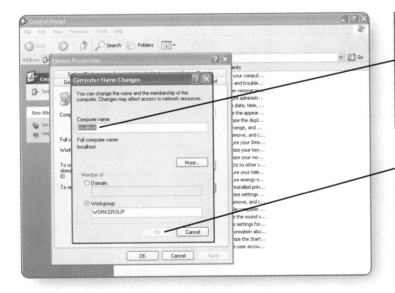

NOTE

You can enter a new name for your computer, if you like. We'll keep ours as localhost.

16. Click on OK. The Computer Name Change window will close.

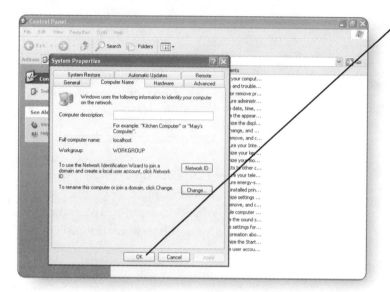

17. Click on OK. The System Properties window will close.

18. Open a Web browser. Internet Explorer 6 is the recommended browser.

19. Type **http://** followed by the name of your computer and press the Enter key. The Windows XP Professional IIS default start page will be displayed. This page indicates that your Web server is up and running.

NOTE

You can customize the home page that is displayed when you enter http://localhost as a URL. You need to create a Web page and save it as either default.asp or index.htm within the c:\inetpub\ wwwroot folder.

TIP

Localhost will be used as the Web server name throughout this book. Please substitute localhost with the name of your computer (if IIS is running locally) or Web server.

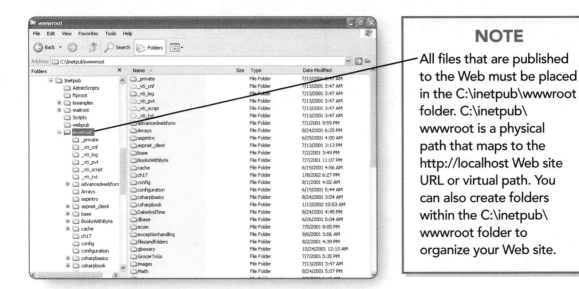

NOTE

All files that are published to the Web must be placed in the C:\inetpub\wwwroot folder. C:\inetpub\ wwwroot is a physical path that maps to the http://localhost Web site URL or virtual path. You can also create folders within the C:\inetpub\ wwwroot folder to organize your Web site.

Creating IIS Virtual Directories and Applications

Any folder on your server can be Web-enabled by creating a virtual directory. As an example, the folder C:\csharpbook can be accessed through the http://localhost/csharpbook URL by making C:\csharpbook a virtual directory. A folder that resides within the Web root (C:\inetpub\wwwroot) can also be made into a separate ASP.NET application. This allows custom read, write, and directory browsing privileges to be set. Separate ASP.NET configurations can also be used.

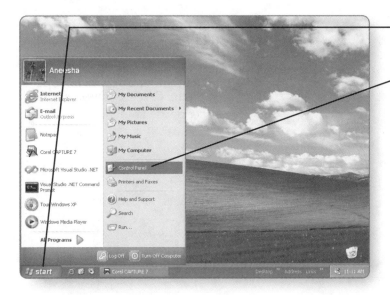

1. Click on Start. The Start menu will appear.

2. Click on Control Panel. The Control Panel window will open.

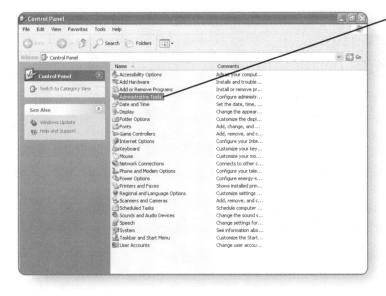

3. Double-click on Administrative Tools. The Administrative Tools window will open.

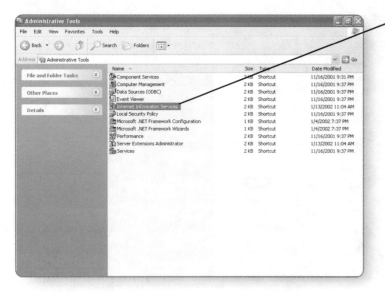

4. Double-click on Internet Information Services. The Internet Information Services Management Console will open.

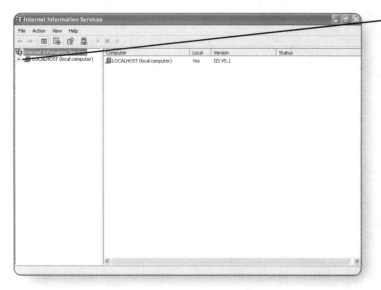

5. Click on the **+** next to the name of the server. The node will expand.

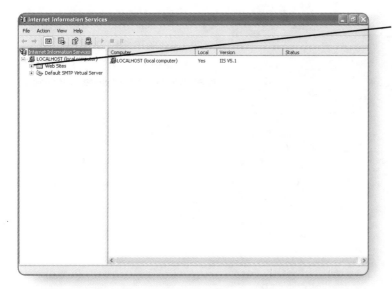

6. Click on the **+** next to Web Sites. The node will expand.

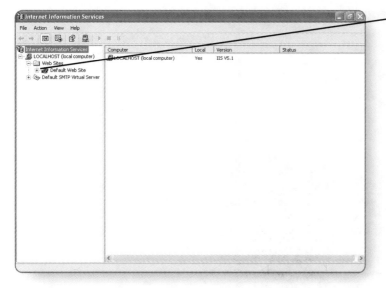

7. Click on the **+** next to Default Web Site. The node will expand. All of the folders within the Web root will be displayed.

8. Right-click on the folder that must be made into a virtual directory or ASP.NET application. A menu will be displayed.

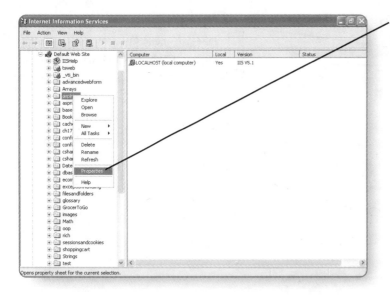

9. Click on Properties. The Properties window will open.

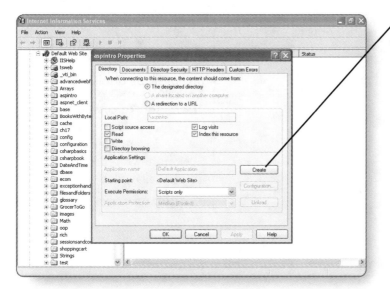

10. Click on Create. The folder will become a Web application.

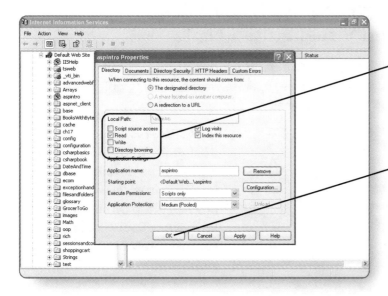

NOTE

You can also allow Web site visitors to have write and directory browsing privileges.

11. Click on OK. The Properties window will close.

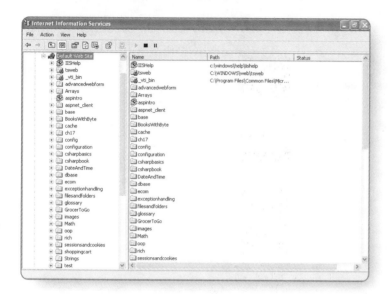

TIP

In Chapter 16, "Configuring and Deploying Web Applications," you will learn how to customize the configuration of an ASP.NET application by using the web.config and global.asax files.

Installing .NET, ASP.NET, and Visual Studio.NET

All the examples in this book require that ASP.NET be installed. The three separate ways for you to obtain and install ASP.NET are outlined as follows:

1. ASP.NET is included in the .NET Framework Redistributable which can be downloaded for free from http://www.asp.net/download/aspx. The .NET Framework Redistributable is approximately 21MB in size and includes everything you need to get started with ASP.NET, C#, ADO.NET, and Web Services. Documentation is not included but can be accessed from the Web. This download is recommended to get you started quickly.

2. The .NET Framework SDK is approximately 131MB. You can download the .NET Framework from http://www.asp.net/download.aspx. It includes command line tools, documentation, and tutorials. This download includes everything you need to develop all types of .NET applications.

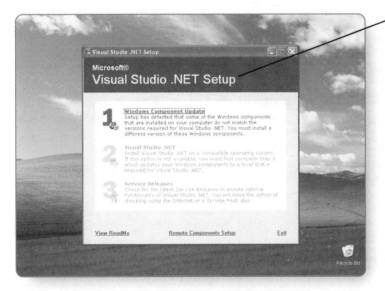

3. You can also purchase Visual Studio.NET which is a powerful development environment that supports C# and VB.NET development. Visual Studio.NET has an excellent feature set that will improve your productivity tremendously. It is not free, but is well worth the money if you are serious about moving to .NET.

NOTE
The entire .NET Framework SDK is included with VS.NET.

Testing C# and ASP.NET

We will now create a simple ASP.NET page in C# that prints the current date and time. This will serve as your first page as well as help you test your installation.

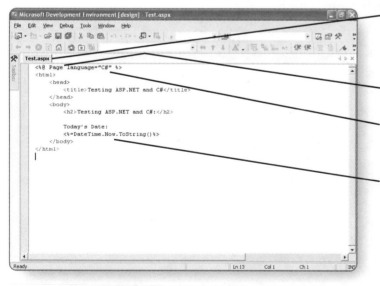

1. Create a new page with an .aspx extension. All ASP.NET code must have an .aspx extension.

2. Insert a Page directive.

3. Set the language attribute to C#.

4. Type **<%=DateTime.Now. ToString()%>**. This code will print the current date and time to the page. The <%= and the %> delimiters print data to the page while DateTime.Now.ToString() returns the current date and time as string.

NOTE

All the code in this book was written with VS.NET but any text editor can also be used. Other popular editors include the following:

- Notepad

- ASP Express (http://aspexpress.com)

- Sharp Develop (http://www.icsharpcode.net/OpenSource/SD/)

- Antechinus C# Programming Editor (http://www.c-point.com/csharp.htm)

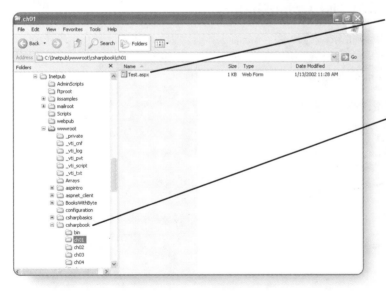

5. Save the file to your Web root (C:\inetpub\wwwroot).

NOTE

All the source code for this book can be downloaded from http://www.premier pressbooks.com/downloa ds.asp. You will need to copy the code to your Web root folder (C:\inetpub\wwwroot).

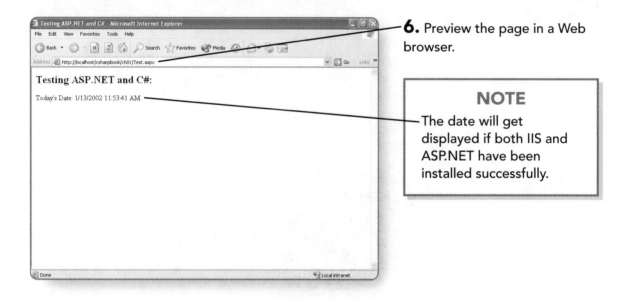

6. Preview the page in a Web browser.

NOTE

The date will get displayed if both IIS and ASP.NET have been installed successfully.

2

Introducing ASP.NET

ASP.NET is not just an upgrade to ASP! In many respects, it is brand new technology developed to simplify the design and development of database-driven Web sites. ASP.NET delivers improved performance and scalability. It also changes the way Web applications are programmed by letting you process client-side events on the server. ASP.NET applications are compiled, and you can write them in C#. In this chapter, you'll learn to:

- Use C# to build ASP.NET applications.
- Convert classic ASP applications to ASP.NET.
- Use HTML server controls.
- Use built-in ASP.NET objects such as `Response`, `Request`, and `Server`.

Using C# to Build Your First ASP.NET Application

Microsoft designed ASP.NET to address numerous problems associated with Web development. ASP.NET changes the programming model for developing dynamic Web applications. ASP.NET has the following advantages over classic ASP:

- Programming logic is separated from page layout. This is particularly important when both programmers and designers need to work on the same file.

- ASP.NET has an enhanced feature set. You no longer need third-party components to send email or upload files to a server. You can also validate data entry and cache page output with ease. This sort of built-in functionality is not available in classic ASP or traditional server-side scripting languages such as CGI (Common Gateway Interface) scripts written in Perl.

- Server-side code is compiled the first time a page is requested. All other requests are much faster because they are served from the cached version of the compiled code. The cached copy is deleted when the code gets updated.

- ASP.NET is not programmed with scripting languages. You can use compiled languages such as VB.NET, JScript.NET, and C#. While you are restricted to using one language per page, elements of your application can be programmed in different languages. We will use C# throughout this book because it is a modern, object-oriented language with an elegant syntax. C# is also the obvious choice because it will help you structure complex Web applications. In fact, ASP.NET was built in C#.

- ASP.NET applications can target multiple browsers as well as mobile devices.

- Server-side code can respond to events that occur in a Web browser. This eliminates the need to write client-side code in JavaScript. With ASP.NET, you can concentrate on the logic and not the information transfer between the browser and server.

The best way to understand and appreciate ASP.NET is to actually evaluate a simple page coded in classic ASP and then look at how easy it is to build the same page in ASP.NET. The example that follows highlights the difficulties associated with building dynamic applications and provides a theoretical platform for the introduction to ASP.NET.

The example includes a form with a text box, drop-down list, and submit button. The user must enter her name and favorite programming language and then click on the submit button to transfer the data to the server. Once the server receives the data, the data entered by the user appears on the page. The form fields also retain the data previously entered by the user:

1. You must put ASP code between <% and %> delimiters. The code is VBScript, which is a scripting language. VBScript does not get compiled.

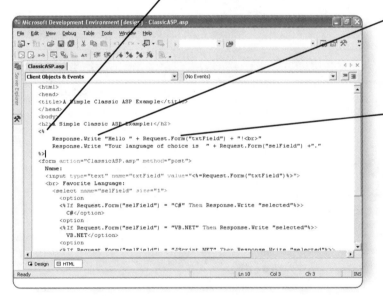

2. The Response.Write method prints data to the page. You use it to display the data entered by the user.

3. The Request.Form method retrieves the data entered into a form field. You must pass the name of the form field as a parameter to the Request.Form method. The data entered into the text box and the drop-down list is printed to the page with the Response.Write method.

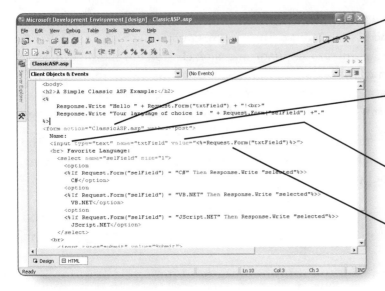

4. The form includes an `action` attribute that posts the data entered back to the same page.

5. You use the `<input>` tag to insert a text box. The `type` attribute must be set to `text`.

6. The `value` attribute displays data in the text box.

7. The `Request.Form` method retrieves the data the user entered into a text box. The text box retains its state.

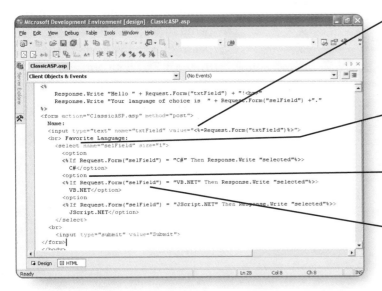

8. The `<%=` and `%>` delimiters print data to the page. This tag in effect replaces the `Response.Write` method.

9. You use the `<select>` tag to insert a drop-down list.

10. The `<option>` tags define the items in the drop-down list.

11. Retaining state in a drop-down list involves some programming. You must insert code in each option tag to decide which option is selected when the page reloads.

In general, you can spot the following shortcomings:

- ASP code is mixed with HTML. This mixture is hard to trace and does not let you easily change the layout without making some adjustments in the code as well.

- No state is retained when round trips are made to the server. You must manually program this aspect. Getting drop-down lists, check boxes, and radio buttons to remember their original value requires a lot of code. Can you imagine writing code to retain state on a larger form?

- The client (the browser) and the server use different programming models. ASP renders HTML, which is displayed in a browser. The user enters data that is submitted back to the server for processing. You cannot respond to events that occur within the browser. You must use the `Request.Form` method to retrieve the posted form data.

Now for the exciting part—the conversion to ASP.NET. Although ASP.NET is different, it is not difficult:

1. Change the file extension to .aspx. All ASP.NET pages must use this extension.

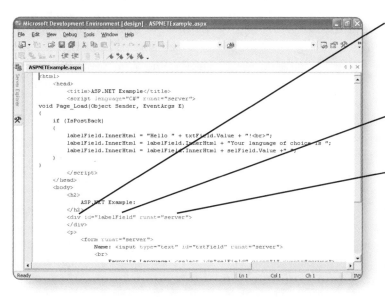

2. Insert opening and closing `<div>` tags. You use this tag to display the data entered by the user.

3. The `<div>` tag must have a unique ID.

4. You must place a `runat` attribute set to `server` within the opening `<div>` tag. The `runat="server"` means that server-side code can access the tag properties.

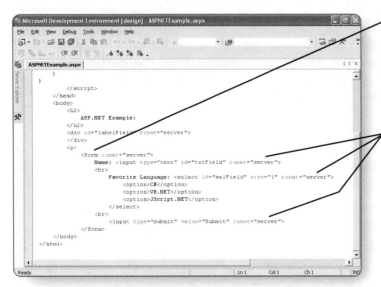

5. The form tag does not require action and method attributes any more. You just need to include runat="server" in the opening form tag.

6. Insert the runat="server" attribute in all form fields.

7. Insert opening and closing <script> tags. You must place all methods within these tags. This is known as a script declaration block.

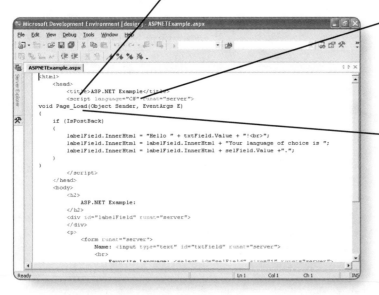

8. Set the language attribute to C#. Because this book focuses on developing Web applications in C#, you will program ASP.NET in C#.

9. Insert a Page_Load method. You place the void keyword in front of the method name because the method does not return any data. The Page_Load event occurs when ASP.NET loads the page.

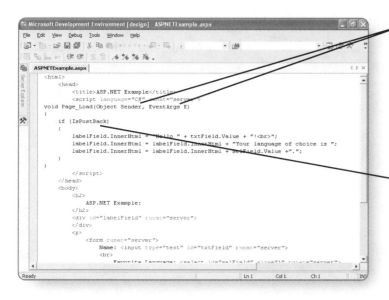

10. The Page_Load method takes two parameters. The first parameter, which must be type Object, contains the object that fired the event. The second parameter contains data associated with the object.

11. You don't want to execute the code within the Page_Load method unless the form is posted. The IsPostback property returns True if the form has been submitted back to the server.

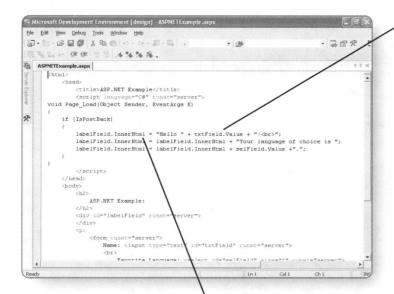

12. You can now access the data entered by typing the ID of the form element followed by a period and the name of the property that holds the data (the value).

NOTE

You can use the same dot notation to change the data that is displayed in a form element.

13. The <div> tag has label1 as its ID. A <div> tag has an InnerHtml property that contains the text and HTML formatting of the data displayed. You will assign some text that indicates what the user entered. When a page is displayed, the text will appear where the <div> tag is located on the page.

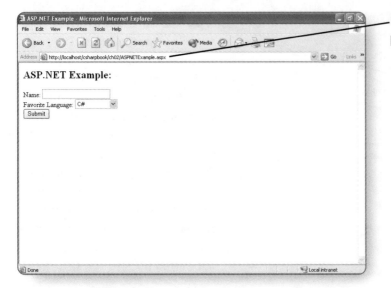

14. Preview the page in a Web browser. The form will appear.

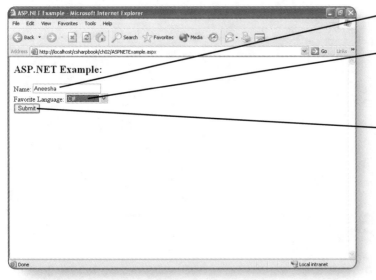

15. Enter your name.

16. Select your favorite language. (I hope you choose C#.)

17. Click the Submit button. The form data will be sent to the server.

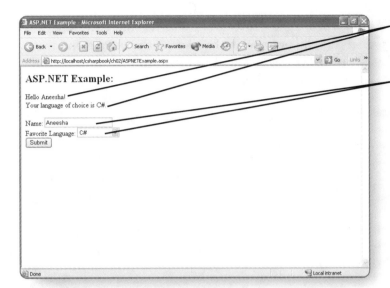

18. The data you entered will appear in a sentence.

19. The form elements automatically retain their state during round trips to the server.

By looking at the source code that ASP.NET generated, you can get a better understanding of what it is doing behind the scenes.

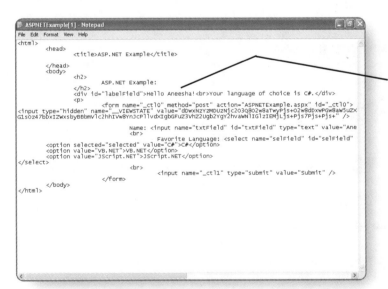

20. View the source code of the page that is generated.

21. The text appears within the ⟨div⟩ tags.

22. The method and action attributes for the form were inserted. You did not have to hand-code the action and method attributes. This allows you to change the file name without breaking the code.

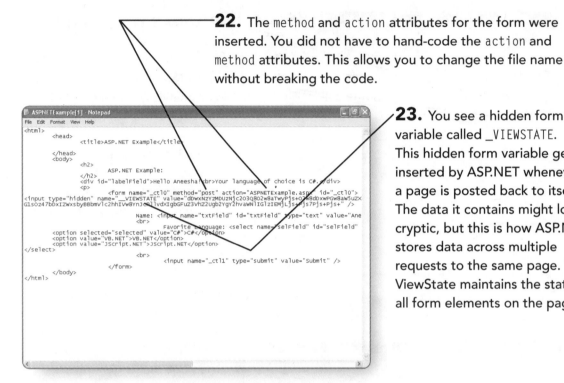

23. You see a hidden form variable called _VIEWSTATE. This hidden form variable gets inserted by ASP.NET whenever a page is posted back to itself. The data it contains might look cryptic, but this is how ASP.NET stores data across multiple requests to the same page. The ViewState maintains the state of all form elements on the page.

Converting ASP to ASP.NET

Migrating from ASP to ASP.NET is a simple 5-step process.

1. Change the file extension to .aspx.

2. Insert a runat=server attribute in all form elements that you want to access from ASP.NET code.

3. Place methods in a special script block.

4. Set the language attribute on the script tag to C#.

5. Use dot notation to set and retrieve form element properties. You can manipulate any HTML tag that includes the runat="server" attribute from server-side code. You can dynamically set or retrieve these properties.

Using HTML Server Controls

In ASP.NET, code on the server can access any HTML element, provided that the element contains the runat="server" attribute. All HTML tag attributes become properties that can be accessed through dot notation.

You use the img tag to insert an image:

```
<img src="img1.gif" >
```

You use the src attribute to specify the image that must be displayed. To convert this tag to an HTML server control, you give it a unique ID and insert the runat="server" attribute:

```
<img src="img1.gif" id="imgBannner" runat="server" />
```

You must place the / before the closing > of the tag. You must use this notation when there is no matching closing tag.

You can now access the src attribute as a property on the server. From the server-side code, you can learn the name of the image as well as change the image displayed:

```
imgBannner.Src = "newimg.gif";
```

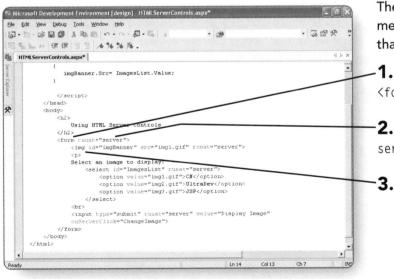

The code that follows uses a C# method to change the image that is displayed:

1. Insert opening and closing <form> tags.

2. Set the runat attribute to server.

3. Insert an img tag.

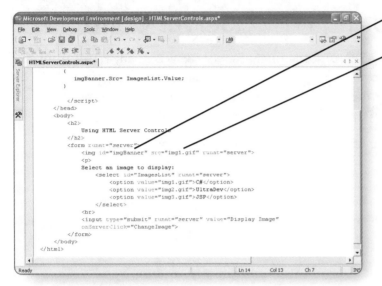

4. Set the ID.

5. Assign an image to the src attribute. This image will initially be displayed.

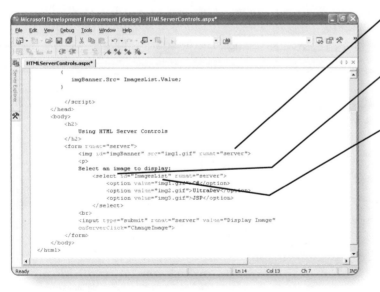

6. Set the runat attribute to server.

7. Insert opening and closing select tags.

8. Set the ID.

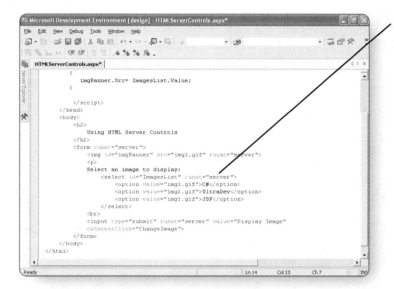

9. Set the `runat` attribute to server.

10. Insert opening and closing `option` tags for each image the user can select.

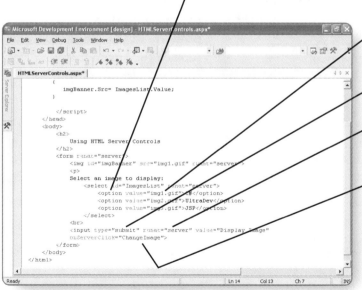

11. Set the `value` attribute to the image file name.

12. Insert a submit button.

13. Set the `runat` attribute to server.

14. Set the `onServerClick` event to `ChangeImage`. The `ChangeImage` method will execute on the server when the user clicks the button.

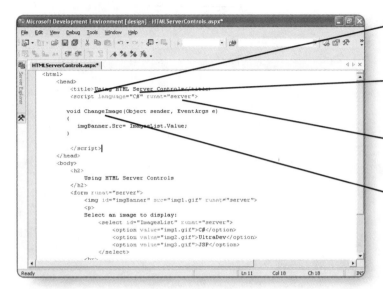

15. Insert opening and closing script tags.

16. Set the language attribute to C#.

17. Set the runat attribute to server.

18. Insert a void method named ChangeImage. A void method does not return a value.

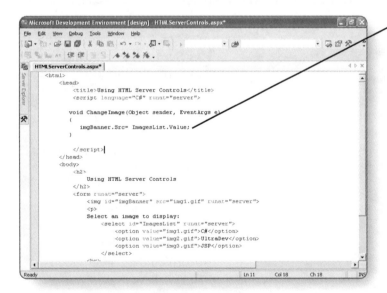

19. Assign the Value property of the drop-down list to the Src property of the image. This will replace the image that is currently displayed.

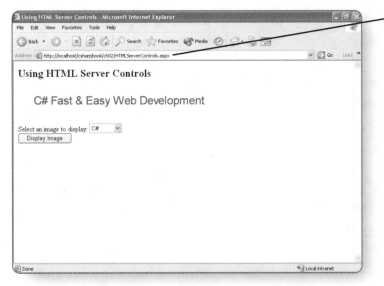

20. Preview the page in Web browser. An image will appear.

21. Select an image from the drop-down list. The option will be selected.

22. Click on the Display Image button. Your selection will be sent to the server.

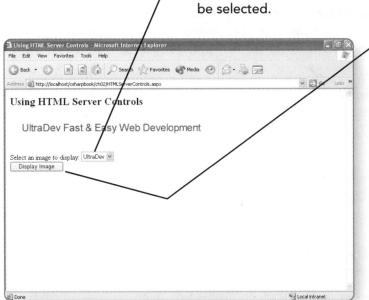

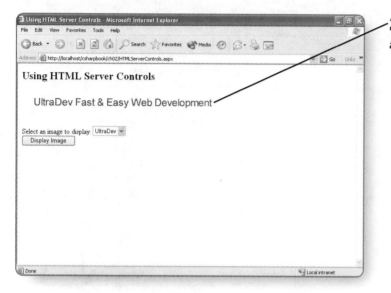

23. The selected image will appear.

Migrating from ASP to ASP.NET

You can still run existing ASP applications, but only files with an .aspx extension are processed by ASP.NET. Following are a few additional differences between ASP and ASP.NET:

- You can't declare functions and subroutines within the <% and %> tags. You must use a script declaration block. Functions are known as methods in C#:

```
<%
    Sub SayHello
        Response.Write "Hello from ASP"
    End Sub
%>
```

The preceding code becomes the following when using C# and ASP.NET:

```
<script language="C#" runat="server">
    void SayHello()
    {
        Response.Write("Hello from ASP");
```

```
        }
</script>
```

- You can't mix HTML and ASP.NET code:

```
<%
    Sub SayHello
        Size = 3
        Message = "Hello from ASP"
%>
        <font size = <%= Size %>> <%= Message %>
</font>
<%
    End Sub
%>
```

The preceding code becomes the following when you use C# and ASP.NET:

```
<script language="C#" runat="server">
    void SayHello()
    {
        int Size = 3;
        string Message = "Hello from ASP.NET and C#";
        Response.Write("<font size=" + Size + " >");
        Response.Write(Message);
        Response.Write("</font>");
    }
</script>
```

- You can still use the <% %> and <%= %> tags to insert code in a page, but you must use the @page directive to specify the language being used:

```
<%@ Page Language="C#" %>
<%
    Response.Write("Hello from C#");
%>
```

NOTE

The Page directive is used to specify page-level attributes. These attributes are used when the page gets processed and compiled.

NOTE

The <% %> tag is known as a code-render block in ASP.NET.

Intrinsic ASP.NET Objects

ASP.NET has built-in objects that receive and send data back to a browser:

- The Request object retrieves the data submitted to the server.

- The Response object sends data back to the browser.

- The Server object includes a number of useful methods. You can encode HTML as well as find the physical path to a file.

Using the Response Object

The Response object contains methods that send data to a browser. The Write method is the most important method because, as its name suggests, it prints data to the page. The Write method can print HTML code, text, or variables to the ASP.NET page:

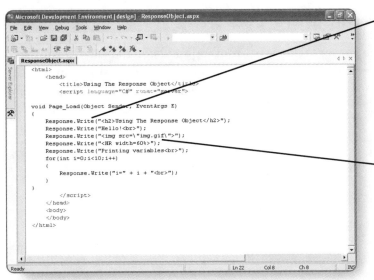

1. Type **Response.Write** to call the Write method of the Response object. You use dot notation to separate the object name and method.

NOTE

The Write method must be followed by parentheses.

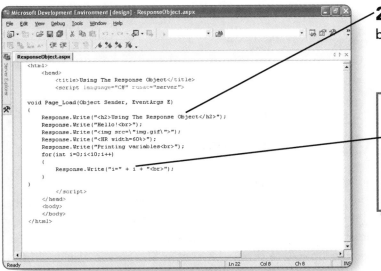

2. Place the text to print between quotation marks.

NOTE

You can use the Response.Write method to write HTML to the browser.

TIP

You do not need to put variables within quotation marks.

Redirecting Users

The `Response.Redirect` method forwards the user to another page. A user may have bookmarked pages that no longer exist. To prevent a file-not-found error, you should redirect the user to the new location:

1. Pass the path of the file to the `Response.Redirect` method.

> **NOTE**
> No content will appear.

Passing Data between ASP.NET Pages

Earlier in this chapter, you learned to post data back to the same page that generated the form. You will now take a look at how you can transfer data between pages in your Web application. The `form` tag contains a `method` attribute that specifies how data should be sent to the server. You could set this attribute to either `Get` or `Post`. The `action` attributes specifies the file that the data must be submitted to:

```
<form action="Get | Post" method = "processingfile.aspx" >
```

Form elements must be placed within the opening and closing form tags.

```
</form>
```

Using the Get Method

The Get method appends the data to the end of the URL of the file that will process the data.

You place a question mark after the file name. The form field name is followed by a + sign and the value entered by the user. This is a key-value pair. You use the ampersand (&) to separate key-value pairs. The data after the ? is known as the query string.

CAUTION

There is a limit to the amount of data you can append to the query string. You should not use the Get method to transfer large amounts of data. Because the data is visible in the URL, the Get method is not a good choice for transferring sensitive data.

Here is a form that uses the Get method.

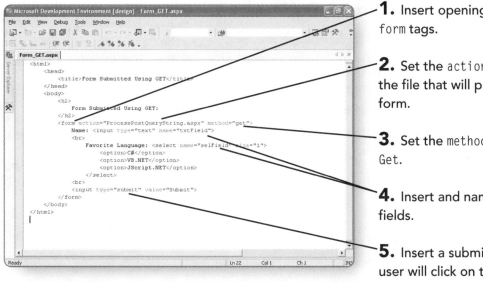

1. Insert opening and closing form tags.

2. Set the action attribute to the file that will process the form.

3. Set the method attribute to Get.

4. Insert and name your form fields.

5. Insert a submit button. The user will click on this button to send the data to the server.

Processing the Get Request

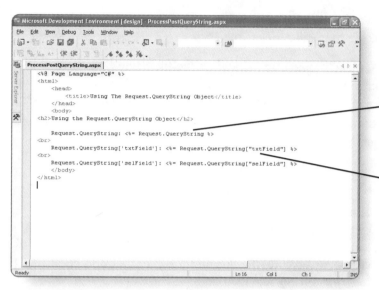

The Request.QueryString method is used to retrieve data sent to a server using the Get method.

1. Retrieve the Request.Query String property. This will return the entire query string.

2. Place the name of the form field you want to retrieve between the square brackets of the Request.QueryString method.

Using the Post Method

The Post method sends the form data in the header of the request to the server. You can transfer larger amounts of data with the Post method. You should use the Post method to send sensitive information to a server:

1. Insert opening and closing form tags.

2. Set the action attribute to the file that will process the form.

3. Set the method attribute to Post.

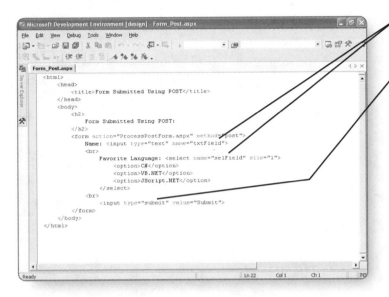

4. Insert and name your form fields.

5. Insert a submit button. The user will click on this button to send the data to the server.

Processing the Post Method

The Request.Form method is used to retrieve data posted to the server using the Post method.

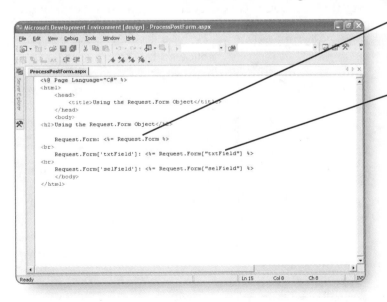

1. Retrieve the Request.Form property. This will return all the form fields.

2. Place the name of the form field you want to retrieve between the square brackets of the Request.Form method.

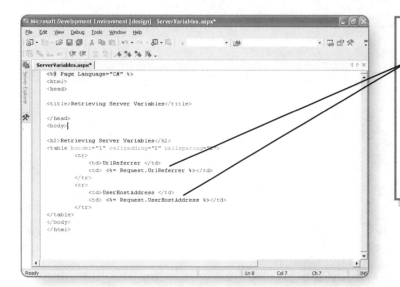

NOTE

The Request object can also be used to retrieve server variables such as the user's IP address (UserHostAddress) and the page that made the request from the server (UrlReferrer).

Detecting Browser Properties

The Browser property of the Request object can be used to determine browser capabilities. You can determine the features that a browser supports and render code accordingly.

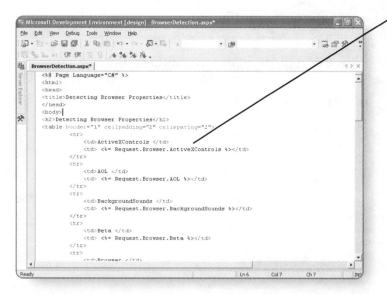

1. Type Request.Browser followed by the browser property.

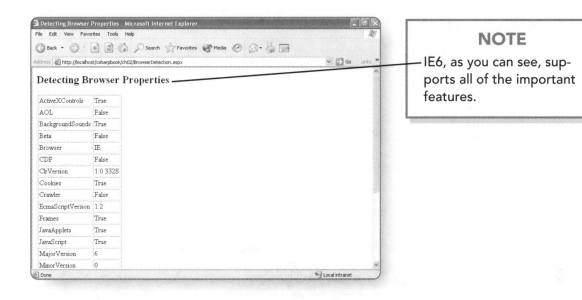

NOTE

IE6, as you can see, supports all of the important features.

Using the Server Object

The Server object contains a few handy methods. The HtmlEncode method replaces special characters so that you can display HTML code on a page. The UrlEncode method can format name-value pairs for inclusion in a query string. The MapPath method returns the physical path to a file. The ResolveUrl method returns the virtual path to a file.

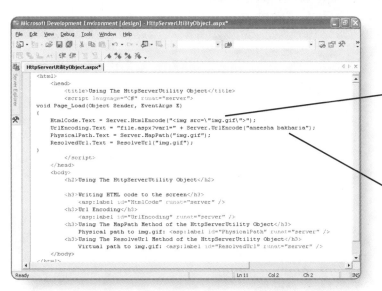

1. Pass the HTML code to the Server.HtmlEncode method. The HTML will appear instead of being rendered to the page.

2. Pass the name-value pair to the Server.UrlEncode method. The data will be encoded.

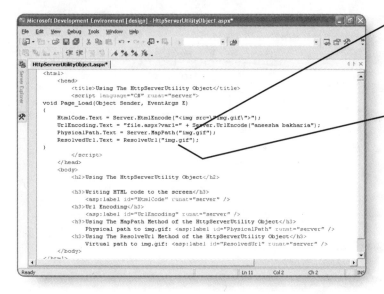

3. Pass a file name to the Server.MapPath method. The physical path of the file will return.

4. Pass a file name to the ResolveUrl method. The virtual path to a file will be returned.

3

C# Basics

C# is elegant, simple, powerful, and easy to learn. This chapter introduces the basic building blocks of the C# language—statements, expressions, operators, variables, and constants. You will use these concepts in every program you write. In this chapter, you'll learn to:

- Perform basic arithmetic.
- Understand operator precedence.
- Declare variables and constants.
- Work with expressions.
- Use the increment and decrement operators.
- Create methods.
- Comment your code.

Basic C# Syntax

The best way to learn C# is to jump right in and take a look at the code. This section examines the fundamental syntax of the C# language. I cover statements, code formatting, case sensitivity, braces, and the Response.Write method. I also explain how you can embed C# code in an ASP.NET page:

1. Web pages that include C# code must have an .aspx extension.

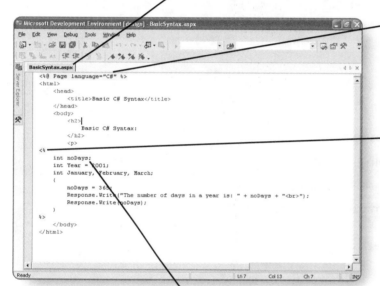

2. You must insert a Page directive at the top of the page and set the language attribute to C#. This will inform ASP.NET that the page contains C# code.

3. You must place C# code inserted within a Web page inside the <% and %> delimiters. The <% and %> tags form a code render block. The language attribute of the page directive must be set before a code-render block is used.

4. Every code statement must end with a semicolon. A statement is C# code that performs a task. A statement could be a single line or span multiple lines of code. When a statement spans multiple lines, the semicolon only needs to be placed at the end of the final line that completes the statement. You will receive an error if a statement does not end with a semicolon (;).

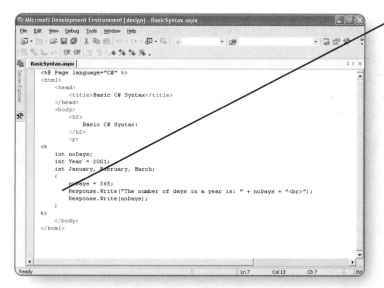

5. You can use blank space, tabs, and line and paragraph breaks to format your code. The use of this *whitespace* makes your code more readable. Whitespace is ignored by the compiler. Properly formatted code is easier to understand, modify, and debug.

6. C# is case sensitive. This means that you must always use the correct combination of uppercase and lowercase characters. For example, `theTime`, `TheTime`, `thetime`, and `THETIME` all refer to different variables.

7. Statements placed within opening and closing braces are grouped together. You must use braces in matching pairs. Matching braces constitute a code block.

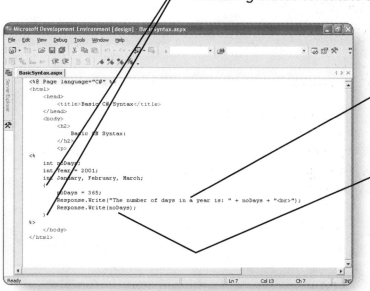

8. You use the `Response.Write` method to print data to the Web page:

- You must enclose text in quotation marks before you pass it to the `Response.Write` method.

- You can simply pass a variable to the `Response.Write` method. Don't enclose variable names in the quotation marks if you want to display the contents of the variable and not its name.

Performing Basic Arithmetic

Operators perform a mathematical action that involves two values and returns a result. The addition operator (+), for example, returns the sum of two values. You use operators to perform subtraction, multiplication, division, and more.

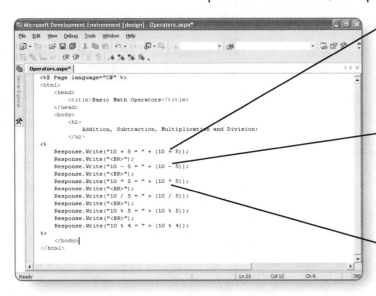

1. Type + between two values. The + operator performs addition. The Response.Write method will print the result to the Web page.

2. Type – between two values. The – operator performs subtraction. The Response.Write method will print the result to the Web page.

3. Type * between two values. The * operator performs multiplication. The Response.Write method will print the result to the Web page.

4. Type / between two values. The / operator performs integer division and does not return a remainder. The Response.Write method will print the result to the Web page.

5. Type % between two values. The % operator is known as the modulus operator. The % operator returns the remainder from integer division. The Response.Write method will print the result to the Web page.

Table 3.1 displays the arithmetic operators available in C#.

Table 3.1 Arithmetic Operators

Operator	Performs	Example	Result
+	Addition	10 + 5	15
-	Subtraction	10 - 5	5
*	Multiplication	10 * 5	50
/	Division	10 / 5	2
%	Modulus	10 % 4	2

Operator Precedence

An expression can use any combination of arithmetic operators. The C# compiler follows the rules of basic arithmetic when determining the order in which operators should be evaluated. This simply means that multiplication and division have higher precedence than addition and subtraction. Expressions are evaluated from left to right on operators with the same level of precedence. The direction of evaluation is known as associativity. You can also use parentheses to group the values that must be calculated first. Table 3.2 details the order of operator precedence in C#.

```
Microsoft Development Environment [design] - OperatorPrecedance.aspx*
File  Edit  View  Debug  Tools  Window  Help

OperatorPrecedance.aspx*
<%@ Page language="C#" %>
<html>
    <head>
        <title>Operator Precedence</title>
    </head>
    <body>
        <h3>
            Operator Precendance:
        </h3>
<%
    Response.Write("20 - 5 * 3 + 4 / 2 = " + (20 - 5 * 3 + 4 / 2));
    Response.Write("<BR>");
    Response.Write("(20 - 5) * (3 + 4) / 2 = " + ((20 - 5) * (3 + 4) / 2));
%>
    </body>
</html>
```

1. In this expression, the basic rules of precedence apply. The program will perform multiplication and division before addition and subtraction.

The expression will be evaluated as follows:

$$20 - 5 * 3 + 4 / 2$$
$$= 20 - 15 + 2$$
$$= 7$$

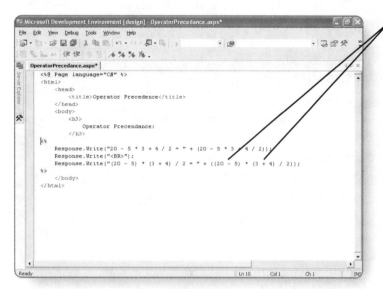

2. This expression uses parentheses to define the order of precedence:

$$(20 - 5) * (3 + 4)/2$$
$$= 15 * 7/2$$
$$= 15 * 3.5$$
$$= 52.5$$

Table 3.2 Operator Precedence in C#

Category	Operator(s)	Associativity
Primary	(x) x.y f(x) a[x] x++ x— new typeof sizeof checked unchecked	Left
Unary	+ — ! ~ ++x —x (T)x	Left
Multiplicative	* / %	Left
Additive	+ —	Left
Shift	<< >>	Left
Relational	< > <= >= is	Left
Equality	== !=	Right
Logical AND	&	Left
Logical XOR	^	Left
Logical OR	|	Left
Conditional AND	&&	Left
Conditional OR	||	Left
Conditional	?:	Right
Assignment	= *= /= %= += -= <<= >>= &= ^= |=	Right

Declaring Variables

A variable associates a name with a value that is stored in memory. You can simply refer to the variable by name whenever you need to use it in a calculation. A variable can store numeric, text, or character-based data. You must declare first variables because C# is a strongly-typed language. Table 3.3 contains a list of all the data types that can be stored in a variable. Declaring a variable involves specifying a name for the variable and the type of data that it will store.

Here is the syntax for declaring a variable:

```
data_type variable_name;
```

Table 3.3 C# Data Types

Type	Size in Bits	Range
sbyte	8	–128 to 127
byte	8	0 to 255
short	16	–32,768 to 32,767
ushort	16	0 to 65,535
int	32	–2,147,483,648 to 2,147,483,647
uint	32	0 to 4,294,967,295
long	64	–9,223,372,036,854,775,808 to 9,223,372,036,854,775,807
ulong	64	0 to 18,446,744,073,709,551,615
char	16	0 to 65,535
float	32	$1.5 * 10^{-45}$ to $3.4 * 10^{38}$ (7-digit precision)
double	64	$5.0 * 10^{-324}$ to $1.7 * 10^{308}$ (15 to 16 precision)
decimal	128	$1.0 * 10^{-28}$ to $7.9 * 10^{28}$ (28 to 29 decimal places)

The following C# statement declares a variable called `myName` as a string:

```
string myName;
```

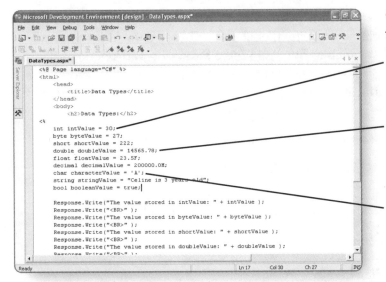

C# supports the following data types:

- **Integers**. Integers are nondecimal numbers (`int myTestScore = 5;`).

- **Floating-point numbers**. These numbers have a decimal component (`float myFraction = 3.2;`).

- **Characters**. Character variables can store only a single character. You must enclose the character in single quotation marks (`char myCharacter = 'A';`).

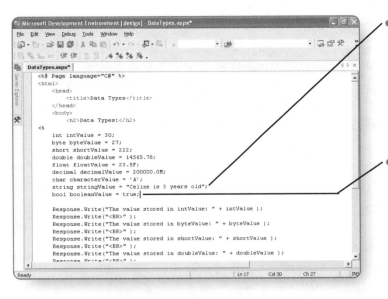

- **Strings**. Strings can be a combination of characters and numbers. You enclose strings in quotation marks so they are not confused with variable names (`string myString = "C# is cool!";`).

- **Booleans**. A Boolean variable can store only a True or False value (`bool performedCalculation = TRUE;`).

Always adhere to the following guidelines when naming variables:

- Variable names cannot contain blank spaces.

- Don't name variables after C# reserved keywords. These keywords are part of the C# language and cannot serve as variable names. Appendix B, "C# Quick Reference," contains a comprehensive list of all C# keywords.

- Always use the same capitalization when referring to variables. In C#, `myName` and `myname` are two different variables.

- Don't include operators (=, +, −, /, *, or %) in the variable's name.

- Don't begin a variable name with a number.

NOTE

A variable can begin with an underscore (_) or dollar sign ($).

NOTE

Always use variable names that describe the data being stored. This habit makes your code easier to understand. For example, `netSales` is a better name than `x73E2` for a variable that will hold a net sales amount.

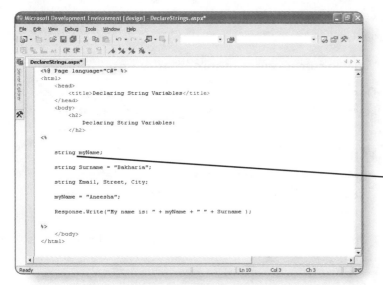

Declaring Strings

A string can contain words, characters, and numbers. I take a look at declaring string variables and initializing them. You use the `string` keyword to declare a string variable:

1. Type **string** followed by the variable name and a semicolon. This declares a single variable as a string.

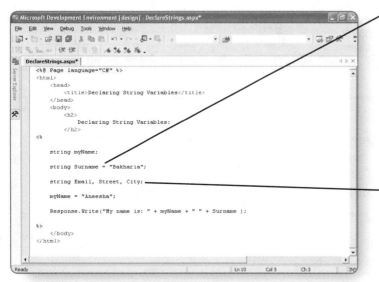

2. Use the equal sign (=) to assign a value to the variable when it is being initialized. This is known as explicit initialization. You must enclose the string in quotation marks.

TIP

You can initialize more than one variable of the same type by separating each variable name with a comma.

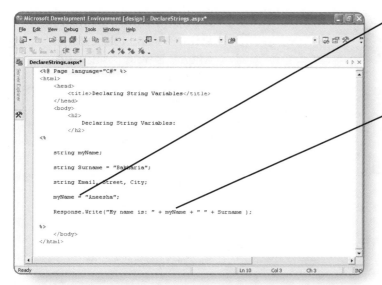

3. Type = to assign a value to a variable. You must place the value on the right side of the equal sign.

4. Use the Response.Write method to print the value of a variable.

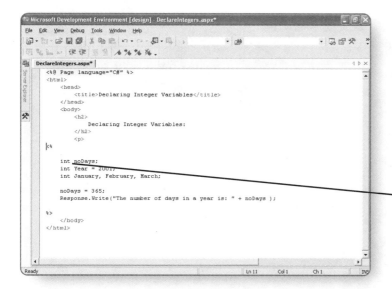

Declaring Integers

The four standard types of integers are sbyte, short, int, and long. Integers store numeric data, and you declare them with the keyword int. Let's take a look at declaring integer variables in detail:

1. Type **int** followed by the variable name and a semicolon. This declares a single variable as an integer.

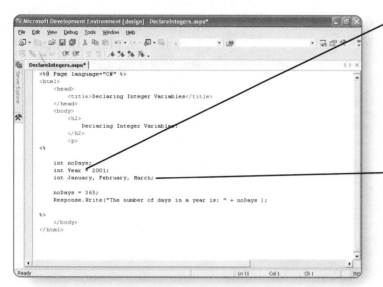

2. Use the equal sign (=) to assign a value to the variable when it is being initialized (performing explicit initialization).

TIP
You can initialize more than one variable of the same type by separating each variable name with a comma.

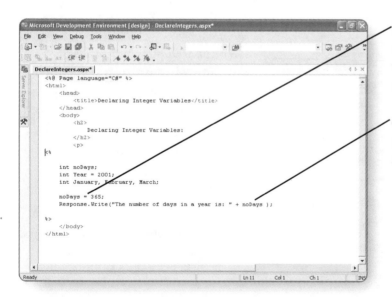

3. Type = to assign a value to a variable. You must place the value on the right side of the equal sign.

4. Use the `Response.Write` method to print the value of a variable.

Working with Constants

You use constants to store values that must not change during the execution of your code. Constants are really just variables that must be initialized and can't be assigned new values:

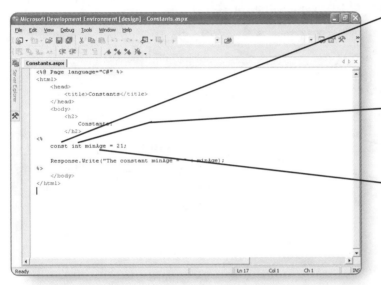

1. Type the **const** keyword. The const keyword tells the complier that the variable will be declared as a constant.

2. Type the keyword used to define the type of data that the constant must store.

3. Type a name for the constant.

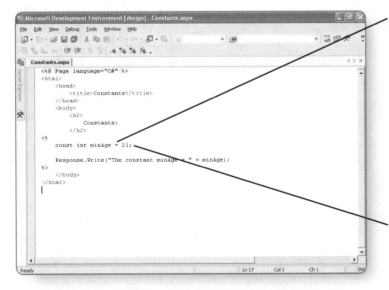

4. Assign an initial value to the constant. You use the equal-to (=) operator to assign a value.

NOTE

You must initialize a constant when you declare it.

5. Type a semicolon at the end of the line. Each constant declaration must end with a semicolon.

Working with Expressions

An expression is a statement that returns a value. You use the assignment operator (=) to store the result returned by an expression in a variable. The following example stores the sum of two values in a variable:

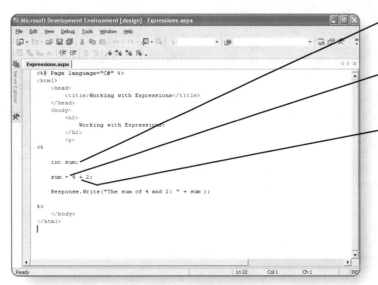

1. Declare a variable named sum as an integer.

2. Type = after the variable name.

3. Type + between the two values. I perform addition in this example, but you can use any other operator.

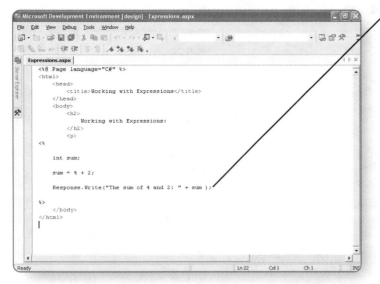

4. Type ; at the end of the expression. You must put a semicolon at the end of an expression.

NOTE

As a general rule, the value returned by the left-hand side is assigned to the variable on the right-hand side of the equal sign.

Compound Assignments

Compound assignments allow you to perform a calculation that involves a particular variable and assigns the result to the same variable. Compound assignment operators perform addition, subtraction, multiplication, and division. Table 3.4 contains a list of compound assignment operators as well as their equivalent syntax.

Table 3.4 Compound Assignment Operators

Compound Assignment Operators	Example	Equivalent Syntax
+=	value += 5	value = value + 5
–=	value –= 5	value = value – 5
/=	value /= 5	value = value / 5
*=	value *= 5	value = value * 5

The following example uses the addition compound assignment operator (+=):

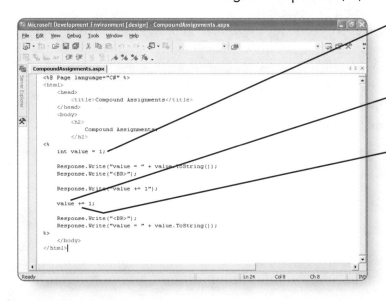

1. Declare a variable as an integer and assign an initial value.

2. Type the name of the variable.

3. Type += after the variable name. The += operator will add a value to the variable and store the result in the variable.

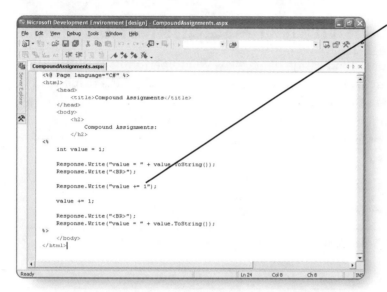

```
Microsoft Development Environment [design] - CompoundAssignments.aspx
File  Edit  View  Debug  Tools  Window  Help

CompoundAssignments.aspx
<%@ Page language="C#" %>
<html>
    <head>
        <title>Compound Assignments</title>
    </head>
    <body>
        <h2>
            Compound Assignments:
        </h2>
<%
    int value = 1;

    Response.Write("value = " + value.ToString());
    Response.Write("<BR>");

    Response.Write("value += 1");

    value += 1;

    Response.Write("<BR>");
    Response.Write("value = " + value.ToString());
%>
    </body>
</html>
```

```
Ready                                    Ln 24    Col 8    Ch 8         INS
```

4. Type the value that must be added. You could also store it in a variable.

> **NOTE**
> Remember to place a semicolon at the end of the statement.

Using the Increment and Decrement Operators

Increasing or decreasing the value of a variable by 1 is a calculation frequently performed in programming. The operation is simple, but the increment (++) and decrement (−−) operators shorten the syntax. You use the increment operator to add 1 to a value; the decrement operator subtracts 1 from the value. Both the increment and decrement operators are available in prefix and postfix versions.

Using the Prefix Increment and Decrement Operators

The prefix operators increment the variable before it is used in a calculation:

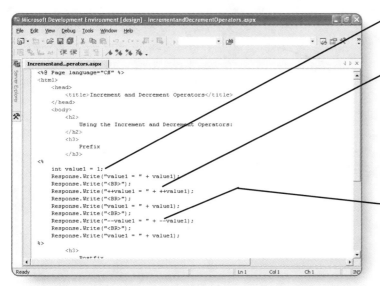

1. Declare an integer variable with an initial value of 1.

2. Type ++ in front of the variable name. Placing the ++ operator as a prefix means that the variable will be incremented and then printed to the Web page.

3. Type -- in front of the variable name. Placing the -- operator as a prefix means that the variable will be decreased by 1 and then printed to the Web page.

Using the Postfix Increment and Decrement Operators

The postfix operators first perform the calculation and then increment or decrement the variable:

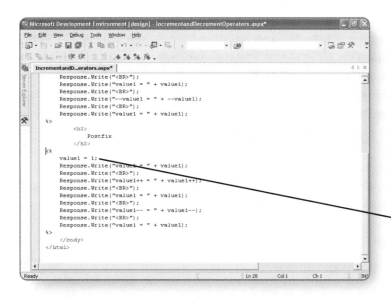

1. Declare an integer variable with an initial value of 1.

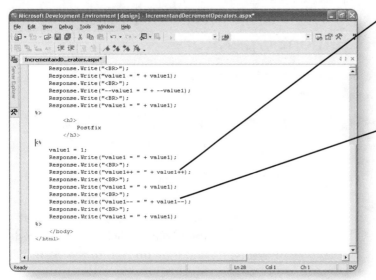

2. Type ++ after the variable name. Placing the ++ operator as a postfix means that the variable will be displayed and then incremented.

3. Type –– after the variable name. Placing the –– operator as a postfix means that the variable will be displayed and then decreased by 1.

NOTE

The increment and decrement operators are known as unary operators. That just means that you can only apply them to a single value or variable.

Creating Methods

Methods store code in a reusable format. Methods or functions reduce code repetition and maintenance by storing code in a central location. In ASP.NET, methods must be placed with code declaration blocks. This facilitates the separation of code and layout.

This is the syntax for declaring a method:

```
Data_type methodname(data_type argument1, data_type
argument2, …, data_type
argumentN)
{
          insert code here;
}
```

You have already used a number of methods (such as
`Response.Write`), but you will now learn to create your own.

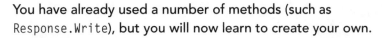

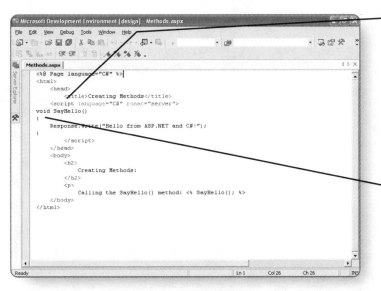

1. Insert opening and closing
`<script>` tags. Set the `language`
attribute to C#. Set the `runat`
attribute to server. The `<script>`
tags are known as code
declaration blocks. All methods
must be placed within the
`<script>` tags.

2. Type **void** followed by a
method name. A void method
does not return any data.

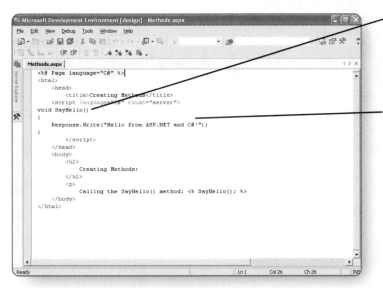

3. Type opening and closing
parentheses after the method
name. This method will not
accept any arguments.

4. Place the code within
opening and closing braces.

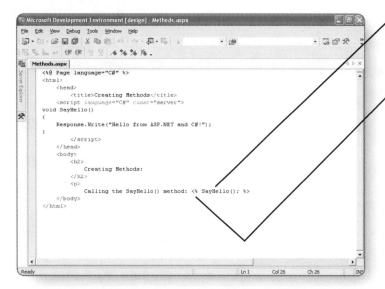

5. Type the method name followed by parentheses to call the method.

6. You use the <% and %> tags to call a method from within a page.

Returning Data from a Method

The `return` keyword is used to return data from a method. The type of data that gets returned must be defined as part of the method declaration.

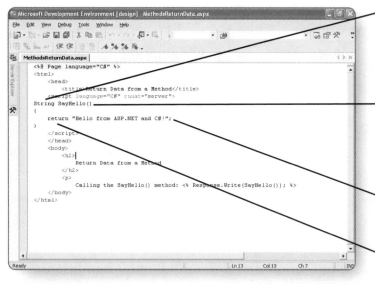

1. Type the data type followed by a method name. The method will return a value that matches this data type.

2. Type opening and closing parentheses after the method name. This method will not accept any arguments.

3. Place the code within opening and closing braces.

4. Type the `return` keyword followed by the data you want to return.

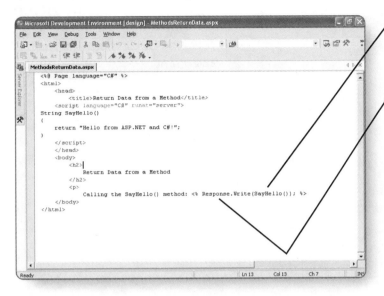

5. Type the method name followed by parentheses to call the method.

6. You use the <% and %> tags to call a method from within a page. The `Response.Write` method will print the returned data to the page.

Passing Arguments to a Method

Data passed to a method can be used by the code inside the method. In the example that follows, a method that calculates percentages requires two arguments to be passed to it. This method gets reused to calculate various percentages.

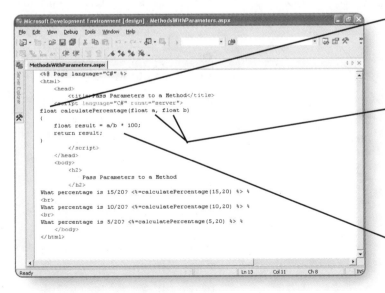

1. Type the data type followed by a method name. The method will return a value that matches this data type.

2. Type opening and closing parentheses after the method name. Declare the arguments that the method accepts. Multiple arguments must be separated by a comma.

3. Place the code within opening and closing braces.

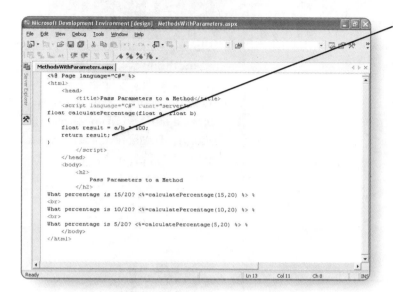

4. Type the return keyword followed by the data you want to return.

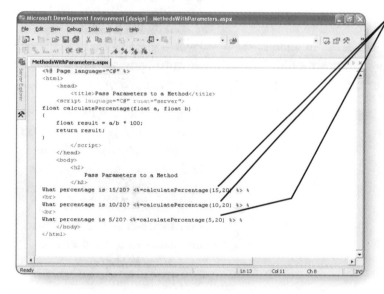

5. Type the method name followed by parentheses to call the method. Pass arguments to the method within the parentheses. Multiple arguments must be separated by a comma.

6. You use the <%= and %> tags to call a method from within a page.

Commenting Your Code

Comments are just sentences that describe how a program works. Documenting your code using comments is important because it helps other programmers understand your code. Even you will appreciate your own comments when you return to edit the code in a few months' time. Comments are ignored by the C# compiler.

You can comment code on a Web page in a number of ways. I describe all of them, but it is up to you to select the method that is most appropriate:

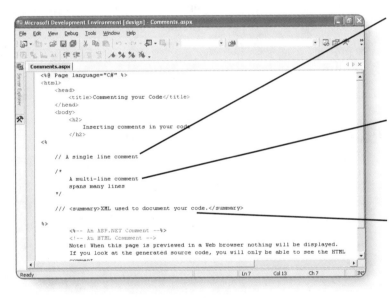

● **A single-line comment**. You use the // symbol to tell the C# compiler to treat the rest of the text on the current line as a comment.

● **A multiline comment**. A lengthy comment that spans more than one line must appear between /* and */ delimiters.

● **XML comment**. You use the /// symbol to inform the compiler that an XML-formatted comment follows. Using XML lets you structure your comments so they can be extracted and reformatted into HTML documentation.

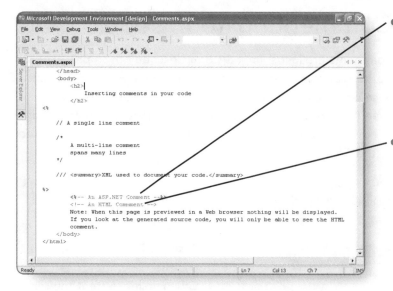

- **ASP.NET comment**. You use the <%-- and --%> delimiters to define comments in ASP.NET. You can use these delimiters to insert either single or multiline comments.

- **HTML comment**. You can also still use generic HTML comments. It is important to note that HTML comments are sent to the browser and inserted in the HTML source code.

NOTE

Don't forget to update your comments when you modify code.

4

Creating Web Forms

Although HTML server controls introduced an innovative event-driven model for developing ASP.NET applications, the syntax used to access properties was not consistent across all controls. This was mainly due to the fact that HTML server controls mapped directly to their HTML counterpart tags. HTML tags don't exactly use a standard notation to describe their attributes. Web server controls address these issues. They provide a common set of properties that you can manipulate via C# code that resides on the server. Using server controls, you can create intuitive Web interfaces to take advantage of Internet Explorer's dynamic HTML capabilities while still delivering pure HTML to other browsers. In this chapter, you'll learn to:

- Implement a variety of controls including text boxes, labels, buttons, radio buttons, and check boxes.

- Generate dynamic tables.

- Create a quiz.

- Generate Web controls dynamically.

Using the Label Control

A Label control displays text on a page. You can put a Label control anywhere on a page. You use the Text property to specify or change the text that is displayed. When a user clicks a button, you can update the contents of a Label control:

1. Insert a Label control. You must place the asp: prefix in front of the control name.

2. Set the id.

3. Set the runat attribute to server.

4. Set the Text attribute. This string will be displayed.

5. Insert a Button control. You must place the asp: prefix in front of the control name.

6. Set the id.

7. Set the runat attribute to server.

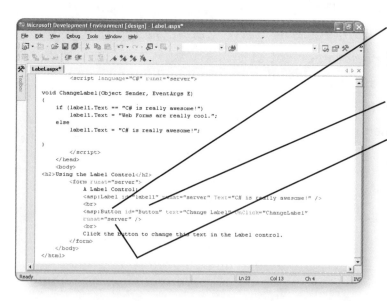

USING THE LABEL CONTROL

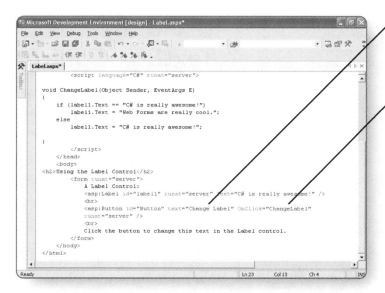

8. Set the `Text` attribute. This text will appear as a label on the button.

9. Set the `OnClick` event to `ChangeLabel`. When the user clicks the button, the `ChangeLabel` method will execute.

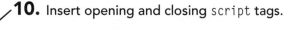

10. Insert opening and closing `script` tags.

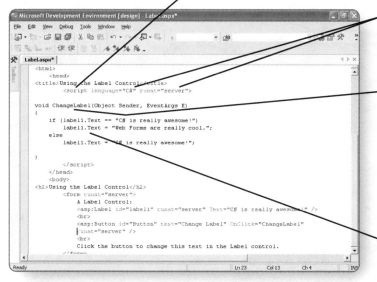

11. Set the `language` attribute to `C#` and the `runat` attribute to `server`.

12. Insert a `ChangeLabel` method. Put the `void` keyword in front of the method name because the method does not return any data. The `ChangeLabel` method will execute when the user clicks the button.

13. Assign a string to the `Text` property of the Label control. This string will replace the text that the label currently displays.

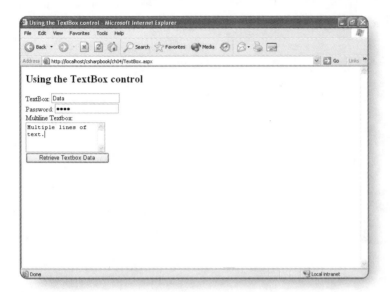

Using the TextBox Control

The TextBox control encompasses the two HTML free-form text-entry fields: the single-line input field and the multiline input field. The mode attribute allows you to specify whether a text box, multiline text box, or password entry field is displayed. The Text property retrieves the data that has been entered:

1. Insert opening and closing form tags.

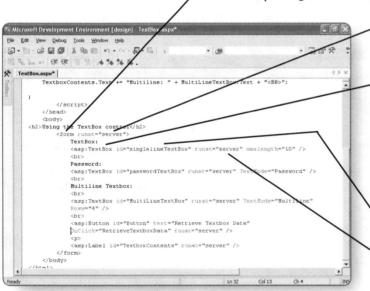

2. Set the runat attribute to server.

3. Insert a TextBox control. You must put the asp: prefix in front of the control name. A single-line text box is ideally used to capture small amounts of structured data, such as a name or address.

4. Set the id.

5. Set the runat attribute to server.

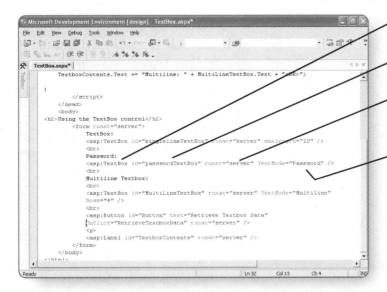

6. Insert a TextBox control.

7. Set the id.

8. Set the runat attribute to server.

9. Set the TextMode attribute to Password. Each character the user enters will be masked by an asterisk so that the password isn't visible.

10. Insert a TextBox control.

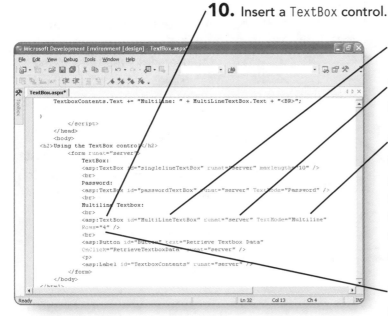

11. Set the id.

12. Set the runat attribute to server.

13. Set the TextMode attribute to Multiline. This is a replacement for the <textarea> tag in HTML. This mode allows the user to enter paragraphs of text. You can gather comments and feedback from the user.

14. Set the Rows to the number of lines the multiline text box should span.

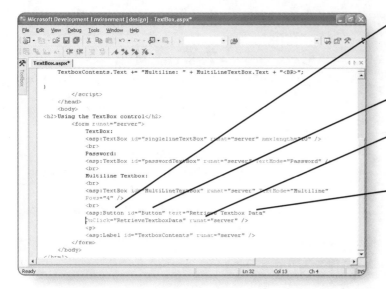

15. Insert a Button control. You must put the asp: prefix in front of the control name.

16. Set the id.

17. Set the runat attribute to server.

18. Set the Text attribute. This text will appear as a label on the button.

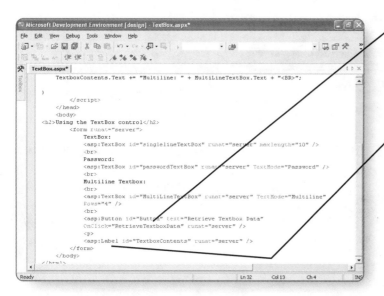

19. Set the OnClick event to RetrieveTextBoxData. When the user clicks the button, the RetrieveTextBoxData method will execute.

20. Insert a Label control. This control will display the data entered when the user clicks the button.

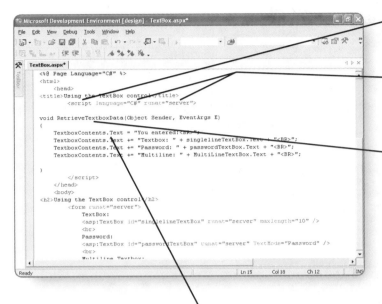

21. Insert opening and closing script tags.

22. Set the language attribute to C# and the runat attribute to server.

23. Insert a RetrieveText BoxData method. Put the void keyword in front of the method name because the method does not return any data. The RetrieveTextBoxData method will execute when the user clicks the button.

24. Assign data retrieved from the TextBox controls to the Text property of the Label control.

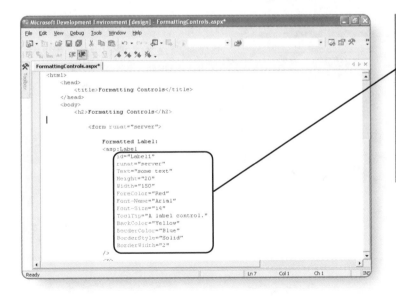

NOTE

You can also format a control by setting the Height, Width, ForeColor, Font-Name, Font-Size, BackColor, BorderColor, BorderStyle, and BorderWidth properties.

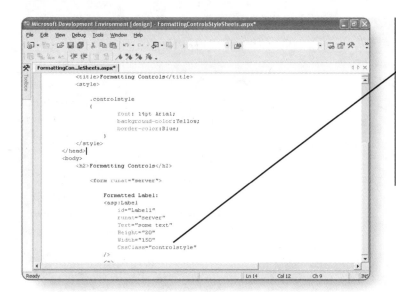

NOTE

To format multiple controls with the same settings, it is much easier to create a style sheet and assign the style to the Cssclass property of each control.

Using the Button Control

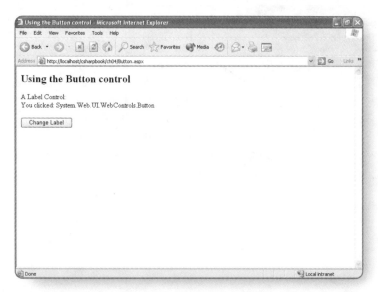

The Button control's main function is to execute a method when it gets clicked. The onClick event specifies the method that must execute:

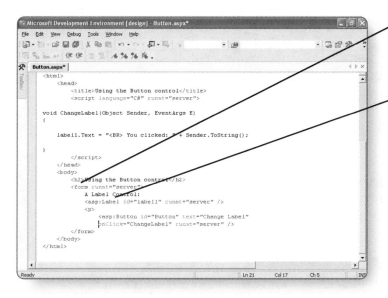

1. Insert opening and closing `form` tags. Set the `runat` attribute to `server`.

2. Insert a `Label` control. You must put the `asp:` prefix in front of the control name. Set the `id`. Set the `runat` attribute to `server`.

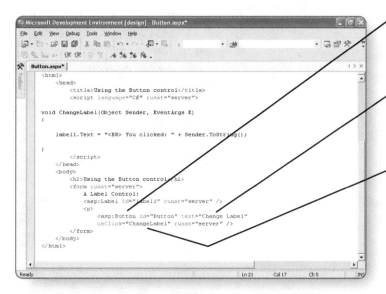

3. Insert a `Button` control. Set the `id`. Set the `runat` attribute to `server`.

4. Set the `Text` attribute. This text will appear as a label on the button.

5. Set the `OnClick` event to `ChangeLabel`. When the user clicks the button, the `ChangeLabel` method will execute.

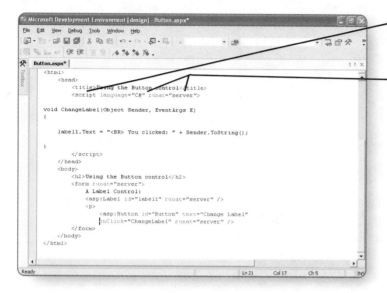

6. Insert opening and closing `script` tags.

7. Set the `language` attribute to `C#` and the `runat` attribute to `server`.

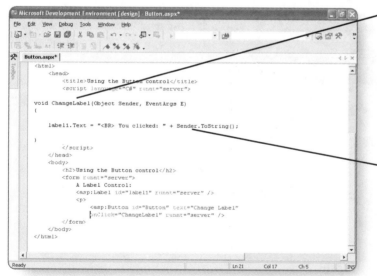

8. Insert a `ChangeLabel` method. Put the `void` keyword in front of the method name because the method does not return any data. The `ChangeLabel` method will execute when the user clicks the button.

9. Print the `Sender` object to the page. The `Sender` object is passed as the first parameter to the `ChangeLabel` method and contains information about the button that was clicked. You must use the `ToString` method to convert the `Sender` object to a string.

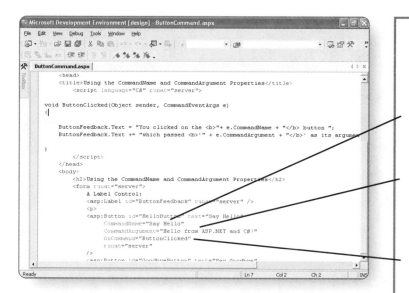

NOTE

The `Button` control has the following additional properties:

- The `CommandName` property, which defines the method that must be executed.

- The `CommandArgument` property, which passes a value to the method being executed.

- The `OnCommand` property, which sets the event that the button must respond to. In most cases this will be the `ButtonClicked` event.

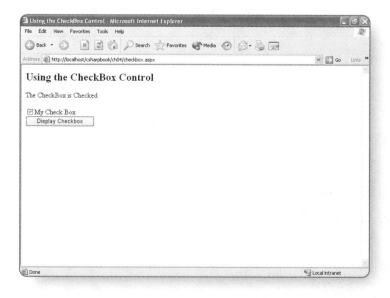

Using the CheckBox Control

The `CheckBox` control allows the user to make a choice. A check box collects Yes/No or True/False data. A check mark appears inside the check box when an option is selected. The `Text` property defines the label displayed beside the check box:

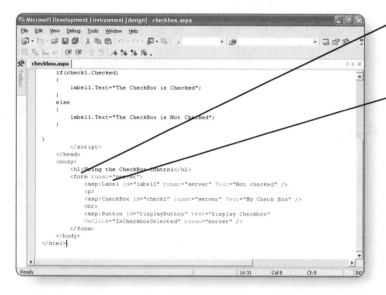

1. Insert opening and closing form tags. Set the `runat` attribute to `server`.

2. Insert a `Label` control. Set the `id`. Set the `runat` attribute to `server`.

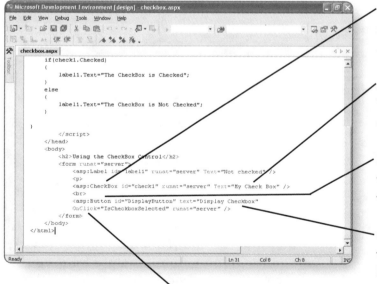

3. Insert a `CheckBox` control. Set the `id`. Set the `runat` attribute to `server`.

4. Set the `Text` attribute. The text will appear beside the check box.

5. Insert a `Button` control. Set the `id`. Set the `runat` attribute to `server`.

6. Set the `Text` attribute. This text will appear as a label on the button.

7. Set the `OnClick` event to `IsCheckboxSelected`. When the user clicks the button, the `IsCheckboxSelected` method will execute.

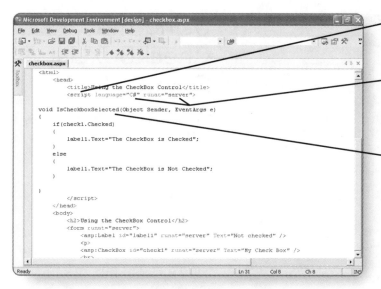

8. Insert opening and closing `script` tags.

9. Set the `language` attribute to `C#` and the `runat` attribute to `server`.

10. Insert an `IsCheckboxSelected` method. Put the `void` keyword in front of the method name because the method does not return any data. The `IsCheckboxSelected` method will execute when the user clicks the button.

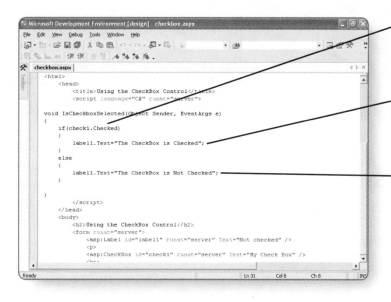

11. The `Checked` property will be `True` if the check box has been selected.

12. Set the `Text` property of the label to `"Checked"` if the `Checked` property is `True`.

13. Set the `Text` property of the label to `"Not Checked"` if the `Checked` property is `False`.

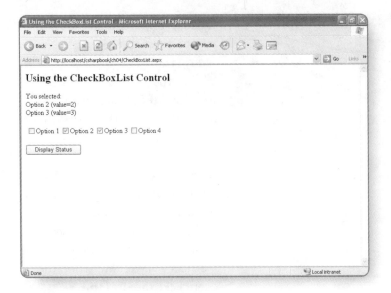

Using the CheckBoxList Control

The CheckBoxList control enables you to easily display and process a group of check boxes. You must define each check box within an <asp:ListItem> tag. The Text attribute displays the label, but the value attribute contains the value that gets posted back to the server:

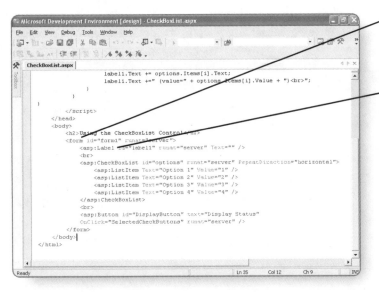

1. Insert opening and closing form tags. Set the runat attribute to server.

2. Insert a Label control. Set the id. Set the runat attribute to server.

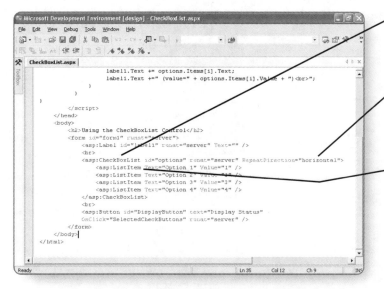

3. Insert a `CheckBoxList` control. Set the `id`. Set the `runat` attribute to `server`.

4. Set the `RepeatDirection` attribute. This can be horizontal or vertical.

5. Insert a `ListItem` control for each check box you want to include.

6. Set the `Text` attribute. The text will appear beside the check box.

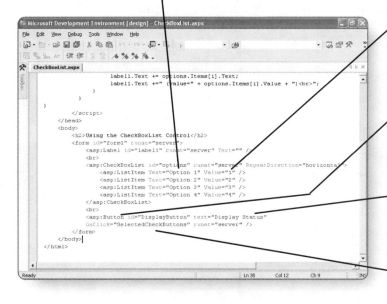

7. Set the `Value` attribute. The `Value` will be posted back to the server when the check box is selected.

8. Insert a `Button` control. Set the `id`. Set the `runat` attribute to `server`.

9. Set the `Text` attribute. This text will appear as a label on the button.

10. Set the `OnClick` event to `SelectedCheckButtons`. When the user clicks the button, the `SelectedCheckButtons` method will execute.

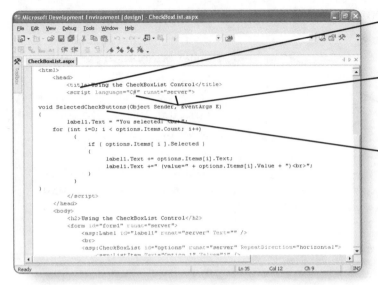

11. Insert opening and closing script tags.

12. Set the language attribute to C# and the runat attribute to server.

13. Insert a SelectedCheck Buttons method. Put the void keyword in front of the method name because the method does not return any data. The SelectedCheckButtons method will execute when the user clicks the button.

14. The Items.Count property returns the number of check boxes contained in the CheckBoxList control.

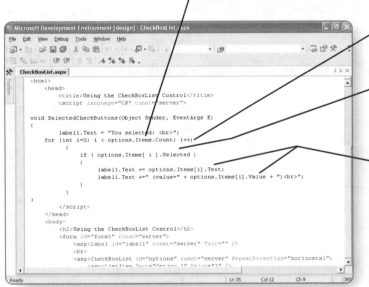

15. Use a for loop to iterate through each check box.

16. The Selected property will return True if the current check box is checked.

17. Display the Text and Value properties of the check boxes that have been selected.

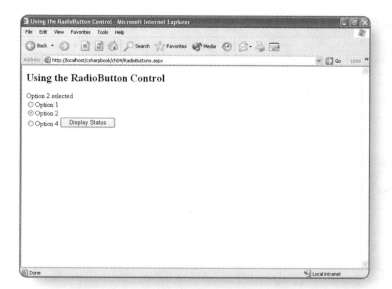

Using the RadioButton Control

Radio buttons present the user with a group of options from which he can select only one at a time. You must implement radio buttons in groups. When a user clicks a radio button, the previously selected one is deselected:

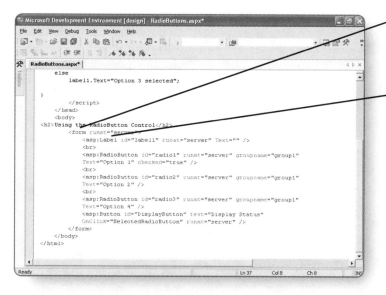

1. Insert opening and closing form tags. Set the runat attribute to server.

2. Insert a Label control. Set the id. Set the runat attribute to server.

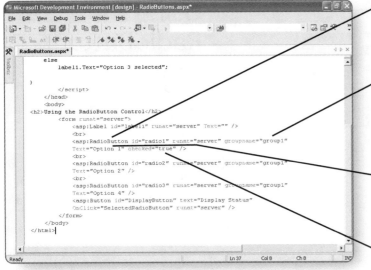

3. Insert a RadioButton control. Set the id. Set the runat attribute to server.

4. Set the groupname attribute. Only a single radio button in a group can be selected at any one time.

5. Set the Text attribute. The text will appear beside the radio button.

6. Set the checked attribute to true to select the option by default.

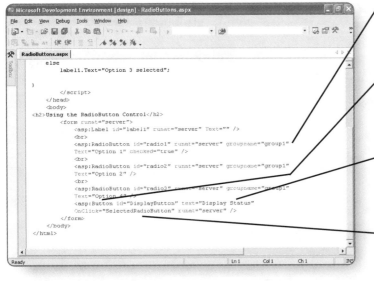

7. Insert additional RadioButton controls for each option in the group.

8. Insert a Button control. Set the id. Set the runat attribute to server.

9. Set the Text attribute. This text will appear as a label on the button.

10. Set the OnClick event to SelectedRadioButton. When the user clicks the button, the SelectedRadioButton method will execute.

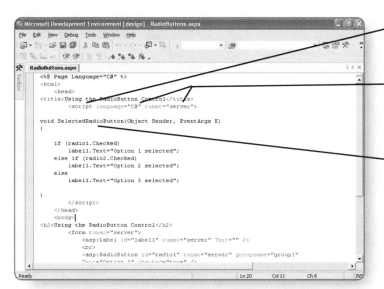

11. Insert opening and closing `script` tags.

12. Set the `language` attribute to `C#` and the `runat` attribute to `server`.

13. Insert a `SelectedRadio Button` method. Put the `void` keyword in front of the method name because the method does not return any data. The `Selected RadioButton` method will execute when the user clicks the button.

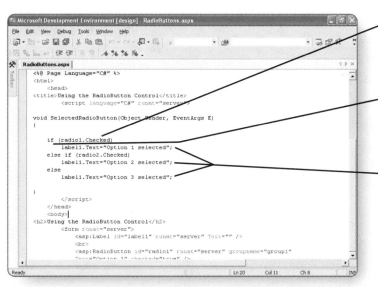

14. The `Checked` property will be `True` if the `RadioButton` has been selected.

15. Use an `if` statement to determine which radio button is selected.

16. Use the label to display the selected radio button.

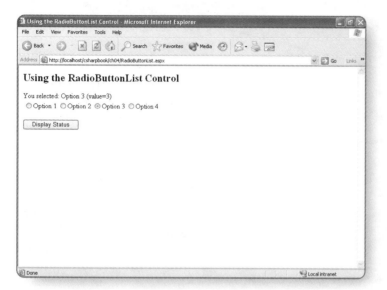

Using the RadioButtonList Control

The RadioButtonList control works just like the CheckBoxList control. It allows you to easily determine which option has been selected. Using the RadioButtonList control is easier than using the CheckBox control.

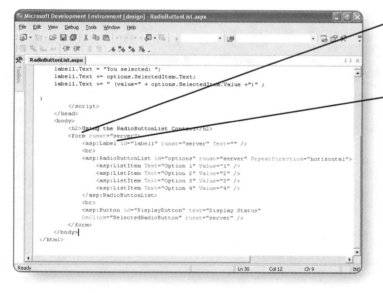

1. Insert opening and closing form tags. Set the runat attribute to server.

2. Insert a Label control. Set the id. Set the runat attribute to server.

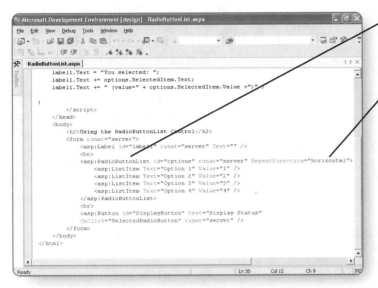

3. Insert a RadioButtonList control. Set the id. Set the runat attribute to server.

4. Set the RepeatDirection attribute. This can be horizontal or vertical.

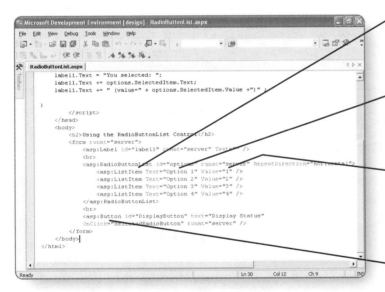

5. Insert a ListItem control for each radio button you want to include.

6. Set the Text attribute. The text will appear beside the radio button.

7. Set the Value attribute. The Value will be posted back to the server when the user selects the radio button.

8. Insert a Button control. Set the id. Set the runat attribute to server.

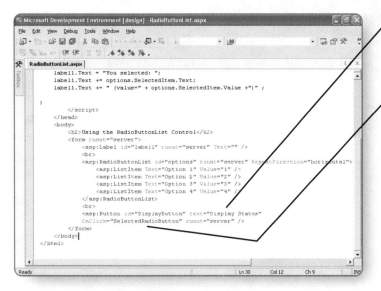

9. Set the `Text` attribute. This text will appear as a label on the button.

10. Set the `OnClick` event to `SelectedRadioButton`. When the user clicks the button, the `SelectedRadioButton` method will execute.

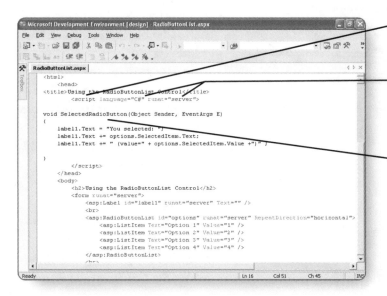

11. Insert opening and closing `script` tags.

12. Set the `language` attribute to `C#` and the `runat` attribute to `server`.

13. Insert a `SelectedRadio Button` method. Put the `void` keyword in front of the method name because the method does not return any data. The `SelectedRadioButton` method will execute when the user clicks the button.

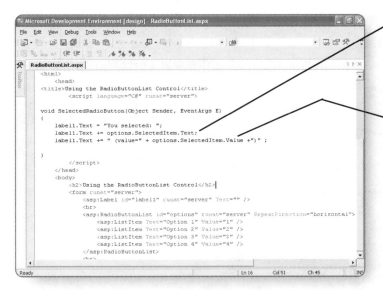

14. The SelectedItem.Text property will return the label displayed beside the selected radio button.

15. The SelectedItem.Value property will return the value of the selected radio button.

Using the ListBox Control

The ListBox control is probably the most flexible control that you will encounter. It provides a practical alternative to the RadioButton and RadioButton List controls. You can implement the ListBox control as a selection list, a scrolling selection list, or a multi-select list:

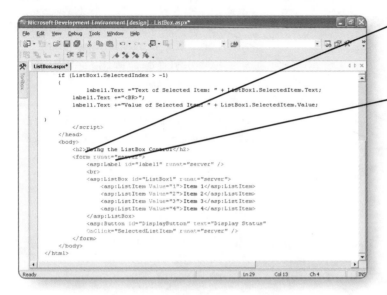

1. Insert opening and closing form tags. Set the `runat` attribute to `server`.

2. Insert a `Label` control. Set the `id`. Set the `runat` attribute to `server`.

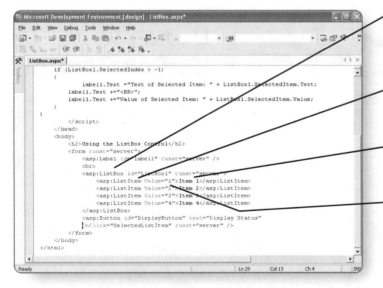

3. Insert a `ListBox` control. Set the `id`. Set the `runat` attribute to `server`.

4. Insert a `ListItem` control for each item you want to include.

5. Set the `Text` attribute. This text will be displayed.

6. Set the `Value` attribute. The `Value` will be posted back to the server when the user selects the item.

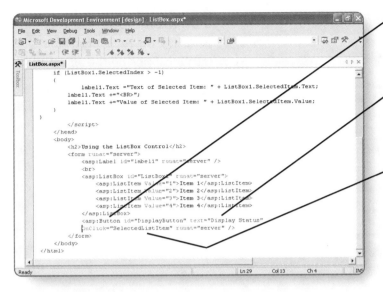

7. Insert a `Button` control. Set the `id`. Set the `runat` attribute to `server`.

8. Set the `Text` attribute. This text will appear as a label on the button.

9. Set the `OnClick` event to `SelectedListItem`. When the user clicks the button, the `SelectedListItem` method will execute.

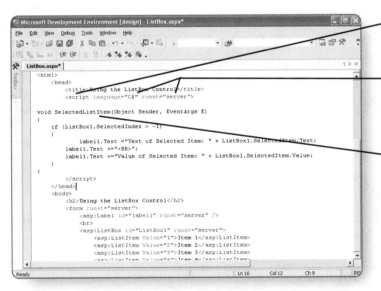

10. Insert opening and closing `script` tags.

11. Set the `language` attribute to `C#` and the `runat` attribute to `server`.

12. Insert a `SelectedListItem` method. The `SelectedListItem` method will execute when the user clicks the button.

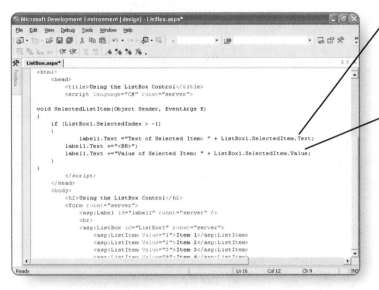

13. The `SelectedItem.Text` property will return the label displayed beside the selected radio button.

14. The `SelectedItem.Value` property will return the value of the selected radio button.

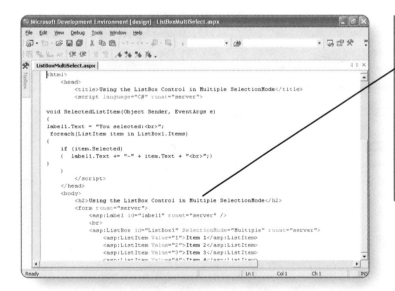

NOTE

The `ListBoxMultiSelect.aspx` file contains an example of a `ListBox` control that allows multiple items to be selected. The `SelectionMode` attribute must be set to multiple to enable this feature.

Populating a DropDownList Dynamically

A drop-down list displays only a single value at a time, but you can expand it to display all the items when the user clicks the down arrow. You can dynamically add the data items contained in the DropDownList control. This feature is known as data binding. The following example uses an array as a data source. As this book progresses, you will learn to bind controls to a database:

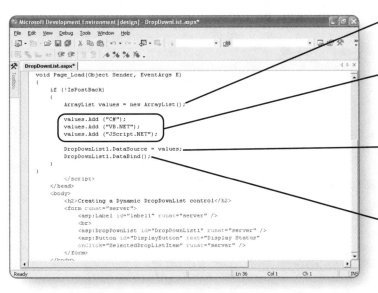

1. Declare an ArrayList by calling the ArrayList constructor.

2. Call the add method of the ArrayList object to add items to the ArrayList.

3. Assign the ArrayList object to the DataSource property of the DropDownList.

4. Call the DataBind method of the DropDownList to bind the data to the control.

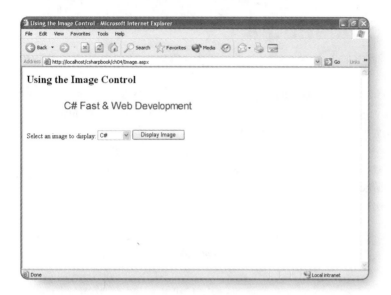

Using the Image Control

The Image control inserts an image, either a GIF or a JPEG. You can programmatically set the ImageUrl property, which specifies the path to the image:

1. Insert opening and closing form tags. Set the runat attribute to server.

2. Insert an Image control. Set the id. Set the runat attribute to server.

3. Set the ImageUrl attribute to the path of the image.

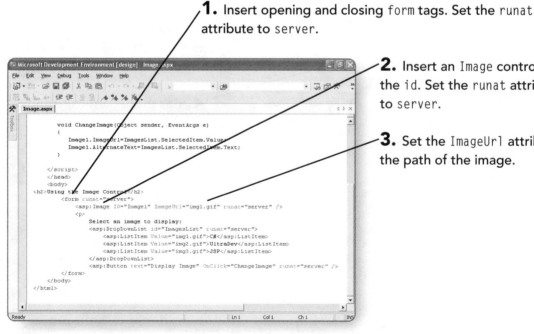

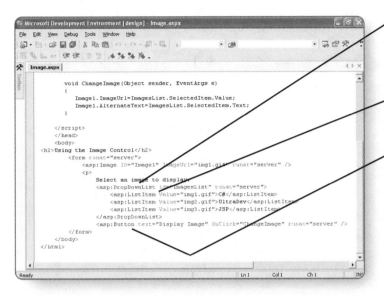

4. Insert a DropDownList control. Set the id. Set the runat attribute to server.

5. Insert a ListItem control for each image the user can select.

6. Insert a Button control. Set the id. Set the runat attribute to server.

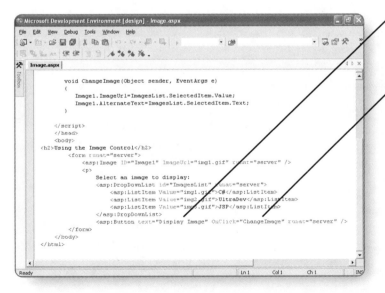

7. Set the Text attribute. This text will appear as a label on the button.

8. Set the OnClick event to ChangeImage. When the user clicks the button, the ChangeImage method will execute.

9. Insert opening and closing `script` tags.

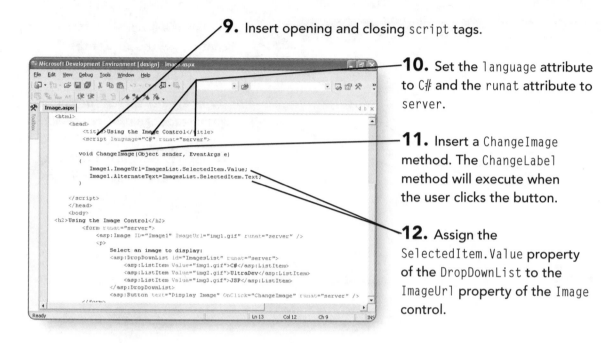

10. Set the `language` attribute to `C#` and the `runat` attribute to `server`.

11. Insert a `ChangeImage` method. The `ChangeLabel` method will execute when the user clicks the button.

12. Assign the `SelectedItem.Value` property of the `DropDownList` to the `ImageUrl` property of the `Image` control.

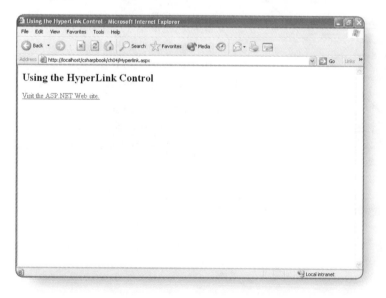

Using the HyperLink Control

The `HyperLink` control, as its name suggests, creates a link to another page. You use the `NavigateUrl` property to specify the link:

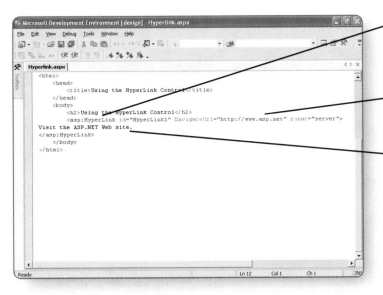

1. Insert a HyperLink control. Set the id. Set the runat attribute to server.

2. Set the NavigateUrl attribute.

3. Place the link text within the opening and closing <asp:HyperLink> tags.

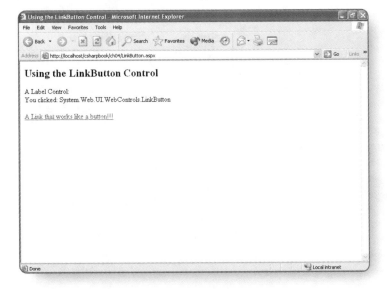

Using the LinkButton Control

The LinkButton control inserts a link in a page that works just like a button. The LinkButton control can respond to the onClick event and execute a method that resides on the server:

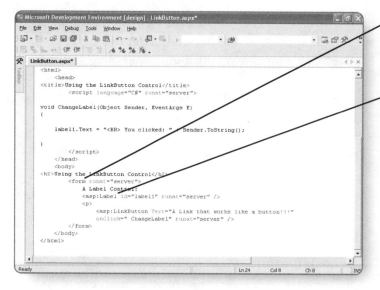

1. Insert opening and closing `form` tags. Set the `runat` attribute to `server`.

2. Insert a `Label` control. You must put the `asp:` prefix in front of the control name. Set the `id`. Set the `runat` attribute to `server`.

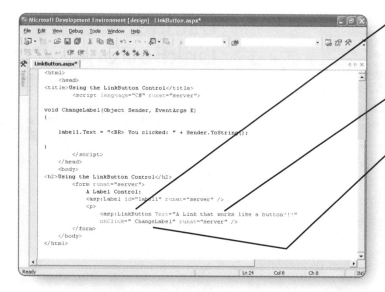

3. Insert a `LinkButton` control. Set the `runat` attribute to `server`.

4. Set the `Text` attribute. This text will appear as a link.

5. Set the `OnClick` event to `ChangeLabel`. When the user clicks the link, the `ChangeLabel` method will execute.

6. Insert opening and closing `script` tags.

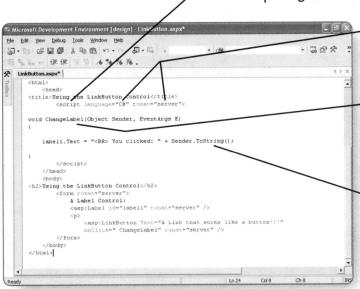

7. Set the `language` attribute to `C#` and the `runat` attribute to `server`.

8. Insert a `ChangeLabel` method. The `ChangeLabel` method will execute when the user clicks the link.

9. Print the `Sender` object to the page. The `Sender` object is passed as the first parameter to the `ChangeLabel` method and contains information about the object that fired the event. You must use the `ToString` method to convert the `Sender` object to a string.

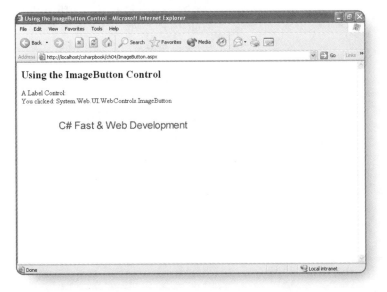

Using the ImageButton Control

The `ImageButton` control inserts an image the user can click to perform a certain function. The `ImageUrl` property specifies the image to display. The `ImageButton` control can respond to an `onClick` event:

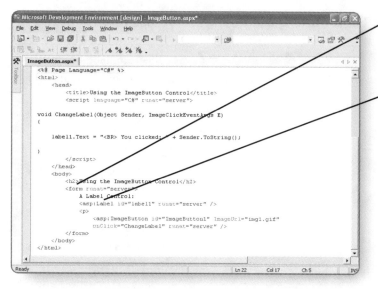

1. Insert opening and closing form tags. Set the runat attribute to server.

2. Insert a Label control. You must put the asp: prefix in front of the control name. Set the id. Set the runat attribute to server.

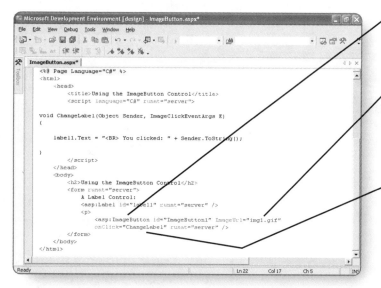

3. Insert an ImageButton control. Set the id. Set the runat attribute to server.

4. Set the ImageUrl attribute. This image will behave as a button and allow you to click on it.

5. Set the OnClick event to ChangeLabel. When the user clicks the image, the ChangeLabel method will execute.

6. Insert opening and closing script tags.

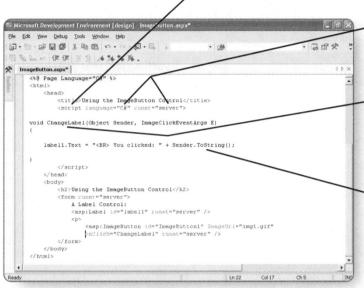

7. Set the language attribute to C# and the runat attribute to server.

8. Insert a ChangeLabel method. The ChangeLabel method will execute when the user clicks the image.

9. Print the Sender object to the page. The Sender object is passed as the first parameter to the ChangeLabel method and contains information about the object that fired the event. You must use the ToString method to convert the Sender object to a string.

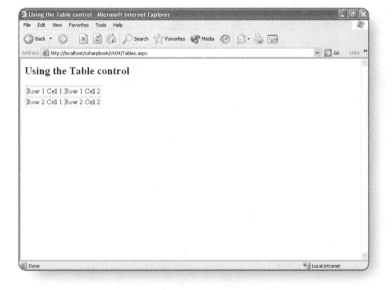

Using the Table Controls

ASP.NET also contains controls that generate HTML tables. Using the syntax required to build a table with these controls is simpler than using the HTML counterparts. You need only three controls: table, tablerow, and tablecell:

1. Insert a `Table` control.

2. Set the `id`.

3. Set the `BorderStyle` attribute.

4. Set the `GridLines` attribute.

5. Set the `runat` attribute to `server`.

6. Insert a `TableRow` control for each row to insert in the table.

7. Insert a `TableCell` control for each column to place in the row.

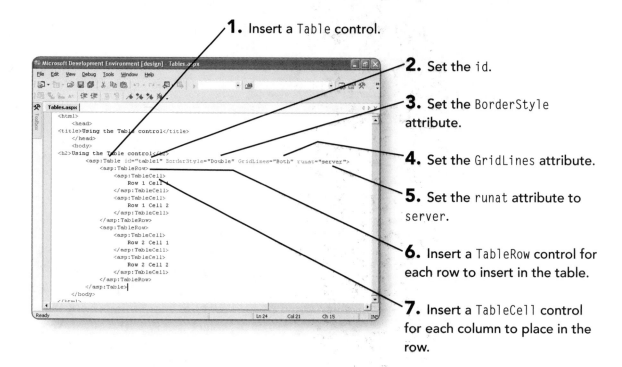

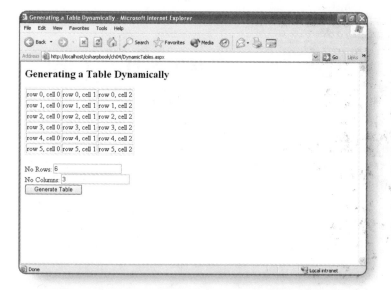

Creating a Table Dynamically

The following example creates a table dynamically. The user gets to specify the number of rows and columns in the table. You need to create a `tablerow` object for each row in the table, add `tablecell` objects to each row, and then add the `tablerow` objects to the `Table` control:

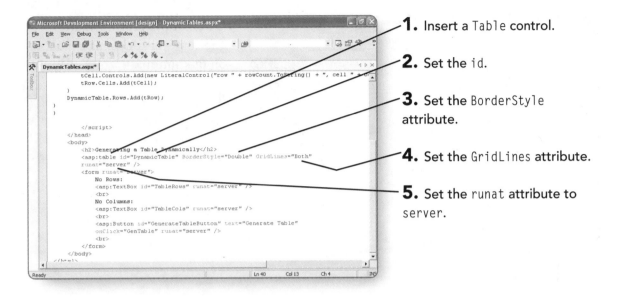

1. Insert a `Table` control.

2. Set the `id`.

3. Set the `BorderStyle` attribute.

4. Set the `GridLines` attribute.

5. Set the `runat` attribute to server.

6. Insert opening and closing `form` tags. Set the `runat` attribute to `server`.

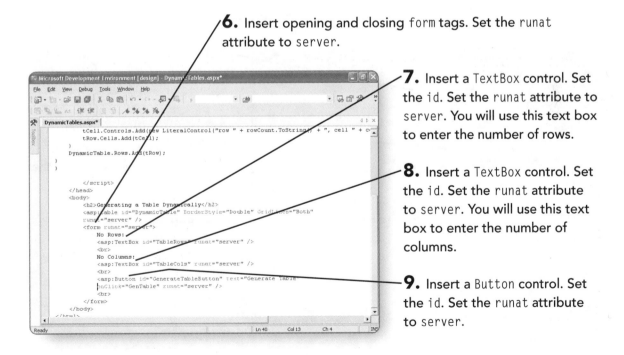

7. Insert a `TextBox` control. Set the `id`. Set the `runat` attribute to `server`. You will use this text box to enter the number of rows.

8. Insert a `TextBox` control. Set the `id`. Set the `runat` attribute to `server`. You will use this text box to enter the number of columns.

9. Insert a `Button` control. Set the `id`. Set the `runat` attribute to `server`.

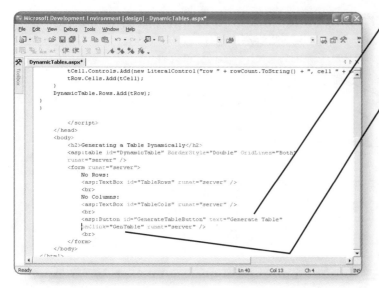

10. Set the `Text` attribute. The text will appear as a label on the button.

11. Set the `OnClick` event to `GenTable`. When the user clicks the image, the `GenTable` method will execute.

12. Insert opening and closing `script` tags.

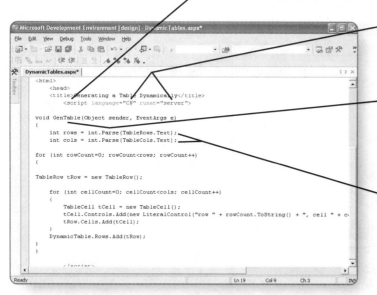

13. Set the `language` attribute to `C#` and the `runat` attribute to `server`.

14. Insert a `GenTable` method. The `GenTable` method will execute when the user clicks the button.

15. Retrieve the number of rows and columns that the table must contain.

16. Use a `for` loop to repeatedly create a new table row until the number of rows is reached.

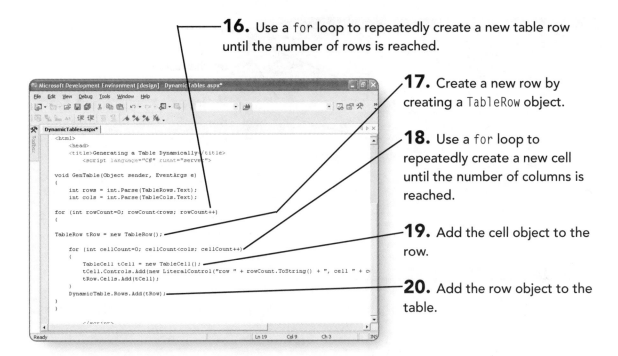

17. Create a new row by creating a `TableRow` object.

18. Use a `for` loop to repeatedly create a new cell until the number of columns is reached.

19. Add the cell object to the row.

20. Add the row object to the table.

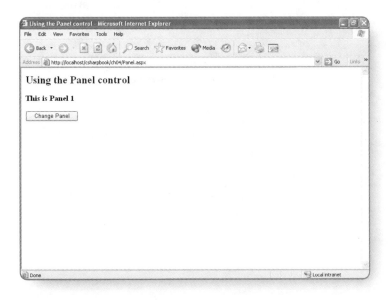

Using the Panel Control

The `Panel` is a container control. This basically means that the `Panel` control can hold other controls. You can have multiple panels on a page and enable or disable them as required. You can set the `Visible` property to `True` or `False`:

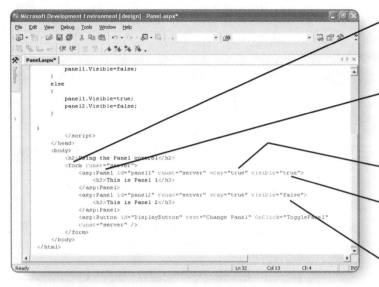

1. Insert opening and closing form tags. Set the runat attribute to server.

2. Insert a Panel control. Set the id. Set the runat attribute to server.

3. Set the wrap attribute.

4. Set the visible attribute to True.

5. Insert another Panel control and set the visible attribute to False. This panel will not appear.

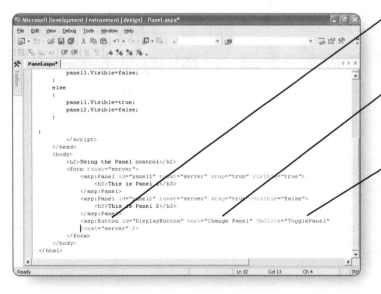

6. Insert a Button control. Set the id. Set the runat attribute to server.

7. Set the Text attribute. This text will appear as a label on the button.

8. Set the OnClick event to TogglePanel. When the user clicks the button, the TogglePanel method will execute.

9. Insert opening and closing `script` tags.

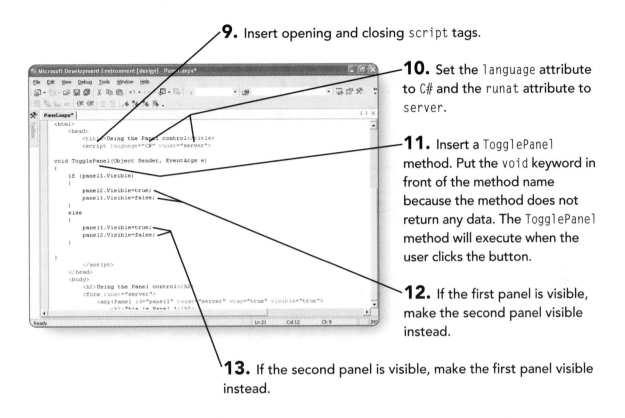

10. Set the `language` attribute to `C#` and the `runat` attribute to `server`.

11. Insert a `TogglePanel` method. Put the `void` keyword in front of the method name because the method does not return any data. The `TogglePanel` method will execute when the user clicks the button.

12. If the first panel is visible, make the second panel visible instead.

13. If the second panel is visible, make the first panel visible instead.

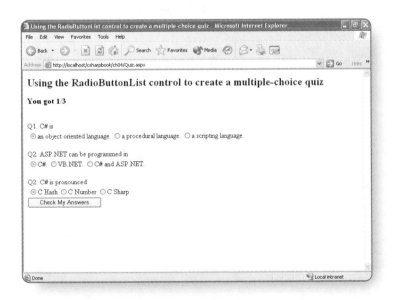

Creating a Quiz

The quiz uses a `RadioButtonList` control to display each possible answer to a question. You can easily grade the quiz by comparing the option selected by the user to the correct answers:

1. Insert opening and closing form tags. Set the `runat` attribute to `server`.

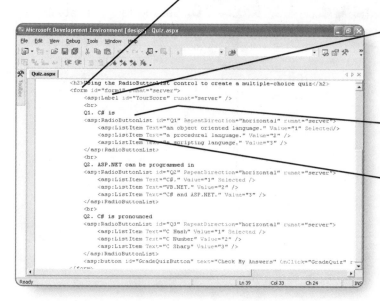

2. Insert a `Label` control. Set the `id`. Set the `runat` attribute to `server`. This label will be used to display the quiz score.

3. Insert a `RadioButtonList` for each question in the quiz.

4. Insert a `ListItem` for each answer to a question.

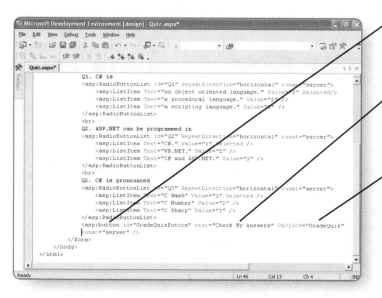

5. Insert a `Button` control. Set the `id`. Set the `runat` attribute to `server`.

6. Set the `Text` attribute. This text will appear as a label on the button.

7. Set the `OnClick` event to `GradeQuiz`. When the user clicks the button, the `GradeQuiz` method will execute.

8. Insert opening and closing `script` tags.

9. Set the `language` attribute to `C#` and the `runat` attribute to `server`.

10. Insert a `GradeQuiz` method. The `GradeQuiz` method will execute when the user clicks the button.

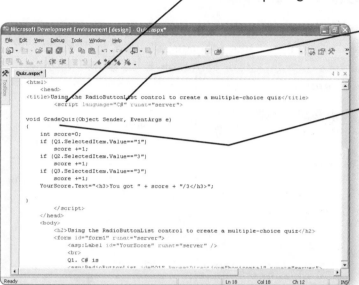

```
<html>
    <head>
<title>Using the RadioButtonList control to create a multiple-choice quiz</title>
        <script language="C#" runat="server">

void GradeQuiz(Object Sender, EventArgs e)
{
    int score=0;
    if (Q1.SelectedItem.Value=="1")
        score +=1;
    if (Q2.SelectedItem.Value=="3")
        score +=1;
    if (Q3.SelectedItem.Value=="3")
        score +=1;
    YourScore.Text="<h3>You got " + score + "/3</h3>";

}

        </script>
    </head>
    <body>
        <h2>Using the RadioButtonList control to create a multiple-choice quiz</h2>
        <form id="form1" runat="server">
            <asp:Label id="YourScore" runat="server" />
            <br>
            Q1. C# is
```

11. Declare an integer variable that will store the number of correct answers.

12. If the answer for a question is correct, add a value of 1 to the score.

13. Use the `Label` control to print the quiz score to the page.

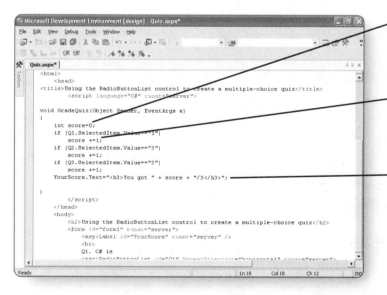

```
<html>
    <head>
<title>Using the RadioButtonList control to create a multiple-choice quiz</title>
        <script language="C#" runat="server">

void GradeQuiz(Object Sender, EventArgs e)
{
    int score=0;
    if (Q1.SelectedItem.Value=="1")
        score +=1;
    if (Q2.SelectedItem.Value=="3")
        score +=1;
    if (Q3.SelectedItem.Value=="3")
        score +=1;
    YourScore.Text="<h3>You got " + score + "/3</h3>";

}

        </script>
    </head>
    <body>
        <h2>Using the RadioButtonList control to create a multiple-choice quiz</h2>
        <form id="form1" runat="server">
            <asp:Label id="YourScore" runat="server" />
            <br>
            Q1. C# is
```

Databinding

Databinding is a powerful and innovative feature. Databinding, as its name suggests, allows data that is stored in an Array, ArrayList, or hash table to be bound (displayed) by a control. The DropDownList, CheckBoxList, and RadioButtonList controls all support databinding. The example that follows will bind the data stored in an ArrayList to each of these controls. In the case of the CheckBoxList control, a checkbox will be inserted for each item in the list.

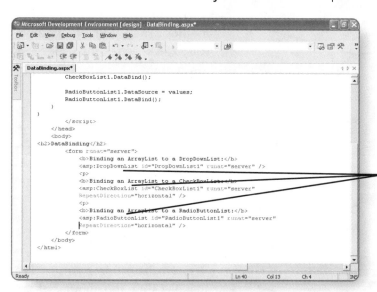

1. Insert DropDownList, CheckBoxList, and RadioButtonList controls.

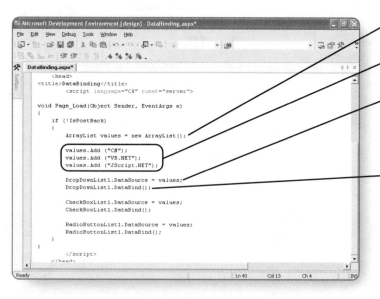

2. Create an ArrayList.

3. Add data to the ArrayList.

4. Set the DataSource property of the DropDownList control to the name of the ArrayList.

5. Call the DataBind method of the DropDownList control. Each item in the ArrayList will be added to the control.

6. Set the `DataSource` property of the `CheckBoxList` control to the name of the `ArrayList`.

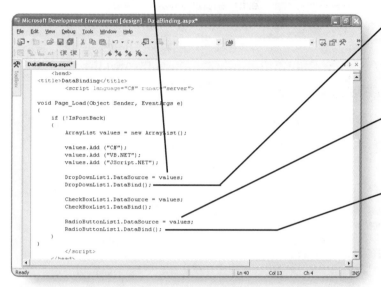

7. Call the `DataBind` method of the `CheckBoxList` control. Each item in the `ArrayList` will be added to the control.

8. Set the `DataSource` property of the `RadioButtonList` control to the name of the `ArrayList`.

9. Call the `DataBind` method of the `RadioButtonList` control. Each item in the `ArrayList` will be added to the control.

Binding Controls to Variables and Methods

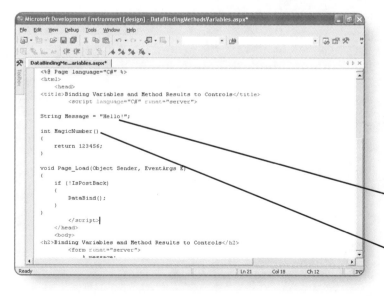

Methods that return data and variables can also be bound to a control. A new syntax that uses the `<%#` and `%>` delimiters must be used to bind a method or variable to a control. The `DataBind` method must be called to dynamically bind the data to a page.

1. Declare and initialize a variable.

2. Declare a method that returns data. The `return` keyword is used to do this.

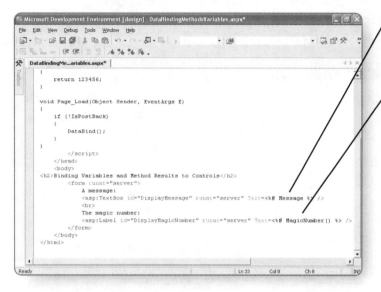

3. Type the name of the variable between the <%# and %> delimiters.

4. Type the name of the method between the <%# and %> delimiters.

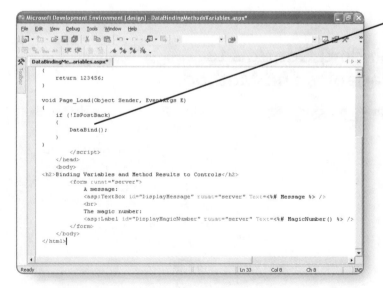

5. Call the DataBind method. This will dynamically bind the data to the page.

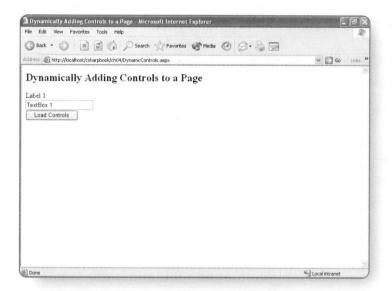

Dynamically Adding Controls to a Page

You can add controls to a page at any time. You will add a Label and textbox control to a panel. You need to create Label and textbox objects and then set their Text and Id properties. The Controls.Add method will insert the controls on the panel. This feature is very powerful because it allows you to dynamically build a page based upon user input.

1. Insert opening and closing form tags. Set the runat attribute to server.

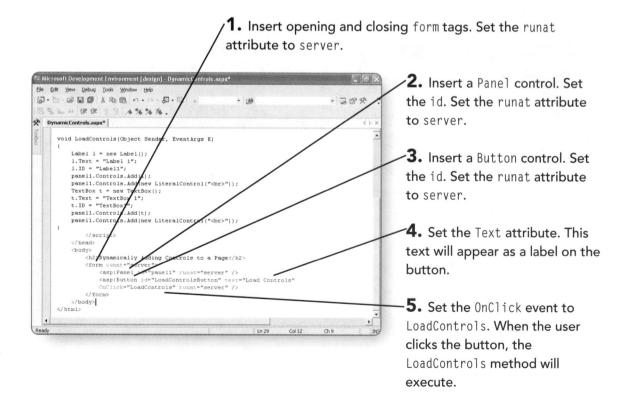

2. Insert a Panel control. Set the id. Set the runat attribute to server.

3. Insert a Button control. Set the id. Set the runat attribute to server.

4. Set the Text attribute. This text will appear as a label on the button.

5. Set the OnClick event to LoadControls. When the user clicks the button, the LoadControls method will execute.

6. Insert opening and closing `script` tags.

7. Set the `language` attribute to `C#` and the `runat` attribute to `server`.

8. Insert a `LoadControls` method. The `LoadControls` method will execute when the user clicks the button.

9. Create a new `Label` object.

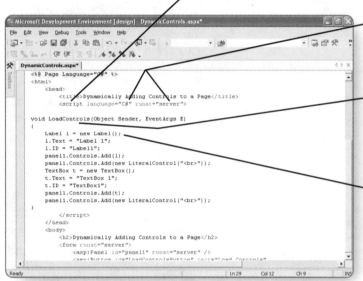

10. Set the `Text` property of the `Label` object.

11. Set the `id` of the label.

12. Add the label to the panel.

13. Create a new `TextBox` object.

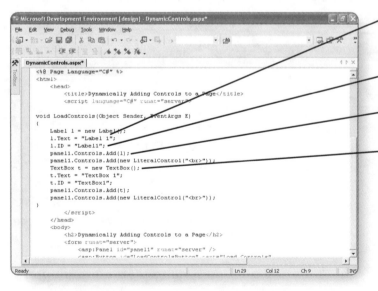

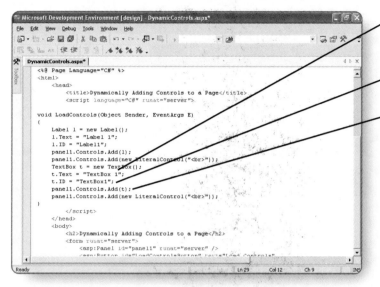

14. Set the Text property of the textbox object.

15. Set the id of the textbox.

16. Add the TextBox to the panel.

5

Controlling the Flow of C# Code

The ability to process information logically is fundamental to the success of any Web application. C# provides numerous decision-making constructs that enable you to evaluate data and execute the appropriate code. A loop, or iteration control, is another important C# programming construct. A loop provides a convenient way for code to be repeated. In this chapter, you'll learn to:

- Use logical and comparison operators.
- Use the if and switch statements to make decisions.
- Implement for, foreach, while, and do loops.
- Use the break and continue keywords to exit a loop.

Making Decisions

A C# program is a list of instructions that are usually executed in a linear manner. To build programs that can respond to different scenarios, you need the ability to analyze data and make decisions. C# offers a variety of ways to change the flow of program execution. The following programming constructs are implemented in C#:

- the if statement
- the switch statement
- the conditional operator (?:)

CAUTION

The C# syntax found in this chapter does not resemble the Visual Basic syntax at all. If you are a Visual Basic programmer, you may find the syntax a little complex initially, but the examples and interactive exercises presented in this chapter will quickly bring you up to speed. Programmers with some experience in Java or C++ will have no trouble adjusting to the C# syntax. There are, however, a number of subtle differences that will be highlighted throughout this chapter. The tips and cautions in this chapter will save you from spending hours debugging your code.

Using Logical and Comparison Operators

Comparison operators compare data values against one another and return either a true or false result. Comparison operators allow string and numeric data to be compared for equality, inequality, and size. The result of a comparison test can be used by an if statement to make a decision. Table 5.1 includes a list of all the available comparison operators.

NOTE

A true or false result is also known as a Boolean result. Comparison operators are also sometimes referred to as relational operators.

Table 5.1 Comparison Operators

Comparison Operator	Title	Description
==	equal to	Compares two values and returns true if they are equal.
!=	not equal to	Compares two values and returns true if they are not equal.
>	greater than	Compares two values and returns true if the value on the left of the operator is greater than the value on the right.
<	less than	Compares two values and returns true if the value on the left of the operator is less than the value on the right.
>=	greater than or equal to	Compares two values and returns true if the value on the left of the operator is greater than or equal to the value on the right.
<=	less than or equal to	Compares two values and returns true if the value on the left of the operator is less than or equal to the value on the right.

CAUTION

The data on either side of a conditional operator must be of the same type. You can't compare a string to an integer.

The And (&&), Or (||), and Not (!) operators are known as logical operators. Logical operators enable you to combine two or more comparison tests into a compound expression. A description of the available logical operators is found in Table 5.2, and a list of logical expressions and their results is listed in Table 5.3.

Table 5.2 Logical Operators

Logical Operator	Title	Description
&&	And	Returns true if both values are true.
||	Or	Returns true if either value is true.
!	Not	Inverts the true or false result.

Table 5.3 Example Logical Expressions

Expression	Example	Result
True && True	(3>2) && (4>1)	True
True && False	(3>2) && (4<1)	False
False && True	(3<2) && (4>1)	False
False && False	(3<2) && (4<1)	False
True || True	(3>2) || (4>1)	True
True || False	(3>2) || (4<1)	True
False || True	(3>2) || (4>1)	True
False || False	(3<2) || (4<1)	False
!(True)	!(3>2)	False
!(False)	!(3<2)	True

Using the if Statement

The if statement is used to conditionally execute code statements. An if statement enables you to execute one or more code statements based on the Boolean result returned by an expression. The if statement is the most commonly used decision-making programming structure.

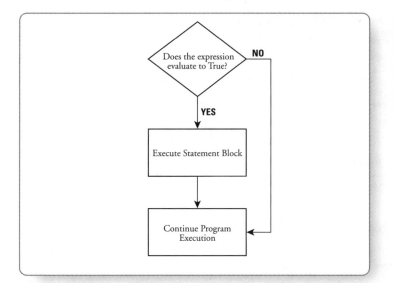

NOTE

The flowchart illustrates the logic behind an if statement.

The basic syntax for an if statement follows:

```
if (expression)
{
// insert code statements that must be executed when
condition is true here;
}
```

- The if keyword must be followed by a condition.

- The expression, also called a conditional, must be placed in parentheses. The expression must return a Boolean value.

- The code that must be executed if the expression evaluates to true must be placed within curly braces.

NOTE

Curly braces are used to group code statements that must be executed together. Each statement must end with a semicolon.

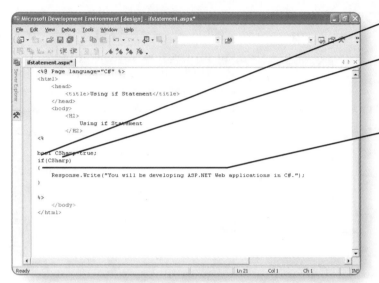

1. Type the if keyword.

2. Type an expression between the parentheses that follow the if keyword.

3. Type an opening brace ({). This will mark the beginning of the if code block.

CAUTION

C# requires all expressions used in an if statement to return a Boolean value (that is, either true or false). Unlike C and C++, an expression in C# that returns an integer can't be used. This means that you can't substitute an integer value of 1 for true or an integer value of 0 for false. If the expression does not return a Boolean value, you will receive the following error message:

```
Error CS0029: Cannot implicitly convert type 'int' to 'bool'.
```

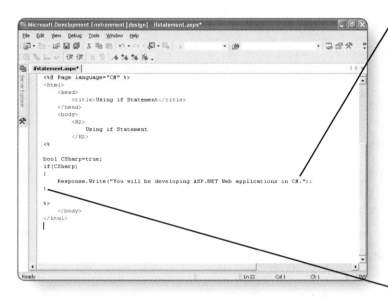

```
Microsoft Development Environment [design] - ifstatement.aspx*
File   Edit   View   Debug   Tools   Window   Help

ifstatement.aspx*

<%@ Page language="C#" %>
<html>
    <head>
        <title>Using if Statement</title>
    </head>
    <body>
        <H2>
            Using if Statement
        </H2>
<%

bool CSharp=true;
if(CSharp)
{

    Response.Write("You will be developing ASP.NET Web applications in C#.");

}

%>
    </body>
</html>
```

4. Type the code to be executed if the expression is `true`.

TIP

It is common practice to indent the code embedded in an `if` statement. This is not required but does make your code easier to read and debug.

5. Type a closing brace (}). This will end the `if` code block.

Using the else Clause of an if Statement

The `if` statement simply executes a group of statements if a condition is found to be true. The `else` clause is used in conjunction with the `if` statement to specify the code that should be executed if the condition is `false`. The `else` clause is an optional part of the `if` statement.

YES — Does the expression evaluate to True? — NO

Execute if Statement Block

Execute else Statement Block

Continue Program Execution

NOTE

This image is a graphical representation of an `if` statement that includes an `else` clause.

The basic syntax for implementing an if else clause follows:

```
if (expression)
{
// insert code statements that must be executed when
condition is true here;
}
else
{
// insert code statements that must be executed when
condition is false here;
}
```

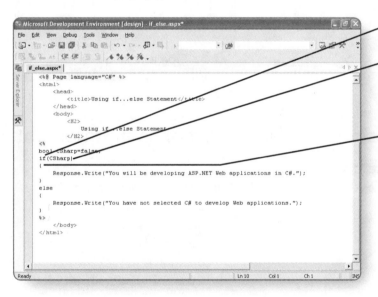

1. Type the if keyword.

2. Type an expression between the parentheses that follow the if keyword.

3. Type an opening brace. This will mark the beginning of the if code block.

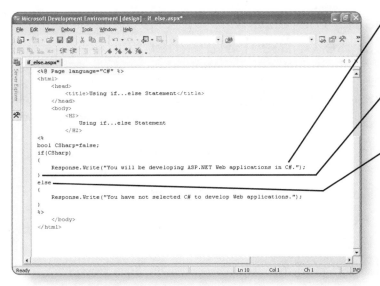

4. Type the code to be executed if the expression is true.

5. Type a closing brace. This will end the if code block.

6. Type the else keyword.

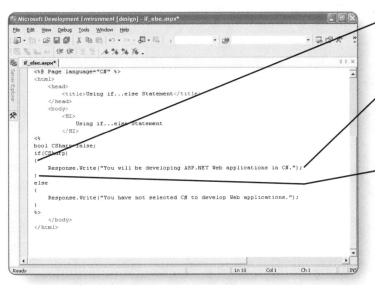

7. Type an opening brace. This will mark the beginning of the else code block.

8. Type the code to be executed if the expression is false.

9. Type a closing brace. This will end the else code block.

Using the else if Clause of the if Statement

The if statement enables only a single condition to be evaluated. What if you want to process multiple scenarios? C# provides a solution: You can test for additional conditions by using the else if clause. There is no limit on the number of else if clauses that can be used.

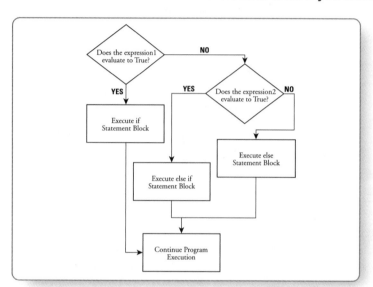

NOTE

This image is a graphical representation of an if statement that includes an else if clause.

The basic syntax for implementing an if else clause follows:

```csharp
if (expression1)
{
// insert code statements that must be executed when
condition1 is true here;
}
else if (expression2)
{
// insert code statements that must be executed when
condition2 is true here;
}
else
{
// insert code statements that must be executed when
both condition1 and condition2 are false here;
}
```

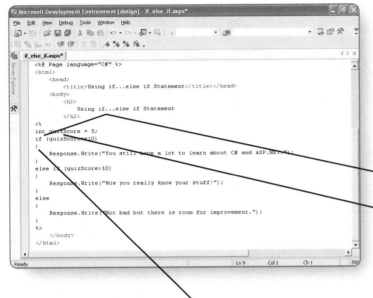

NOTE

Only one condition can be `true`. Once the code for a `true` condition has been executed, the rest of the clauses are ignored.

1. Type the `if` keyword.

2. Type an expression within the parentheses that follow the `if` keyword.

3. Type an opening brace. This will mark the beginning of the `if` code block.

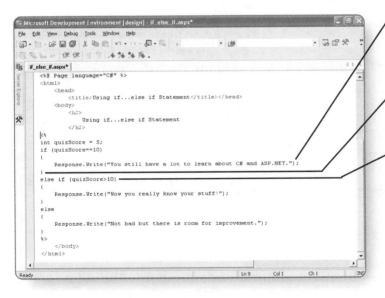

4. Type the code to be executed if the expression is `true`.

5. Type a closing brace. This will end the `if` code block.

6. Type `else if` followed by an expression. The expression must be placed within parentheses.

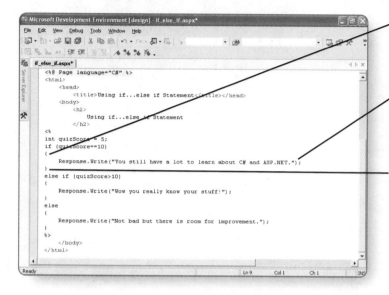

7. Type an opening brace. This will mark the beginning of the `else if` code block.

8. Type the code to be executed if the expression proves `true`.

9. Type a closing brace. This will end the `else if` code block.

NOTE

No restriction is placed on the number of `else if` clauses you can include.

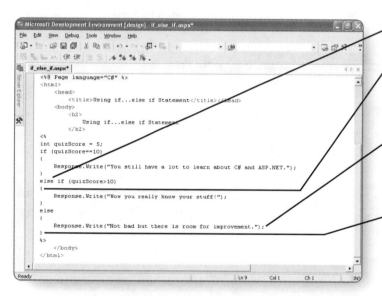

10. Type the `else if` keyword.

11. Type an opening brace. This will mark the beginning of the `else if` code block.

12. Type the code that will be executed if the expression is `false`.

13. Type a closing brace. This will end the `else` code block.

NOTE

The `if-else` statement in this example produces this message: *Not bad but there is room for improvement.*

Using the Conditional Operator

The conditional operator is really just an `if else` statement with compacted syntax. It is used when you want to return one of two values based on the result of a Boolean expression. The syntax for the conditional operator:

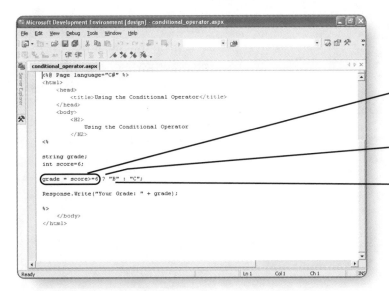

```
condition ? value to return
if condition is true : value
to return if condition is
false
```

1. Type a valid Boolean expression.

2. Type **?** after the expression.

3. Type the value that must be returned if the expression evaluates to `true`.

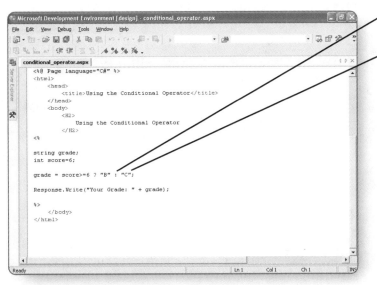

4. Type **:**.

5. Type the value that must be returned if the expression evaluates to `false`.

NOTE

The following `if` statement is equivalent to the conditional operator:

```
if (score>=6)
        grade = "B";
else
        grade = "C";
```

Using the switch Statement

If you have many conditions to test, multiple else if clauses can become difficult to implement and maintain. The switch statement provides a viable alternative to nested else if statements, particularly if the expression needs to be evaluated only once. The switch statement enables you to define a case for each value that must be compared to the result of an expression. The code embedded in a case block will be executed when the result of the expression matches the case value. The default case block will be executed if no match is found.

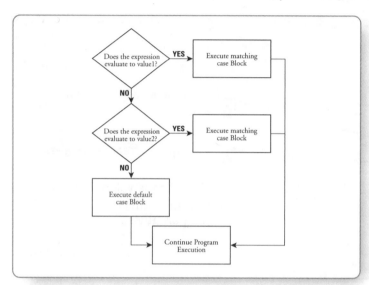

NOTE

This flowchart models a switch statement.

The syntax for a switch statement follows:

```csharp
switch (expression)
{
case value1
    // insert code statements that must be executed when
expression evaluates to value1;
    break;
case value2:
    // insert code statements that must be executed when
expression evaluates to value2;
    break;
default:
    // insert code statements that must be executed when
none of the cases match;
    break;
}
```

- The switch keyword is followed by the expression that must be evaluated.

- The case keyword is followed by a value. The expression will be matched against this value.

- A colon (:) is used to terminate the case.

- A break statement must be placed at the end of each case block. This will exit the switch statement.

- The default keyword defines a default case. This default case will execute if none of the other cases are matched.

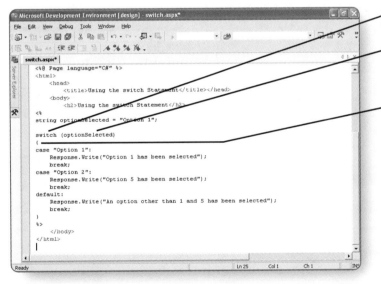

1. Type the switch keyword.

2. Type an expression within the parentheses.

3. Type an opening brace. This will mark the beginning of the switch code block.

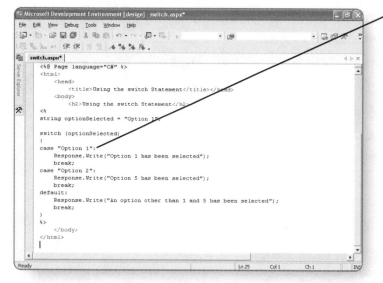

4. Type the `case` keyword followed by the value that must be returned by the expression to match this `case`. Each `case` statement must end with a colon (:).

NOTE

In Java, the expression can only return a simple data type, such as an int or char. This is not the case with C#. The expression can return sbyte, byte, short, ushort, uint, long, ulong, char, and string data. This provides the great flexibility that Visual Basic programmers are already accustomed to.

5. Type the code that will be executed if the `case` is matched.

CAUTION

Case values must be constants or an error will be produced.

6. Type the `break` keyword. All case blocks must end with a `break` statement. This will exit the `switch` statement so that no other cases are tested.

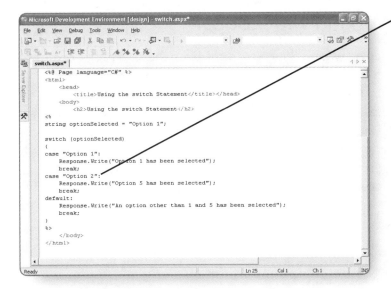

7. Type all of the case blocks that you require.

CAUTION

Each case must be terminated with a `break` statement. The `break` statement is used to exit the `switch` statement. C# does not allow many cases to be executed. This is known as fall-through. In some other languages, omitting the `break` statement results in the code for each remaining case being executed.

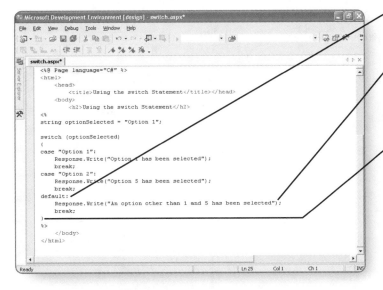

8. Type the `default` keyword followed by a colon.

9. Type the code that must be executed if none of the cases match the result.

10. Type a closing brace. This will end the `switch` code block.

Working with Loops

Imagine writing the code to calculate the salary for a company that has 50,000 employees. It would just not make sense to copy the code 50,000 times to print a pay slip for every employee. Loops allow you to repeat sections of code until a criterion is met. Loops are essential when you need to perform the same calculation using different data. C# has a set of looping constructs that allow code blocks to be executed repeatedly. C# has four types of loops:

- for
- foreach
- while
- do-while

The concepts involved in implementing a loop are usually difficult to grasp, especially for a first-time programmer. The interactive tutorials in this chapter were designed with that in mind and will enhance your understanding so that you can immediately start building your own loops in C#. You will be able to interactively change loop parameters and view the output produced.

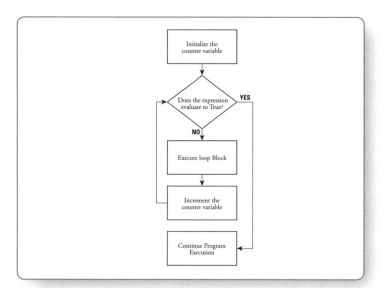

Using the for Loop

The for loop is the most convenient loop. It allows code to be executed a specified number of times and uses a counter that is incremented each time the loop is executed.

NOTE

The flowchart for a for loop.

The syntax for a `for` loop follows:

```
for (counter=start_value; counter < max_value ; increment
counter)
{
// insert code that must be executed until the test
condition becomes true;
}
```

The `counter` variable keeps track of the number of iterations through the loop and is initialized before the loop begins. It is incremented after each iteration through the loop. When the `counter` is equal to the `max_value` variable, the execution of the loop stops.

The interactive `for` loop exercise will enable you to set the start and end values of the loop counter variable and see the output that the loop produces.

TIP

All source code can be downloaded from the Premier Press Web site at http://www.premierpressbooks.com/downloads.asp.

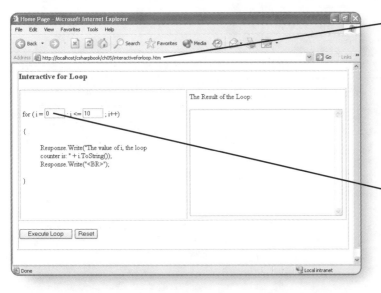

1. Open the interactiveforloop.htm file in a Web browser. This file is in the ch05 folder. (This file contains the syntax of a `for` loop.) You can test the loop by entering an initial value and an end value for the loop counter variable.

2. Type the initial value of the loop counter variable.

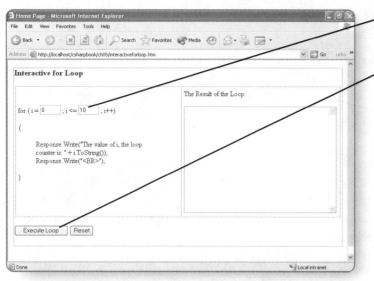

3. Type the value that will end the loop.

4. Click on Execute Loop. The results will be displayed.

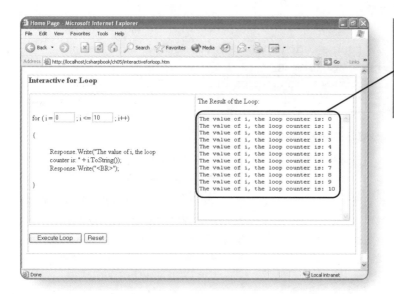

NOTE

The value of the loop counter at each iteration of the loop is displayed.

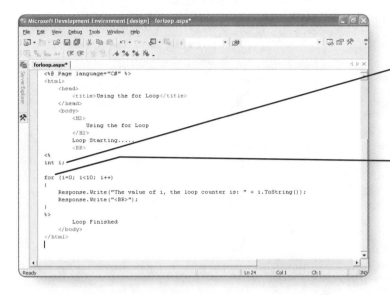

Now you'll write some C# code to create a for loop.

1. Declare a variable as an integer. This variable will be used to count repetitions of the loop.

2. Type the for keyword followed by parentheses.

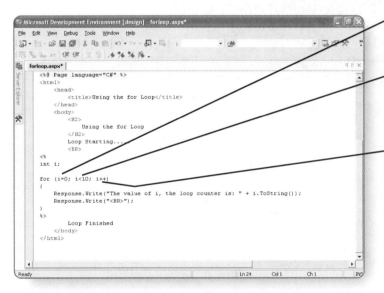

3. Assign an initial value to the loop counter variable.

4. Type a Boolean expression that will determine when the loop will end.

5. Increment the loop counter variable.

NOTE

Each control parameter passed to the for loop must be separated by a semicolon.

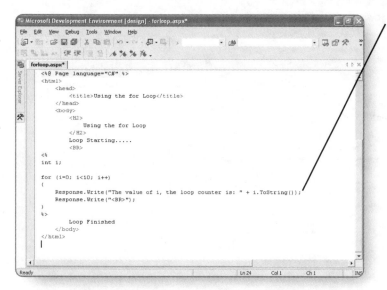

6. Within the braces, type the code that will be repeated.

Using the foreach Loop

On many occasions, the ability to loop through all the elements in a group of data will be beneficial. C# provides a foreach loop to simplify looping through the contents of an object that stores many items such as an array. You are not required to specify the upper bounds of an array before you loop through all the elements.

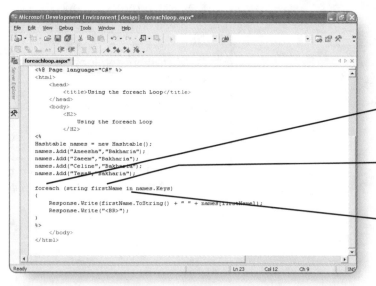

1. Type the foreach keyword followed by parentheses.

2. Declare a variable that will store the element.

3. Type the in keyword.

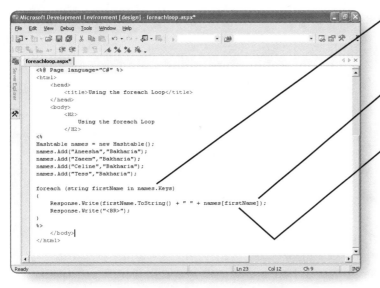

4. Type the name of the object or collection you want to loop through.

5. Within the braces, type the code that will be repeated.

6. The variable will store the value of each element in the collection.

Using a while Loop

The while loop is handy if you need to execute code until a condition is met. This can be achieved without knowing how many times the loop needs to execute before the condition becomes true.

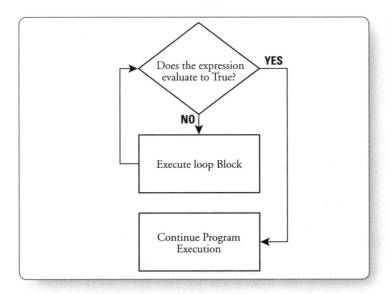

NOTE
The flowchart for a while loop.

The syntax for a while loop follows:

```
while (expression)
{
  // insert code that must be executed while the test
  condition is true;
}
```

The while loop begins by evaluating the test condition. If it evaluates to true, the code within the loop body is executed.

The interactive exercise presented in this section will enable you to create a while loop that uses a counter to determine the number of times a loop should be executed. The counter variable is initialized before the while loop begins. The counter has to be incremented inside the loop code block.

1. In your Web browser, open the interactivewhileloop.htm file from the Premier Web site (http://www.premierpressbooks.com/downloads.asp). A Web page that contains the syntax of a while loop will be displayed. You can test the loop by typing an initial value and an end value for the loop counter variable.

2. Type the initial value of the loop counter variable.

3. Type the value that will end the loop.

4. Click on Execute Loop.

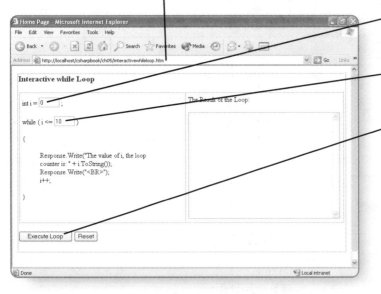

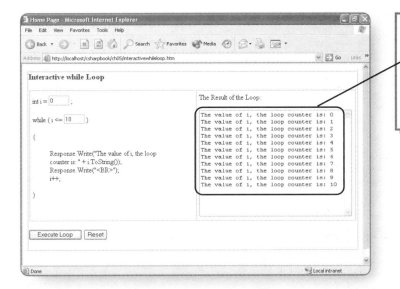

NOTE

The results will be displayed. You will now write the C# code to implement a while loop.

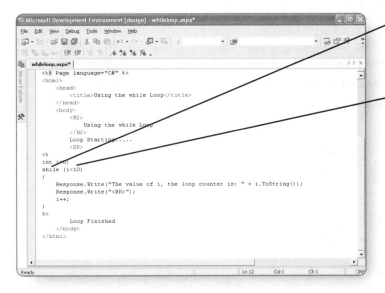

1. Type the while keyword followed by a pair of parentheses.

2. Type a Boolean expression that will determine when the loop will end. Do not place a semicolon after the expression.

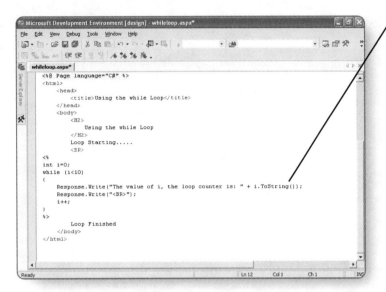

3. Within the braces, type the code that will be repeated.

Using a do while Loop

The do while loop is very similar to the while loop; the difference is that the condition is evaluated after the execution of the loop iteration. This means that the code will be executed at least once.

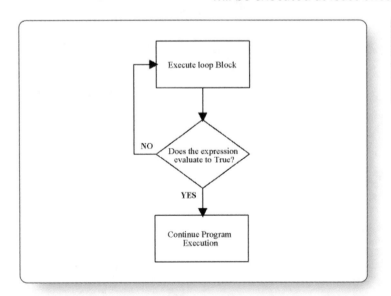

NOTE

The flowchart for a do while loop.

The syntax for a do while loop follows:

```
do
{
    // insert code that must be executed while the test
    condition is true;
} while (expression);
```

The following interactive exercise illustrates that no matter what you define as the start and stop values of a do while loop, the code embedded in the loop always gets executed once.

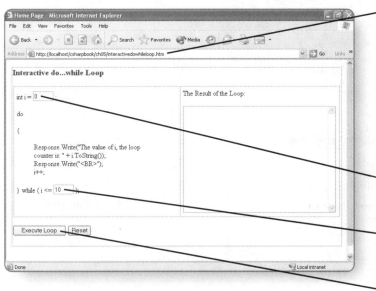

1. In your Web browser, open the interactivedowhileloop.htm file. A Web page that contains the syntax of a do while loop will be displayed. You can test the loop by typing both an initial value and an end value for the loop counter variable.

2. Type the initial value of the loop counter variable.

3. Type the value that will end the loop.

4. Click on Execute Loop.

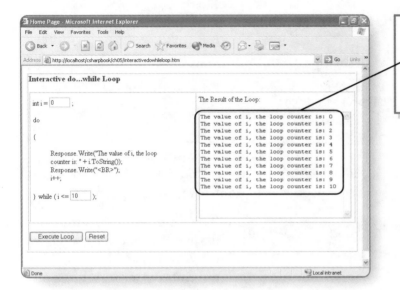

NOTE

The results will be displayed. Now you'll build a do while loop.

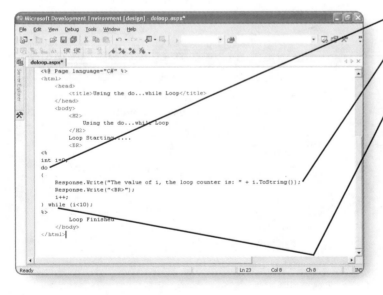

1. Type the do keyword.

2. Type the code that will be repeated between the braces.

3. Type the while keyword followed by a pair of parentheses.

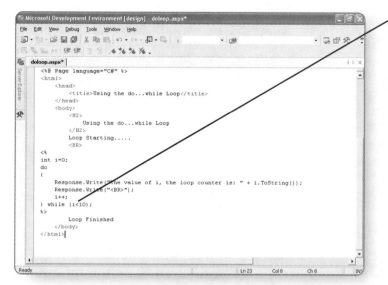

4. Type a Boolean expression that determines the end of the loop. A semicolon must be placed after the expression.

Exiting Loops

A loop will stop only when the test condition evaluates to true. You can, however, exit a loop when a special condition arises. The break and continue keywords can be used to abruptly terminate the execution of a loop.

Using the break Statement

The break statement was used earlier in this chapter to exit a switch statement. The break statement can also be used to terminate a loop. After the break statement is encountered, execution is transferred to the first code statement after the closing loop braces.

In the interactive exercise that follows, you will define the condition that will terminate the loop. The loop will not produce any output after the break statement.

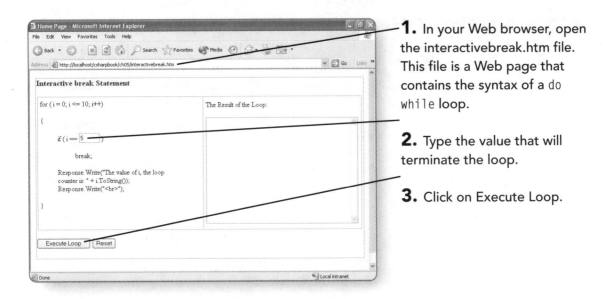

1. In your Web browser, open the interactivebreak.htm file. This file is a Web page that contains the syntax of a do while loop.

2. Type the value that will terminate the loop.

3. Click on Execute Loop.

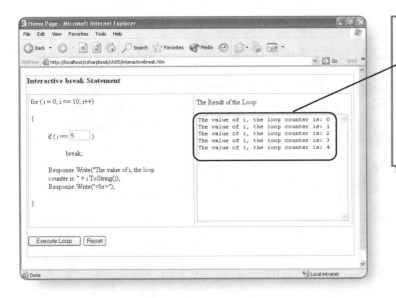

NOTE

The results will be displayed. The following includes a break statement to exit a loop when a certain condition becomes true.

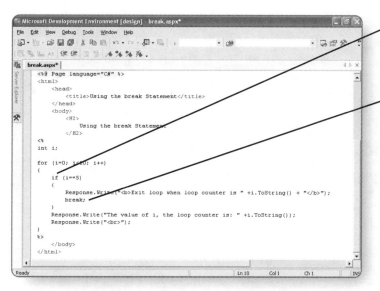

1. Use an `if` statement to test for the condition that will exit the loop.

2. Type the `break` keyword. When the `break` keyword is encountered during execution, the loop will end.

Using the continue Statement

The `continue` statement is very similar to the `break` statement, but instead of stopping the loop, it starts over at the next iteration. When the `continue` statement is executed, the remaining code statements within the loop are ignored, and the loop returns to the beginning.

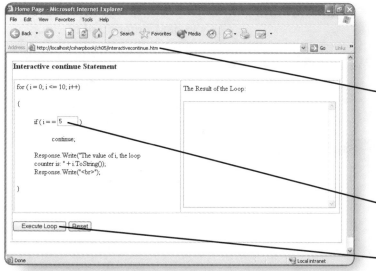

In this exercise, you will be able to specify the condition that will cause the rest of the code in the current iteration to be skipped.

1. In your Web browser, open the interactivecontinue.htm file. This file is a Web page that contains the syntax of a `continue` statement.

2. Type the value that will stop the current iteration.

3. Click on Execute Loop.

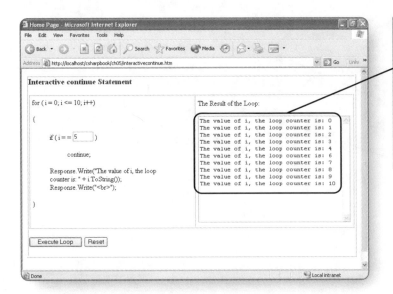

NOTE

The results will be displayed. Now you'll insert a `continue` statement in a loop so that a loop iteration can be skipped.

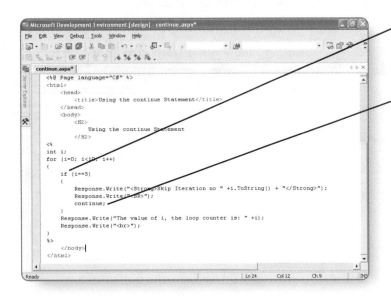

1. Use an `if` statement to test for the condition that will stop the current iteration of the loop.

2. Type the `continue` keyword. When the `continue` keyword is encountered during execution, the next iteration of the loop will begin.

6

Programming in C#

This chapter focuses on the base .NET classes that are essential for creating sophisticated applications in C#. I cover both the String and Math classes in detail because they are a fundamental part of any programming language. It is almost impossible to write a useful program that does not involve string manipulation or mathematical processing. In this chapter, you'll learn to:

- Create and manipulate strings.
- Utilize regular expressions.
- Use the Math class.
- Work with dates.
- Work with arrays.

Working with Strings

A string is a collection of characters—numbers, letters, punctuation marks, and spaces. Strings store real data such as the text you want to print to the screen or the data just entered by a user. The String class has properties and methods that allow you to manipulate the data stored in a string variable. Table 6.1 provides a summary of the methods and properties encapsulated in the String class.

Table 6.1 The String Class

Method	Purpose
Compare	Compares two strings for equality
Concat	Joins two strings together
IndexOf	Returns the first occurrence of a character or string
LastIndexOf	Returns the last occurrence of a character or string
PadLeft	Add spaces at the beginning of a string
PadRight	Adds spaces at the end of a string
Substring	Extracts a portion of a string
ToLower	Converts a string to lowercase
ToUpper	Converts a string to uppercase
Trim	Removes leading and trailing spaces
TrimEnd	Removes trailing spaces
TrimStart	Removes leading spaces

Creating Strings

You must place a string within opening and closing quotation marks. You can include special whitespace characters such as a tab or new line, but you must precede these characters with a backslash (\). The backslash is also known as the escape character. Placing the @ symbol before the opening quotation mark of a string creates a verbatim string. Verbatim strings do not need to contain the escape character and can span multiple lines without producing a syntax error.

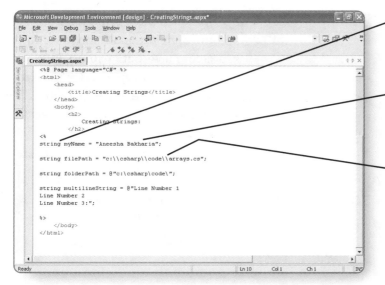

1. You use the `string` keyword to declare a variable that stores a string.

2. The text stored in a string must be enclosed in quotation marks.

3. You can insert special characters in a string as long as they are preceded by a backslash (\).

Table 6.2 shows some common whitespace characters and their escape sequences.

Table 6.2 Escape Sequences

Escape Sequence	Special Character
\'	Single quotation mark
\"	Double quotation mark
\\	Backslash
\t	Tab
\b	Backspace
\r	Carriage return
\f	Form feed

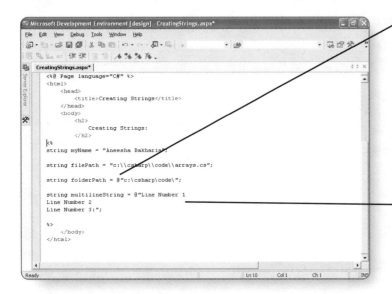

4. Place the @ symbol before the opening quotation mark to create a verbatim string. In a verbatim string, you don't need to use the \ escape character. The verbatim string gets used as is.

NOTE

A verbatim string can span multiple lines.

Determining the Length of a String

When you declare a string, you are really creating a `string` object. All `string` objects have a `Length` property that returns the number of characters (spaces included) stored in a string.

You can access the properties and methods of an object through dot notation.

The syntax to access the property of an object follows:

objectName.propertyName

Here is the syntax for accessing an `object` method:

objectName.methodName( )

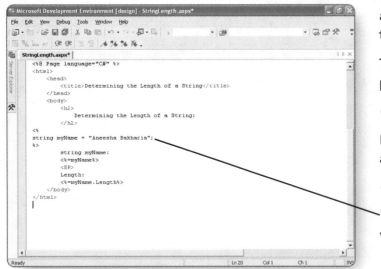

1. Declare and initialize a string variable.

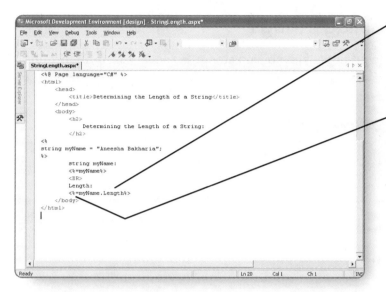

2. Type **.Length** after the variable name. This will access the Length property of the string.

3. Use the <%= %> tag to print the number of characters stored in the string to the page.

Converting Numbers to Strings

You use the ToString method to convert a numeric value to a string. This is handy when you want to store a number in a string variable:

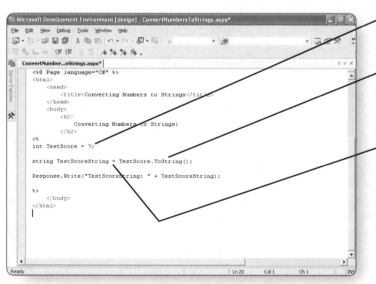

1. Declare and initialize an integer variable.

2. Type **.ToString** after the variable name. This will call the ToString method.

3. Use the = sign to assign the result to a string variable.

Joining Strings

The process of combining strings is known as *concatenation*. It is easy to join strings in C#. You can use the + operator or the Concat method to combine strings:

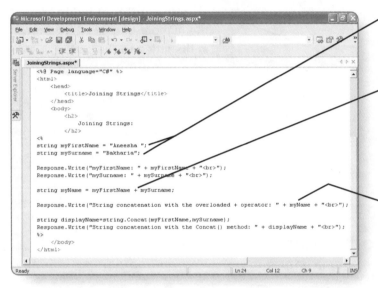

1. Declare and initialize the string variables that you want to concatenate.

2. Place the + operator between the two variable names. This will concatenate the strings and assign the result to the myName variable.

3. Use the Response.Write method to print the data stored in the myName variable to the page. The combined string will appear.

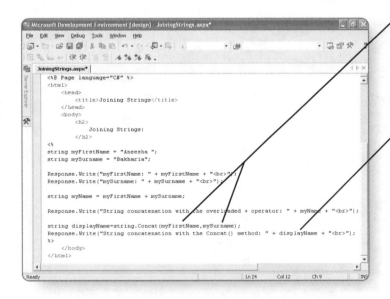

4. Pass the string variables that must be concatenated to the string.Concat method and assign the result to the displayName variable.

5. Use the Response.Write method to print the data stored in the displayName variable to the page. The combined string will appear.

Changing Case

The ToUpper and ToLower methods change the case of a string. You can use them to format data before it is displayed or stored and processed:

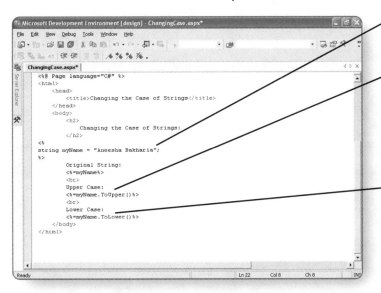

1. Declare and initialize a string variable.

2. Type **.ToUpper** after the name of the string variable. This will call the ToUpper method. The ToUpper method converts all the characters to uppercase.

3. Type **.ToLower** after the name of the string variable. This will call the ToLower method. The ToLower method converts all the characters to lowercase.

Comparing Strings

You use the Compare method to test two strings for equality. By default, the Compare method is case sensitive, but you can turn that off. You can also compare strings using the is-equal-to (==) or not-equal-to (!=) operators:

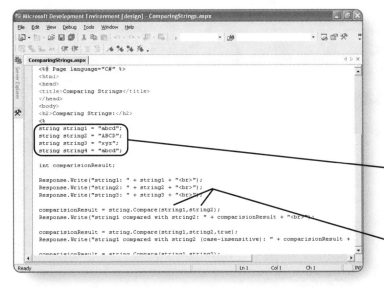

1. Declare and initialize the strings that you want to use in the comparison.

2. Pass the strings to the string.Compare method. The Compare method is case sensitive.

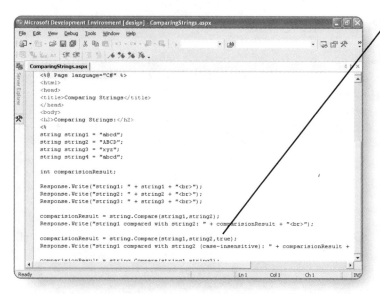

3. Pass True as the third parameter passed to the Compare method. This will force the Compare method to ignore case when making a comparison.

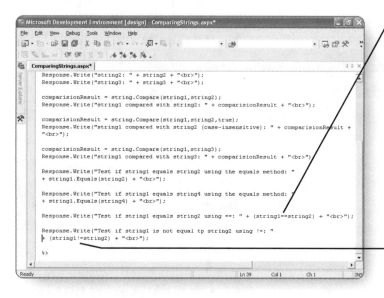

4. Placing the == operator between two strings will also test for equality.

5. The != operator will return True when the two strings are not equal.

Searching and Replacing

The `Replace` method is powerful. It allows you to search for and replace all occurrences of a specified character or phrase. You can also use the `Replace` method to replace individual characters:

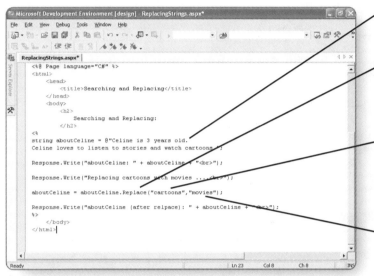

1. Declare and initialize a string variable.

2. Type **.Replace** after the variable name. This will call the `Replace` method.

3. Pass the text that you are searching for as the first parameter to the `Replace` method.

4. Pass the replacement text as the second parameter to the `Replace` method.

Trimming and Padding Strings

When a user enters data, he can accidentally type additional spaces. This whitespace must be removed before the data is processed and stored. The `string` class has methods that remove leading and trailing spaces from a string. There are even methods that can insert a specified number of spaces at either the beginning or end of a string:

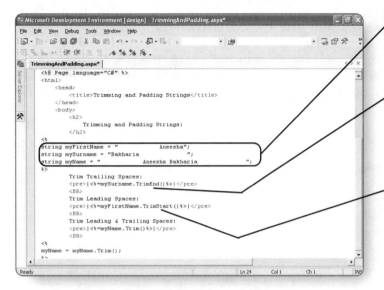

1. Declare and initialize strings that contain leading and trailing spaces.

2. Type **.TrimEnd** after the variable name to call the `TrimEnd` method. This will remove trailing spaces from the string.

3. Type **.TrimStart** after the variable name to call the `TrimStart` method. This will remove leading spaces from the string.

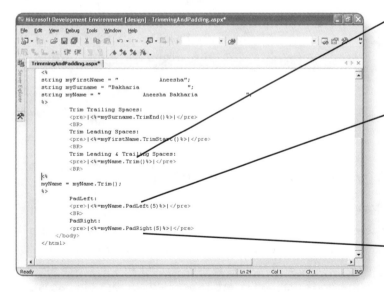

4. Type **.Trim** after the variable name to call the `Trim` method. This will remove both leading and trailing spaces from the string.

5. Type **.PadLeft** after the variable name to call the `PadLeft` method. Pass the number of spaces that must be inserted at the start of the string. Leading spaces will appear.

6. Type **.PadRight** after the variable name to call the `PadRight` method. Pass the number of spaces that must be inserted at the end of the string. Trailing spaces will appear.

Working with Substrings

The `IndexOf` method finds the first occurrence of a character or sequence of characters in a string. The `IndexOf` method returns the location where the substring is found. If the substring is not found, the method returns `-1` (indicating a false result). You use the `Substring` method to extract a potion of a string. The example that follows uses the `IndexOf` and `Substring` methods to separate the sentences found in a paragraph:

1. Declare a string and store a paragraph of text in it.

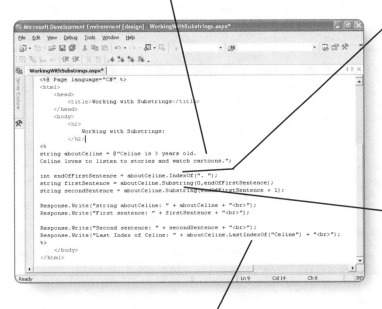

2. Type **.IndexOf** after the variable name to call the `IndexOf` method. You must pass the text you are searching for as a parameter. The `IndexOf` method will return the first position of the text if it is found. If no match is found, it returns a value of `-1`.

3. Type **.Substring** after the variable name to call the `Substring` method. You must pass the start and end positions of the text you want to extract to the method.

NOTE

The `LastIndexOf` method returns the position of the last instance of the matching pattern.

Creating an Online Psychiatrist

The online psychiatrist application uses the string-manipulation techniques covered in this chapter. Basically, the problems you enter will be rephrased. Dr Sharp is the name of the virtual psychiatrist who offers a free 24-hour service to all C# programmers. Dr Sharp can cure your programming blues:

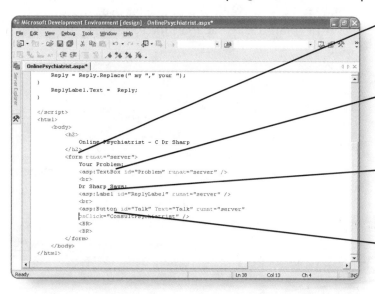

1. Insert opening and closing `<form>` tags. Set the `runat` attribute to `server`.

2. Insert a `textbox` control. This is where you will enter your problem.

3. Insert a `Label` control. This is where Dr Sharp's response will appear.

4. Insert a `Button` control. When you click the button, the `ConsultPsychiatrist` method will execute.

5. Set the `language` attribute of the `Page` directive to `C#`.

6. Insert opening and closing `<script>` tags. Set the `language` attribute to `C#`.

7. Insert the `ConsultPsychiatrist` method.

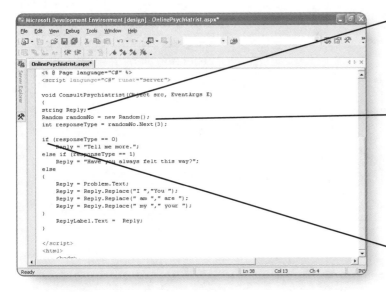

8. Declare a string variable named Reply. This variable will store the psychiatrist's response before it is printed to the screen.

9. Generate a random number between 0 and 2. The random number will determine the psychiatrist's response. Store the random number in the responseType variable.

10. Use an if statement to determine what must be stored in the Reply variable.

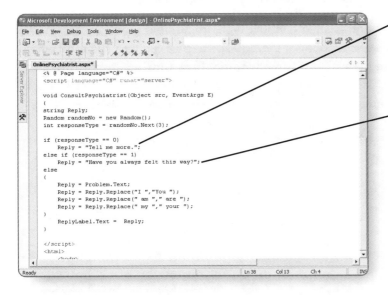

11. If the responseType variable is equal to 0, then store "Tell me more." in the Reply variable.

12. If the responseType variable is equal to 1, then store "Have you always felt this way?" in the Reply variable.

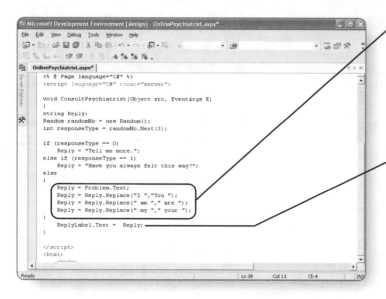

```
<% @ Page language="C#" %>
<script language="C#" runat="server">

void ConsultPsychiatrist(Object src, EventArgs E)
{
string Reply;
Random randomNo = new Random();
int responseType = randomNo.Next(3);

if (responseType == 0)
    Reply = "Tell me more.";
else if (responseType == 1)
    Reply = "Have you always felt this way?";
else
{
    Reply = Problem.Text;
    Reply = Reply.Replace("I ","You ");
    Reply = Reply.Replace(" am "," are ");
    Reply = Reply.Replace(" my "," your ");
}
    ReplyLabel.Text =  Reply;
}

</script>
<html>
```

13. If the responseType variable is equal to 2, then the user's problem will be re-phrased. "I" will change to "You," "am" will change to "are," and "my" will change to "your."

14. Assign the Reply variable to the Text property of the ReplyLabel. This will display the psychiatrist's response on the Web page.

Using the StringBuilder Class

A string is an immutable type. Immutable types are assigned a specific amount of storage space that can't be changed when the data is modified or copied. Each time you add more data to a string, the program actually creates a new string object in memory. The StringBuilder class is more efficient when you need to dynamically build strings. When you create a StringBuilder object, it is allocated enough memory to store data that is appended to the string as well. The StringBuilder class has an Append method that you use to concatenate data to a string. It also has a Replace method:

```
<%@ Page language="C#" %>
<html>
    <head>
        <title>Comparing Strings</title>
    </head>
    <body>
        <h2>
             Comparing Strings:
        </h2>
<%
StringBuilder aboutCeline = new StringBuilder();

aboutCeline.Append("Celine is 3 years old. ");

aboutCeline.Append("Celine loves to listen to stories and watch cartoons.");

aboutCeline.Replace("cartoons","movies");

Response.Write("aboutCeline: " + aboutCeline + "<br>");
%>
    </body>
</html>
```

1. Create a StringBuilder object. You must use the new keyword when calling the StringBuilder constructor.

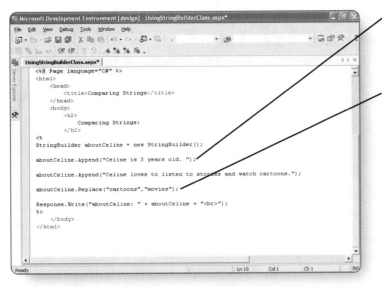

2. Use the `Append` method to add data to the `StringBuilder` object.

3. Use the `Replace` method to search for and replace portions of text.

Working with Regular Expressions

Although the `string.Replace` method is useful, it is not flexible. It will only allow you to search for and replace a sequence of characters. You can use it to search for an exact email address (as in someone@somecompany.com), but you can't use it to find all the email addresses in a document. With a regular expression, on the other hand, you can define the pattern that an email address follows. Regular expressions are so powerful that they let you define matching patterns for just about any data. You can use regular expressions to validate, search, and format data in a string.

A single regular expression can make many lines of C# code redundant. Unfortunately, as the complexity of a regular expression increases, it becomes difficult to understand what it is attempting to match. Regular expressions can be cryptic, particularly if you have never used them before. This section introduces the basic concepts behind creating regular expressing patterns. It is by no means conclusive, but it will whet your appetite. Table 6.3 introduces the syntax for regular expressions.

Table 6.3 Constructing Regular Expressions

Regular Expression	Matches
A sequence of characters	All words that begin, contain, and end with the characters. For example, "in" will match in, inner, and working.
Period (.)	The period is a wildcard character. The regular expression r.m will match all words that begin with an r and end with an m, regardless of the number of characters between the r and the m. For example, it will match rm, ram, and room.
Opening and closing square brackets ([ ])	You can use opening and closing square brackets to specify a range of characters to match. For example, r[aue]n will match an, run, and ren.

Quantifiers determine the number of times a given sequence should be repeated:

*	0 or more times
+	1 or more times
?	0 or 1 times
{n}	n times
{n,m}	n to m times

To match a three-digit number, you use [0-9]{3}.

You can also use the following notations to match common patterns:

\d	Matches any digit from 0 to 9
\D	Matches any nondigit character
\w	Matches any characters from A to Z or 0 to 9
\W	Matches any nonalphanumeric character
\s	Matches whitespace such as a tab or a carriage return
\S	Matches any nonwhite space character

Let's build a regular expression to match a Social Security number. A Social Security number looks like: 111–111–111. It has three digits, a hyphen, three digits, a hyphen, and another set of three digits. The regular expression is `[0-9]{3}\-[0-9]{3}\-[0-9]{3}`. You have to escape the hyphen because it is a part of the syntax to define a range in a regular expression. You can also simplify the regular expression by replacing `[0-9]` with `\d`: `\d{3}\-\d{3}\-\d{3}`.

Matching

The `System.Text.RegularExpressions` namespace contains all the necessary classes you need to utilize regular expressions. You can use the `Regex` class in particular to match a pattern to a string. The following example extracts all the email addresses found in a string:

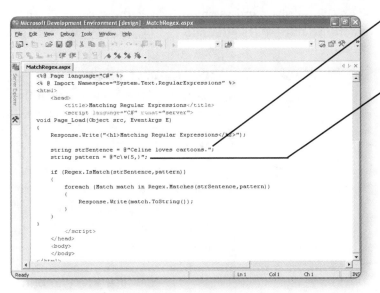

1. Declare a string variable. The variable will store the text that must be searched.

2. Declare a variable called `pattern` as a string. This variable will store the regular expression.

TIP

Make the regular expression a verbatim string by placing @ in front of the string. This way, you don't need to escape the backslash character, and you can simplify the regular expression.

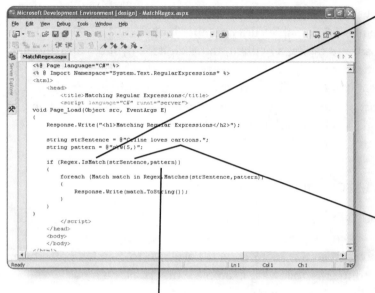

3. Use the `IsMatch` method of the `Regex` class to determine whether a match is found in the string. The `IsMatch` method is available as a static method, so there is no need to create an instance of the `Regex` class before using it. The `IsMatch` method will return `True` if it makes a match within the string.

4. Pass the string as the first parameter to the `IsMatch` method.

5. Pass the regular expression pattern as the second parameter to the `IsMatch` method.

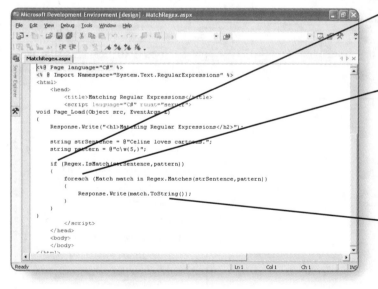

6. Use an `if` statement to execute steps 5 and 6 only if the `IsMatch` method returns `True`.

7. Use a `foreach` loop to iterate through all the matches that are present. The `Regex.Matches` method will return a collection of match objects.

8. Use `Response.Write` to print the matching portion of the string to the page.

Replacing

The Regex class also contains a Replace method, which substitutes text whenever a pattern is matched. The following example removes the path portion of a file name:

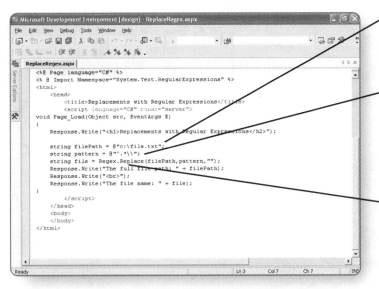

1. Declare a string variable. The variable will store the file name and path.

2. Declare a variable called pattern as a string. This variable will store the regular expression that identifies all characters preceding a \.

3. Call the Regex.Replace method and store the result in a string variable. The Replace method produces a modified string that must be stored in a variable.

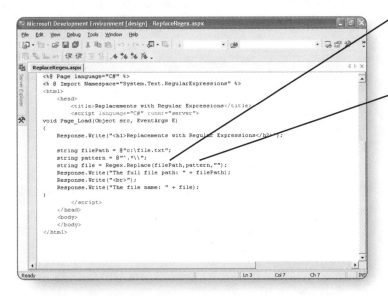

4. Pass the string that must be searched as the first parameter to the Regex.Replace method.

5. Pass the regular expression pattern as the second parameter to the Regex.Replace method.

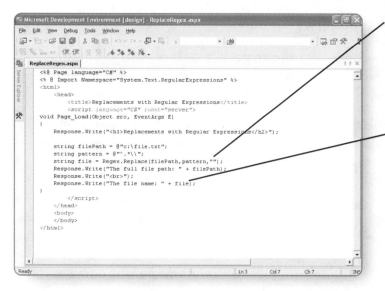

6. Pass the replacement text as the third parameter. In this case, you won't specify any text because you want to delete the matching text, the file path.

7. Use the `Response.Write` method to print the modified string to the page.

Using the Math Class

The `Math` class contains methods that perform common mathematical functions such as finding the square root of a number or the cosine of an angle. It also allows you to access various mathematical constants such as π. Table 6.4 contains a description of important methods in the `Math` class.

Table 6.4 The Math Class

Method	Description
Sin	Returns the sine of an angle
Cos	Returns the cosine of an angle
Tan	Returns the trigonometric tangent of an angle
ASin	Returns the arc sine of an angle
ACos	Returns the arc cosine of an angle
ATan	Returns the arc tangent of an angle
ATan2	Converts rectangular coordinates to polar coordinates

Table 6.4 The Math Class *(continued)*

Method	Description
Sqrt	Returns the square root of a number
Pow	Returns the result of raising a number to a specified power
Exp	Returns the result of e raised to a specified power
Log	Returns the natural logarithm of a number
Abs	Returns the absolute value of a number
Min	Returns the greater of two numbers
Max	Returns the smaller of two numbers
Sign	Returns whether a number is positive or negative

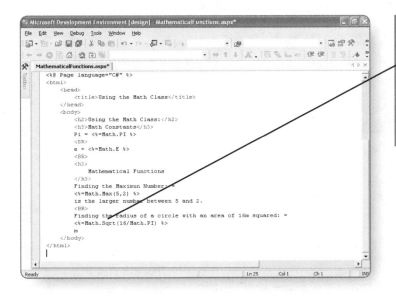

NOTE
The example that follows calculates the radius of a circle. It uses the Math.Sqrt method and the Math.PI constant.

Generating Random Numbers

Generating random numbers is simple in C#, thanks to the Random class. The Next method returns a random number between 0 and the number you pass to the method. You can easily modify the following script to display random images or quotes:

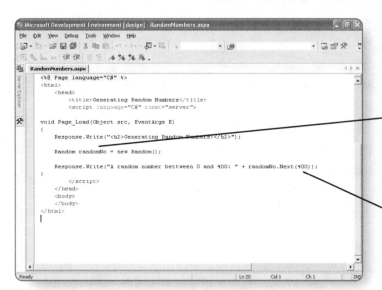

1. Create a new Random object called randomNo. You must use the new keyword when calling the Random constructor.

2. Call the Next method of the randomNo object. Pass the maximum value to the Next method. The program will return a random number between 0 and this maximum value.

Formatting Dates

The DateTime class contains methods that allow you to display the date in different formats. The Now method returns the current date and time:

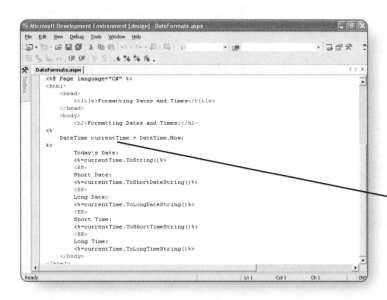

1. Create a new DateTime object called currentTime.

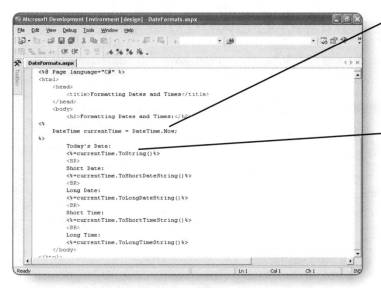

2. Call the `Now` property of the `DateTime` class and store the result in the `currentTime` object. The `Now` method will return the current date and time.

3. Use the `ToString` property to convert the date to a string so it can be printed to the page (11/6/2002 12:09:55 AM).

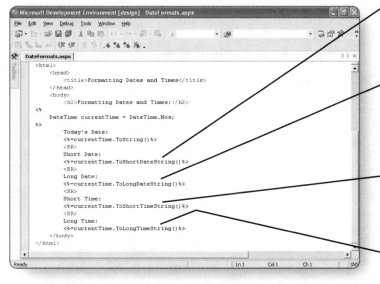

4. Use the `ToShortDateString` method to display the date in a short format (11/6/2002).

5. Use the `ToLongDateString` method to display the date in a long format (Wednesday, November 06, 2002).

6. Use the `ToShortTimeString` method to display the time in a short format (12:09 AM).

7. Use the `ToLongTimeString` method to display the time in a long format (12:09:55 AM).

Counting Down to a Date

You use the TimeSpan class to determine the difference between two dates. You can use it to count down to Christmas:

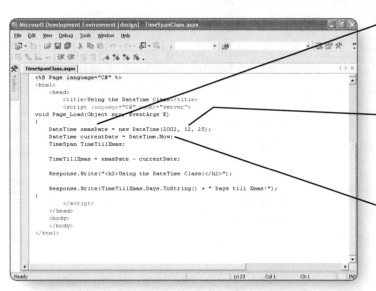

1. Create a DateTime object called xmasDate. You must use the new keyword when calling the DateTime constructor.

2. Pass the date that you want to count down to as a parameter to the DateTime constructor.

3. Create another DateTime object called currentDate and store the current date in it.

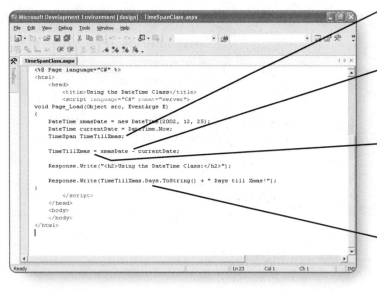

4. Create a TimeSpan object called TimeTillXmas.

5. Type – between the xmasDate and currentDate object names. This will subtract the dates.

6. Store the result in the TimeSpan object. TimeTillXmas will contain the time difference between the two dates.

7. Print the Days property of the TimeSpan object. This will return the time difference in days.

Working with Arrays

Let's say you had to process the test results for all the students in a class. You could declare a new variable to store each student's result, but this would be repetitive. Imagine having to remember the name of each variable when you wanted to print all the test scores or calculate the average. This is why arrays were invented. An array is a structure that allows you to easily reference data items of the same type. You can define a new array called TestScores and store each student's grade as a new element in the array. Each element that gets stored is assigned an index sequentially. You can use this index when you refer to the element. The sequential nature of the index allows you to programmatically process the data stored in an array with a loop.

NOTE

The index numbering in an array starts at 0 instead of 1, as is the case with some other languages.

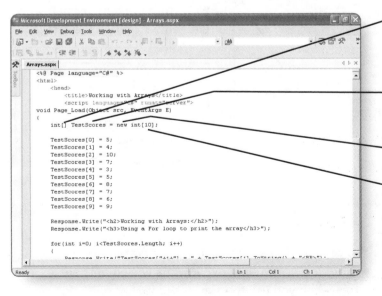

1. Declare an array by typing square brackets after the data type keyword.

2. Type the name of the array after the square brackets.

3. Create an array object.

4. Define the size of the array by entering the size in the square brackets after the type keyword.

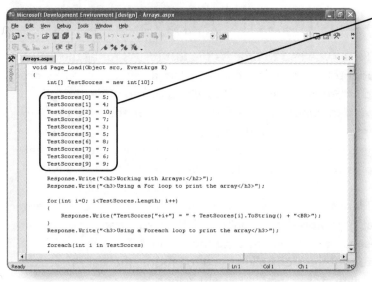

5. Assign a value to each element in the array. Individual elements are referenced with the same name but have a different index. You place the index in square brackets after the name of the array.

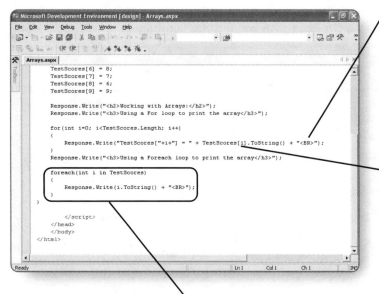

6. Use a `for` loop to iterate through the array and print each element. The `Length` property will return the number of elements stored in the array.

NOTE

You reference the contents of each element by its index.

7. You can also use a `foreach` loop to iterate through the array. You don't need to know how many elements are in the array when you use the `foreach` loop.

Reversing and Sorting Arrays

The Sort method arranges the elements in an array in ascending order. This might be useful when you want to print each element to the screen in alphabetical order. The Reverse method, as its name suggests, reverses the order of elements in an array:

1. Declare and initialize an array that will store string values.

2. Call the Array.Sort method and pass the name of the array to the method. The elements in the array will be sorted in ascending order.

3. Call the Array.Reverse method and pass the name of the array to the method. The ordering of elements in the array will be reversed.

Working with ArrayLists

An `ArrayList` is a special type of array that lets you add and remove elements dynamically:

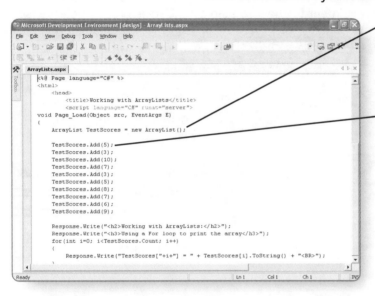

1. Create a new `ArrayList` object. You must use the `new` keyword when calling the `ArrayList` constructor.

2. Call the `Add` method of the `ArrayList` object to insert a new element. Pass the value that must be stored in the element to the `Add` method.

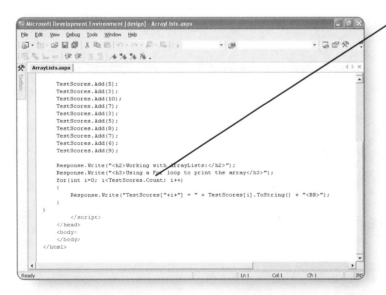

3. The `Count` property contains the number of elements in the `ArrayList` object. You can use this property when you want to iterate the contents of the `ArrayList`.

NOTE

An `ArrayList` is just like a vector in Java.

7

Understanding Object-Oriented Programming

C# is an object-oriented programming language. Essentially, an object-oriented programming language allows you to group methods with the data that they manipulate. Using an object-oriented programming language to develop a Web application helps you structure your code so it is easier to build, maintain, and reuse. Object-oriented programming is ideally suited to modeling real-world examples. In this chapter, you'll learn how to:

- Create a class to define objects.
- Declare instance variables.
- Declare methods.
- Overload methods.
- Implement inheritance.

What Is Object-Oriented Programming?

Object-oriented programming was designed to simplify the process of building complex real-world applications. Before object-oriented programming was introduced, programs were coded in a procedural manner. You had a lot of variables and a lot of functions that used and changed the data stored in these variables. It was hard to associate a function with the data that it changed. This made complex and lengthy procedural programs hard to debug, maintain, and re-use.

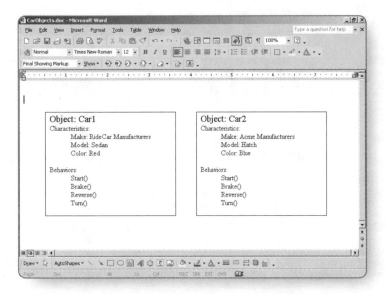

Object-oriented programming addresses all of these issues by introducing a new concept: the object. Objects are like real-world entities—they have attributes and behaviors. In other words, an object's attributes model its characteristics (data), and its methods describe the functions that an object can perform. A class defines both the properties of an object and the code used to manipulate these properties. The process of integrating an object's properties and behaviors is known as *encapsulation*. To utilize an object, you don't need to know anything about its inner workings. You only require access to its attributes and methods.

NOTE

A circle is a good example of an object. It has attributes (radius, center point, and a diameter) and functions that can be performed on it (calculating the diameter, calculating the circumference, calculating the area).

Polymorphism (Greek for many forms) is the ability of a method to perform a specific task even though different parameters are being passed to it. The `Response.Write` method is a good example. This method prints the data that is passed to it to the requested Web page. It does not matter what type of data is being passed to it; integers, strings, and Boolean values will all be printed to the page. Without polymorphism you would have to use different methods such as `Response.WriteInt()`, `Response.WriteString()`, or `Response.WriteBool()` to print data to a Web page. I'm sure you will agree that it is much easier to remember `Response.Write`.

Inheritance is the third important aspect of object-oriented programming. Inheritance is important because it enables you to easily re-use as well as extend existing functionality. If you create objects to model the characteristics of an animal and a cat, you don't have to specify everything a cat has in common with other animals. The cat object can simply inherit from the animal object, which contains the core characteristics. Inheritance promotes code re-use because you model your code in a hierarchical manner.

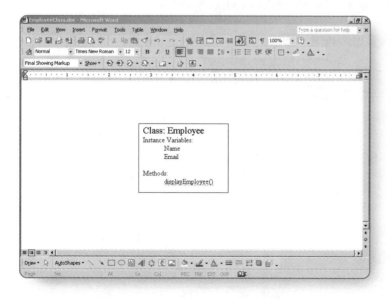

Understanding Classes and Objects

A class describes the structure of an object. The object's attributes are defined in the form of instance variables or data members. You must place the code used to manipulate these instance variables in methods. A method models the behavior of an object. A method is also sometimes called a function. An object is an instance of a class.

Instance Variables

Variables contained in a class are known as instance variables, data members, or fields. Every time an object is created, new instance variables are created. Each object has instance variables with the same names, but the data they store is different.

Methods

Code that has access to instance variables must be inside a method. A method is a function contained in a class. Methods have access to the data stored in an object's instance variables.

Creating a Class

A class defines the instance variables and the methods associated with an object. All classes must be named. Here is a look at the basic syntax used to create a class:

1. Type the class modifier. This is usually public, which means the class is visible to all other classes.

2. Type the class keyword.

3. Type the name of the class.

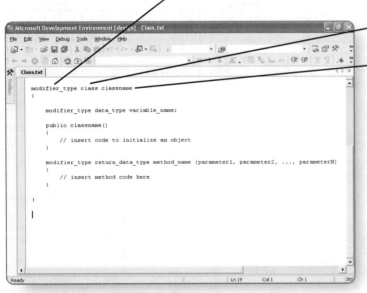

```
modifier_type class classname
{

    modifier_type data_type variable_name;

    public classname()
    {
        // insert code to initialize an object
    }

    modifier_type return_data_type method_name (parameter1, parameter2, ..., parameterN)
    {
        // insert method code here
    }

}
```

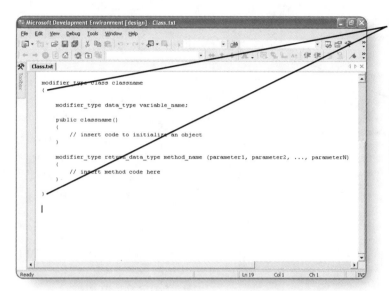

4. You must place a class block after the class name.

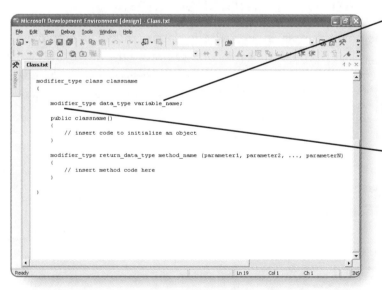

5. You must declare instance variables and methods within a class block. Declare an instance variable by typing the data type of the variable followed by the name of the variable.

6. An instance variable can have a type modifier such as public or private. A public variable or method can be accessed from other classes. A private variable or method can only be accessed within the class.

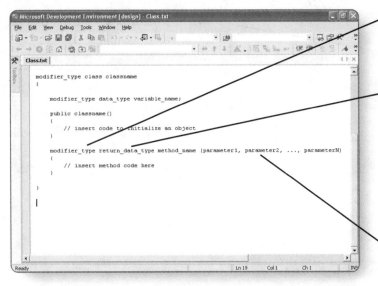

7. A method can have a type modifier such as `public` or `private`.

8. You must also specify a return type for a method. The return type indicates whether the method returns a string or integer. The return type is `void` if the method does not return a value.

9. You can pass parameters to a method. Commas must separate the parameters.

Creating an Employee Class

The next example creates a basic class to model an employee. This class needs instance variables to store the name and email address of the employee and must also have a method to display employee details:

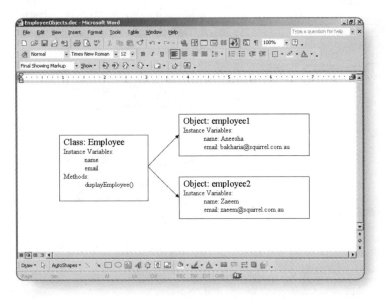

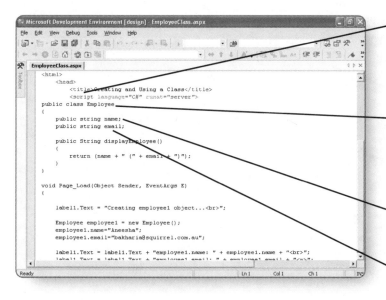

1. Insert opening and closing `<script>` tags. Set the `language` attribute to `C#`. Set the `runat` attribute to `server`.

2. Create a public class called `Employee`. The name of the class and the name of the file must be identical.

3. Declare the `name` variable as a string.

4. Declare the `email` variable as a string.

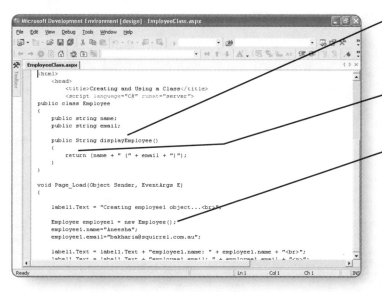

5. Declare a public method called `displayEmployee` with a `string` return type.

6. Use the `return` keyword to return the employee details.

7. Create an instance of the `Employee` class.

NOTE

You create a class instance (in other words, an object) by typing the class name followed by the name of the object and then using the `new` keyword to call the constructor method and assign the result to the object. A constructor method has the same name as the class.

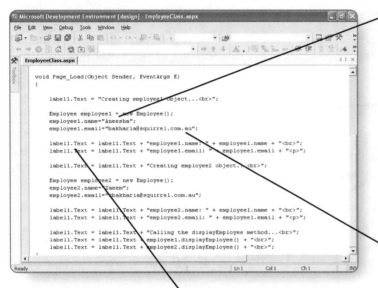

8. Set the `name` instance variable of the object.

NOTE

You reference an instance variable of an object by typing the object name, a period (.), and the name of the instance variable.

9. Set the `email` instance variable of the object.

10. Use the `Text` property of a label control to print the result from the `displayEmployee` method to the page.

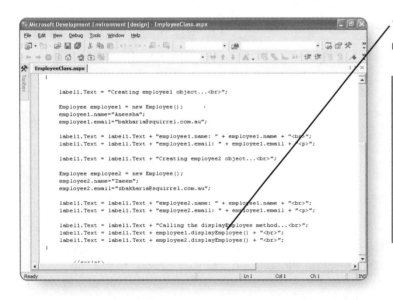

11. Call the `displayEmployee` method.

NOTE

You call an object's method by typing the object name, a period (.), and the name of the method. Parentheses must follow the method name.

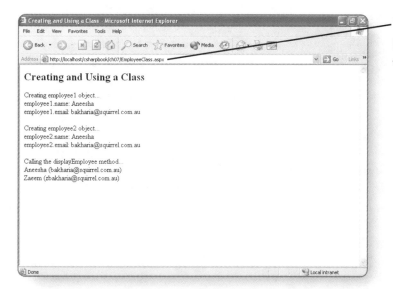

12. Preview the page in a Web browser. You will see the instance variables of the `Employee` objects.

Using Constructors

Constructors are special methods that let you set the properties of an object when the object is initialized. A constructor must be a public method that returns no value. The constructor must have the same name as the class.

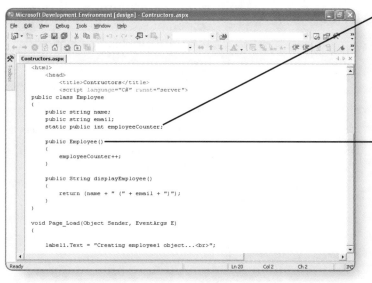

1. Declare a static variable. Static variables store data common to all object instances. The `employeeCounter` static variable in this example will contain a count of all objects created.

2. Create a public method that has the same name as the class. The constructor will increment the `employeeCounter` static variable. The constructor is called when an object is created. The `employeeCounter` static variable will therefore contain the number of objects that have been created.

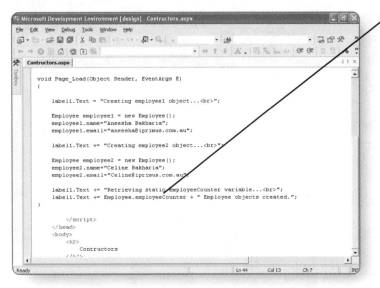

3. The `employeeCounter` static variable can be accessed as a property of the class. You need a period between the class name and the static variable's name.

Overloading Methods

Method overloading simply means that you can create many methods with the same name to do the same task but have each method respond to a different set of arguments. Method overloading is the first type of polymorphism that you will encounter.

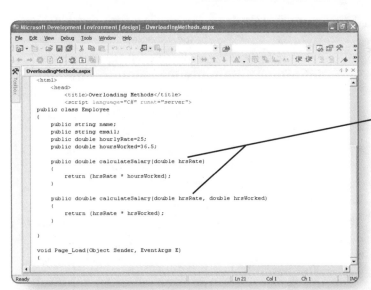

1. Create two methods with the same name. The methods must accept a different number of parameters.

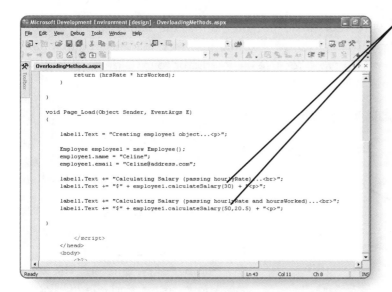

2. Pass parameters in the correct order and data type to the method that is being called. The matching method will be executed.

Overloading Constructor Methods

You can include many constructor methods in a class, but each method must accept a different list of parameters. Overloaded constructor methods are used to assign data to instance variables when an object is created.

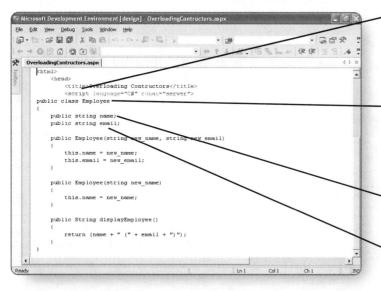

1. Insert opening and closing `<script>` tags. Set the `language` attribute to `C#`. Set the `runat` attribute to `server`.

2. Create a public class called `Employee`. The name of the class and the name of the file must be identical.

3. Declare the `name` variable as a string.

4. Declare the `email` variable as a string.

5. Create a public method that has the same name as the class. This is a constructor method—a public method that has no return type. You use a constructor to initialize an object when it is created.

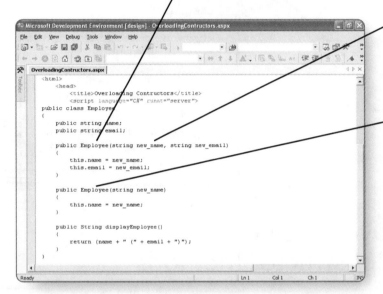

6. The constructor accepts two parameters and sets the name and email address properties when the object gets created.

7. You can have many constructor methods, each of which you pass a different number of parameters. This is known as method-overloading. The constructor that matches the number of parameters you pass to it will execute when the object is created.

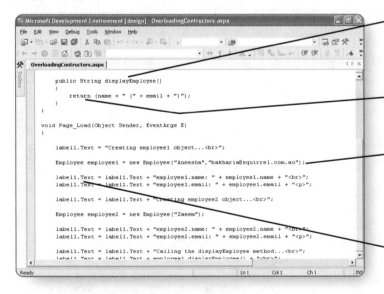

8. Declare a public method called `displayEmployee` with a `string` return type.

9. Use the `return` keyword to return the employee details.

10. Create an instance of the `Employee` class. Pass the name and email address to the `Employee` constructor.

11. Use the `Text` property of a label control to print the employee object properties to the page.

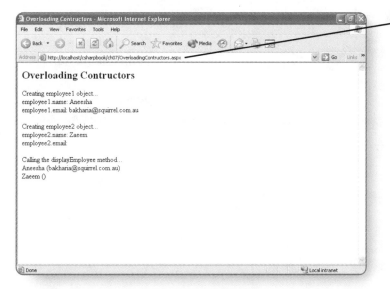

12. Preview the page in a Web browser. You will see the instance variables of the `Employee` objects that have been set using constructors.

Creating Properties

A property is a special type of instance variable/data member that has built-in methods to assign and retrieve its data. Properties are very important because they restrict direct access to instance variables. The idea is that you make all public instance variables private and provide properties for data access. This way you are not exposing the internal structure of your class and can make changes without affecting the way the object is used.

Properties have get and set code blocks that are executed when data is assigned to or retrieved from an instance variable. This is handy if you'd like to perform validation before data is assigned to an instance variable.

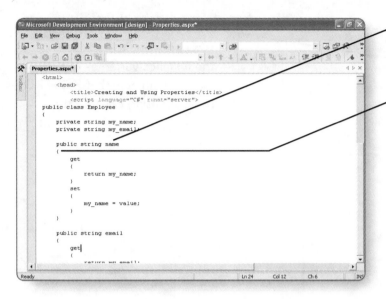

1. Declare a public variable. The data type must be placed in front of the variable name.

2. Type opening and closing braces after the variable name.

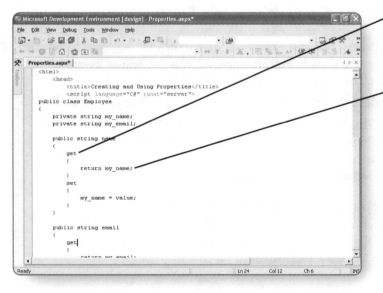

3. Type **get** followed by opening and closing braces. This is called the get code block.

4. Type **return** followed by the name of a private instance variable.

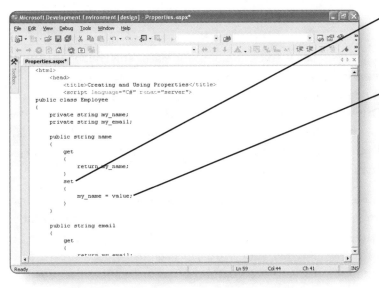

5. Type **set** followed by opening and closing braces. This is called the set code block.

6. Assign the `value` keyword to the private instance variable. Value is a special parameter that is passed to the set code block when data is assigned to a property.

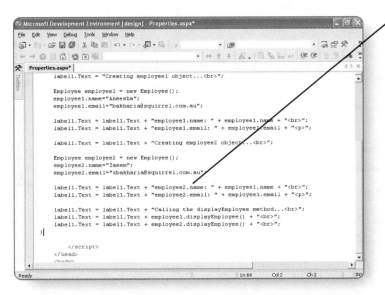

7. Data is assigned to and retrieved from a property in the same manner as an instance variable. A period must be placed between the object name and the property name.

Inheritance

Once you create a class, you can use it to define another class. This means that you don't need to create an entirely new class for each object to be modeled. You should first decide what characteristics your objects have in common and create a base class from them. Other classes can then inherit the properties and methods from a base class. A class that inherits from a base class is known as a derived class. Organizing your classes into hierarchical relationships is important in creating reusable code that you can easily maintain and extend.

For example, you can model a generic `Employee` class and create derived classes for the different types of employees. The `Employee` class can contain the fundamental characteristics of an employee—and then be subclassed to define classes for full-time, part-time, and contract employees. A derived class can use existing features from a base class, override features, and even extend or add new features.

NOTE

- A base class is also known as a parent class.

- A derived class is also called a child or subclass.

NOTE

While many calluses can inherit from a base class, each class can only inherit from a single class. C# does not directly support multiple inheritance.

The syntax for a subclass is

```
modifier_type class classname:parentclassname
{
    instance variable declarations;
    method declarations;
}
```

1. Create an `Employee` class. The `Employee` class has instance variables to store an employee's name and email address. The class also included various constructor methods and a method that prints an employee's details.

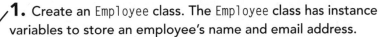

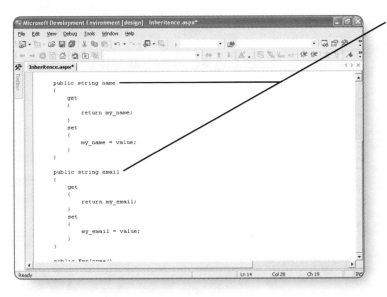

2. Declare the instance variables that can be accessed by a derived class with the protected access modifier. The protected and private access modifiers are very similar. Both restrict access to the instance variables from outside the class but protected allows access by derived classes.

3. Declare properties to access the instance variables.

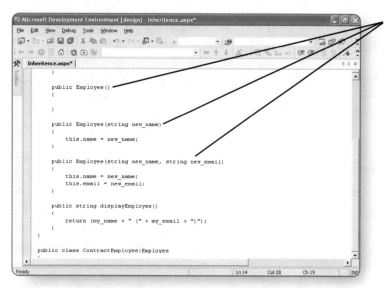

4. Declare overloaded constructors to handle different object initialization parameters.

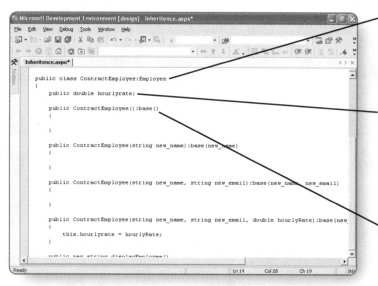

5. Declare a derived class called ContractEmployee. A colon must be placed between the derived class and the base class.

6. Declare an instance variable that stores the hourly rate of pay for a contract employee. This is a unique property of a contract employee.

7. Constructors from the base class are included by typing :base() after the constructor name.

NOTE

You will need to pass parameters to the base constructors that accept parameters.

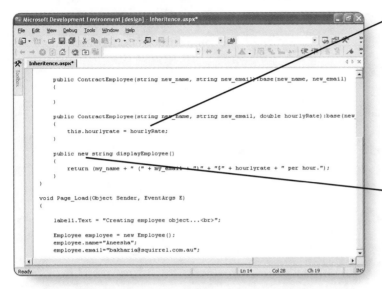

8. Type code inside a construct to extend the functionality contained in the base class. In this example, the base class is used to set the name and email properties, while the derived class sets the hourly rate for a contract employee.

9. The new keyword must be used to override an existing method. The displayEmployee method in the contractEmployee class replaces the displayEmployee method in the base class.

Using Namespaces

A namespace is a collection of related classes. As the number of classes you create or use increases, it is inevitable that naming conflicts will arise. Namespaces resolve naming conflicts because separate namespaces can contain classes with the same name. It is a good practice to place all classes that relate to a particular project within the same namespace.

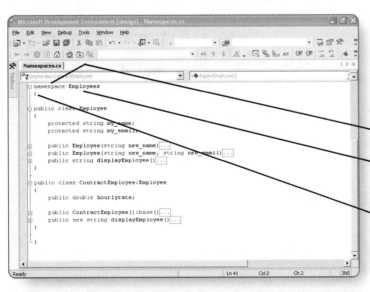

1. Type **namespace**.

2. Type the name of the namespace.

3. Type opening and closing braces after the namespace declaration.

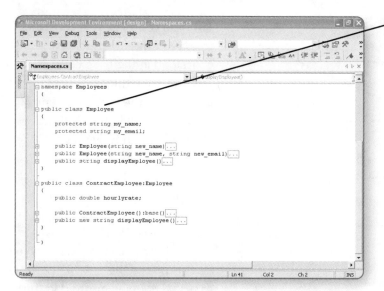

4. Insert the classes with the namespaces code block.

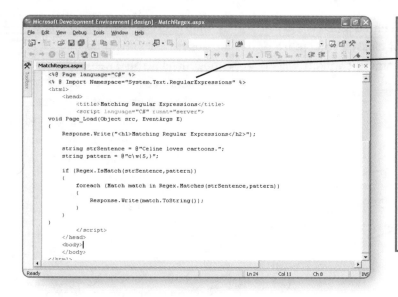

NOTE

All of the base.NET classes are packaged into a namespace. In Chapter 6, "Programming in C#," you had to use the `import` attribute of the page directive to import the `System.Text.RegularExpressions` namespace before you could use the `Regex` class.

8

Handling Exceptions and Tracing

As a programmer, you should strive for perfection in your code. You should always endeavor to produce bug-free code that is capable of handling every possible scenario in the real world. Although these goals might have been impossible to achieve a few years ago, improvements in the way you debug ASP.NET applications and the introduction of exception handling both go a long way to help you build the perfect application. With the techniques introduced in this chapter, you'll be able to write reliable, versatile, and manageable code. In this chapter, you'll learn to:

- Use the `try-catch` error-handling mechanism.
- Handle common exceptions.
- Implement page- and application-level tracing.
- Display generic and specific error pages.
- Enable the .NET debugger.

Bugs and Exceptions

I want to make an important distinction between bugs and exceptions. Bugs occur when your program does not perform the way it should. They are usually caused by an error in the program code. Most likely, the code won't compile because of an error in your C# syntax; a syntax error has occurred. Sometimes, your code will compile but won't work as intended due to an inherent logical error in your program design. You must fix these bugs before the code is released.

On the other hand, exceptions are unusual circumstances that can arise while your program is running. These errors are known as syntax errors. Exceptions are present in code that successfully compiles and can occur at any time. For example, an exception is thrown when you try to access a file that does not exist in the specified location. The user could have moved the file. Your failure to handle this exception adequately can result in a cryptic error message, program termination, and the loss of unsaved data. However, you can prevent these problems by taking advantage of the exception-handling mechanisms of C#. Always remember that handling exceptions is the key to building robust code.

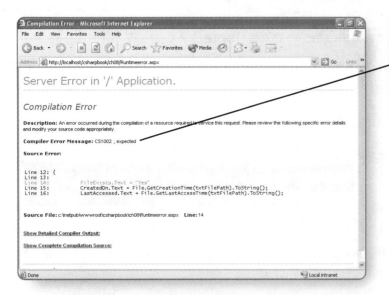

NOTE

This error message is displayed when a syntax error occurs.

Handling Exceptions

Implementing exception handling was not always straightforward. Exception-handling code was mixed with regular code—usually in a series of `if` statements, which made it difficult to trace the flow of program execution. It was difficult not only to structure but also to maintain and debug your code.

C# introduces an improved model that separates program code and exception-handling code. It has numerous advantages: Code is smaller in size, easier to trace, and robust. You can use three new code blocks to handle exceptions: the `try`, `catch`, and `finally` blocks.

Any code that might throw an exception must appear within a `try` block. You put the corresponding code that will gracefully handle the exception inside a matching `catch` block.

Here is the general syntax for implementing exception handling in C#:

```
try
{
    // Insert the code that could cause an exception here.
}
catch (Exception e)
{
    // Insert the exception-handling routine here.
}
finally
{
    // Insert code that must be executed even if
    // an exception is not thrown.
}
```

The `catch` statement must specify the type of exception that it handles. The `catch` statement looks like a method declaration. It takes the name of the class representing the exception that the block must handle and a parameter name. An `Exception` object is passed from the `try` block to a matching `catch` block when an exception is thrown. This object must be a subclass of `System.Exception`.

Code in a `finally` block is always executed, whether an exception occurs or not. You put the `finally` block after the `catch` block. The `finally` block is optional.

The following code attempts to perform a mathematical impossibility—divide a number by zero:

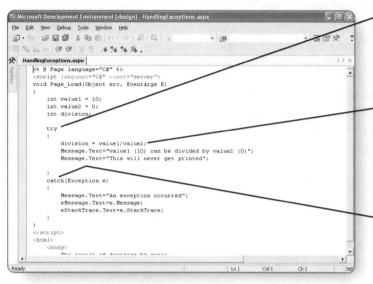

1. Insert a try block. A try block consists of the try keyword followed by opening and closing braces.

2. Place the code that will attempt to divide by zero within the try block. Code that could potentially throw an exception must appear within a try block.

3. Insert a catch block.

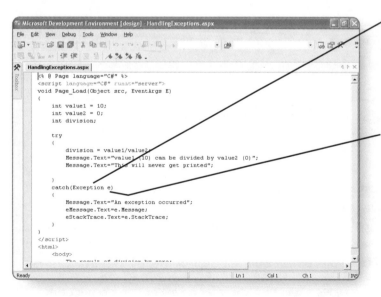

4. Pass the Exception object to the catch block. Exception is the superclass for all exceptions and therefore allows the catch block to handle all exceptions.

5. Type the name you want to use to refer to the Exception object. This name will be handy when you need to retrieve the object's properties.

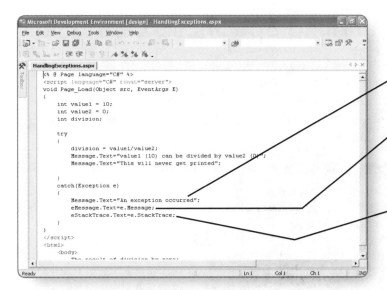

6. Insert the exception-handling code within the catch block.

7. Print a generic error message to the Web page.

8. Print the Message property of the Exception object to the Web page.

9. Print the StackTrace to the Web page. The stack trace lists all the methods that were successfully called before the exception occurred.

NOTE

After an exception is caught, execution does not return to the try block. The catch block is ignored when no exception occurs.

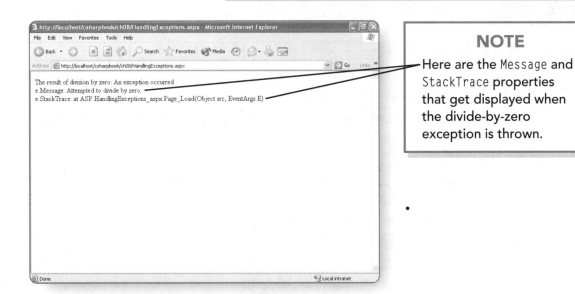

NOTE

Here are the Message and StackTrace properties that get displayed when the divide-by-zero exception is thrown.

Handling Specific Exceptions

Rather than always use the generic `Exception` object, you can catch specific exceptions. In such a way, you can tailor your exception-handling routines to meet the requirements of your Web application. It also allows you to display specific error messages.

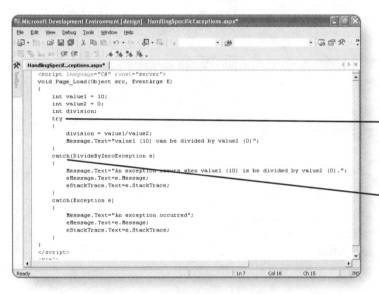

C# exceptions are derived from the `Exception` class, which appears in the `System.Exception` namespace. Table 8.1 contains common exception classes.

1. Insert a `try` block. Place the code that will attempt to divide by zero within the `try` block.

2. Insert a `DivideByZeroException` catch block. This `catch` block will only be executed when division-by-zero occurs.

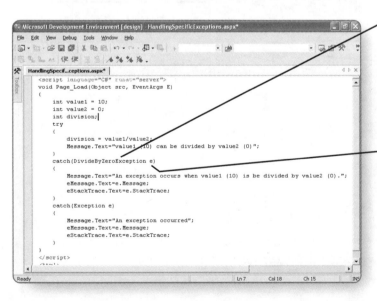

3. Pass the `DivideByZeroException` object to the `catch` block. A `DivideByZeroException` object will be created when an integer is divided by zero.

4. Type the name you want to use to refer to the exception object. You will use this name to refer to the object's properties.

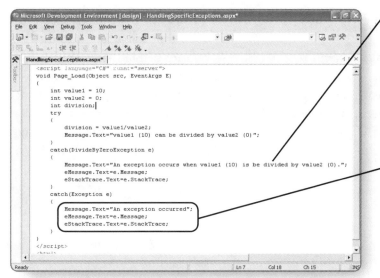

```
Microsoft Development Environment [design] - HandlingSpecificExceptions.aspx*
File  Edit  View  Debug  Tools  Window  Help

HandlingSpecif...ceptions.aspx*
<script language="C#" runat="server">
void Page_Load(Object src, EventArgs E)
{
    int value1 = 10;
    int value2 = 0;
    int division;
    try
    {
        division = value1/value2;
        Message.Text="value1 (10) can be divided by value2 (0)";
    }
    catch(DivideByZeroException e)
    {
        Message.Text="An exception occurs when value1 (10) is be divided by value2 (0).";
        eMessage.Text=e.Message;
        eStackTrace.Text=e.StackTrace;
    }
    catch(Exception e)
    {
        Message.Text="An exception occurred";
        eMessage.Text=e.Message;
        eStackTrace.Text=e.StackTrace;
    }
}
</script>
<html>
```
Ready   Ln 7   Col 18   Ch 15   INS

5. Use the DivideByZeroException catch block to print a specific error message to the Web page. This message will inform the user that division by zero has occurred.

6. Insert a generic exception handler. You must pass this catch block the Exception object.

Table 8.1 C# Exception Classes

Exception	Gets Thrown When
System.DivideByZeroException	A numeric value has been divided by zero
System.ArithmeticException	Invalid arithmetic has been performed
System.IndexOutOfRangeException	An array is incorrectly indexed
System.NullReferenceExample	Object pointers are not initialized
System.IO.IOException	Input/Output operations, such as reading from a file, fail

Ordering Multiple Exceptions

You can use multiple catch blocks to handle the different exceptions that may occur in your code. The catch block that contains a matching exception object will be executed. The order in which you place catch clauses is important because exceptions are matched sequentially. The program might never reach the catch clause for an exception if it is placed after the catch clause for its superclass:

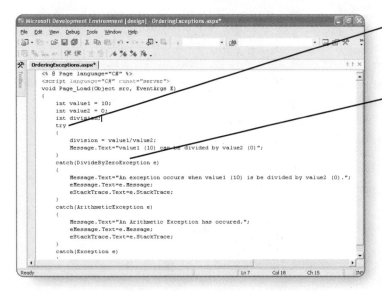

1. Insert a `try` block. Place the code that will attempt to divide by zero within the `try` block.

2. Insert a `DivideByZeroException` catch block. This `catch` block will only be executed when division by zero occurs. The `DivideByZeroException` must appear before the `ArithmeticException` because `DivideByZeroException` is a subclass of `ArithmeticException`.

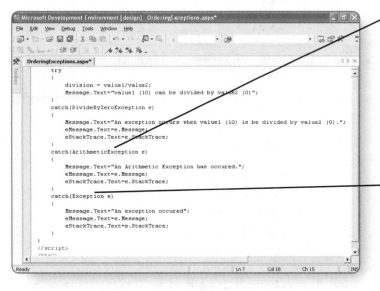

3. Insert an `ArithmeticException` catch block. The `ArithmeticException.catch` block must appear after the `DivideByZeroException`; otherwise, a runtime error will occur.

4. Insert an `Exception` catch block. The `Exception` class is a superclass of all exception classes and must appear last.

Tracing in ASP.NET

Printing the contents of variables to the screen as your application executes is a handy way to identify the location of a bug. This practice is known as *tracing*. Tracing a Web application also involves monitoring the requests and responses made by a Web page. In classic ASP, you used the `Response.Write` method to implement tracing. It was a cumbersome method because you had to delete the `Response.Write` methods before your Web site went live and then insert them again if you ever needed to do additional troubleshooting. Tracing in ASP.NET is more sophisticated. Basically, you can embed trace statements in your code with the `Trace.Write` method and decide when you want them enabled without adding any performance overhead.

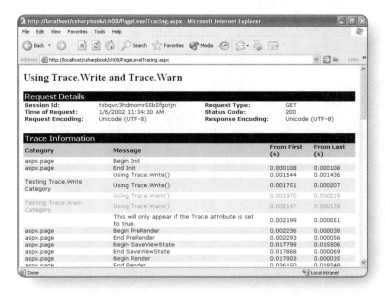

NOTE

When tracing is enabled, you see information from the following categories:

- **Request details**. This list contains all the data that was sent to the server using the `Get` method.

- **Trace information**. This data is printed using the `Trace.Write` method.

- **Cookies collection**. This list contains all cookies associated with the current user.

- **Headers collection**. This list contains the headers that were sent to the server from a browser.

- **Server variables**. This is a list of all server variables.

- **Control tree**. This is a list of all Web controls that were processed on the current page.

Page-Level Tracing

You must set the `Trace` attribute of the `Page` directive to `True` to turn on tracing for the current page. You can then use the `Trace.Write` and `Trace.Warn` methods to print tracing information. The `Trace.Warn` method prints to the page in red:

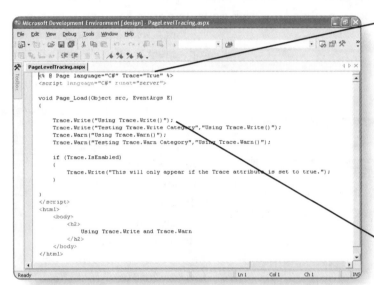

1. Set the `Trace` attribute of the `Page` directive to `True`. This will enable tracing for the current page.

NOTE

You can turn off tracing for a particular page by setting the `Trace` attribute to `False`.

2. Use the `Trace.Write` method to print debugging information to the page.

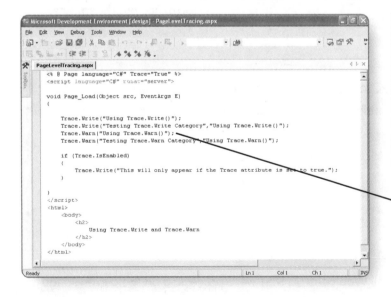

NOTE

Trace statements can be categorized. The `Trace.Write` and `Trace.Warn` methods can take a category as their first parameter.

3. Use the `Trace.Warn` method to print debugging information to the page in red.

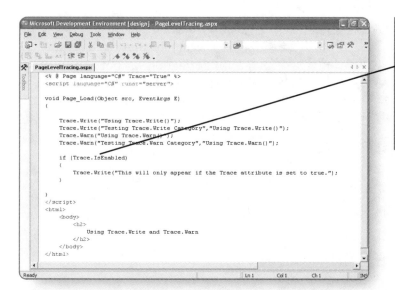

Application-Level Tracing

The ability to turn tracing on or off at the application level is
a powerful feature of ASP.NET. You enable tracing at the
application level by including a trace tag in the web.config
configuration file. The web.config file is XML-based and must
be stored in the root directory
of your Web application:

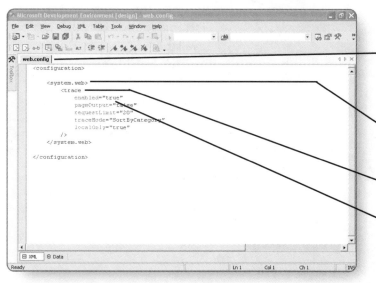

1. Create a new web.config file
and save it to the root directory
of your Web application.

2. Insert opening and closing
`<system.web>` tags.

3. Insert a `trace` tag.

4. Set the `enabled` attribute to
`True`. This will turn on tracing for
all the pages in the same folder
as the web.config file.

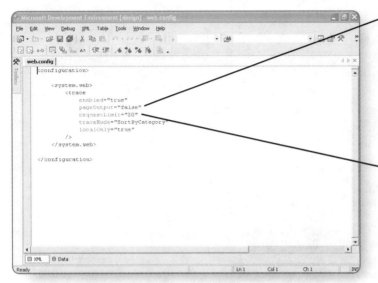

5. Set the `pageOutput` to `False`. This means that trace information will not appear at the end of each page. You will access the trace information using the trace.axd utility, which is covered in the next section.

6. Set the `requestLimit` to `20`. The `requestLimit` specifies the number of times page-tracing information must be collected. The default value is 10.

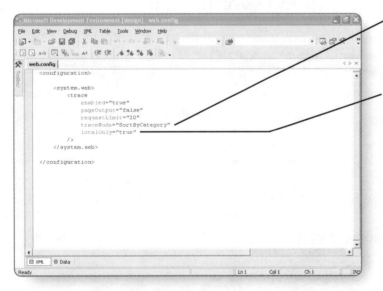

7. Set the `traceMode` to `SortByCategory`. `SortByTime` is the default.

8. Set the `localOnly` attribute to `True`. This means that trace information will only be available to `localhost` users. You will be able to display tracing information even while your application is being accessed by external users.

Using the trace.axd Utility

You can access tracing information for each page in your application with the trace.axd utility. The trace.axd utility will only collect trace information until the requestLimit is reached. You set the requestLimit in the web.config file:

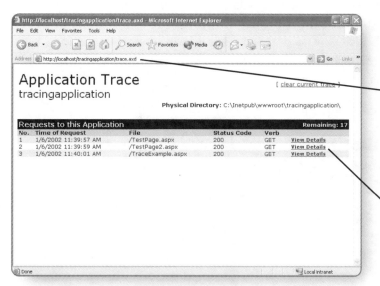

1. Request the pages in your Web application that you want to trace.

2. Load the trace.axd utility by typing **trace.axd** after the folder name in the URL. A list of all requested pages will be displayed, sorted by time.

3. Click on the View Details link. The trace information for the page will appear.

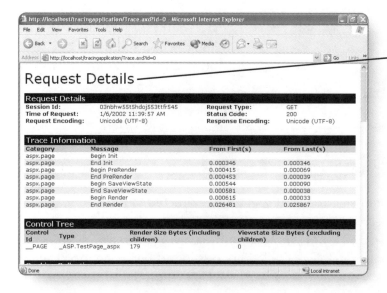

NOTE

Here is an example of trace information produced by trace.axd.

Creating Customized Error Pages

When a runtime error occurs, the stack trace and location of the error are displayed. Although this information is crucial to you as a programmer, it is not something you want Web site visitors to see. With ASP.NET, you can enjoy the best of both worlds: viewing detailed error information when testing locally while displaying custom errors to visitors. You specify custom error pages in the web.config file:

1. Create a new web.config file.

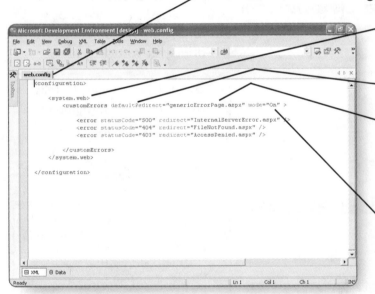

2. Insert opening and closing `<system.web>` tags.

3. Insert a `customErrors` tag.

4. Set the `defaultRedirect` attribute to the page that must be displayed when an exception is thrown.

5. Set the `mode` attribute to `On`. You can also set the `mode` attribute to `Off` or `RemoteOnly`.

Creating the Error Page

When an error occurs, you are redirected to the error page specified in the web.config file. The generic error page should display a user-friendly error message. You can also include contact details for help desk or support personnel. You can easily display the name of the file that produced the error after it is retrieved by the `Request.QueryString` method:

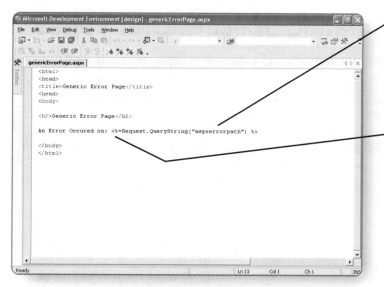

1. Pass `aspxerrorpath` to `Request.QueryString`. The `aspxerrorpath` variable contains the name and path of the page where the error occurred.

2. Use the `<%=` and `%>` tags to print the file name of the page that produced the error.

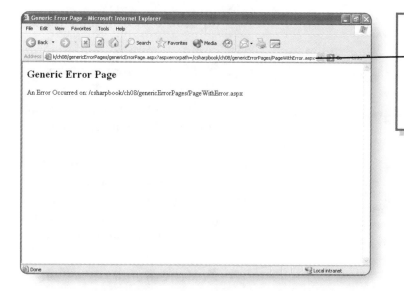

NOTE

The path of the page that produced an error is passed to the error page in the `QueryString`.

Creating Specific Error Pages

You can configure your Web application to display different error messages for internal server, file not found, or access denied errors. You use the customErrors tag to specify the pages that will handle these specific errors:

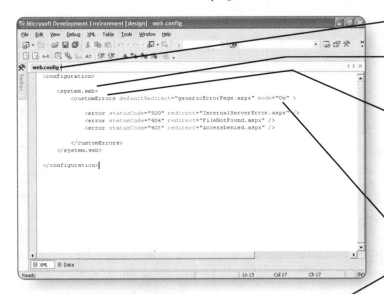

1. Create a new web.config file.

2. Insert opening and closing ⟨system.web⟩ tags.

3. Insert a customErrors tag. Set the defaultRedirect attribute to the page that must be displayed when a generic exception is thrown.

4. Set the mode attribute to On.

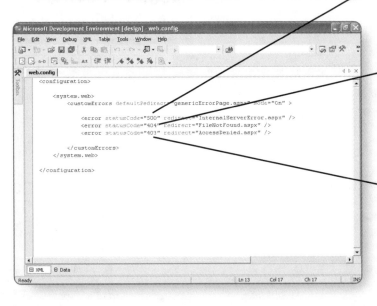

5. Insert an error tag and set the status code to 500. Set the redirect attribute to the file that will handle internal server errors.

6. Insert an error tag and set the status code to 404. Set the redirect attribute to the file that must be displayed when the requested file can't be found.

7. Insert an error tag and set the status code to 403. Set the redirect attribute to the file that must be displayed when the user does not have the appropriate access privileges to view the requested page.

Using the .NET Framework SDK Debugger

The .NET Framework SDK Debugger is a powerful troubleshooting tool. It allows you to step through your code, monitor variables, display the stack, and view request, response, and session details.

You enable debugging by inserting a compilation tag with its debug attribute set to True in the web.config file.

You start the debugger by launching DbgClr.exe on the Web server. You will have to attach the debugger to the aspnet_wp.exe process and load your source code files.

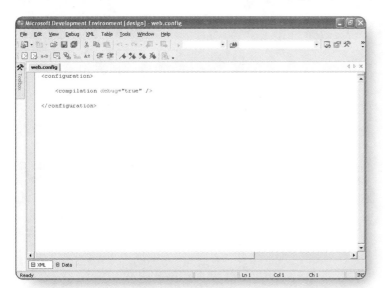

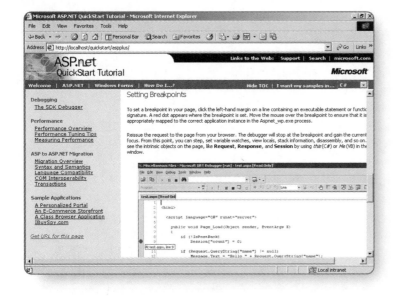

9

Validating User Input

Ensuring that the data entered by a user is in the correct format is critical to the success of all Web applications. You will often need to check that the user has not left mandatory fields blank and has entered essential contact information, such as a phone number or e-mail address, correctly. Validation prevents errors from occurring when data is being processed or stored in a database. Implementing form validation used to be a tedious and time-consuming chore, but ASP.NET has totally revolutionized the process. ASP.NET comes with a set of powerful validation controls that can easily be implemented to perform both client- and server-side validation. In this chapter, you'll learn to:

- Use the `RequiredField` validation control.
- Use the `Compare` validation control.
- Use the `Range` validation control.
- Use the `RegularExpression` validation control.

Understanding Validation in ASP.NET

Initially, validation may seem to be a trivial task, but its importance will quickly become obvious as the size and complexity of your Web application increases. In many situations, the validation requirements of individual forms in your application will vary considerably. Programming to meet these requirements will take up precious development time and usually result in unmanageable ASP code.

Validation can either be implemented on the client (that is, Web browser) or server sides. Although client-side validation provides the user with immediate feedback, it is hard to target multiple browsers. Server-side validation, on the other hand, caters to all browsers but is less responsive, slower, and increases network bandwidth.

ASP.NET has addressed all of these issues with a set of validation controls, as shown in Table 9.1. These controls are capable of detecting blank fields, performing field comparisons, matching regular expressions, and checking that a value is within a specified range. The validation controls take advantage of the enhanced DHTML functionality that Internet Explorer 4+ supports and are able to dynamically display error messages in an intuitive manner. No data will be posted to the server until all the validation requirements are met. Validation occurs on both the client and the server sides. This may seem like a duplication of functionality, but it actually prevents users from copying your forms, removing the client-side validation, and posting the data to the server for processing. Client-side validation will not be performed for browsers that do not support complex DHTML.

The validation controls will enable you to do the following:

- Perform client-side validation if an Internet Explorer 4+ browser is being used.
- Provide immediate feedback in the form of customized error messages.
- Submit data to the server only after the client-side validation is successful.
- Check that fields satisfy multiple conditions.
- Create custom validation routines in C#.
- Easily implement and modify form validation.

Table 9.1 List of Available Validation Controls

Validation Control	Description
RequiredField Validator	Ensures that data has been entered into mandatory fields.
Compare Validator	Compares the data entered into fields.
Range Validator	Checks whether the data entered is within a specified range.
RegularExpression Validator	Matches the data to a regular expression.
Custom Validator	Defines custom client- and server-side methods to perform validation.
ValidationSummary	Displays all validation error messages at a specified location on the page.

Using the RequiredField Validator

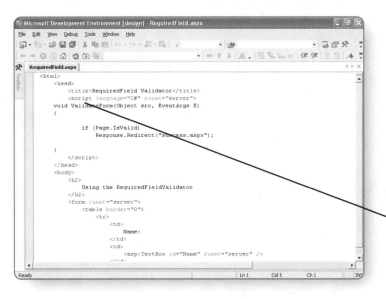

The RequiredField validator is the simplest validation control. It is used to test whether a field has been left blank. The RequiredField validator is not concerned with the format of the data that is entered. This control should be used to validate fields that gather mandatory user information.

1. Insert a method. This method will perform validation when a button control is clicked.

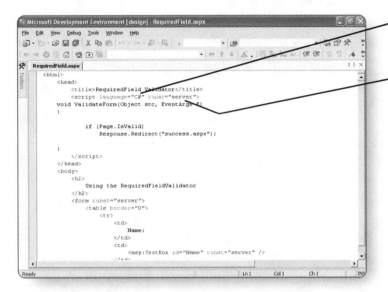

2. Set the `language` attribute to `C#`.

3. Set the `runat` attribute to `server`. The form will be processed on the server.

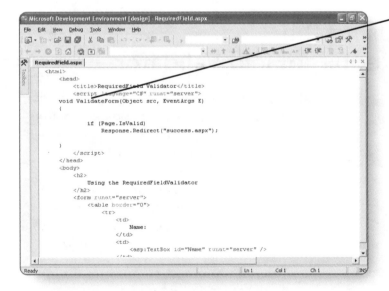

4. Insert a `Page_Load` method. This method will be executed each time the page is loaded.

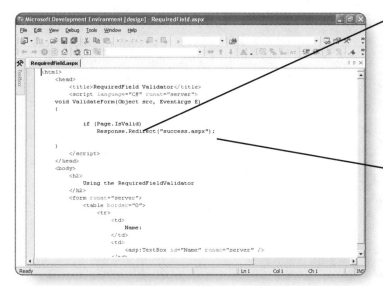

5. Use an `if` statement to test whether the `Page.IsValid` property is `true` and then process the form. The `Page.IsValid` property will only return `true` if no validation errors have occurred.

6. Insert the C# code that will process the data. In this example, the `Response.Redirect` method is used to redirect the user to a page that will acknowledge form submission.

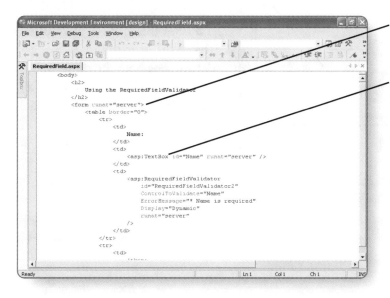

7. Insert opening and closing `<form>` tags.

8. Insert a `TextBox` control. This will be a mandatory field. Set the `id` and `runat` attributes. The `id` attribute is used to name the control. Each field that requires validation must be given a unique `id`.

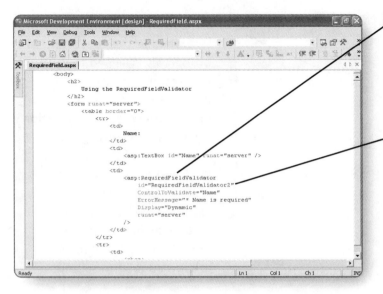

9. Insert the RequireField Validator control. This is done by inserting opening and closing <asp:RequiredFieldValidator> tags.

10. Name the validation control by setting the id attribute.

11. Specify the id of the control that must not be left blank.

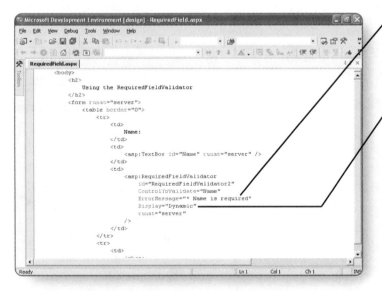

12. Assign a custom error message to the ErrorMessage attribute. The error message will be displayed if the validation fails.

13. Set the Display attribute. The Display attribute determines how the page will be rendered before and after a validation error gets written to the page. The error message will only take up space when the validation fails if the Display is set to Dynamic. Setting the Display attribute to Static means that space will always be reserved for the error message.

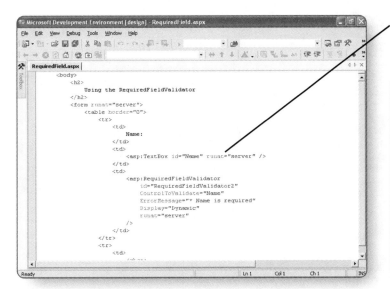

14. Set the runat attribute to server.

NOTE

The appearance of the error message can also be changed by setting various CSS attributes, such as BackColor, ForeColor, and Font-Size. The CssClass attribute can be used to specify a style sheet.

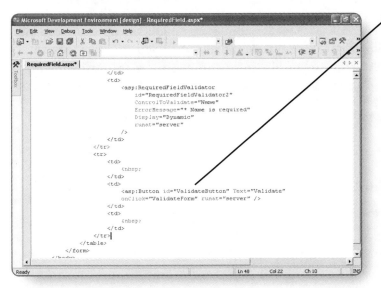

15. Insert a Button control. Assign the name of the method validation to the on-Click attribute.

NOTE

There is also an initialValue attribute that specifies the default value that a form control displays, such as Enter your name. This value will be ignored when validation occurs. This is ideal for drop-down lists that load with a default value.

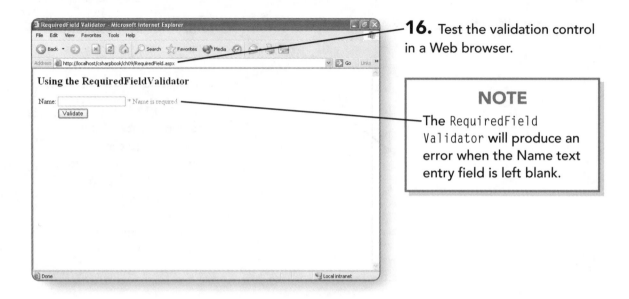

16. Test the validation control in a Web browser.

Using the Compare Validator

The CompareValidator control compares the data entered into two fields. This control is handy when you need the user to confirm a password. You can also compare the data entered into a field with a constant.

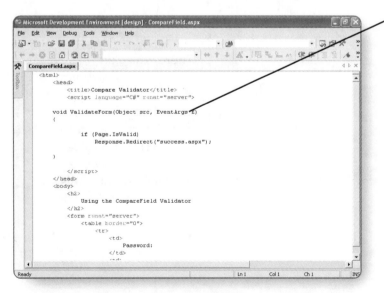

1. Insert a method. This method will perfom validation when a button control is clicked.

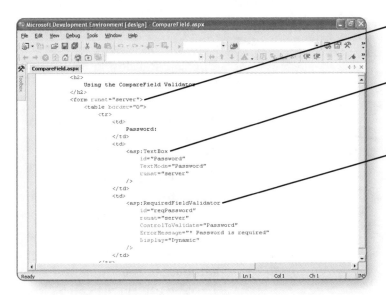

2. Insert opening and closing `<form>` tags.

3. Insert a `TextBox` control and set the `TextMode` attribute to `Password`.

4. Use the `RequiredFieldValidator` control to ensure that the field is not left blank.

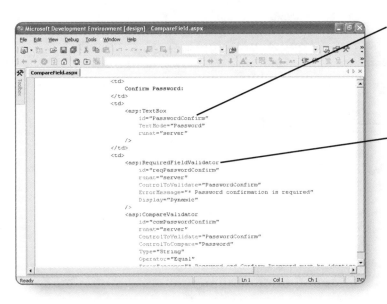

5. Insert a Password Confirmation field. A `TextBox` control with the `TextMode` property set to `Password` must be used.

6. Use the `RequiredFieldValidator` control to ensure that the Password Confirmation field is not left blank.

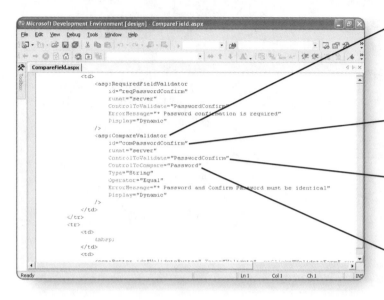

7. Insert the `CompareValidator` control. This is done by inserting opening and closing `<asp:CompareValidator>` tags.

8. Name the validation control by setting the `id` attribute.

9. Use the `ControlToValidate` attribute to specify the control that must be validated.

10. Use the `ControlToCompare` attribute to specify control that must be used in the comparison.

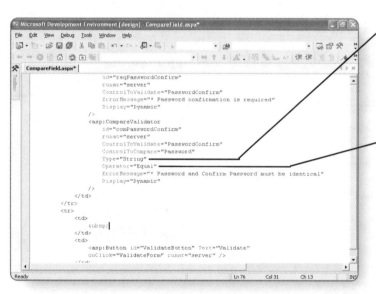

11. Specify the type of data being compared. The `Type` attribute could be set to `String`, `Integer`, `Double`, `DateTime`, or `Currency`.

12. Specify the comparison operator. This could be `Equal`, `GreaterThan`, `GreaterThanEqual`, `LessThan`, `LessThanEqual`, or `NotEqual`.

NOTE

`DataTypeCheck` is an additional operator that does not perform a comparison. It is used to ensure that the data entered matches the specified type. It provides a simple way to verify the format of data entered by a user.

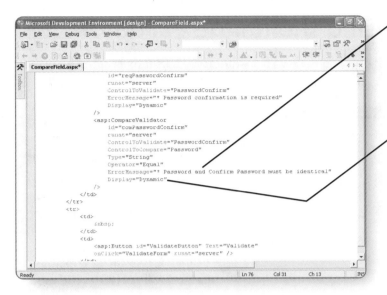

13. Assign a custom error message to the ErrorMessage attribute. The error message will be displayed if the validation fails.

14. Set the Display attribute to Dynamic.

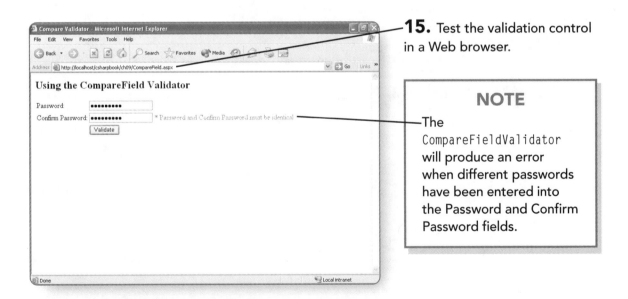

15. Test the validation control in a Web browser.

> **NOTE**
>
> The CompareFieldValidator will produce an error when different passwords have been entered into the Password and Confirm Password fields.

Using the Range Validator

Date and numeric values entered by a user must often be within a particular range. The `RangeValidator` enables you to easily apply this type of validation to your form fields. All you need to do is specify the type of value that must be within the range as well as the range limits. The maximum and minimum values can also be set dynamically from other form fields.

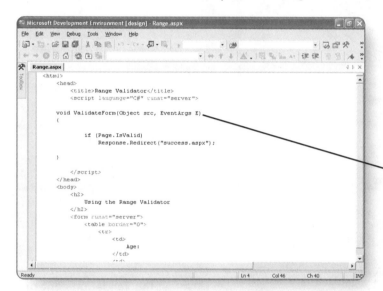

1. Insert a method. This method will perform validation when a button control is clicked.

2. Insert opening and closing `<form>` tags.

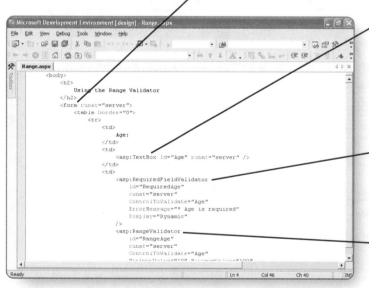

3. Insert a `TextBox` control. The `RangeValidator` will be used to validate this field. Set the `id` and `runat` attributes. In this example, we will require the user to be between 10 and 100 years old.

4. Use the `RequiredField Validator` control to ensure that the field is not left blank.

5. Insert the `RangeValidator` control. This is done by inserting opening and closing `<asp:RangeValidator>` tags.

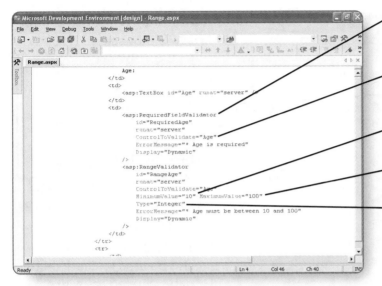

6. Name the validation control by setting the `id` attribute.

7. Specify the control that must be validated.

8. Specify the minimum value.

9. Specify the maximum value.

10. Specify the `Type` of values that fall within the range. This could be an `Integer` or a `Date`.

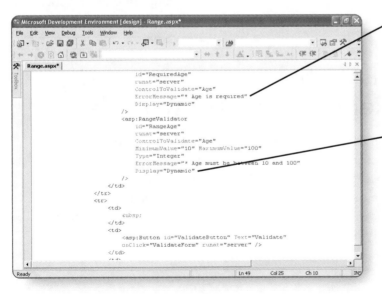

11. Assign a custom error message to the `ErrorMessage` attribute. The error message will be displayed if the validation fails.

12. Set the `Display` attribute to `Dynamic`.

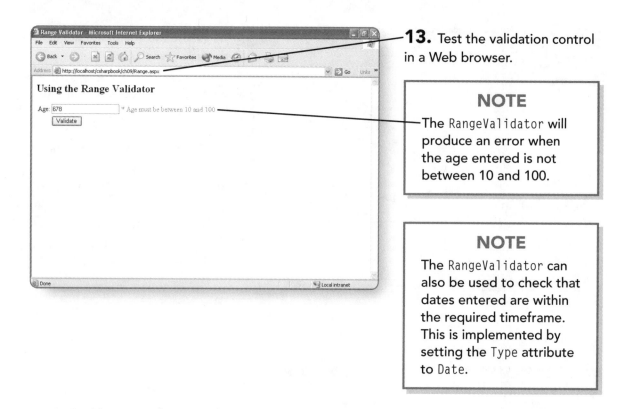

13. Test the validation control in a Web browser.

NOTE

The RangeValidator will produce an error when the age entered is not between 10 and 100.

NOTE

The RangeValidator can also be used to check that dates entered are within the required timeframe. This is implemented by setting the Type attribute to Date.

Using the RegularExpression Validator

E-mail addresses, phone numbers, social security numbers, and credit card numbers all follow a pattern. The RegularExpressionValidator control enables you to match the data required in a field to an expression. With a basic knowledge of regular expressions you will find this control very powerful.

NOTE

You might find it handy to refresh your knowledge of regular expressions by returning to Chapter 6, "Programming in C#", where the theory was first introduced.

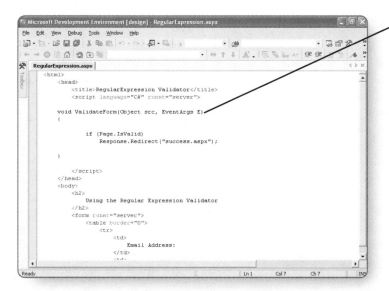

1. Insert a method. This method will perform validation when a button control is clicked.

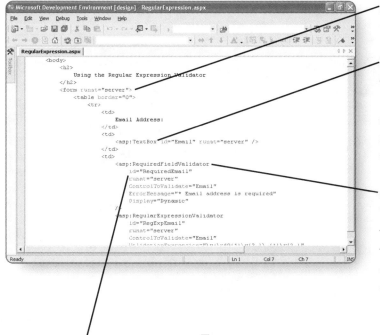

2. Insert opening and closing `<form>` tags.

3. Insert a `TextBox` control. This field will be validated by the `RegularExpressionValidator` control. Set the `id` and `runat` attributes. In this example we will validate an email address.

4. Use the `RequiredField Validator` control to ensure that the field is not left blank. Insert the `RegularExpressionValidator` control. This is done by inserting opening and closing `<asp:Regular ExpressionValidator>` tags.

5. Name the validation control by setting the `id` attribute.

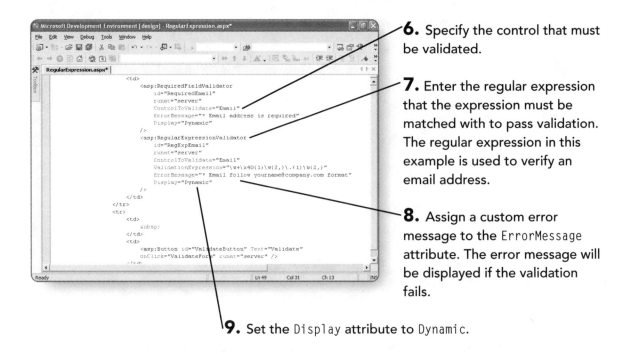

6. Specify the control that must be validated.

7. Enter the regular expression that the expression must be matched with to pass validation. The regular expression in this example is used to verify an email address.

8. Assign a custom error message to the ErrorMessage attribute. The error message will be displayed if the validation fails.

9. Set the Display attribute to Dynamic.

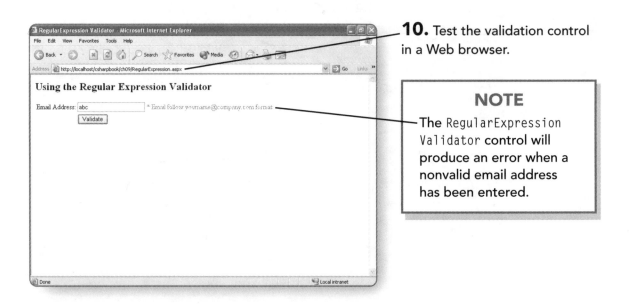

10. Test the validation control in a Web browser.

NOTE

The RegularExpression Validator control will produce an error when a nonvalid email address has been entered.

Using the Summary Validator

The SummaryValidator control collects and displays the error messages generated by all the validation controls implemented on the current ASP.NET page. A paragraph, list, or pop-up alert box can be used to display the error messages at the insertion point of the control.

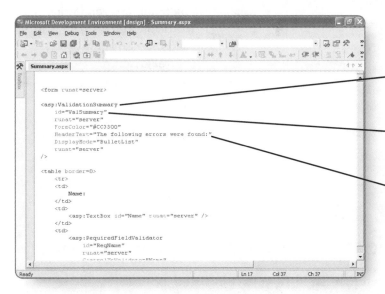

1. Insert the ValidationSummary control.

2. Name the validation control by setting the id attribute.

3. Specify the heading that must be displayed.

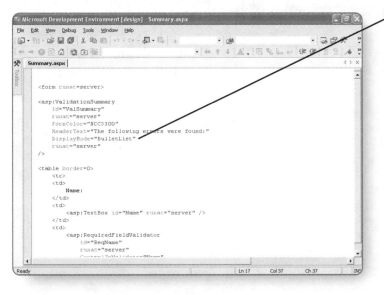

4. Specify DisplayMode. This could be set to

- BulletList. Errors are displayed in a bulleted list using the <li> tags.

- SingleParagraph. Errors are all displayed in the same paragraph.

- List. Errors are separated by line breaks (
 tags).

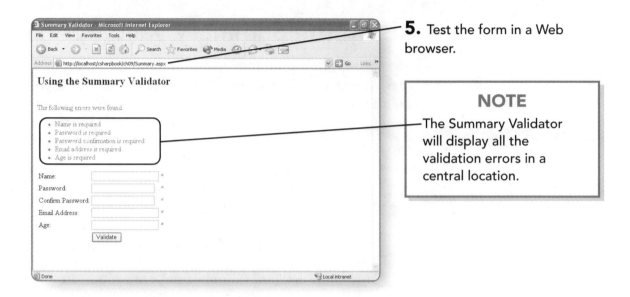

5. Test the form in a Web browser.

The Summary Validator will display all the validation errors in a central location.

Forcing Server-Side Validation

If Internet Explorer 4+ is being used, both client- and server-side validation will be performed. This occurs by default. You can, however, disable client-side validation by setting the `ClientTarget` attribute of the `Page` directive to `"DownLevel"`. `"UpLevel"` is the default value.

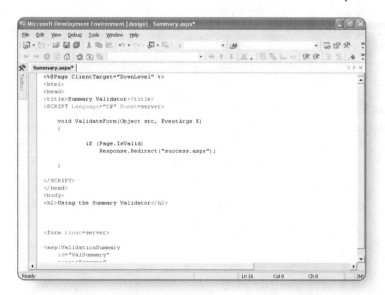

10

Creating Advanced Web Interfaces

Designing an intuitive and user-friendly interface for a Web application has never been a simple task. You had to write JavaScript code to respond to events that occur in a browser and then process the data that was sent to the server in classic ASP. It was also a nightmare to implement cross-browser compatible solutions. Luckily, this is no longer the case. ASP.NET WebControls generate rich user interface elements if you use Internet Explorer 5.5 and HTML 3.2 compliant code for other browsers. This means that you can target multiple browsers while still taking advantage of the rich feature set that Internet Explorer brings to Web interface development. In this chapter, you'll learn to use the:

- `AdRotator` control.
- `Calendar` control.
- `Toolbar`, `TreeView`, `TabStrip`, and `MultiPage` Internet Explorer WebControls.
- Mobile Internet Toolkit.

Using the AdRotator Control

Banner ads are everywhere. Banner ads are rectangular images that you can click on to find out more about a particular product or service. With the AdRotator control, you can easily implement a banner ad rotation system.

Each banner that you want to place in rotation must be described in an XML document. You need to specify the path of the banner image, the URL that the banner will link to, alternate text that will appear when the user moves her mouse over the image, a keyword used to filter ads, and the number of impressions:

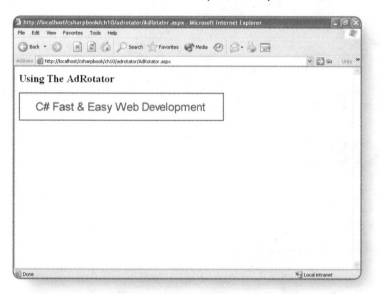

1. Insert opening and closing <Advertisements> tags.

2. Insert opening and closing <Ad> tags for each banner.

3. Specify the path to the image between opening and closing <ImageUrl> tags.

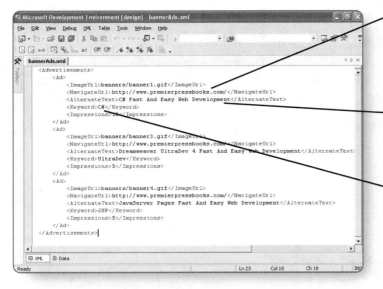

4. Specify the URL that the banner should link to when clicked between opening and closing `<NavigateUrl>` tags.

5. Specify the alternate text between opening and closing `<AlternateText>` tags.

6. Specify a keyword that can be used to filter the ads between opening and closing `<Keyword>` tags.

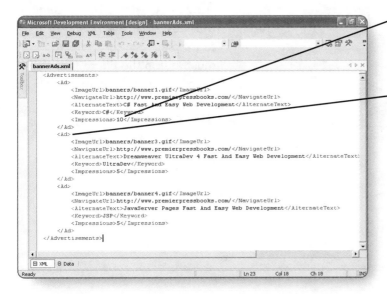

7. Specify the percentage of impressions between opening and closing `<Impressions>` tags.

8. Insert a new `<Ad>` tag for each banner ad you want to place in rotation.

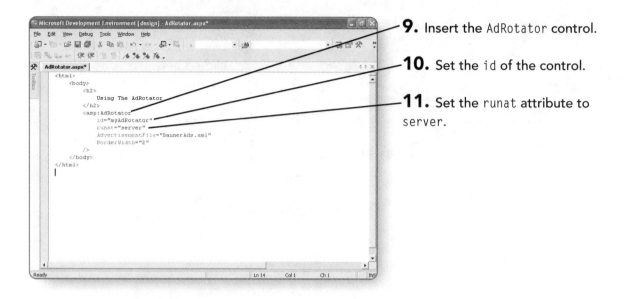

9. Insert the AdRotator control.

10. Set the id of the control.

11. Set the runat attribute to server.

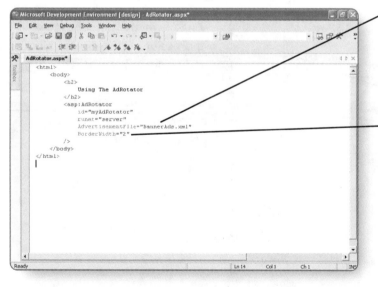

12. Specify the XML document that describes each banner to be placed in rotation. You must assign the file to the AdvertisementFile attribute.

13. Specify the pixel width of the border that surrounds each banner.

Using the Calendar Control

The Calendar control provides a user-friendly interface for users to select and specify dates. The calendar initially shows the current month, but users have the ability to navigate to any month of the year. A user can select a date by just clicking on it. You will insert a Calendar control on a Web page and display the date that the user selects in a label control. The SelectedDate property of the Calendar control contains the date specified by the user.

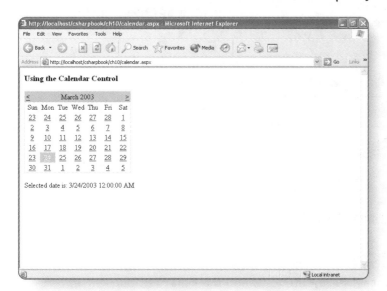

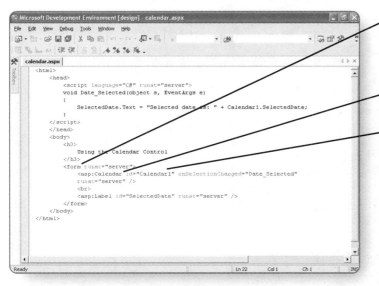

1. Insert opening and closing `<form>` tags. Set the runat attribute to server.

2. Insert the Calendar control.

3. Set the id of the Calendar control.

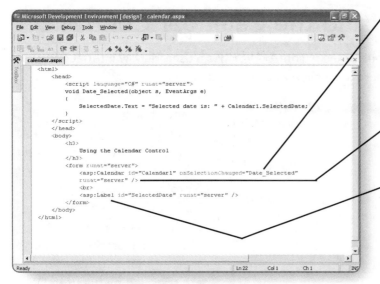

4. Set the `onSelectionChanged` event to `Date_Selected`. The `Date_Selected` method will execute when a user selects a date by clicking on it.

5. Set the `runat` attribute to `server`.

6. Insert a `Label` control. The `Date_Selected` method will use this label to display the date the user has selected using the `Calendar` control.

7. Insert opening and closing `<script>` tags. Set the `language` attribute to `C#` and the `runat` attribute to `server`.

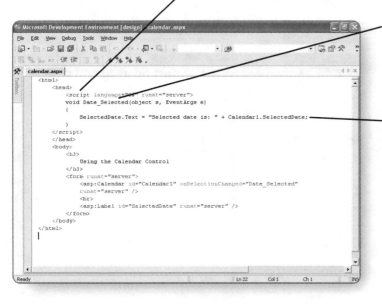

8. Insert a `Date_Selected` method. This method will execute when the user selects a date.

9. Assign the `SelectedDate` property of the `Calendar` control to the label's `text` property. This will display the date that the user has selected.

Using the Internet Explorer WebControls

The `TreeView`, `Toolbar`, `TabStrip`, and `MultiPage` controls are popular interface elements implemented in Windows applications. These intuitive controls that aid user navigation are now available for Web development, thanks to a set of server controls that Microsoft developed for use in ASP.NET. These controls provide richer user interaction to Internet Explorer users (version 5.5+) while still delivering HTML 3.2-compliant content to other browsers.

NOTE

The Internet Exploer WebControls were not included in version 1 of ASP.NET. They were still in beta when this book was published. You will be able to download the Internet Explorer WebControls from **http://www.asp.net** when they are released. Please check **http://www.premierpressbooks.com/downloads.asp** for updated source code and errata for this chapter when the Internet Explorer WebControls become available.

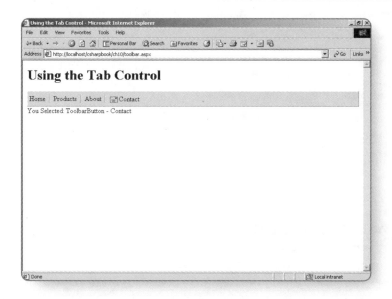

Using the Toolbar Control

A toolbar contains buttons that allow quick access to frequently used application features. A toolbar has always been an essential interface element for Windows-based applications, and now it is available for use in Web applications as well. You will build a method to identify the button that has been clicked:

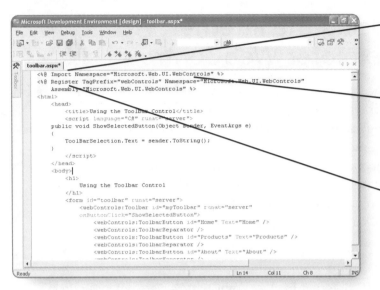

1. Insert the @Import directive. You use the Import directive to import a namespace.

2. Set the Namespace attribute to Microsoft.Web.UI.WebControls. This namespace contains the Toolbar WebControl.

3. Insert a Register directive. You use the Register directive to associate a tag prefix with a namespace at its corresponding assembly.

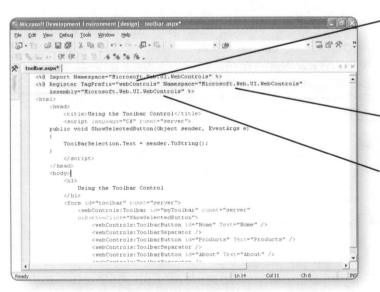

4. Set the TagPrefix attribute. This prefix is a shortened name used instead of the namespace, which is quite lengthy.

5. Set the Namespace attribute to Microsoft.Web.UI.WebControls.

6. Set the Assembly attribute to Microsoft.Web.UI.WebControls.

NOTE

You must place the Import and Register directives at the beginning of the page before you define or reference programmatically any WebControl elements.

7. Insert opening and closing `<form>` tags. Set the `runat` attribute to `server`. You must put the toolbar inside `<form>` tags.

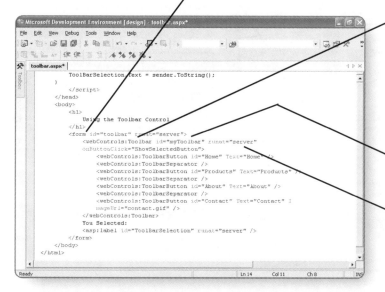

8. Insert the `Toolbar` WebControl. You must put the `tag` prefix that you defined in the `Register` directive before the name of the WebControl element.

9. Set the `id` of the `Toolbar` control.

10. Set the `runat` attribute to `server`.

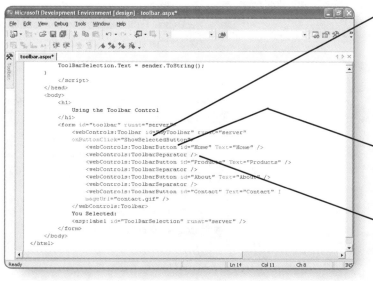

11. Set the `OnButtonClick` event to `ShowSelectedButton`. The `ShowSelectedButton` method will execute each time the user clicks a button on the toolbar.

12. Insert a `ToolbarButton` element. Set the `id` and the `text` attributes of the button.

13. Insert a `ToolbarSeparator` element.

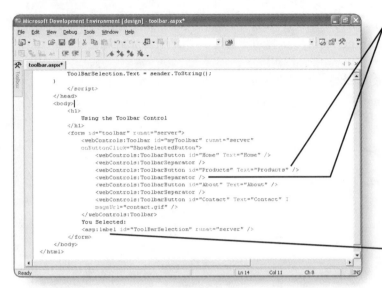

14. Insert additional `ToolbarButton` and `ToolbarSeparator` elements as required.

NOTE

You can display an image on a toolbar button with the `ImageUrl` attribute.

---

15. Insert a `Label` control. This label will display the name of the button clicked.

16. Insert opening and closing `<script>` tags. Set the `language` attribute to `C#` and the `runat` attribute to `server`.

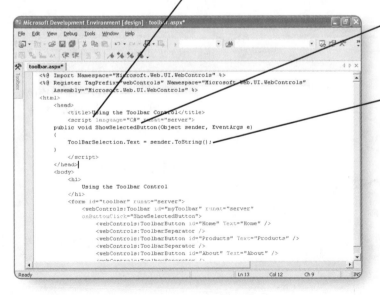

17. Insert a `ShowSelectedButton` method. This method will execute when the user clicks a button.

18. Display the `id` of the button clicked. This is retrieved from the sender object that is passed to the method as a parameter. You must use the `ToString` method to convert the sender object to a string before it is assigned to the `Text` property of the label.

> ### NOTE
>
> You can include the following additional interface elements in a toolbar:
>
> ```
> ToolbarCheckButton
> ToolbarCheckGroup
> ToolbarDropDownList
> ToolbarLabel
> ToolbarSeparator
> ToolbarTextBox
> ```

Using the MultiPage Control

With the `MultiPage` control, you can separate content into manageable chunks that fit on a single screen. The user can then use buttons to navigate between the pages. You place each page within a `PageView` tag. You use the `SelectedIndex` property, which starts at 0, to display the pages within the control:

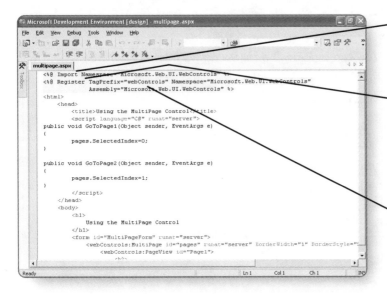

1. Insert the @Import directive. Set the Namespace attribute to Microsoft.Web.UI.WebControls.

2. Insert a Register directive. You use the Register directive to associate a tag prefix with a namespace at its corresponding assembly.

3. Set the TagPrefix attribute. This prefix is a shortened name used instead of the namespace, which is quite lengthy.

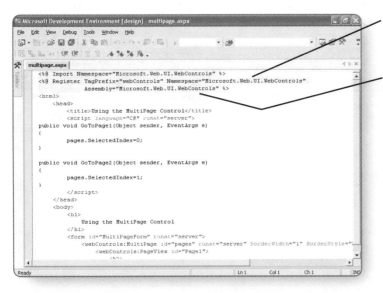

4. Set the Namespace attribute to Microsoft.Web.UI.WebControls.

5. Set the Assembly attribute to Microsoft.Web.UI.WebControls.

6. Insert opening and closing ⟨form⟩ tags. Set the runat attribute to server. You must put the MultiPage control inside ⟨form⟩ tags.

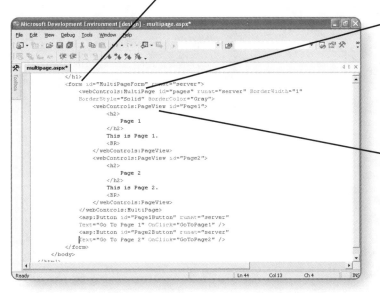

7. Insert the MultiPage WebControl. You must place the tag prefix that you defined in the Register directive before the name of the WebControl element.

8. Insert a PageView element. The PageView element inserts a new page in the MultiPage control. Set the id so that each page can be uniquely identified.

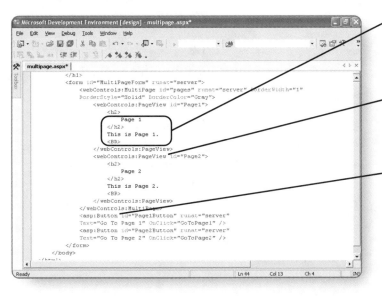

9. Insert the HTML code for each page within the PageView opening and closing tags.

10. Insert additional PageView elements to add pages to the MultiPage control.

11. Insert a Button control. This button will display the first page in the MultiPage control. Set the runat attribute to server. Set the OnClick event to GoToPage1. The GoToPage1 method will execute when the user clicks the button.

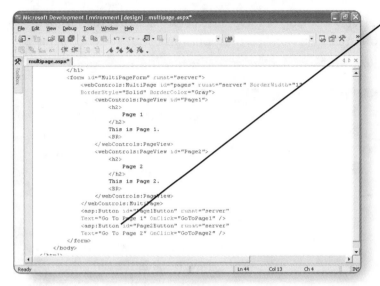

12. Insert another `Button` control. This button will display the second page in the `MultiPage` control. Set the `runat` attribute to `server`. Set the `OnClick` event to `GoToPage2`. The `GoToPage2` method will execute when the user clicks the button.

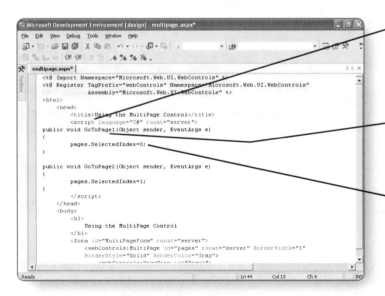

13. Insert opening and closing `<script>` tags. Set the `language` attribute to `C#`. Set the `runat` attribute to `server`.

14. Insert a `GoToPage1` method. This method will display the first page.

15. Set the `SelectedIndex` property of the `MultiPage` control to the index of the page to be displayed, which is 0 because page numbering begins at 0.

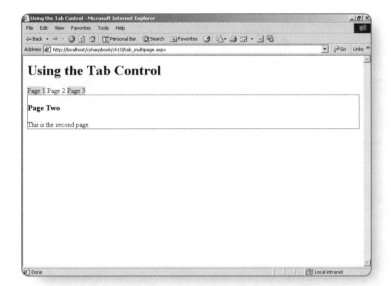

Using the TabStrip Control

The TabStrip control inserts tabs that you can use to navigate the pages contained in a MultiPage control. Only one page is displayed at a time. Using tabs to switch between pages is easy to implement, visually appealing, and intuitive:

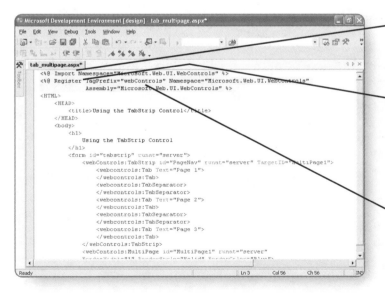

1. Insert the @Import directive. Set the Namespace attribute to Microsoft.Web.UI.WebControls.

2. Insert a Register directive. You use the Register directive to associate a tag prefix with a namespace at its corresponding assembly.

3. Set the TagPrefix attribute. This prefix is a shortened name used instead of the namespace, which is quite lengthy.

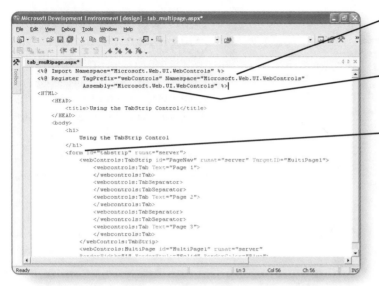

4. Set the `Namespace` attribute to `Microsoft.Web.UI.WebControls`.

5. Set the `Assembly` attribute to `Microsoft.Web.UI.WebControls`.

6. Insert opening and closing `<form>` tags. Set the `runat` attribute to `server`. You must place the `TabStrip` and `MultiPage` controls inside `<form>` tags.

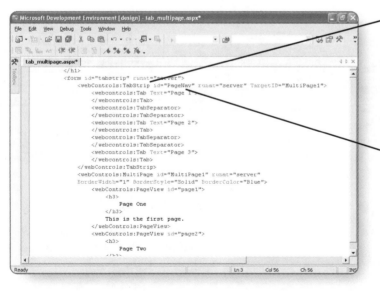

7. Insert the `TabStrip` WebControl. You must place the tag prefix that you defined in the `Register` directive before the name of the WebControl element.

8. Set the `TargetID` to the ID of the `MultiPage` control that the `TabStrip` will navigate.

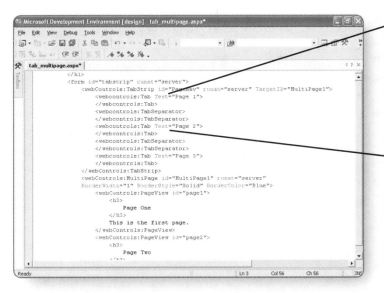

9. Insert a `Tab` element. Set the `text` attribute of the `Tab` element. This text will appear on the tab and should indicate which page will be loaded when the user selects the tab.

10. Insert additional `Tab` elements for each tab you want to insert.

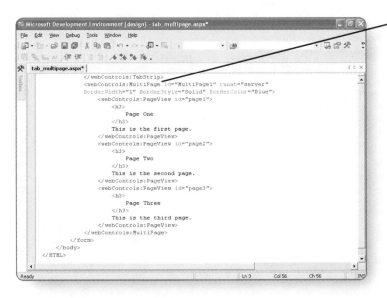

11. Insert the `MultiPage` control. Use the `PageView` tag to add pages to the control.

Using the TreeView Control

The `TreeView` control displays hierarchical data. Windows Explorer uses a `TreeView` control to navigate the files and folders on your computer, so most users will be familiar with the control. You can use the `TreeView` control to display the structure of your organization or Web site. Many Web sites use the `TreeView` control to implement centralized site navigation. It is ideally suited to data that has parent-child relationships. Each item is called a *node*. The node at the top of the hierarchy is called the *root*. The root has subnodes or child nodes. Nodes can be expanded or collapsed. You can bind data from a database or XML document to a `TreeView` control. I illustrate here a simple hand-coded example:

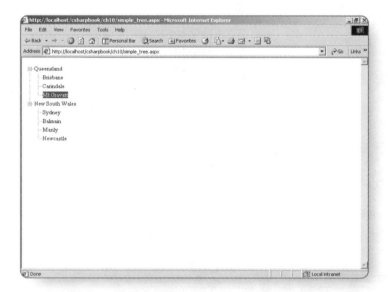

1. Insert the `@Import` directive. Set the `Namespace` attribute to `Microsoft.Web.UI.WebControls`.

2. Insert a `Register` directive. Set the `TagPrefix` attribute.

3. Set the `Namespace` attribute to `Microsoft.Web.UI.WebControls` and the `Assembly` attribute to `Microsoft.Web.UI.WebControls`.

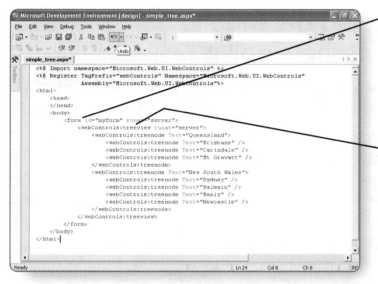

4. Insert opening and closing `<form>` tags. Set the `runat` attribute to `server`. You must place the `TreeView` control within opening and closing `<form>` tags.

5. Insert the `TreeView` `WebControl`. You must place the tag prefix you defined in the `Register` directive before the name of the WebControl element. Set the `runat` attribute to `server`. Set the `type` attribute to `folder`.

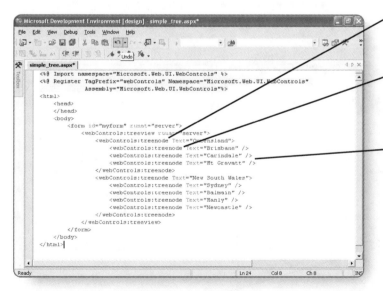

6. Insert a `treenode` element and set the `text` attribute.

7. Insert `treenode` elements within another `treenode` element to create child nodes.

8. Insert additional nodes and subnodes as required.

Using the Mobile Internet Toolkit

The Mobile Internet Toolkit simplifies the development of applications for mobile devices by allowing you to leverage your existing skills. There is no longer a need to learn the Wireless Markup Language (WML) to build applications for WAP (Wireless Application Protocol) devices. The Mobile Internet Toolkit includes TextBox, Label, and Command controls that you can use to construct WAP applications to target a variety of mobile devices.

I illustrate the use of the Mobile controls with a simple example that retrieves the data a user has entered into a form and displays it. You will use the Form, Label, TextBox, and Command mobile server controls. You will place two forms on the page. The first form will display the interface, and the second form will only be activated after the first form is submitted. A Label control on the second form will display the data the user has entered.

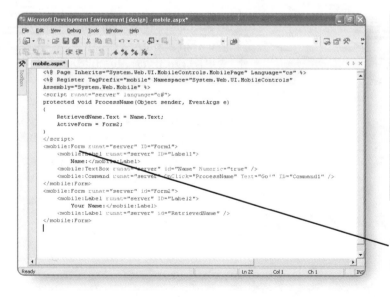

> **NOTE**
>
> The Mobile Toolkit is an add-on to ASP.NET. You can download it from **http://www.asp.net/download.aspx**. You must install the toolkit before you can use the mobile server controls.

1. Insert a Form control. Set the runat attribute to server.

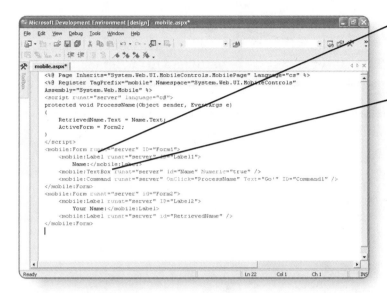

2. Insert a `Label` control. Enter the text that the label must display.

3. Insert a `TextBox` control. Set the `runat` attribute to `server`. Set the `id` attribute. You will use the `id` to retrieve the data the user has entered.

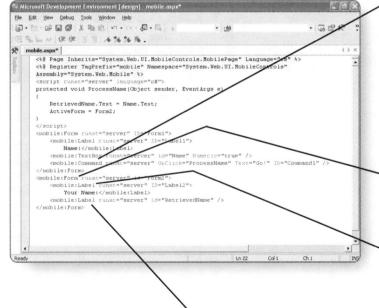

4. Insert a `Command` control. Set the `runat` attribute to `server`. Set the `text` attribute. The text you enter will appear as a label on the button. Set the `OnClick` event to `ProcessName`. The `ProcessName` method will execute when the user clicks the button.

5. Insert a `Form` control. Set the `runat` attribute to `server`. Assign a unique ID to the form.

6. Insert a `Label` control. Enter the `text` that the label must display.

7. Insert a `Label` control with an `id` of `RetrievedName`. This label will display the data the user enters into the first form.

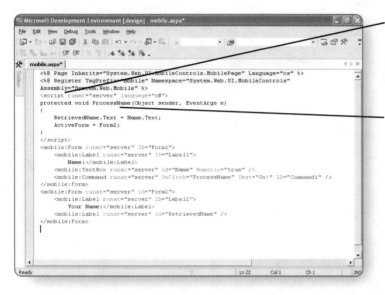

8. Insert opening and closing `<script>` tags. Set the `language` attribute to `C#`. Set the `runat` attribute to `server`.

9. Insert a `ProcessName` method. This method will execute when the first form is submitted.

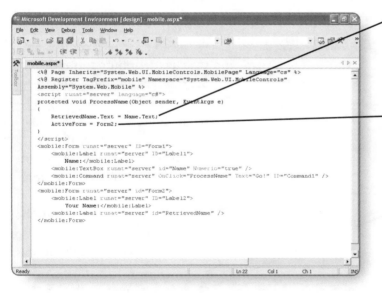

10. Retrieve the data entered by the user and assign the data to the `RetrievedName` label on the second form.

11. Activate the second form by assigning its form ID to `ActiveForm`.

NOTE

You can test mobile applications with a WAP phone simulator that you can download from http://www.microsoft.com/mobile/downloads.

11

Advanced Web Form Techniques

This chapter focuses on the reuse and creation of new user-interface elements. User controls allow you to store a combination of server controls in a central location so that multiple pages can reuse the encapsulated interface and logic. Custom controls, on the other hand, allow you to introduce new interface elements or extend the functionality of existing server controls. Code-Behind, an additional technique to further separate programming logic from layout will also be introduced. In this chapter, you'll learn to:

- Create a simple user control.
- Use properties in a user control.
- Create a simple custom control.
- Set and retrieve properties in a custom control.
- Use the Code-Behind technique.

Working with User Controls

A user control allows you to group together server controls so that you can use them in different pages. Your site probably uses the same header and footer on all pages. You could insert the header and footer on every page or store the code in a central location, where it can easily be updated. A user control provides the perfect solution. You can extract elements of a page, including server controls, save them as a user control, and reuse the encapsulated functionality.

Creating a Simple User Control

The first user control that you will create is extremely simple. It only displays some text on the page. Although this is a trivial example, it does demonstrate the fundamental steps required to create and implement any user control:

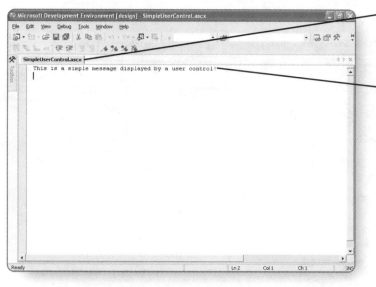

1. Create a page with an .ascx extension. User controls must have this file extension.

2. Type some text. This user control will display a hard-coded text value.

3. Insert a `Register` directive in an .aspx page. This page will use the user control.

4. Set the `TagPrefix` attribute.

5. Set the `TagName` attribute.

6. Set the `Src` attribute. You must set this attribute to the file name of the user control.

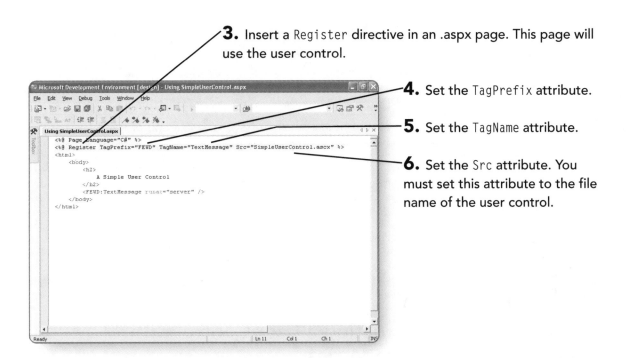

7. Type the `TagPrefix` followed by the `TagName`.

8. Set the `runat` attribute to `server`.

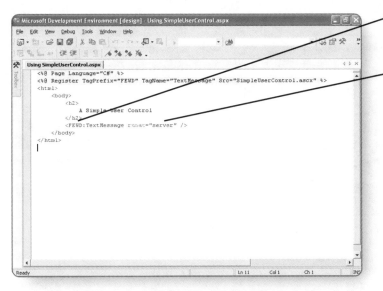

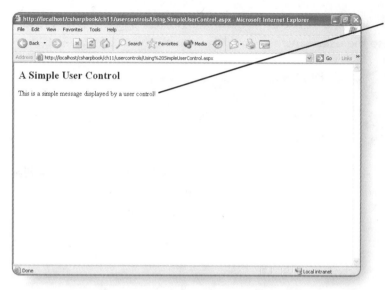

9. Preview the page in a browser. The hard-coded text value will appear.

Creating a User Control with Properties

You will extend the preceding user control to display custom messages in a specified size. You must add public variables to store the size and custom message:

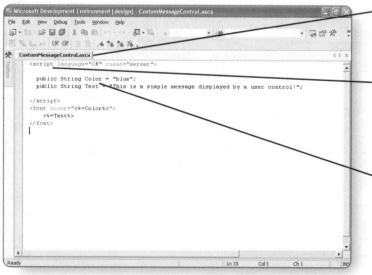

1. Create a page with an .ascx extension. User controls must have this file extension.

2. Insert opening and closing `<script>` tags. Set the `language` attribute to `C#` and the `runat` attribute to `server`.

3. Declare a public string variable called `Color`. This variable will store the default color of the text.

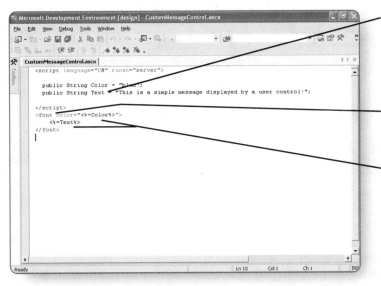

4. Declare a public string variable called Text. This variable will store the default text message.

5. Insert the HTML code that formats the message.

6. Use the <%= and %> delimiters to print the color and text variables within the HTML code.

CAUTION

You can't include the opening and closing <html> and <form> tags in a user control.

7. Insert a Register directive in an .aspx page. This page will use the user control.

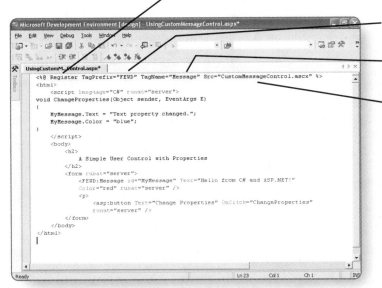

8. Set the TagPrefix attribute.

9. Set the TagName attribute.

10. Set the Src attribute. You must set this attribute to the file name of the user control.

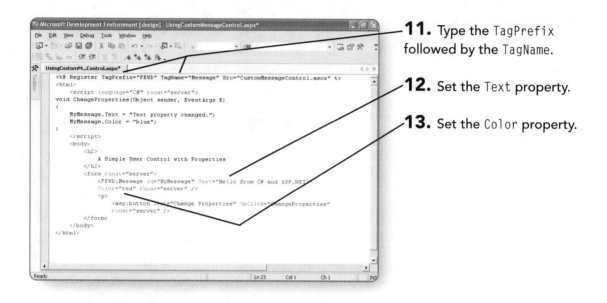

11. Type the TagPrefix followed by the TagName.

12. Set the Text property.

13. Set the Color property.

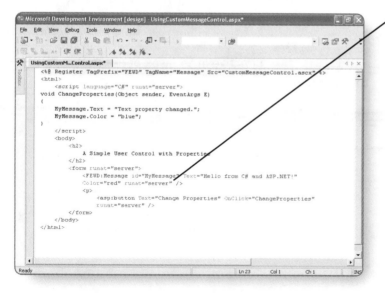

14. Set the runat attribute to server.

NOTE

You can also set the user controls properties programmatically.

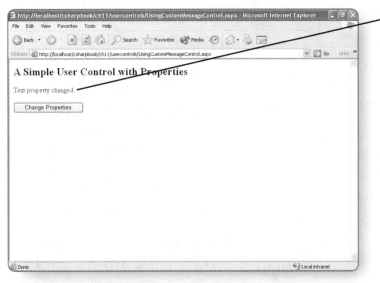

15. Preview the page in a browser. The user control will display custom messages in different colors.

Enhancing the TextBox Server Control

A text box is a common server control. I always find myself placing some text beside a text box to describe the data the user must enter. It serves as a label for the text box. The user control that follows adds a label property to a text box server control. It enables me to specify the label and text a text box must display by default:

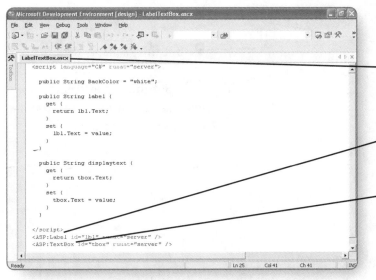

1. Create a page with an .ascx extension. User controls must have this file extension.

2. Insert a `Label` control. Set the `id` and the `runat` attributes.

3. Insert a `TextBox` control. Set the `id` and the `runat` attributes.

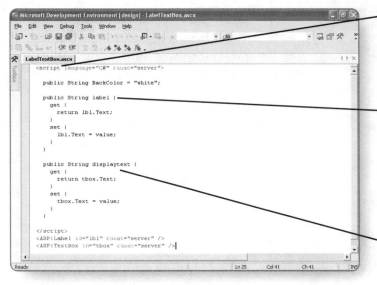

4. Insert opening and closing `<script>` tags. Set the `language` attribute to `C#` and the `runat` attribute to `server`.

5. Declare a string property named `label`. Include `get` and `set` accessor methods. The `set` accessor method must set the `Text` property of the `label` control.

6. Declare a string property named `displaytext`. Include `get` and `set` accessor methods. The `set` accessor method must set the `Text` property of the `TextBox` control.

7. Insert a `Register` directive in an .aspx page. This page will use the user control.

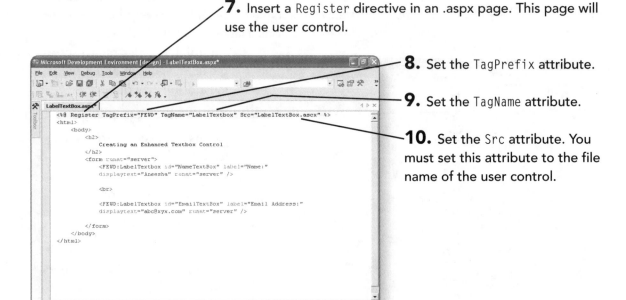

8. Set the `TagPrefix` attribute.

9. Set the `TagName` attribute.

10. Set the `Src` attribute. You must set this attribute to the file name of the user control.

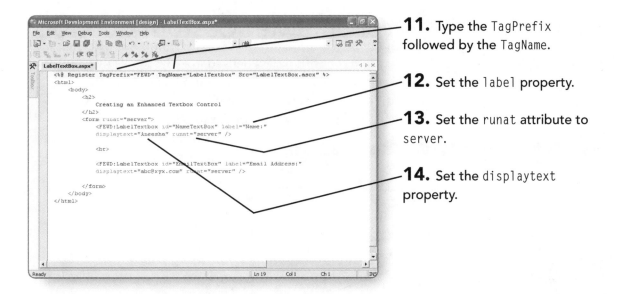

11. Type the `TagPrefix` followed by the `TagName`.

12. Set the `label` property.

13. Set the `runat` attribute to `server`.

14. Set the `displaytext` property.

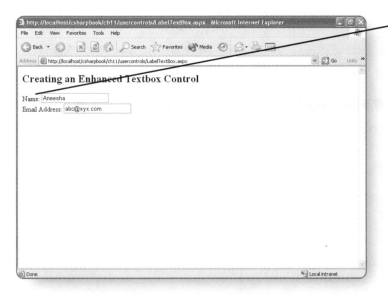

15. Preview the page in a browser. A label will appear beside the text box.

Working with Custom Controls

A custom control is a class derived from `System.Web.UI.Control`. The class must include a `Render` method that accepts an `HtmlTextWriter` object as a parameter. You use the `Write` method of `HtmlTextWriter` object to print HTML to the page. This first custom control will just display some text:

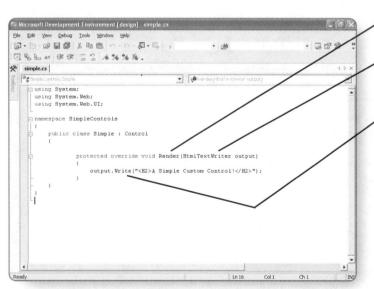

1. Create a file with a .cs extension. You will save the C# class in this file.

2. Import the `System`, `System.Web`, and `System.Web.UI` namespaces.

3. Create a namespace.

4. Create a public class that derives from the `Control` class.

5. Override the `Render` method.

6. Pass an `HtmlTextWriter` object to the `Render` method.

7. Use the `Write` method to print HTML to the page.

WORKING WITH CUSTOM CONTROLS 273

8. Compile the class file by typing the following at the command line:

```
csc /out:bin/SimpleControls.dll /t:library /r:System.dll
/r:System.Web.dll c:\Inetpub\wwwroot\cshrpbook\ch11\
simple.cs
```

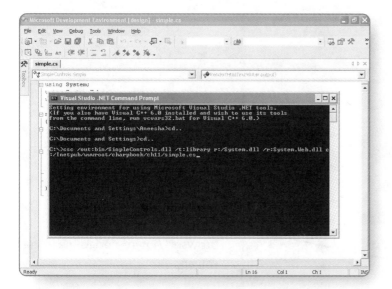

You must save the library file in the /bin subfolder.

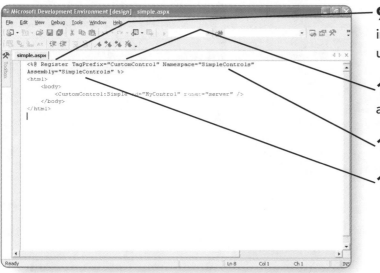

9. Insert a `Register` directive in an .aspx page. This page will use the user control.

10. Set the `TagPrefix` attribute.

11. Set the `Namespace` attribute.

12. Set the `Assembly` attribute.

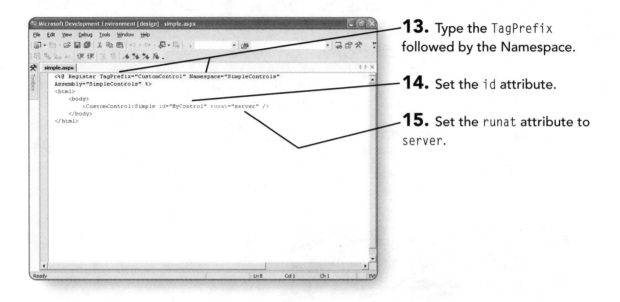

13. Type the `TagPrefix` followed by the Namespace.

14. Set the `id` attribute.

15. Set the `runat` attribute to `server`.

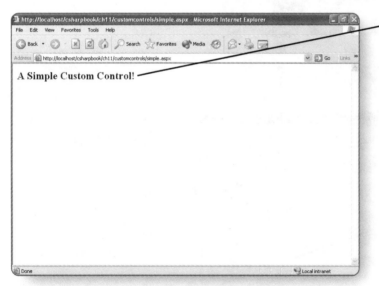

16. Preview the page in a browser. A hard-coded message will appear.

Creating a Custom Control with Properties

In the following custom control, you will implement properties. The ability to set and retrieve property values lets the control display custom messages. You use accessor methods to set and retrieve properties:

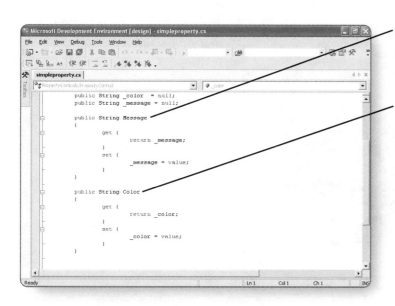

1. Create a file with a .cs extension. You will save the C# class in this file.

2. Import the System, System.Web, and System.Web.UI namespaces.

3. Create a namespace.

4. Create a public class that derives from the Control class.

5. Declare a string property named Message. Include get and set accessor methods.

6. Declare a string property named Color. Include get and set accessor methods.

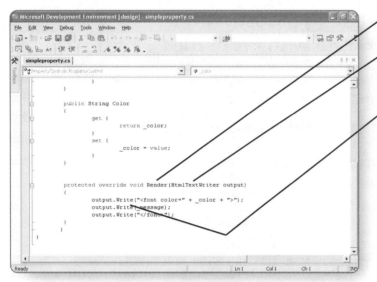

7. Override the `Render` method.

8. Pass an `HtmlTextWriter` object to the `Render` method.

9. Use the `Write` method to print HTML to the page. Include the `Color` and `Message` variables so that you can customize the message.

10. Compile the class file by typing the following at the command line:

```
csc /out:bin/SimpleControls.dll /t:library /r:System.dll
/r:System.Web.dll c:\Inetpub\wwwroot\csharpbook\ch11\
simple.cs
```

You must save the library file in the /bin subfolder.

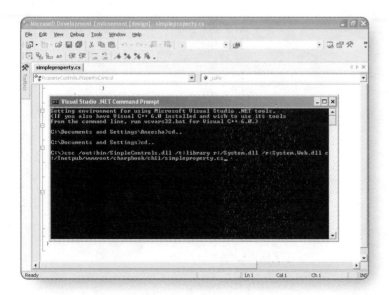

11. Insert a `Register` directive in an .aspx page. This page will use the user control.

12. Set the `TagPrefix` attribute.

13. Set the `Namespace` attribute.

14. Set the `Assembly` attribute.

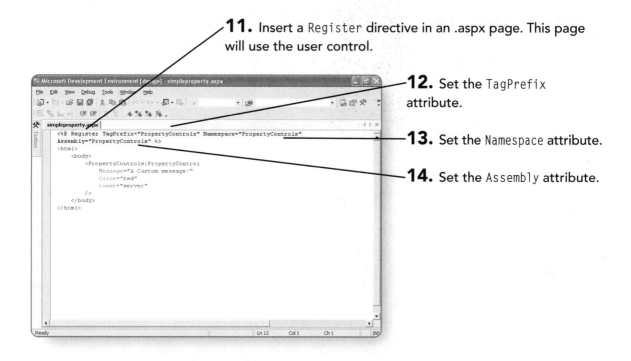

```
<%@ Register TagPrefix="PropertyControls" Namespace="PropertyControls"
Assembly="PropertyControls" %>
<html>
    <body>
        <PropertyControls:PropertyControl
            Message="A Custom message!"
            Color="red"
            runat="server"
        />
    </body>
</html>
```

15. Type the `TagPrefix` followed by the `Namespace`.

16. Set the `Message` property.

17. Set the `Color` property.

18. Set the `runat` attribute to `server`.

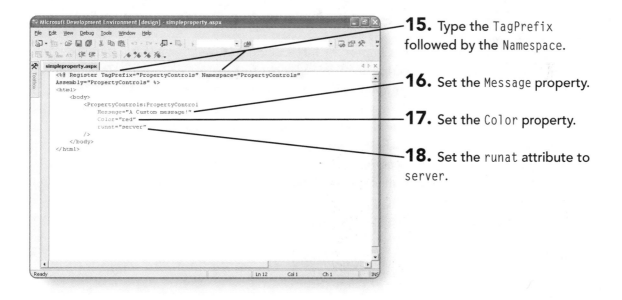

```
<%@ Register TagPrefix="PropertyControls" Namespace="PropertyControls"
Assembly="PropertyControls" %>
<html>
    <body>
        <PropertyControls:PropertyControl
            Message="A Custom message!"
            Color="red"
            runat="server"
        />
    </body>
</html>
```

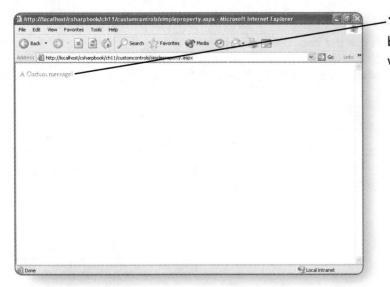

19. Preview the page in a browser. A customized message will appear.

Using Code-Behind to Separate Logic from Layout

In Chapter 2, "Introducing ASP.NET," you learned to use script declaration blocks to separate code and HTML layout. Although script declaration blocks helped you to structure your code, your code and HTML interface still had to be placed within the same file. Code-Behind is a simple technique that enables you to store your C# code in a separate file. Your code must be implemented as a class that is derived from System.Web.UI.Page.

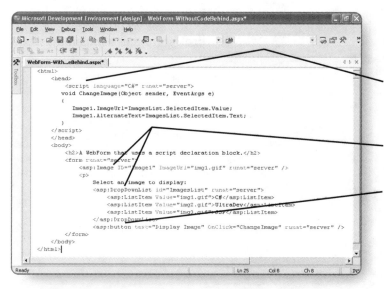

1. Here is a simple WebForm that uses a script declaration block.

- The script declaration block contains a method called `ChangeImage`.

- The WebForm uses an `Image` and a `DropDownList` control.

- A button is used to execute the `ChangeImage` method.

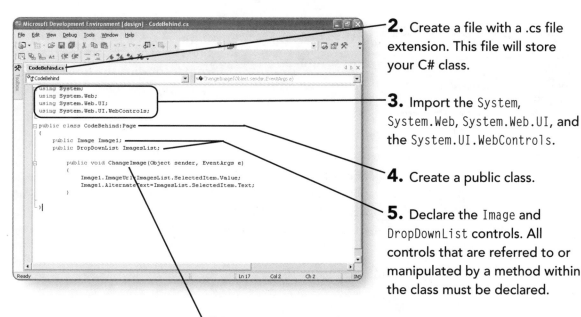

2. Create a file with a .cs file extension. This file will store your C# class.

3. Import the `System`, `System.Web`, `System.Web.UI`, and the `System.UI.WebControls`.

4. Create a public class.

5. Declare the `Image` and `DropDownList` controls. All controls that are referred to or manipulated by a method within the class must be declared.

6. Insert the `ChangeImage` method. This method must be declared as public. This will allow you to call the method from within the .aspx page. In this case, the `onClick` event of a button will call this method.

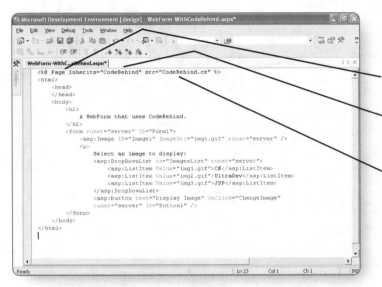

7. Delete the script declaration block from the .aspx file.

8. Insert a Page directive.

9. Set the Inherits attribute to the name of the class.

10. Set the src attribute to the name of the file that contains the C# class. This file will have a .cs extension.

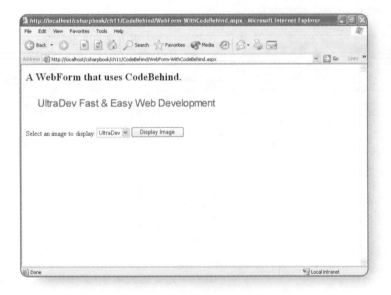

11. Preview the page in a browser. The C# code will be compiled when the page gets requested for the first time.

12

Working with Databases

Databases are a crucial component of many Web applications. All applications that serve dynamic content to many users require an efficient data-storage mechanism. Databases are fast and can store large amounts of information. ADO.NET allows you to access a database from an ASP.NET page and either extract or manipulate the data. In this chapter, you'll learn to:

- Connect to an SQL Server database.
- Use SQL to query a database.
- Use the `DataReader` object.
- Use the `DataSet` object.
- Insert, update, and delete records in a database.
- Use the `Repeater`, `DataList`, and `DataGrid` controls.

ADO.NET—An Overview

ADO.NET is new and improved data retrieval and manipulation architecture. ADO.NET uses a disconnected data model. This means that there is no need to keep an open connection to a database because the retrieved data is stored locally. ADO.NET communicates with a database in discrete transactions. You can then manipulate the local copy of the data without any database interaction. You reconnect to the database only to save the changes. ADO.NET is scalable and less resource-intensive because it does not need to maintain hundreds of concurrent connections.

Essentially, ADO.NET has a DataSet, which stores a subset of a database. The DataSet object consists of tables, constraints, and relationships. You can easily manipulate the data in a DataSet. ADO.NET also has two managed providers. You use the OleDb managed provider to connect to and retrieve data from OLE-compliant databases such as Access, Oracle, and Sybase. The SqlClient managed provider is optimized to access data from SQL Server. The SqlClient namespace contains the SqlConnection, SqlCommand, SqlDataReader, and SqlDataAdapter classes. These classes are optimized for interaction with a SQL Server database and offer a tremendous performance boost. For each SQL Server class there is an equivalent OleDb class that has the same name but starts with OleDb instead of Sql.

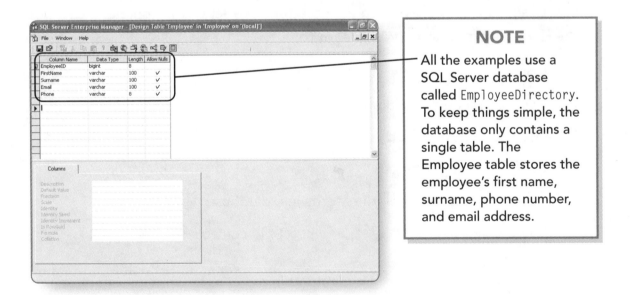

NOTE

All the examples use a SQL Server database called EmployeeDirectory. To keep things simple, the database only contains a single table. The Employee table stores the employee's first name, surname, phone number, and email address.

The examples in this chapter utilize SQL Server instead of Access because SQL Server supports simultaneous connections and is a true client/server database. Access was developed to be a desktop database and is not suitable for Web applications that could be used by hundreds, if not thousands, of users. I have, however, developed OleDb versions for all the examples covered in this chapter. These samples were included in the source code that was downloaded from http://www.premierpressbooks.com/downloads.asp.

Introducing SQL

The Structured Query Language (SQL) was designed to let you query and update database tables. SQL enables you to extract specific information from a database.

You use the Select statement to retrieve data from a database:

```
SELECT * FROM tablename
```

The asterisk is a wildcard character and retrieves all the fields that make up a record in the database. This query will retrieve all of the records in a table.

You can also specify the fields to be retrieved. This is handy if you don't require all the fields:

```
SELECT fieldname1, fieldname2 FROM tablename
```

You must add a where clause to filter data. The where clause retrieves records that match specific criteria:

```
SELECT * FROM tablename WHERE fieldname1='value1'
```

You can use Boolean operators such as AND and OR to define complex search criteria:

```
SELECT * FROM tablename WHERE fieldname1='value1' AND
fieldname2='value2'
SELECT * FROM tablename WHERE fieldname1='value1' OR
fieldname2='value2'
```

Using a DataReader Object

You must make a database connection before you can retrieve data from a database. You need to specify a database-connection string and an SQL query. You pass the SqlConnect object a database-connection string. The ExecuteReader method of the SqlConnection object executes a select query. You can store the returned data in an SqlDataReader object, which can then be bound to a data-aware control:

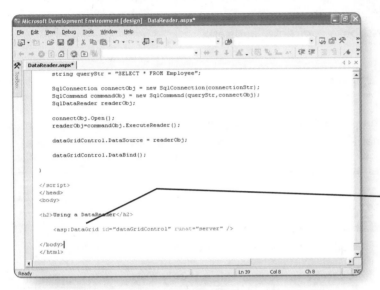

1. Insert a DataGrid control. Set the id and the runat attribute.

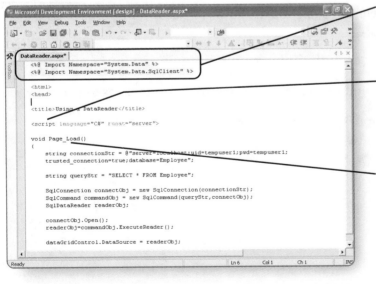

2. Import the System.Data and the System.Data.SqlClient namespaces.

3. Insert opening and closing script tags. Set the language attribute to C# and the runat attribute to server.

4. Insert a Page_Load method.

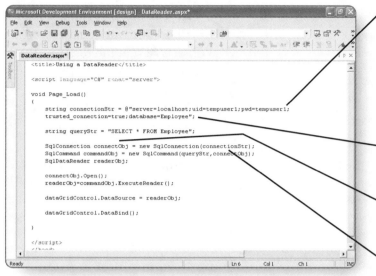

5. Store the connection string in a string variable. You may need to consult your database administrator to obtain the username, password, and server name for your database.

6. Store the SQL query in a string variable.

7. Create an `SqlConnection` object.

8. Pass the connection string to the `SqlConnection` constructor.

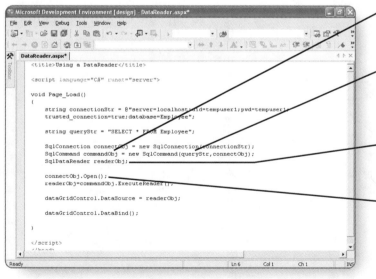

9. Create an `SqlCommand` object.

10. Pass the query and the connection object to the `SqlCommand` constructor.

11. Create an `SqlDataReader` object.

12. Call the `Open` method of the connection object.

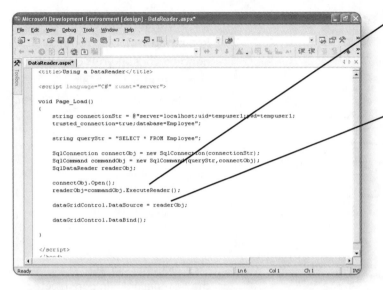

13. Call the `ExecuteReader` method of the `SqlConnection` object. Assign the result to the `SqlDataReader` object.

14. Assign the `SqlDataReader` object to the `DataSource` property of the `DataGrid` control.

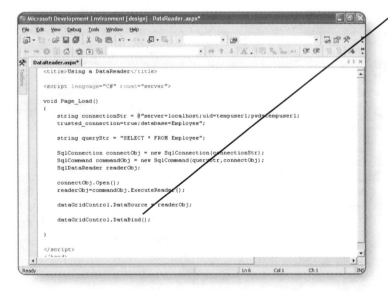

15. Call the `DataBind` method to bind the data to the control.

Using a DataSet Object

A DataSet stores a subset of a database in cache. The disconnected data is stored in XML. The DataSet object is structured like a database. It has DataTable, DataRelation, DataRow, and DataColumn objects.

A DataAdapter object transfers data between a DataSet and a database (or other data source). The Fill method retrieves and binds the data to a DataSet object.

NOTE

In classic ASP, you had to manually print each record to the page. In ASP.NET, however, you simply bind the data to a data-aware control such as a DataGrid. The DataGrid control displays the data in a table. You only need to assign the DataSet object to the DataSource property of the DataGrid and call the DataBind method.

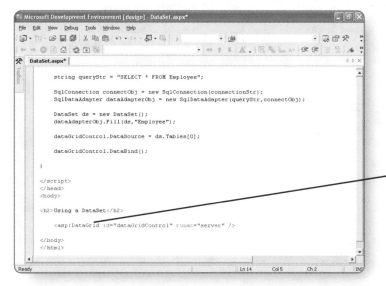

NOTE

You must import the System.Data namespace when you use a DataSet object.

1. Insert a DataGrid control. Set the id and the runat attribute.

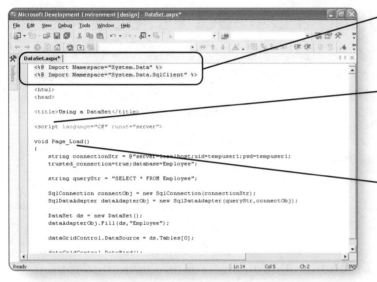

2. Import the `System.Data` and the `System.SqlClient` namespaces.

3. Insert opening and closing `script` tags. Set the `language` attribute to `C#` and the `runat` attribute to `server`.

4. Insert a `Page_Load` method.

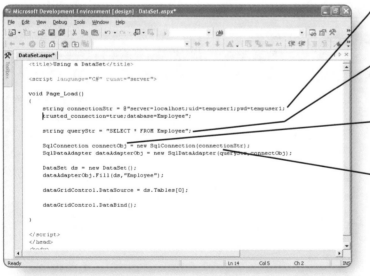

5. Store the connection string in a string variable.

6. Store the SQL query in a string variable.

7. Create an `SqlConnection` object.

8. Pass the connection string to the `SqlConnection` constructor.

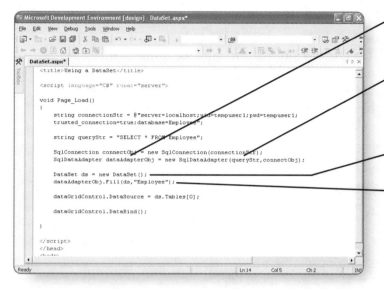

9. Create an `SqlDataAdapter` object.

10. Pass the query and the connection object to the `SqlDataAdapter` constructor.

11. Create a `DataSet` object.

12. Call the `Fill` method of the `SqlDataAdapter` object. You must pass the `DataSet` object to the `Fill` method.

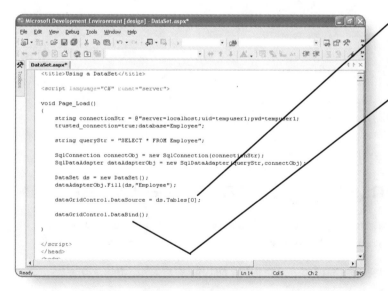

13. Assign the `DataSet` object to the `DataSource` property of the `DataGrid` control.

14. Call the `DataBind` method to bind the data to the control.

TIP

A `DataSet` can also be built programmatically. The DynamicDataSet.aspx file illustrates this concept.

NOTE

The DataAdapterUpdate.aspx file contains an advanced example that uses the Update method of the DataAdapter object to insert, update, and delete data in a database based upon the changes made to a disconnected DataSet object.

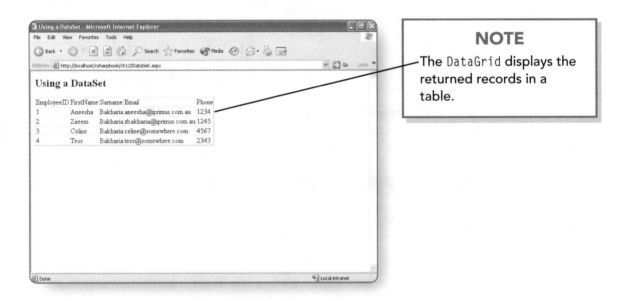

NOTE

The DataGrid displays the returned records in a table.

Inserting Data into a Database

You use the Insert SQL query to add a new record to a database. The syntax for an Insert query follows:

```
INSERT INTO tablename (fieldname1, fieldname2)
Values ("Value1", "Value2")
```

NOTE

You must place the field names and values in the same order.

You must invoke the ExecuteNonQuery method of the OleDbCommand object when a query does not return data. Insert, Delete, and Update queries do not return data:

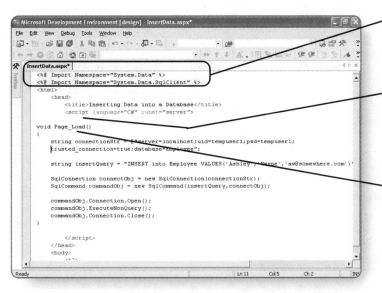

1. Import the System.Data and the System.SqlClient namespaces.

2. Insert opening and closing script tags. Set the language attribute to C# and the runat attribute to server.

3. Insert a Page_Load method.

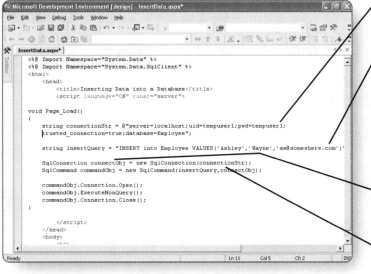

4. Store the connection string in a string variable.

5. Store the Insert SQL query in a string variable.

6. Create an SqlConnection object.

7. Pass the connection string to the SqlConnection constructor.

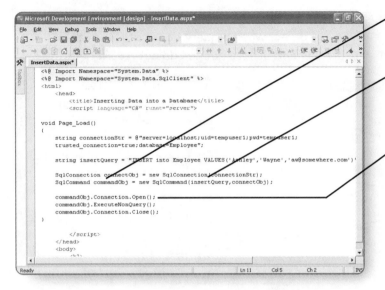

8. Create an `SqlCommand` object.

9. Pass the query and the connection object to the `SqlCommand` constructor.

10. Call the `Open` method of the connection object.

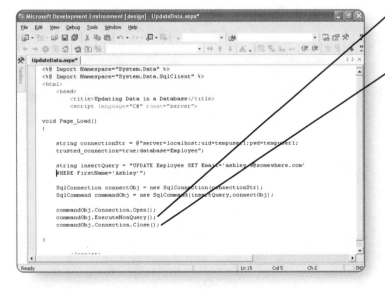

11. Call the `ExecuteNonQuery` method.

12. Call the `Close` method to end the database connection.

Updating Data in a Database

You use the Update SQL query to modify existing records to a database. Following is the syntax for an Update query:

```
UPDATE tablename SET fieldname1="Value1",
fieldname2="Value2",
    WHERE idField='Value'
```

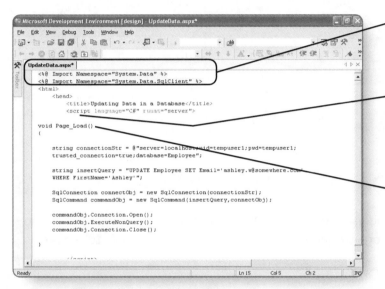

1. Import the System.Data and the System.Data.SqlClient namespaces.

2. Insert opening and closing script tags. Set the language attribute to C# and the runat attribute to server.

3. Insert a Page_Load method.

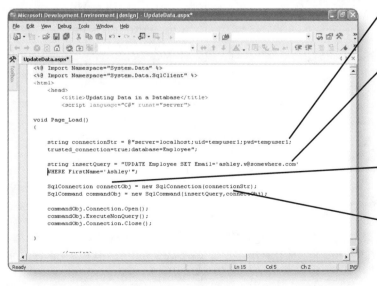

4. Store the connection string in a string variable.

5. Store the Update SQL query in a string variable.

6. Create an SqlConnection object.

7. Pass the connection string to the SqlConnection constructor.

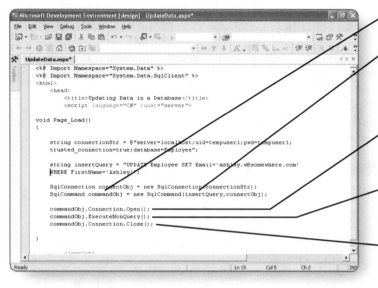

8. Create an SqlCommand object.

9. Pass the query and the connection object to the SqlCommand constructor.

10. Call the Open method of the connection object.

11. Call the ExecuteNonQuery method.

12. Call the Close method to end the database connection.

Deleting Data from a Database

You use the Delete SQL query to remove records that are no longer required. Following is the syntax for a Delete query:

```
DELETE FROM tablename WHERE idField='Value'
```

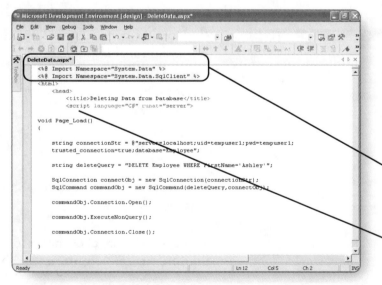

> **CAUTION**
>
> If the criterion is not specific, you might accidentally delete all the records in a table.

1. Import the System.Data and the System.SqlClient namespaces.

2. Insert opening and closing script tags. Set the language attribute to C# and the runat attribute to server.

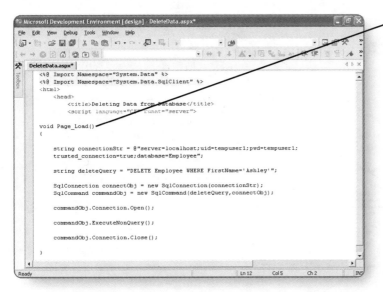

3. Insert a `Page_Load` method.

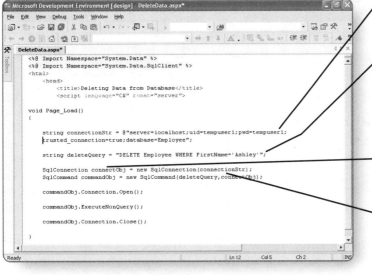

4. Store the connection string in a string variable.

5. Store the `Delete` SQL query in a string variable.

6. Create an `SqlConnection` object.

7. Pass the connection string to the `SqlConnection` constructor.

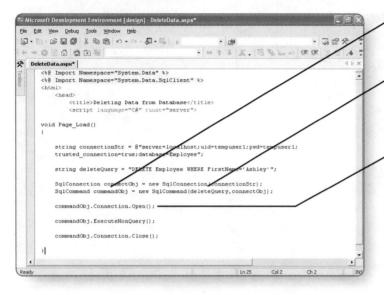

8. Create an `SqlCommand` object.

9. Pass the query and the connection object to the `SqlCommand` constructor.

10. Call the `Open` method of the connection object.

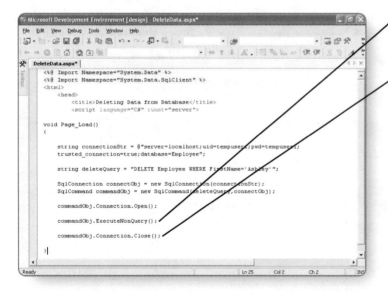

11. Call the `ExecuteNonQuery` method.

12. Call the `Close` method to end the database connection.

Using Parameters

Parameters simplify the syntax used to construct complex queries. Instead of hard coding variables in a query, placeholders are used to indicate the position where a value must be substituted. Placeholders must begin with an @ character.

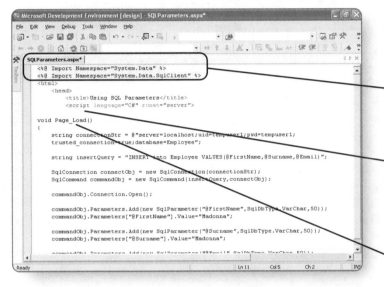

1. Import the System.Data and the System.SqlClient namespaces.

2. Insert opening and closing script tags. Set the language attribute to C# and the runat attribute to server.

3. Insert a Page_Load method.

4. Store the connection string in a string variable.

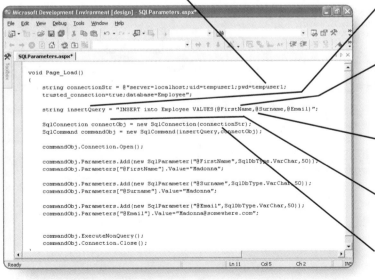

5. Store the SQL query in a string variable.

6. Insert a placeholder for each variable that will be included in the query.

7. Precede each placeholder variable name with the @ symbol.

8. Create an SqlConnection object.

9. Pass the connection string to the SqlConnection constructor.

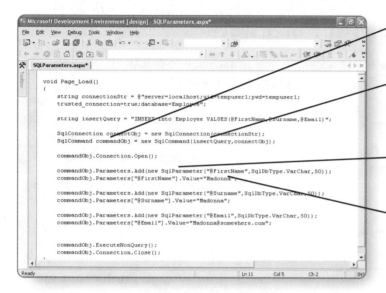

10. Create an `SqlCommand` object.

11. Pass the query and the connection object to the `SqlCommand` constructor.

12. Create a new `SqlParameter` object.

13. You pass the placeholder variable as the first parameter passed to the `SqlParameter` constructor.

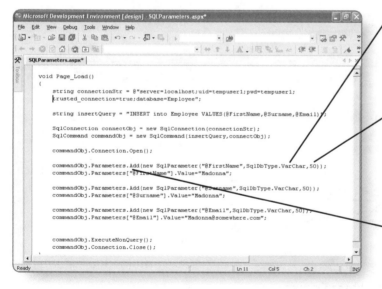

14. You pass the `Sql` data type for the variable as the second parameter passed to the `SqlParameter` constructor.

15. You pass the maximum number of characters that the `SqlParameter` object will store as the third parameter passed to the `SqlParameter` constructor.

16. Pass the `SqlParameter` object to the `Parameters.Add` method of the `SqlCommand` object. This creates a new parameter.

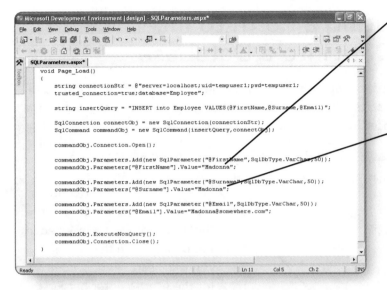

17. Assign the data to the `Value` property of the parameter. The parameter name is passed as an index to the `Parameters` collection.

18. Create and assign values to each placeholder parameter.

19. Repeat steps 12 through 17 for each placeholder variable.

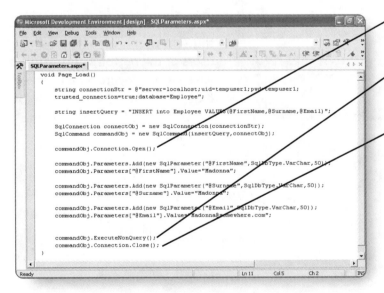

20. Call the `Open` method of the connection object.

21. Call the `ExecuteNonQuery` method.

22. Call the `Close` method to end the database connection.

Using a Form to Insert Data into a Database

The example that follows retrieves the data from a form and inserts it into a database. Parameters are used to simplify the insertion of data retrieved from a form.

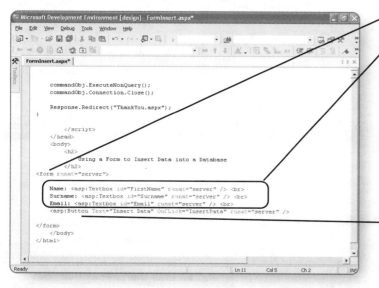

1. Create a form.

2. Insert Web Server controls that are appropriate to capture the data that will be inserted in the database. In this example, you will insert TextBox controls for the user to enter her First Name, Surname, and Email Address.

3. Insert a Button control. Use the Text property to inform the users of the button's purpose which is to execute a method that will retrieve the data that will be entered and insert it into a database.

4. Assign the name of the method that will get executed when the user clicks the button to the OnClick event.

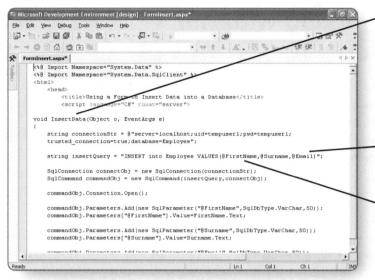

5. Insert the method that will retrieve the data from the form and insert it into a database. This method must be placed within opening and closing `<script>` tags.

6. Store the insert SQL query in a string variable.

7. Insert a placeholder for each Web Server control used for data entry. In this example, placeholder parameters are defined for the FirstName, Surname, and Email Address TextBox controls.

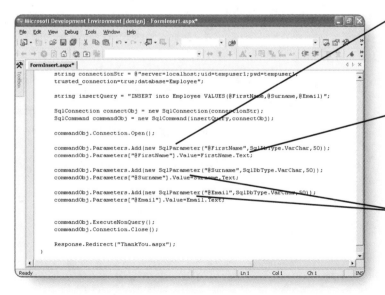

8. Create and add the `SqlParameter` objects to the `Parameters` collection of the `SqlCommand` object.

9. Retrieve the data entered into the `TextBox` controls and assign the data to the `Value` property of the parameter.

10. Repeat steps 8 and 9 for each placeholder parameter in the insert SQL query.

Working with the Repeater Control

The Repeater control, as its name suggests, displays each row of data returned from a database in a customized format. You basically create templates that define how data must be displayed. The Repeater control supports templates for the display of each row of data, alternating rows of data, row separators, headers, and footers.

This example uses the Repeater control to display the data retrieved from a database in a table.

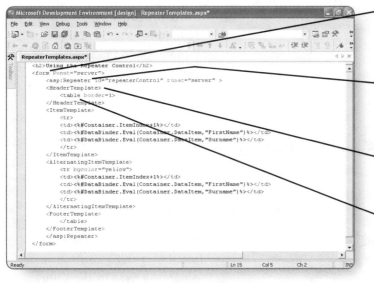

1. Insert opening and closing form tags. Set the runat attribute to server.

2. Insert a Repeater control. Set the id attribute and the runat attribute to server.

3. Insert opening and closing <HeaderTemplate> tags.

4. Insert the HTML code that will be inserted before a row of data is printed such as the opening <table> tag and optional table column headings.

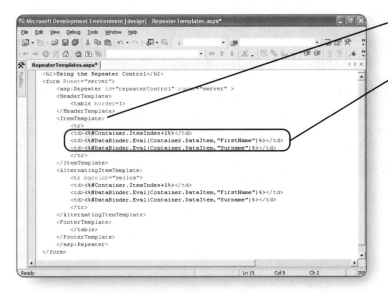

5. Insert opening and closing `<ItemTemplate>` tags

6. Insert the HTML code that will be used to lay out each row of data, such as the HTML code to define a table row with columns for each field of data that will be printed.

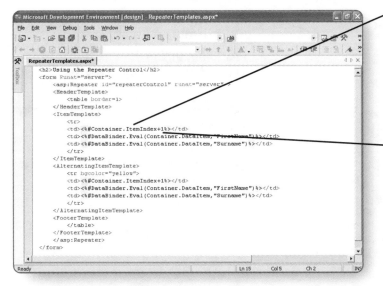

7. You use the `<%#` and `%>` databinding syntax to display the `Container.ItemIndex` property. The `Container.ItemIndex` property is used to number each row.

8. Add a value of 1 to the `Container.ItemIndex` property to start numbering the rows at 1. `Container.ItemIndex` starts at 0.

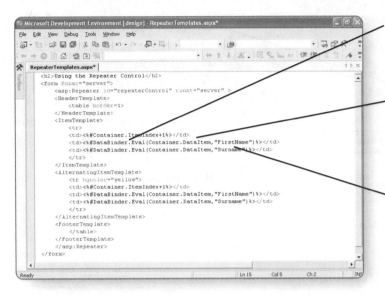

9. You use the `DataBinder.Eval` method to retrieve a data field and print it as a string.

10. You pass the `Container.DataItem` property as the first parameter passed to the `DataBinder` method.

11. You pass the name of the database field as the second parameter passed to the `DataBinder` method.

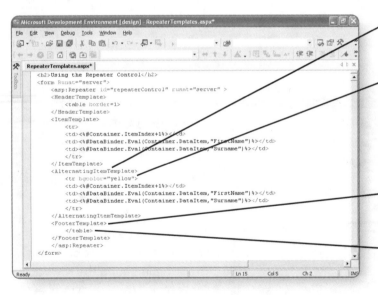

12. Insert opening and closing `<AlternatingTemplate>` tags.

13. Insert the HTML code that will lay out each alternate row of data. This usually involves changing the background color of alternate table rows.

14. Insert opening and closing `<FooterTemplate>` tags.

15. Insert the HTML code that will be displayed after all database data is displayed such as the closing `<table>` tag.

NOTE

The `<ItemTemplate>` tag is the only compulsory tag. All other template tags are optional.

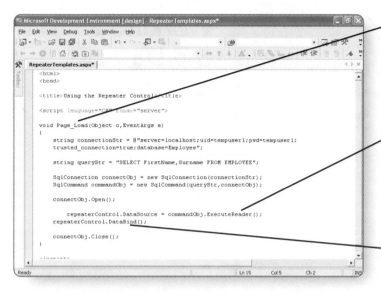

16. Insert a Page_Load method within opening and closing <script> tags. You will retrieve data from a database and bind it to the Repeater control.

17. Assign the data returned by the ExecuteReader method of the SqlCommand object to the DataSource property of the Repeater control.

18. Call the DataBind method of the Repeater control. Data will be bound to the Repeater control.

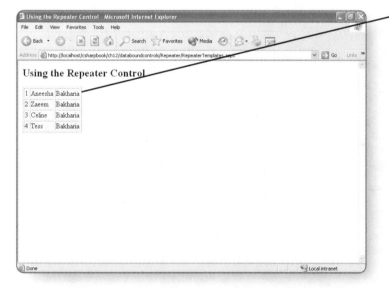

19. Preview the page in a Web browser. The Repeater control will display the data in a table.

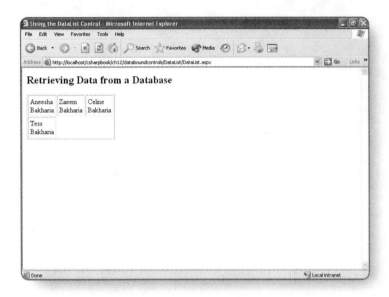

Working with the DataList Control

The DataList control is very similar to the Repeater control— it uses templates to define how each row of data returned from a database is displayed. The DataList control offers advanced functionality for formatting and editing data. The DataList control can display data in multiple columns.

1. Insert opening and closing form tags. Set the runat attribute to server.

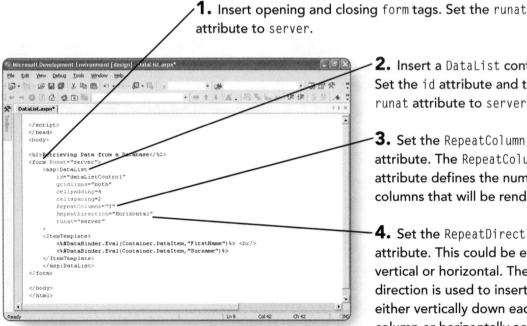

2. Insert a DataList control. Set the id attribute and the runat attribute to server.

3. Set the RepeatColumn attribute. The RepeatColumn attribute defines the number of columns that will be rendered.

4. Set the RepeatDirection attribute. This could be either vertical or horizontal. The direction is used to insert data either vertically down each column or horizontally across cells in a row.

5. Insert opening and closing `<ItemTemplate>` tags.

6. Insert the HTML code that will be used to lay out each cell of data.

7. You use the `DataBinder.Eval` method to retrieve a data field and point it as a string.

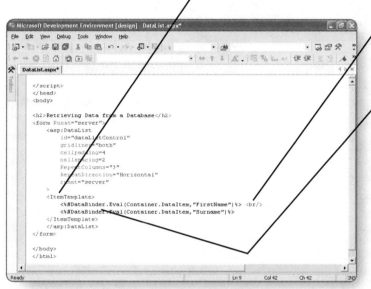

8. You pass the `Container.DataItem` property as the first parameter passed to the `DataBinder` method.

9. You pass the name of the database field as the second parameter passed to the `DataBinder` method.

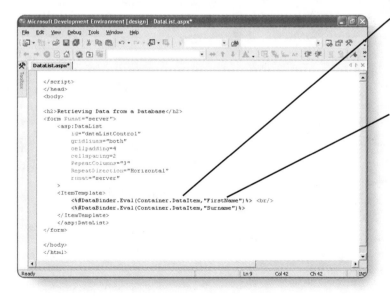

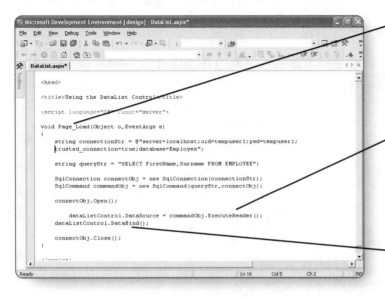

10. Insert a Page_Load method within opening and closing <script> tags. You will retrieve data from a database and bind it to the DataList control.

11. Assign the data returned by the ExecuteReader method of the SqlCommand object to the DataSource property of the DataList control.

12. Call the DataBind method of the DataList control. Data will be bound to the DataList control.

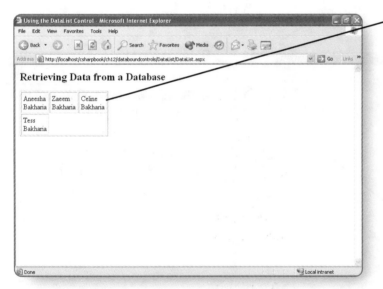

13. Preview the page in a Web browser. The DataList control will display the data in columns across the screen.

> ## NOTE
> The DataList renders the data in a single column table by default. Setting the RepeatLayout attribute to Flow will not generate the data in a table.

Selecting Data in a DataList

The DataList control enables you to define templates for the display of data items that have been selected by a user. You can use the OnItemCommand attribute to specify the method that handles a click event.

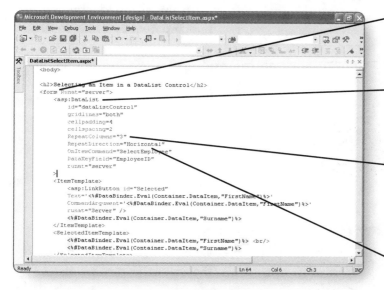

1. Insert opening and closing form tags. Set the runat attribute to server.

2. Insert a DataList control. Set the id attribute and the runat attribute to server.

3. Set the RepeatColumn attribute. The RepeatColumn attribute defines the number of columns that will be rendered.

4. Set the RepeatDirection attribute. This could be either vertical or horizontal. The direction is used to insert data either vertically down each column or horizontally across cells in a row.

5. Set the OnItemCommand attribute to the name of the method that handles the selection of an item in a DataList control. The OnItemCommand will be raised when a user clicks on a button or a link in the DataList control.

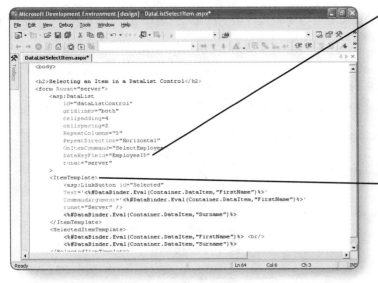

6. Assign the name of the field unique ID field to the `DataKeyField` property. (Sometimes it is also known as the primary key field in a database table.) You will use the `DataKeyField` to identify the selected item by a unique ID.

7. Insert opening and closing `<ItemTemplate>` tags.

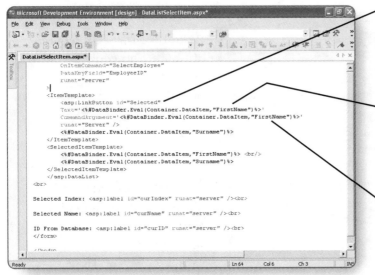

8. Insert a `LinkButton` control. When the `LinkButton` is clicked, the `OnItemCommand` will be raised.

9. Assign a field from the database to the `Text` attribute of the `LinkButton` control. The data will be displayed as a link.

10. Assign a data field to the `CommandArgument` attribute. The `CommandArgument` is passed to the method specified by `OnItemCommand`. You will use the `CommandArgument` to identify the selected item.

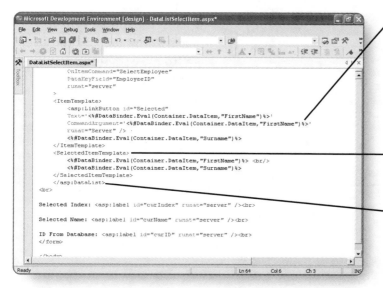

11. Insert the HTML code that will be used to lay out each cell of data. You use the `DataBinder.Eval` method to retrieve a data field and print it as a string.

12. Insert opening and closing `<SelectedItemTemplate>` tags.

13. Insert the HTML code that will format the data of a selected item in a `DataList` control. I have chosen not to include a `LinkButton` control for a selected item.

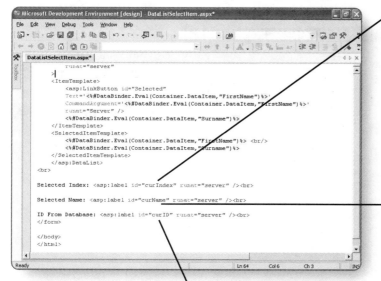

14. Insert a `Label` control called `curIndex`. The `curIndex` label will display the index or position of the selected item as it is displayed in the `DataList` control. This is based upon the order in which data items are bound to cells in a `DataList` control.

15. Insert a `Label` control called `curName`. The `curName` label will display the data passed as a `CommandArgument` from the `LinkButton`.

16. Insert a `Label` control called `curID`. The `curID` label will display the unique ID for the database record that is currently selected. The `id` column is set with the `DataKeyField` attribute of the `DataList` control.

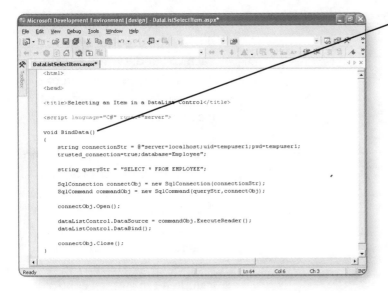

17. Insert a method called BindData, This method retrieves data from a database and binds it to the DataList control.

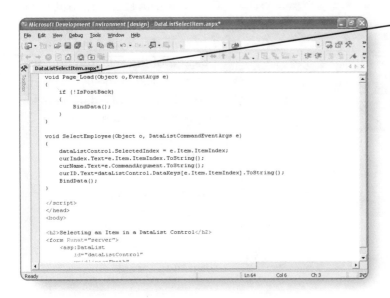

18. Insert a Page_Load method within opening and closing <script> tags. This method calls the BindData method when the page is loaded for the first time.

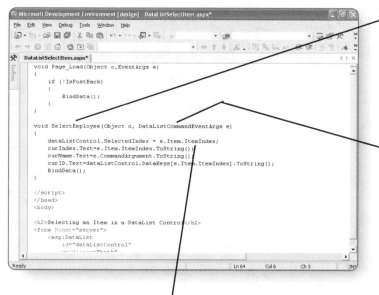

19. Insert the method that handles the selection of an item in a `DataList` control. This method was assigned to the `OnItemCommand` attribute of the `DataList` control.

20. Pass a `DataListCommandEventArgs` object as the second parameter passed to the method that will execute when an item is selected. This object is usually named `e`.

21. Set the `SelectedIndex` property of the `DataList` control to `e.Item.ItemIndex`. This will use the `<SelectedItemTemplate>` to display the selected item.

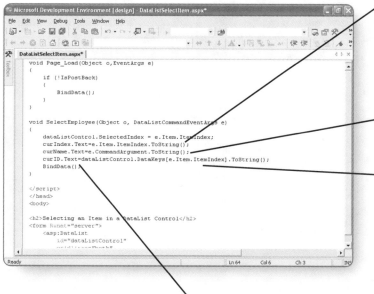

22. Assign `e.Item.ItemIndex.ToString()` to the `Text` property of the `curIndex` label. The index of the selected item in the `DataList` will be displayed.

23. Assign `e.CommandArgument.ToString()` to the `curName` label.

24. Pass `e.Item.ItemIndex` to the `DataKeys` collection of the `DataList` control. This will retrieve the unique ID of the selected item. The `curID` label will display the unique ID.

25. Call the `BindData` method. Data will be bound to the `DataList` control.

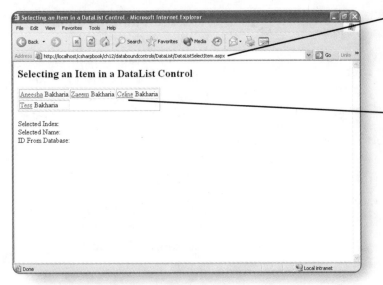

26. Preview the page in a Web browser. The DataList control will display the data in columns across the screen.

27. Click on link to select an item. The `<SelectedItemTemplate>` will be displayed.

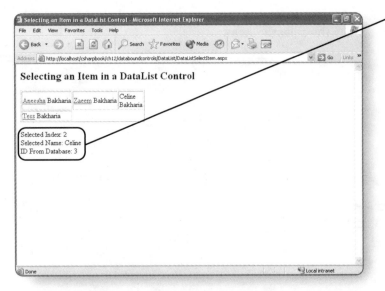

28. The index, name, and ID of the selected item are displayed.

Editing Items in a DataList

With the `EditItemTemplate`, you can display a form for the user to update a currently selected data row. The `EditItemTemplate` can also contain update and cancel buttons or links. The `EditItemIndex` property contains the index of the row being edited. If no row is being edited the `EditItemIndex` property will return -1.

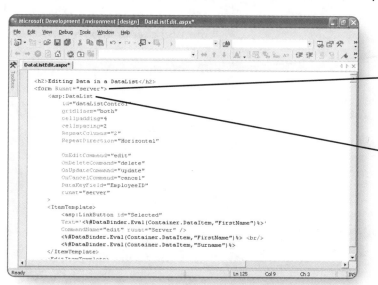

1. Insert opening and closing form tags. Set the `runat` attribute to `server`.

2. Insert a `DataList` control. Set the `id` attribute and the `runat` attribute to `server`.

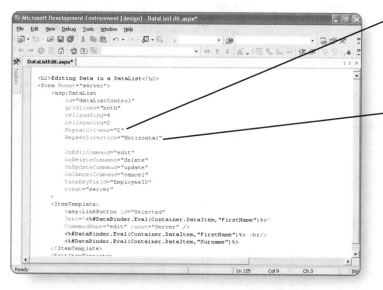

3. Set the `RepeatColumn` attribute. The `RepeatColumn` attribute defines the number of columns that will be rendered.

4. Set the `RepeatDirection` attribute. This could be either vertical or horizontal. The direction is used to insert data either vertically down each column or horizontally across cells in a row.

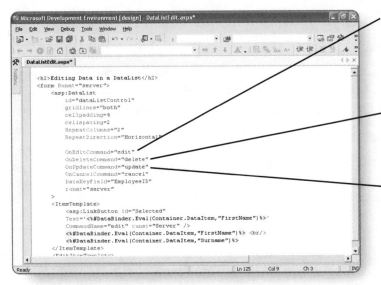

5. Set the OnEditCommand attribute to the name of the method that makes the selected row editable.

6. Set the OnDeleteCommand attribute to the name of the method that deletes a row.

7. Set the OnUpdateCommand attribute to the name of the method of the data in the database.

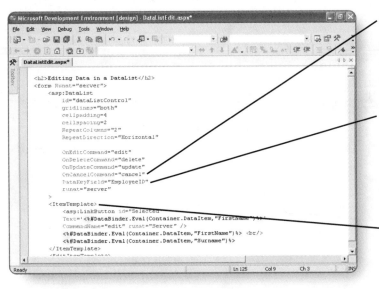

8. Set the OnCancelCommand attribute to the name of the method that cancels the editing of a row.

9. Assign the name of the field unique id field to the DataKeyField property. You will use the DataKeyField to identify the selected item by a unique ID.

10. Insert opening and closing <ItemTemplate> tags.

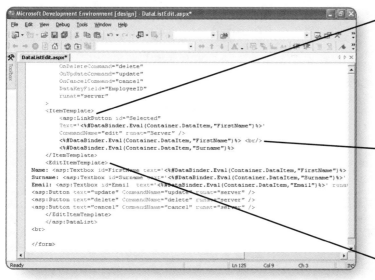

11. Insert a LinkButton control. Set the CommandName attribute to edit. This will fire an edit event when clicked and execute the method specified by the OnEditCommand.

12. Insert the HTML code that will be used to lay out each cell of data. You use the DataBinder. Eval method to retrieve a data field and print it as a string.

13. Insert opening and closing <EditItemTemplate> tags.

14. Insert Web Server controls for editing the data. Use the DataBinder method to assign the data to the controls so the user can edit the data.

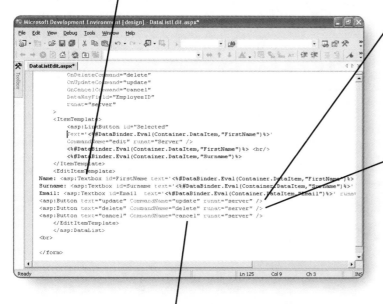

15. Insert an Update button. Set the CommandName attribute to update. This will fire an update event when clicked and execute the method specified by the OnUpdateCommand.

16. Insert a Delete button. Set the CommandName attribute to delete. This will fire a delete event when clicked and execute the method specified by the OnDeleteCommand.

17. Insert a Cancel button. Set the CommandName attribute to cancel. This will fire a cancel event when clicked and execute the method specified by the OnCancelCommand.

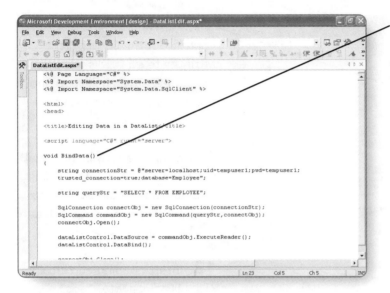

18. Insert a method called `BindData`. This method retrieves data from a database and binds it to the `DataList` control.

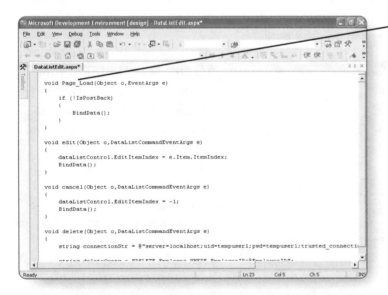

19. Insert a `Page_Load` method within opening and closing `<script>` tags. This method calls the `BindData` method when the page is loaded for the first time.

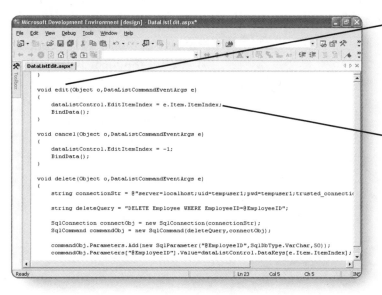

20. Insert an edit method. Pass a `DataListCommandEventArgs` object as the second parameter passed to the edit method. This object is usually named e.

21. Set the `EditItemIndex` property of the `DataList` control to `e.Item.ItemIndex`. This will use the `<EditItemTemplate>` to display the selected item.

22. Insert a cancel method. Pass a `DataListCommandEventArgs` object as the second parameter passed to the cancel method. This object is usually named e.

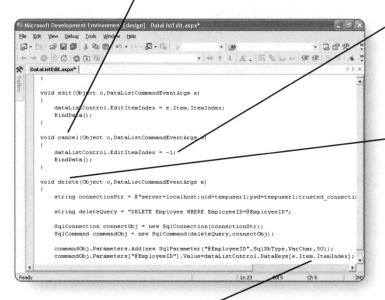

23. Set the `EditItemIndex` property of the `DataList` control to `-1`. This uses the `<ItemTemplate>` to display all the items.

24. Insert a delete method. Pass a `DataListCommandEventArgs` object as the second parameter passed to the delete method. This object is usually named e. The delete method deletes the selected item from the database.

25. The ID of the selected item is retrieved from the `DataKey` collection of the `DataList` control and is used in the delete sql query.

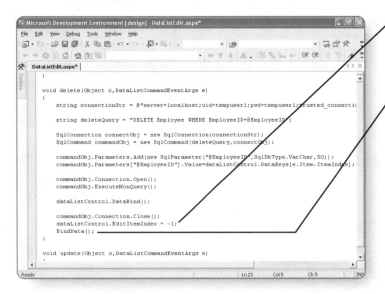

26. Set the EditItemIndex property of the DataList control to -1 after the record is deleted.

27. Call the BindData method. Data will be bound to the DataList control.

28. Insert an update method. Pass a DataListCommandEventArgs object as the second parameter passed to the update method. This object is usually named e. The update method updates the selected item from the database.

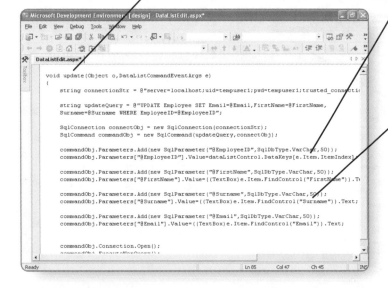

29. The ID of the selected item is retrieved from the DataKey collection of the DataList control and is used in the update SQL query.

30. You use the e.Item.FindControl method to retrieve the updated data from the form.

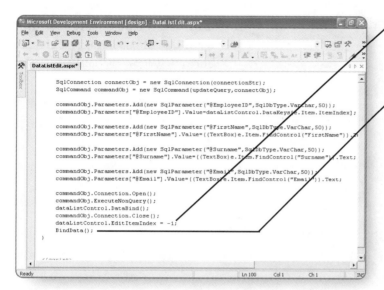

31. Set the `EditItemIndex` property of the `DataList` control to `-1` after the record is updated.

32. Call the `BindData` method. Data will be bound to the `DataList` control.

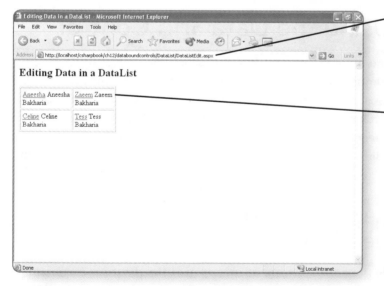

33. Preview the page in a Web browser. The `DataList` control will display the data in columns across the screen.

34. Click on the Edit button. The `<EditItemTemplate>` will be displayed.

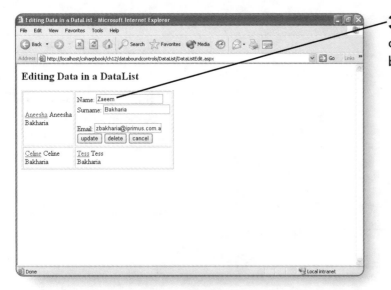

35. You will be able to edit the data. Update, delete, and cancel buttons will be available.

Using the DataGrid Control

The DataGrid control, which has already been used on a number of occasions displays data in a table. While the DataGrid control is the most advanced databound control, t still offers the simplest solution for displaying tabular data. It incorporates many advanced features including in-place editing, column sorting, as well as the ability to page through large data sets.

Customize Column Headings in a DataGrid

By default the DataGrid control uses the database field names as the table column headings, which is not very user-friendly. You need to use the <BoundColumn> tag to specify a new header for each column. The <BoundColumn> tag must be placed within matching <Column> tags.

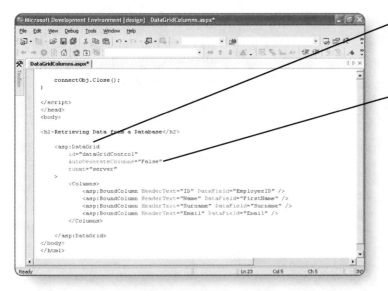

1. Insert a DataGrid control. Set the id attribute and the runat attribute to server.

2. Set the GenerateColumns attribute to false.

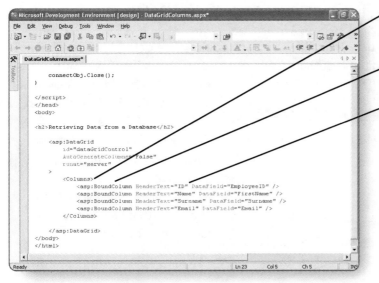

3. Insert opening and closing <Columns> tags.

4. Insert a <BoundColumn> tag.

5. Set the HeaderText attribute to the new column name.

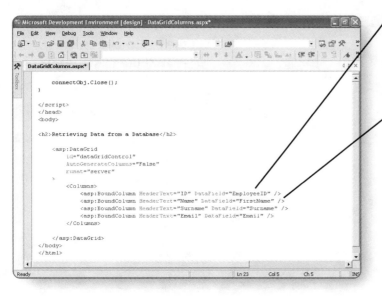

6. Set the `DataField` to the name of the database column that is being replaced by the `HeaderText` attribute.

7. Insert a `<BoundColumn>` tag for each column you want to customize.

Editing Data in a DataGrid

A `DataGrid` allows in-place editing. The data from a row being edited is automatically displayed within a `TextBox` control. The `EditCommandColumn` inserts an Edit button for each row of data. Once the Edit button is clicked, Update and Cancel buttons are displayed. The `OnEditCommand`, `OnCancelCommand`, and `OnUpdateCommand` attributes of a `DataGrid` must specify the methods that handle their associated events.

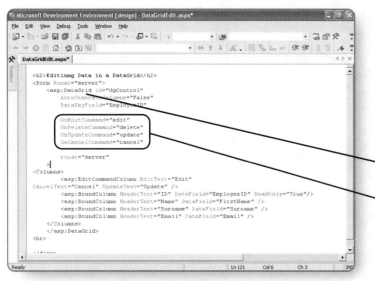

1. Insert a `DataGrid` control.

2. Assign methods to handle the `OnEditCommand`, `OnDeleteCommand`, `OnUpdateCommand`, and `OnCancelCommand` events.

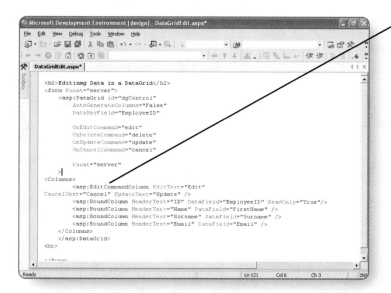

3. Insert an
`<EditCommandColumn>` tag
within opening and closing
`<Columns>` tags.

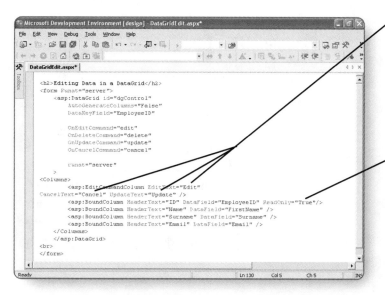

4. Set the `EditText`, `CancelText`,
and `UpdateText` attributes. This
text will be displayed on the
corresponding buttons.

NOTE

Set the `ReadOnly` attribute
to `true` if the column
should not be editable.
This will usually be the
case with id fields.

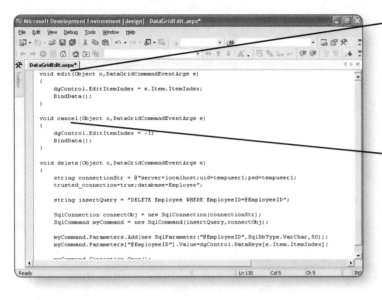

```
void edit(Object o,DataGridCommandEventArgs e)
{
    dgControl.EditItemIndex = e.Item.ItemIndex;
    BindData();
}

void cancel(Object o,DataGridCommandEventArgs e)
{
    dgControl.EditItemIndex = -1;
    BindData();
}

void delete(Object o,DataGridCommandEventArgs e)
{
    string connectionStr = @"server=localhost;uid=tempuser1;pwd=tempuser1;
    trusted_connection=true;database=Employee";

    string insertQuery = "DELETE Employee WHERE EmployeeID=@EmployeeID";

    SqlConnection connectObj = new SqlConnection(connectionStr);
    SqlCommand myCommand = new SqlCommand(insertQuery,connectObj);

    myCommand.Parameters.Add(new SqlParameter("@EmployeeID",SqlDbType.VarChar,50));
    myCommand.Parameters["@EmployeeID"].Value=dgControl.DataKeys[e.Item.ItemIndex];
```

5. The edit method sets the EditItemIndex property of the DataGrid control. This tells the DataGrid to allow the row where the Edit button was clicked to be edited using TextBox controls.

6. The cancel method sets the EditItemIndex property to -1. This tells the DataGrid control that no rows are being edited.

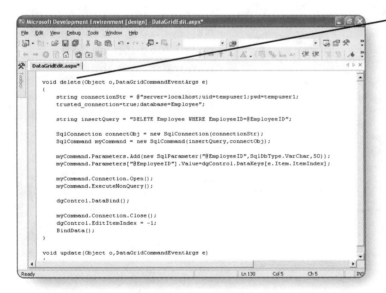

```
void delete(Object o,DataGridCommandEventArgs e)
{
    string connectionStr = @"server=localhost;uid=tempuser1;pwd=tempuser1;
    trusted_connection=true;database=Employee";

    string insertQuery = "DELETE Employee WHERE EmployeeID=@EmployeeID";

    SqlConnection connectObj = new SqlConnection(connectionStr);
    SqlCommand myCommand = new SqlCommand(insertQuery,connectObj);

    myCommand.Parameters.Add(new SqlParameter("@EmployeeID",SqlDbType.VarChar,50));
    myCommand.Parameters["@EmployeeID"].Value=dgControl.DataKeys[e.Item.ItemIndex];

    myCommand.Connection.Open();
    myCommand.ExecuteNonQuery();

    dgControl.DataBind();

    myCommand.Connection.Close();
    dgControl.EditItemIndex = -1;
    BindData();
}

void update(Object o,DataGridCommandEventArgs e)
{
```

7. The delete method deletes the selected item from the database when the Delete button is clicked. The delete method must accept a DataGridCommandEventArgs object that is usually named e as its second parameter. The ID of the selected item is retrieved from the DataKey collection of the DataGrid control and is used in the delete SQL query. Set the EditItemIndex property of the DataGrid control to -1 after the record is deleted and call the BindData method.

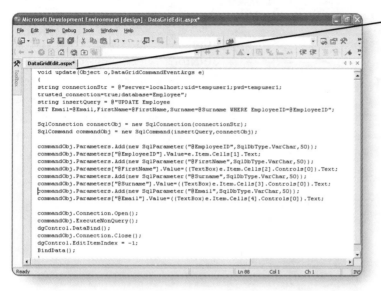

8. The update method updates the selected item in the database. The delete method must accept a `DataGridCommandEventArgs` object that is usually named e as its second parameter. The ID of the selected item is retrieved from the `DataKey` collection of the `DataGrid` control and is used in the update SQL query. To retrieve the updated data from a `TextBox` control in a `DataGrid` column you will need to access the `Text` property of the first control found in the matching cell. `((TextBox)e.Item.Cells[2].Controls[0])`. `Text` will retrieve the data from the `TextBox` in the third column. `e.Item.Cells[1].Text` can be used to return text within a column cell. Set the `EditItemIndex` property of the `DataGrid` control to -1 after the record is updated and call the `BindData` method.

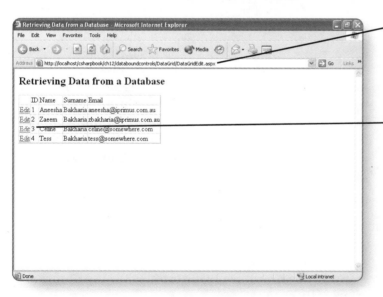

9. Preview the page in a Web browser. The `DataGrid` control will display the data in columns across the screen.

10. Click on the Edit button. `TextBox` controls will be displayed within the current row to allow editing.

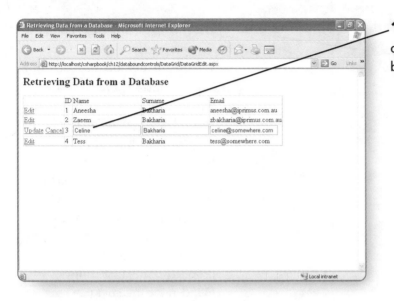

11. You will be able to edit the data. Update, delete, and cancel buttons will be available.

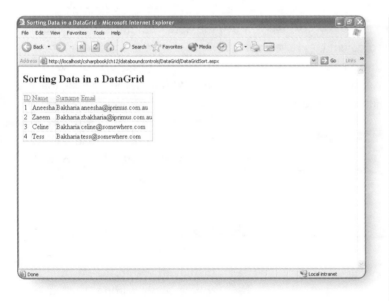

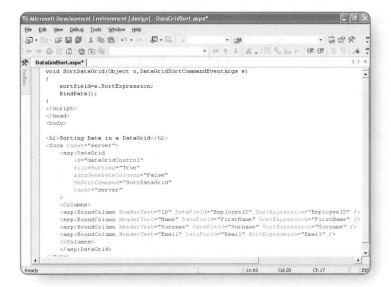

NOTE

Sorting allows a user to click the header of the column that must be sorted. When the `AllowSorting` attribute is set to `true`, each column is rendered as a hyperlink. The `DataGrid` control does not perform the sorting automatically—you will write a method to perform this task when the `SortCommand` event is fired. The DataGridTemplateEdit.aspx file is an additional example that illustrates the implementation of sorting in a `DataGrid` control.

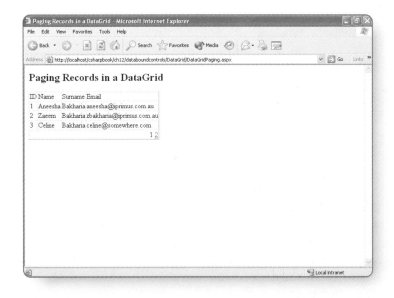

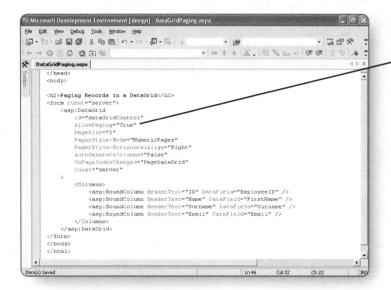

```
</head>
<body>

<h2>Paging Records in a DataGrid</h2>
<form runat="server">
    <asp:DataGrid
        id="dataGridControl"
        AllowPaging="True"
        PageSize="3"
        PagerStyle-Mode="NumericPages"
        PagerStyle-HorizontalAlign="Right"
        AutoGenerateColumns="False"
        OnPageIndexChanged="PageDataGrid"
        runat="server"
    >
        <Columns>
            <asp:BoundColumn HeaderText="ID" DataField="EmployeeID" />
            <asp:BoundColumn HeaderText="Name" DataField="FirstName" />
            <asp:BoundColumn HeaderText="Surname" DataField="Surname" />
            <asp:BoundColumn HeaderText="Email" DataField="Email" />
        </Columns>
    </asp:DataGrid>
</form>
</body>
</html>
```

NOTE

It is not wise to display large amounts of data on a page because the page will take a long time to download and you don't want to overload the user with data. Ideally you should limit the number of records displayed on a page and allow the user to navigate through the returned results. The AllowPaging attribute enables paging. The DataGridTemplateEdit.aspx file is an additional example that illustrates paging in a DataGrid control.

13

Working with Files and Directories

The Windows operating system organizes files into a hierarchical structure that consists of drives, directories, subdirectories, and files. The `System.IO` namespace lets you fully utilize the filing system by encapsulating a variety of useful file- and directory-manipulation classes. Text files serve as a viable data storage alternative to databases. In this chapter, you'll learn to:

- Use the `File`, `FileInfo`, and `Path` classes to determine file properties.
- Create, copy, move, and delete both files and directories.
- List the contents of a directory and all of its subdirectories.
- List the available disk drives on a server.
- Read, write, and append data to a text file.
- Use the HTTP protocol to retrieve the contents of a Web page (screen scraping).
- Upload files to a Web server.
- Create a content management system.

The System.IO Namespace

The System.IO namespace contains both static and instance classes to help you manipulate files and directories. A *static* class allows you to call its methods without creating an object. This is flexible if you only need to use a single method. The File, Directory, and Path classes are static, but the FileInfo and DirectoryInfo classes are *instance* classes.

For example, you can use the Exists method of the File class to determine whether a file exists by passing the file name to the method:

```
File.Exists ("C:/filename.txt");
```

However, if you use the FileInfo class, you must first create a FileInfo object before calling call the Exists method:

```
FileInfo  file = new FileInfo("C:/filename.txt");
File.Exists;
```

Using the File Class

You can use the Exists method of the file class to first check whether a file exists before accessing file properties. You can determine and display the dates the file was created, last accessed, and updated:

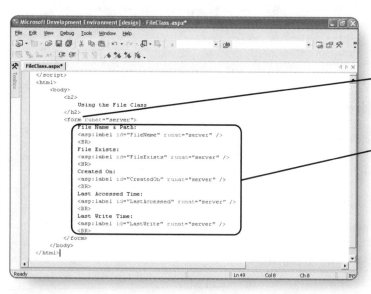

1. Insert opening and closing <form> tags. Set the runat attribute to server.

2. Insert five label controls and set their IDs to FileName, FileExists, CreatedOn, LastAccessed, and LastWrite. The file's properties will be displayed in these labels.

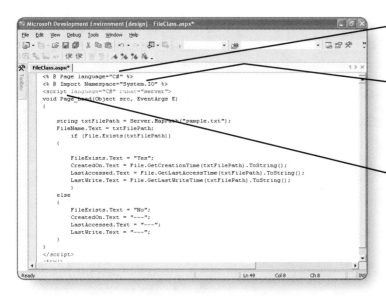

3. Set the `language` attribute of the page directive to `C#`.

4. Import the `System.IO` namespace. The `System.IO` namespace contains the `File` class.

5. Insert opening and closing `<script>` tags. Set the `runat` attribute to `server` and the `language` attribute to `C#`.

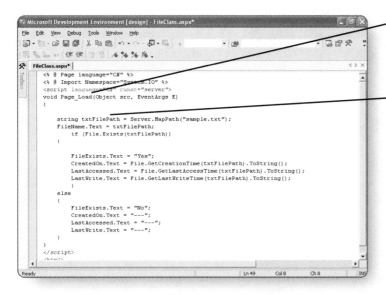

6. Insert a `Page_Load` method. This method will be executed when the page is loaded.

7. Declare a variable called `txtFilePath` as a string. This variable will store the path and name of the file. You will simply pass this variable to all methods that return file properties.

NOTE

Use the `Server.MapPath` method if the file is placed in the same folder as this aspx page.

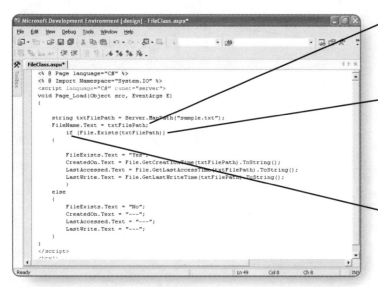

8. Assign the `txtFilePath` variable to the text property of the `FileName` label.

9. Pass the `txtFilePath` variable to the `File.Exists` method. The `Exists` method will return `True` if the file is found in the specified location.

10. Use an `if` statement to display the file properties if the `File.Exists` method returns `True`. Steps 11 through 14 will only be executed if the `File.Exists` method returns `True`.

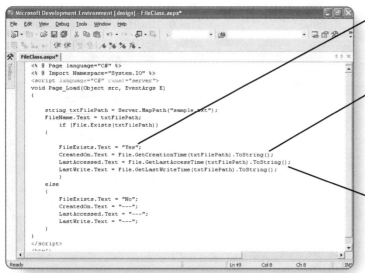

11. Set the `text` property of the `FileExists` label to acknowledge that the file exists.

12. Pass the `txtFilePath` variable to the `File.GetCreationTime` method and assign the result to the `text` property of the `CreatedOn` label.

13. Pass the `txtFilePath` variable to the `File.GetLastAccessTime` method and assign the result to the `text` property of the `LastAccessed` label.

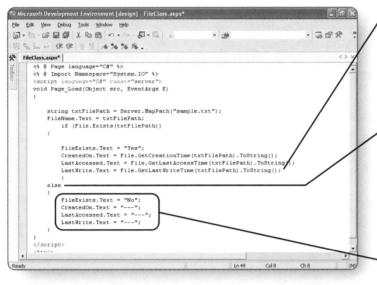

14. Pass the `txtFilePath` variable to the `File.GetLastWriteTime` method and assign the result to the `text` property of the `LastWrite` label.

15. Include an `else` clause for the `if` statement. The code within the `else` clause will only execute if the file does not exist (that is, the `File.Exists` method returns `False`).

16. Inform the user that the file does not exist by setting the `text` property of the `FileExists` label to an appropriate value.

Using the FileInfo Class

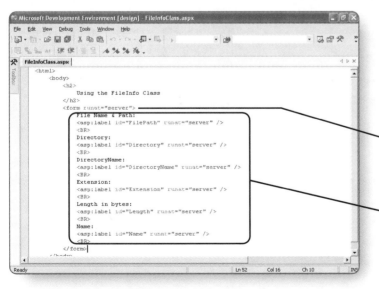

The `FileInfo` class has properties to determine the name, extension, path, and size of the file. The `FileInfo` class is an instance class, so you must first create a `FileInfo` object:

1. Insert opening and closing `<form>` tags. Set the `runat` attribute to `server`.

2. Insert six label controls and set their IDs to `FilePath`, `Directory`, `DirectoryName`, `Extension`, `Length`, and `Name`. The file's properties will be displayed in these labels.

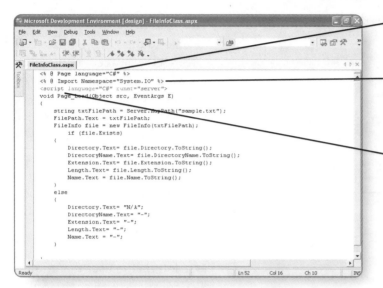

3. Set the `language` attribute of the page directive to `C#`.

4. Import the `System.IO` namespace. The `System.IO` namespace contains the `File` class.

5. Insert opening and closing `<script>` tags. Set the `runat` attribute to `server` and the `language` attribute to `C#`.

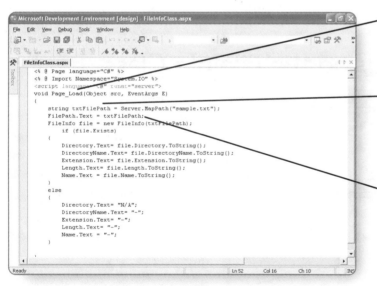

6. Insert a `Page_Load` method. This method will be executed when the page is loaded.

7. Declare a variable called `txtFilePath` as a string. This variable will store the path and name of the file.

8. Assign the `txtFilePath` variable to the `text` property of the `FilePath` label.

9. Create an instance of the `FileInfo` class called `file`.

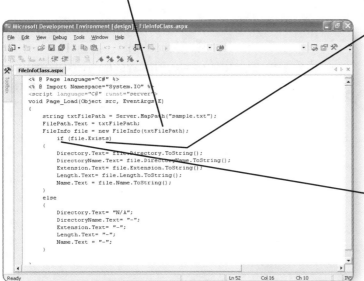

10. Call the `Exists` method of the `FileInfo` object (that is, `File.Exists`). You must pass the `txtFilePath` variable to the `FileInfo` constructor. The `Exists` method will return `True` if it finds the file in the specified location.

11. Use an `if` statement to display the file properties if the `Exists` method returns `True`. Steps 12 through 16 will only execute if the `Exists` method returns `True`.

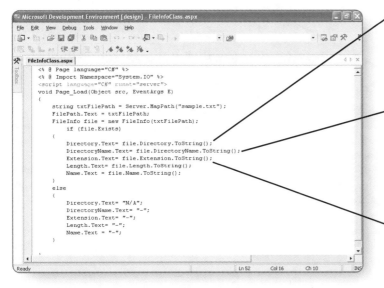

12. Retrieve the `Directory` property and assign the result to the `text` property of the `Directory` label.

13. Retrieve the `DirectoryName` property and assign the result to the `text` property of the `DirectoryName` label.

14. Retrieve the `Extension` property and assign the result to the `text` property of the `Extension` label.

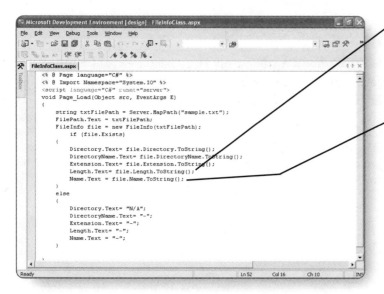

15. Retrieve the Length property and assign the result to the text property of the Length label.

16. Retrieve the Name property and assign the result to the text property of the Name label.

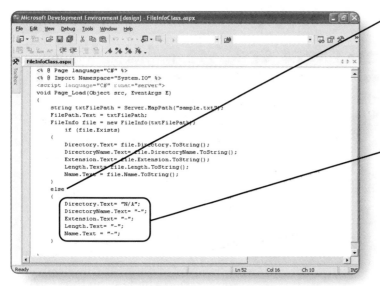

17. Include an else clause for the if statement. The code within the else clause will only execute if the file does not exist (that is, the Exists method returns False).

18. Inform the user that the file does not exist by setting the text property of the FilePath label to the appropriate value.

Using the Path Class

The `Path` class is a static class that allows you to access specific details about a file's path. You can use it to retrieve the extension of a file as well as the location of the Windows temp directory:

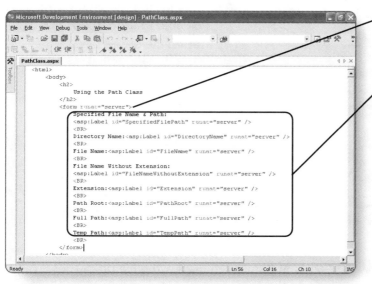

1. Insert opening and closing `<form>` tags. Set the `runat` attribute to `server`.

2. Insert seven label controls and set their IDs to `SpecifiedFileName`, `DirectoryName`, `FileName`, `FileNameWithoutExtension`, `PathRoot`, `FullPath`, and `TempPath`. The file's properties will be displayed in these labels.

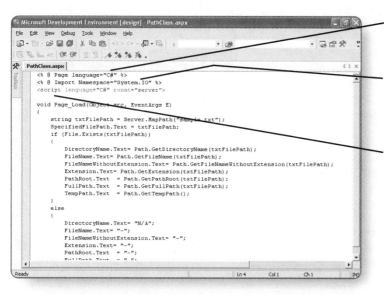

3. Set the `language` attribute of the page directive to `C#`.

4. Import the `System.IO` name space. The `System.IO` namespace contains the `File` class.

5. Insert opening and closing `<script>` tags. Set the `runat` attribute to `server` and the `language` attribute to `C#`.

6. Insert a `Page_Load` method. This method will be executed when the page is loaded.

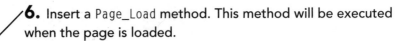

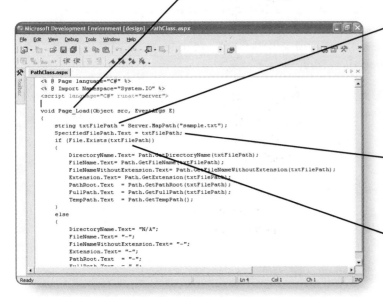

7. Declare a `txtFilePath` variable as a string. This variable will store the path and name of the file. You will simply pass this variable to all methods that return file properties.

8. Assign the `txtFilePath` variable to the `text` property of the `SpecifiedFilePath` label.

9. Pass the variable to the `File.Exists` method. The `Exists` method will return `True` if it finds the file in the specified location.

10. Use an `if` statement to display the file properties if the `File.Exists` method returns `True`. Steps 11 through 17 will only execute if the `File.Exists` method returns `True`.

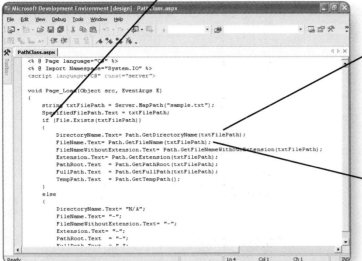

11. Pass the `txtFilePath` variable to the `Path.GetDirectoryName` method and assign the result to the `text` property of the `DirectoryName` label.

12. Pass the `txtFilePath` variable to the `Path.GetFileName` method and assign the result to the `text` property of the `FileName` label.

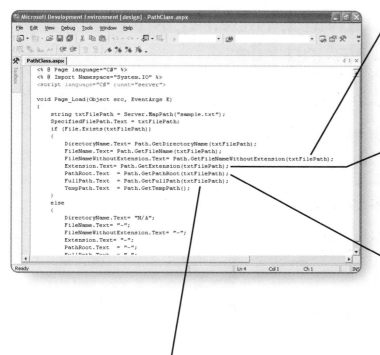

13. Pass the `txtFilePath` variable to the `Path.GetFileNameWithoutExtension` method and assign the result to the text property of the `FileNameWithoutExtension` label.

14. Pass the `txtFilePath` variable to the `Path.GetExtension` method and assign the result to the text property of the `Extension` label.

15. Pass the `txtFilePath` variable to the `Path.GetPathRoot` method and assign the result to the text property of the `PathRoot` label.

16. Pass the `txtFilePath` variable to the `Path.GetFullPath` method and assign the result to the text property of the `FullPath` label.

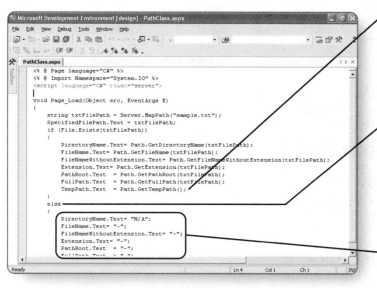

17. Pass the `txtFilePath` variable to the `Path.GetTempPath` method and assign the result to the text property of the `TempPath` label.

18. Include an `else` clause for the `if` statement. The code within the `else` clause will only execute if the file does not exist (that is, the `File.Exists` method returns `False`).

19. Inform the user that the file does not exist by setting the text property of the `FileExists` label to an appropriate value.

Copying, Moving, and Deleting Files

It has never been easier to copy, move, and delete files. The `File` class provides full control over files on your Web server:

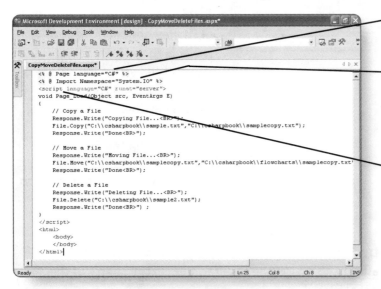

1. Set the `language` attribute of the page directive to `C#`.

2. Import the `System.IO` namespace. The `System.IO` namespace contains the `File` class.

3. Insert opening and closing `<script>` tags. Set the `runat` attribute to `server` and the `language` attribute to `C#`.

4. Insert a `Page_Load` method. This method will execute when the page is loaded.

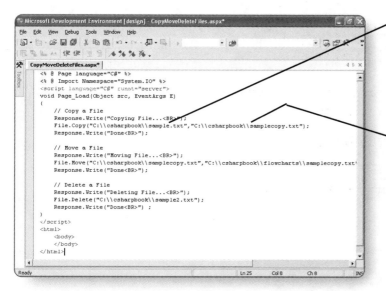

5. Pass the name and path of the source file as the first parameter to the `File.Copy` method. The source file is the file that will be copied.

6. Pass the name and path of the destination file as the second parameter to the `File.Copy` method. The destination file is a copy of the source file. It can be saved in another folder and have a different file name.

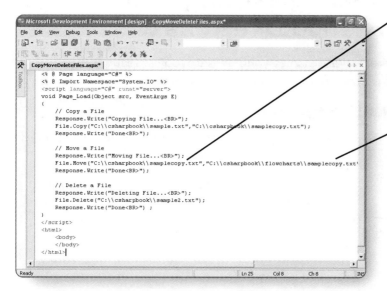

7. Pass the name and path of the source file as the first parameter to the `File.Move` method. The source file is the file that will be moved.

8. Pass the path to the file's new location as the second parameter to the `File.Move` method. The source file will move to this new location.

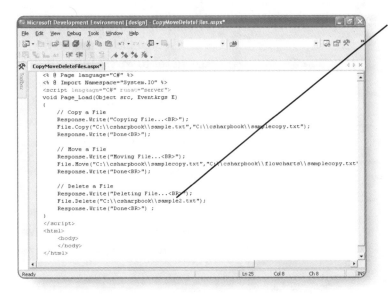

9. Pass the name and path of the file that must be deleted to the `File.Delete` method. The file will be deleted.

Creating, Moving, and Deleting Directories

Directories organize your files into logical sections. The `Directory` class contains methods that copy, move, and delete directories. You can programmatically restructure the hierarchy of content located on your Web server:

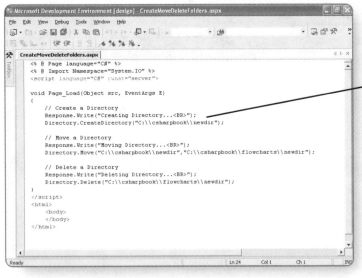

1. Pass the name and path of the directory that must be created to the `Directory.CreateDirectory` method. The directory will be created.

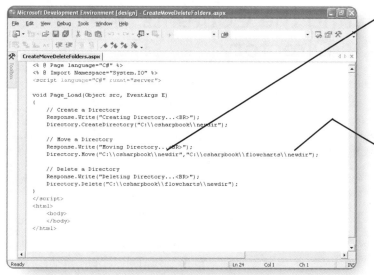

2. Pass the name and path of the source directory as the first parameter to the `Directory.Move` method. The source directory is the directory that will be moved to a new location.

3. Pass the path to the directory's new location as the second parameter to the `Directory.Move` method. The directory will move to the new location.

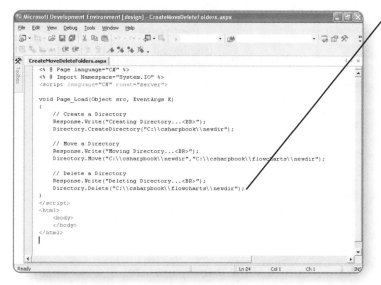

4. Pass the name and path of the directory that must be deleted to the `Directory.Delete` method. The directory will be deleted.

Listing the Contents of a Directory

A directory can contain files as well as subdirectories. The `Directory` class contains methods that allow you to create a custom directory-listing script in C#. The `GetFiles` method returns the lists of files found in the directory, but you use the `GetDirectories` method, as its name suggests, to list the subdirectories:

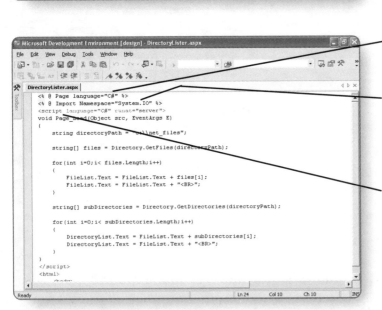

1. Insert a label control called `FileList`. This label will display all the files found in the specified directory.

2. Insert a label control called `DirectoryList`. This label will display all the subdirectories found in the specified directory.

3. Set the `language` attribute of the page directive to `C#`.

4. Import the `System.IO` namespace. The `System.IO` namespace contains the `File` class.

5. Insert opening and closing `<script>` tags. Set the `runat` attribute to `server` and the `language` attribute to `C#`.

6. Insert a `Page_Load` method. This method will execute when the page is loaded.

7. Declare the `directoryPath` variable as a string. This variable will store the path of the directory.

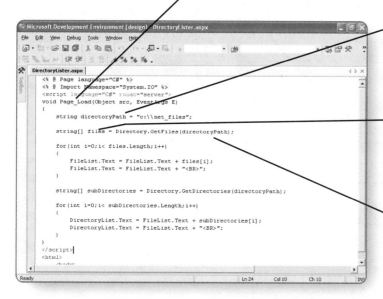

8. Declare an array as a string. The files array will store the list of files found in the current directory.

9. Call the `GetFiles` method and store the result in the files array. You must pass the `directoryPath` variable to the `GetFiles` method. The `GetFiles` method returns the list of files stored in directory.

10. Use a `for` loop to iterate through the array and print the file name of each element stored in the `files` array. The `FileList` label will display each file found in the directory.

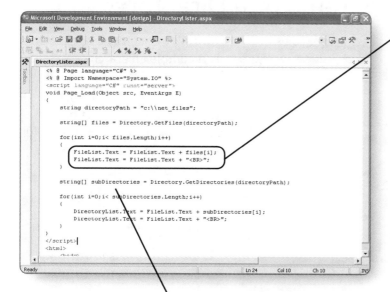

NOTE

You use the `length` property to determine the number of files in the array.

11. Declare an array as a string. The `subdirs` array will store the list of subdirectories found in the current directory.

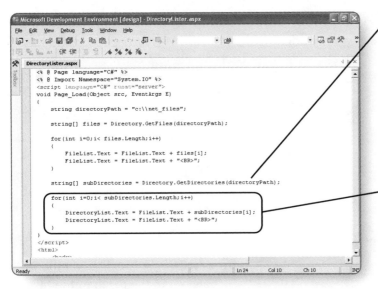

12. Call the GetDirectories method and store the result in the subdirs array. You must pass the directoryPath variable to the GetDirectories method. The GetDirectories method returns the list of subdirectories within the current directory.

13. Use a for loop to iterate through the array and print the directory name of each element stored in the subdirs array. The DirectoryList label will display each subdirectory.

Recursively Listing the Contents of a Directory

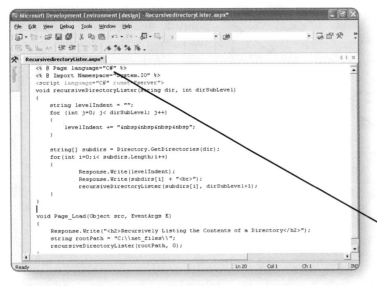

Your files are most likely stored in a complex hierarchy of directories and subdirectories. The previous script lets you display the contents of only a single directory. It is more useful to recursively list the contents of all subdirectories as well. To do this, you use the GetDirectories and GetFiles methods of the Directory class:

1. Set the language attribute of the page directive to C#.

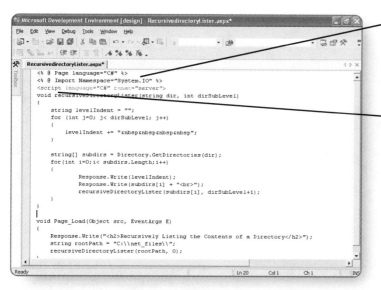

2. Import the System.IO namespace. The System.IO namespace contains the File class.

3. Insert opening and closing <script> tags. Set the runat attribute to server and the language attribute to C#.

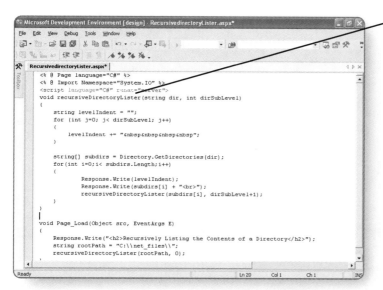

4. Create a void method called recursiveDirectoryLister. You use this method to print the contents of each subdirectory. It takes the path of the directory and the number of levels the subdirectory is from the root directory. You use the dirSubLevel parameter to determine the number of times the directory name must be indented to illustrate the directory location in the file hierarchy.

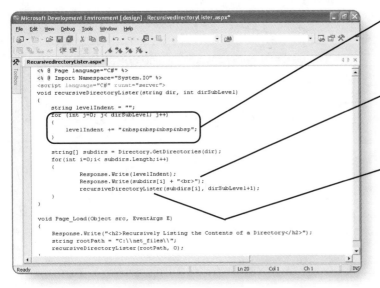

5. Insert four blank spaces for sublevel. Use a `for` loop to do this.

6. Display all the subdirectories with the appropriate indentation.

7. Call the `recursiveDirectory Lister` method for each subdirectory found. You must pass the subdirectory path and sublevel to the `recursive DirectoryLister` method. The level must be incremented each time the method is called.

8. Insert a `Page_Load` method. This method will execute when the page is loaded.

9. Declare the `rootPath` variable as a string. This variable will store the path of the root directory.

10. Call the `recursive DirectoryLister` method. Pass the `rootPath` and the root level as parameters to the method. The starting level is zero.

Working with Drives

The `GetLogicalDrives` method in the `Directory` class returns a list of available drives. The `GetLogicalDrives` method is useful if you ever need to list the drives on a remote server:

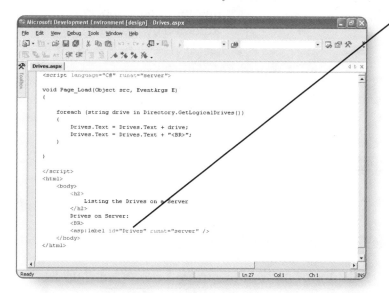

1. Insert a label control called `Drives`. This label will display all the disk drives located on the server.

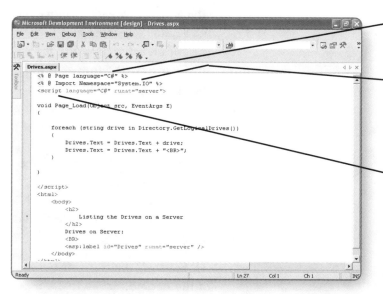

2. Set the `language` attribute of the page directive to `C#`.

3. Import the `System.IO` namespace. The `System.IO` namespace contains the `File` class.

4. Insert opening and closing `<script>` tags. Set the `runat` attribute to `server` and the `language` attribute to `C#`.

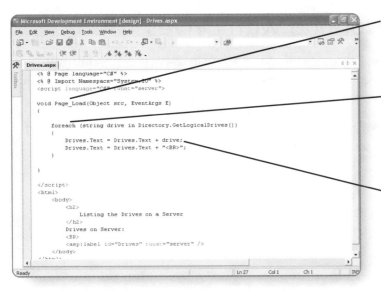

5. Insert a `Page_Load` method. This method will be executed when the page is loaded.

6. Use a `foreach` loop to iterate through the array returned by the `GetLogicalDrives` method.

7. Print each drive to a new line and display the result in the `Drives` label.

Reading Text Files

You will often need the ability to read, process, and display the contents of a text file within a Web page. You use the `OpenText` method of the `File` class to connect to a file from which a `StreamReader` object can read data. You could also use the `include` directive, but it simply inserts the text as is at the specified location. The `include` directive does not allow you to process the data before it is printed to the screen. The example that follows is a source-code viewer. It retrieves the HTML source from the file and encodes it so it can be displayed within a Web page:

1. Set the `language` attribute of the page directive to C#.

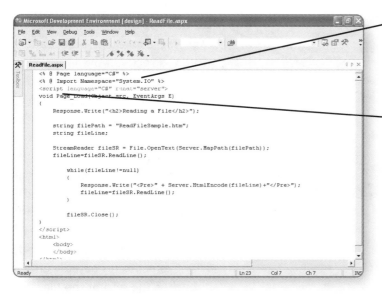

2. Import the `System.IO` namespace. The `System.IO` namespace contains the `File` class.

3. Insert opening and closing `<script>` tags. Set the `runat` attribute to `server` and the `language` attribute to `C#`.

4. Insert a `Page_Load` method. This method will execute when the page is loaded.

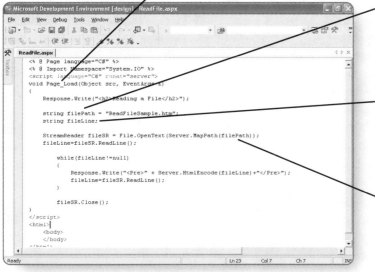

5. Declare the `filePath` variable as a string and assign the name of the file that must be read to the variable.

6. Declare the `fileLine` variable as a string. This variable will store each line of the text file as it is read.

7. Pass the `filePath` variable to the `OpenText` method and assign the result to the `StreamReader` object.

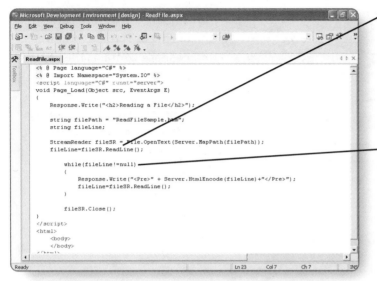

8. Call the ReadLine method of the StreamReader object and store the result in the fileLine variable. The ReadLine method reads the first line of text from the file.

9. Use a while loop to continue reading the file one line at a time until the ReadLine method returns a null value. The method will return null when it reaches the end of the file. Steps 10 and 11 will execute repeatedly until it reaches the end of the file.

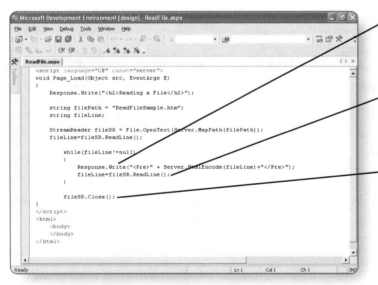

10. Use the Response.Write method to print the fileLine variable.

11. Call the ReadLine method to retrieve another line from the text file.

12. Call the Close method of the StreamReader object. The stream will close.

Writing to Text Files

Data usually gets stored in a database, but such a process is sometimes not worth the overhead, especially if you need to store only a few paragraphs of text. The File class provides a simple yet effective solution for your data storage requirements:

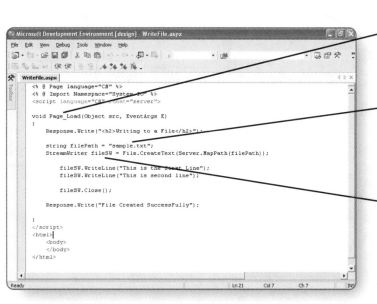

1. Set the language attribute of the page directive to C#.

2. Import the System.IO namespace. The System.IO namespace contains the File class.

3. Insert opening and closing <script> tags. Set the runat attribute to server and the language attribute to C#.

4. Insert a Page_Load method. This method will execute when the page is loaded.

5. Declare the filePath variable as a string and assign the name of the file that must be created to the variable.

6. Create a StreamWriter object.

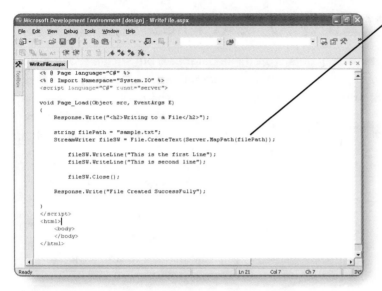

7. Pass the `filePath` variable to the `CreateText` method and assign the result to the `StreamWriter` object.

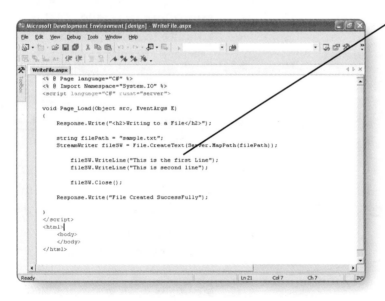

8. Use the `WriteLine` method of the `StreamWriter` object to print a line of text to the file. You must pass the text to the `WriteLine` method as a parameter.

NOTE

The `WriteLine` method prints a line break at the end of each line.

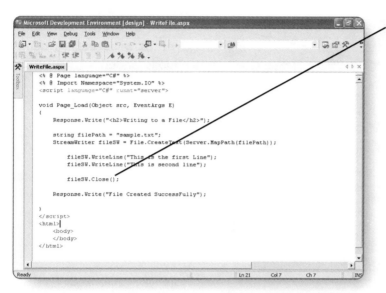

9. Call the `Close` method of the `StreamWriter` object. The stream will close.

Appending Data to a Text File

It is not very useful to overwrite the existing information each time you save data to a file. In fact, the ability to incrementally add data to a file lets you implement a number of practical applications. For instance, you could log user activity, store guestbook entries, and even save posted form data to a text file:

1. Set the `language` attribute of the page directive to `C#`.

2. Import the `System.IO` namespace. The `System.IO` namespace contains the `File` class.

3. Insert opening and closing `<script>` tags. Set the `runat` attribute to `server` and the `language` attribute to `C#`.

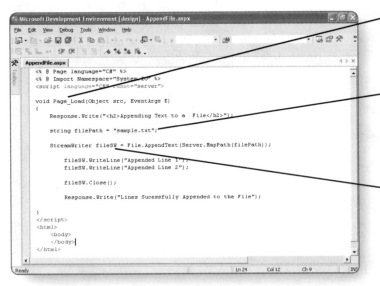

4. Insert a `Page_Load` method. This method will execute when the page is loaded.

5. Declare the `filePath` variable as a string and assign the name of the file that must be created to the variable.

6. Create a `StreamWriter` object.

> **CAUTION**
>
> You will receive a System.Unauthorized AccessException if ASP.NET does not have the appropriate access privileges when writing or appending data to a file. You will have to grant access to ASP.NET. This is a simple task. You need to right-click on the file or folder, select the Security tab, add the ASP.NET account from the users list and then check the write access checkbox.

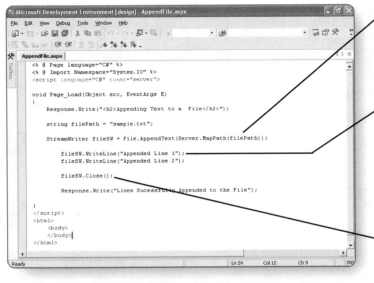

7. Pass the `filePath` variable to the `AppendText` method and assign the result to the `StreamWriter` object.

8. Use the `WriteLine` method of the `StreamWriter` object to add the text at the end of the existing file. You must pass the text to the `WriteLine` method as a parameter.

9. Call the `Close` method of the `StreamWriter` object. The stream will close.

Retrieving a Web Page from the Internet (Screen Scraping)

Using the HTTP protocol to retrieve a Web page that resides on another Web server is known as screen scraping. Although this task was once impossible to achieve without a third-party component, the functionality contained in the System.Net and System.Web namespaces makes screen scraping exceptionally easy:

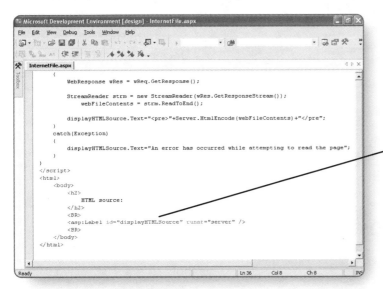

1. Insert a label control called displayHTMLSource. This label will display all the source code of the retrieved file.

2. Set the language attribute of the page directive to C#.

3. Import the System.IO, System.Net, and the System.Web namespaces.

4. Insert opening and closing <script> tags. Set the runat attribute to server and the language attribute to C#.

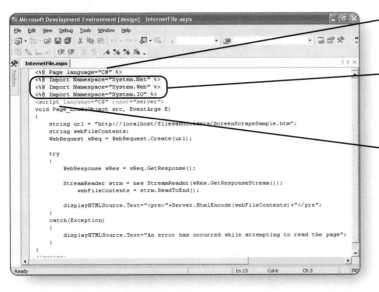

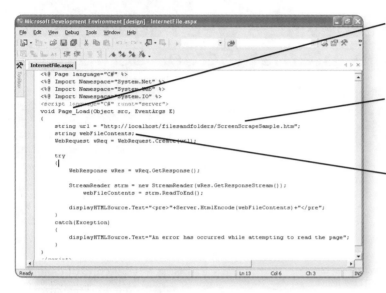

5. Insert a Page_Load method. This method will execute when the page is loaded.

6. Declare the url variable as a string. This variable will store the address of the Web page.

7. Declare the webFileContents variable as a string. This variable will store the contents of the retrieved page.

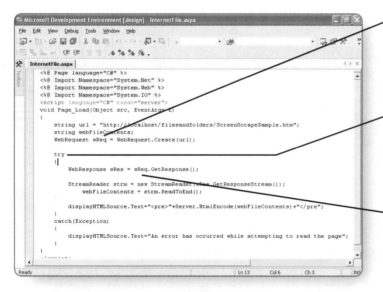

8. Create a new WebRequest object. You must pass the url variable to the WebRequest. Create method.

9. Place the code in a try block because an exception will get thrown if the Web page is not found or the url is not valid.

10. Create a WebResponse object by calling the GetResponse method of the WebRequest object.

11. Create a `StreamReader` object by calling the `StreamReader` constructor. You must pass the `GetResponseStream` method of the `WebResponse` object to the `StreamReader` constructor.

12. Use the `ReadToEnd` method of the `StreamReader` object to obtain the source code of the Web page. You must assign the result to the `webFileContents` variable.

13. Display the source code by assigning the `webFileContents` variable to the text property of the `displayHTMLSource` label. You use the `Server.HtmlEncode` method to encode the source code before it can appear on a Web page.

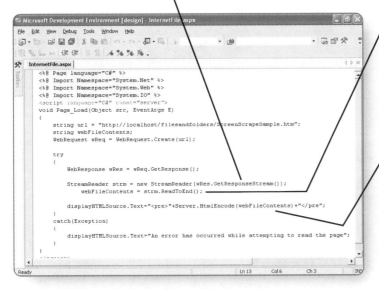

```
Microsoft Development Environment [design] - InternetFile.aspx
File  Edit  View  Debug  Tools  Window  Help

InternetFile.aspx
<%@ Page language="C#" %>
<%@ Import Namespace="System.Net" %>
<%@ Import Namespace="System.Web" %>
<%@ Import Namespace="System.IO" %>
<script language="C#" runat="server">
void Page_Load(Object src, EventArgs E)
{
    string url = "http://localhost/filesandfolders/ScreenScrapeSample.htm";
    string webFileContents;
    WebRequest wReq = WebRequest.Create(url);

    try
    {
        WebResponse wRes = wReq.GetResponse();

        StreamReader strm = new StreamReader(wRes.GetResponseStream());
        webFileContents = strm.ReadToEnd();

        displayHTMLSource.Text="<pre>"+Server.HtmlEncode(webFileContents)+"</pre>";
    }
    catch(Exception)
    {
        displayHTMLSource.Text="An error has occurred while attempting to read the page";
    }
}
```

Processing File Uploads

ASP.NET is able to process file uploads. You can easily upload files of all types without the aid of a third-party component. You can save an uploaded file to a specified location. You can even determine the name, size, and content type of the uploaded file. Users will really appreciate the ability to update their content through a simple Web interface. You can upload files created in Word, Excel, PowerPoint, Acrobat, and just about any other application:

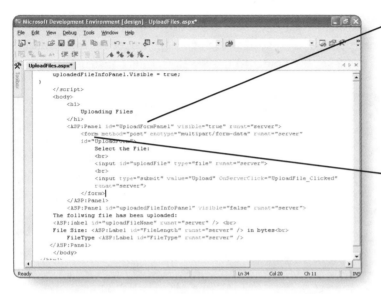

1. Insert a panel control called `UploadFormPanel`. Set the `visible` attribute to `true`. This panel will display when the page loads. The form that allows users to upload files will appear on this panel.

2. Insert opening and closing `<form>` tags within `UploadFormPanel`.

3. Set the `enctype` attribute of the form tag to `"multipart/form-data"`. This step is required when a form sends a file to the server.

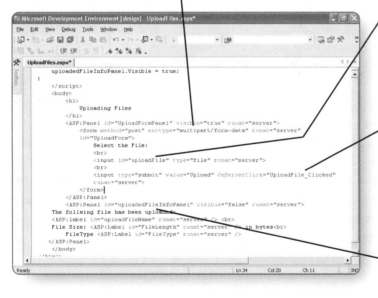

4. Insert an input field called `uploadFile`. Set the `type` attribute to `file`. This will allow users to select the files they want to upload.

5. Insert a submit button. Set the `OnServerClick` attribute to `UploadFile_Clicked`. `UploadFile_Clicked` is the method that will process the file upload.

6. Insert another panel called `uploadedFileInfoPanel`. Set the `visible` attribute to `false`. This panel will only appear when the file has been uploaded. It will display the properties of the uploaded file.

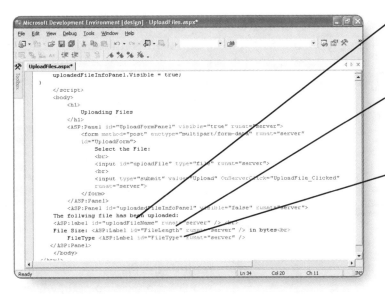

7. Insert a label called `uploadFileName` that will display the name of the uploaded file.

8. Insert a label called `FileLength` that will display the size of the file in bytes.

9. Insert a label called `FileType` that will display the mimetype of the file.

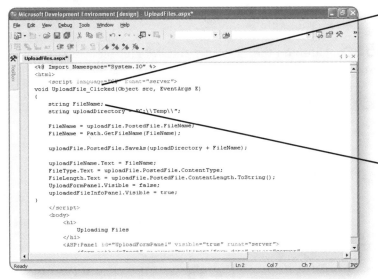

10. Insert the `UploadFile_Clicked` method. This method will execute when the user clicks the Upload button. The method processes the file upload and displays information about the uploaded file.

11. Declare a variable called `FileName` that will store the name and path of the file specified by the user. The path maps to the user's hard drive. You will need to extract the name of the file from the path.

12. Declare a variable called `UploadDirectory`. This variable will specify where the file must be saved on the server.

13. Assign the `uploadFile.PostedFile.FileName` property to the `FileName` variable. The `uploadFile.PostedFile.FileName` property contains the path specified by the user.

14. Use the `GetFileName` method of the `Path` class to retrieve the file name. You don't require the existing path, which maps to the user's hard drive. The file will be saved to a new folder that is specified by the `UploadDirectory` variable.

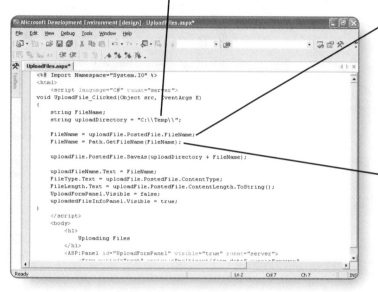

15. Concatenate the `FileName` and `UploadDirectory` variables and pass the result to the `SaveAs` method.

16. Use the `SaveAs` method to save the uploaded file to the server.

17. Print the `FileName`, `ContentType`, and `ContentLength` properties of the uploaded file to their respective labels.

18. Display `uploadFile InfoPanel` by setting its `visible` property to True. You must set the `Visible` property of `UploadFormPanel` to False.

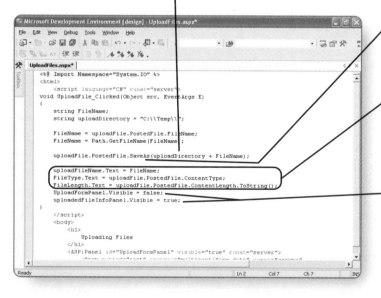

Creating a Content Management System

It is quite possible that millions of users will visit your Web site. Your Web site must therefore always be up-to-date and contain relevant information. In this section, I build an application that allows content experts to maintain their Web pages without any prior knowledge of HTML.

You use most of the file-management techniques covered in this chapter to create an online content management system. The system essentially functions as a browser-based visual HTML editor. In fact, editing a Web page is as easy as using Microsoft Word. Users will be able to:

- View a list of all the files they can update.

- Select the files they want to edit or view.

- Edit the Web page using a browser-based visual HTML editor.

- Save the files back to the Web server.

Take a look at how the content management system will work:

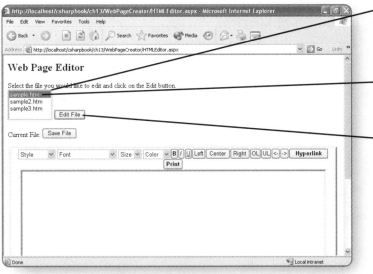

1. A listbox server control will display all of the files in the user's directory.

2. The user will have to select the file she wants to edit.

3. Once the file is selected, the user must click the Edit button.

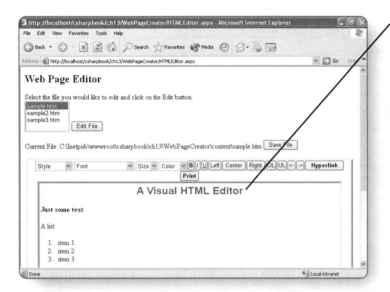

4. The file will appear within the visual editor.

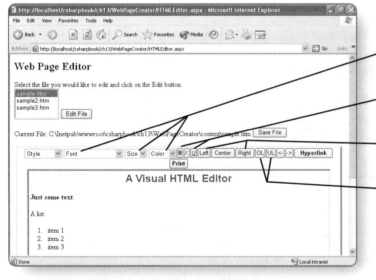

5. The user can format the Web page by:

- Changing the font, size, and color of the text

- Making text bold, italic, or underlined

- Applying left, right, and center justification

- Creating bulleted and numbered lists

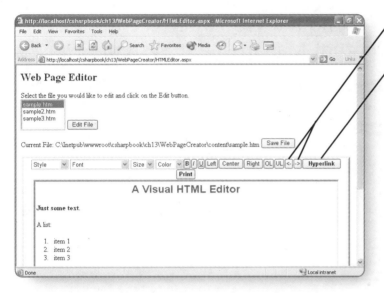

- Indenting or outdenting paragraphs

- Inserting hyperlinks

You will reuse the code developed earlier to list the contents of a directory, retrieve and display a text document, and save a file to the server. The only bit of new functionality you need to implement is the visual Web page editor. The good news is that this is already available by default in Internet Explorer 5.5 because the `<div>` tag supports a `contenteditable` property that lets you select, edit, and format text.

It is beyond the scope of the book to provide a detailed explanation on implementing the visual editor. You can simply reuse the code provided. All you need to remember is that you can retrieve the edited content from the `HtmlEditor.innerHTML` property, where `HtmlEditor` is the ID assigned to the `<div>` tag.

TIP

More information about creating a visual browser-based editor in Internet Explorer appears at **http://msdn.microsoft.com/workshop/c-frame.htm?/workshop/browser/cratewp.asp**.

Creating the Web Interface for the Content Management System

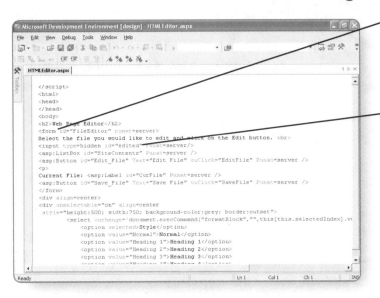

1. Insert opening and closing `<form>` tags. Set the `id` attribute to `FileEditor` and the `runat` attribute to `server`.

2. Insert a hidden form element called `edited`. Set the `runat` attribute to `server`. Once the content of a Web page changes, it is immediately stored inside the hidden field. You can retrieve the edited content from this input field when you need to save the data back to the server.

3. Insert a listbox server control. Set the `id` to `SiteContents`.

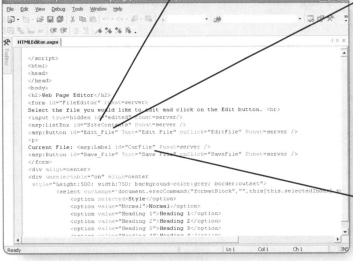

4. Insert a button control. Set the `id` to `Edit_File`. The `Text` attribute will display a label on the button. Set the `onClick` event to `EditFile`. The `EditFile` method will execute when the user clicks the button. The `EditFile` method will load the currently selected file into the visual HTML editor.

5. Insert a label control with an `id` of `CurFile`. This label will display the name of the file currently being edited. Set the `runat` attribute to `server`.

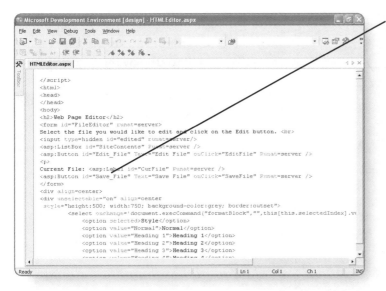

6. Insert a button control. The `SaveFile` method will retrieve the contents of the hidden form field (id="edited") and overwrite the existing file.

Writing the Code for the Content Management System

Here is the C# code that does all the hard work. You'll be surprised at how simple it really is:

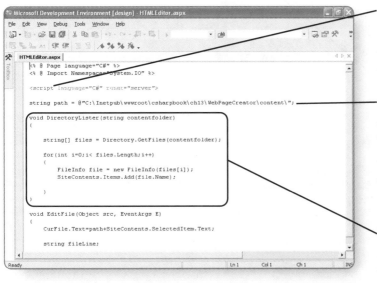

1. Insert opening and closing `<script>` tags. Set the `language` attribute to `C#` and the `runat` attribute to `server`.

2. Store the directory path as a string in a variable named `path`. The directory path is hard-coded, but it could also be dynamic, depending upon your requirements.

3. Insert a `DirectoryLister` method. This method takes the full path to a directory as a parameter. Each file found in the directory is added as an item to the listbox control.

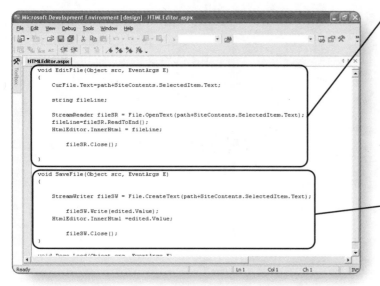

4. Insert an `EditFile` method. This method uses the `CurFile` label to display the name of the currently selected file. It then reads and assigns the contents of the file to `HtmlEditor.innerHTML`. This displays the Web page inside the online visual `Htmleditor`.

5. Insert a `SaveFile` method to overwrite the file with the updated contents.

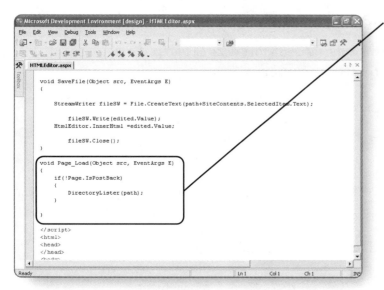

6. Insert a `Page_Load` method to call the `DirectoryLister` method when the content management system is initially loaded.

14

Sending Email Messages

Email is the most popular communication tool used on the Internet today. The ability to send email dynamically from a Web application is a necessity. You can use email to confirm orders, promote new products, and gather user feedback. The process of sending email messages has been simplified with the introduction of the `SmtpMail` object, which is provided by a base .NET class. In this chapter, you'll learn to:

- Use the `SmtpMail` object.

- Send simple email messages.

- Send carbon and blind copies of an email message.

- Change the priority of email messages.

- Send HTML-formatted email messages.

- Process an email form.

Configuring Microsoft SMTP Service

Before you can send email, you must first configure the Simple Mail Transport Protocol (SMTP) server that is part of Internet Information Server (IIS). The SMTP server is usually installed with IIS. If it is not already installed, you need to run Add/Remove Programs from the Control Panel and select the Windows 2000 SMTP Service components.

CAUTION

You cannot use the SMTP service to set up email addresses for your users. It does not support the Post Office Protocol (POP) and can therefore only be used to send email messages. If you require this functionality, you need to purchase and install Microsoft Exchange.

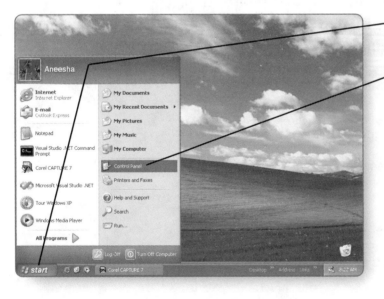

1. Click on Start. The Start menu will appear.

2. Click on Control Panel. The Control Panel window will open.

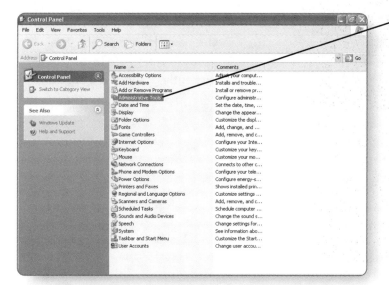

3. Double-click on Administrative tools. The contents of the Administrative tools folder will appear.

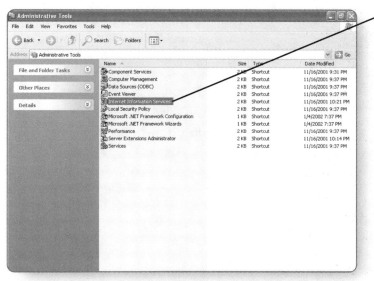

4. Double-click on Internet Information Services Manager. The Internet Information Services Manager snap-in will open.

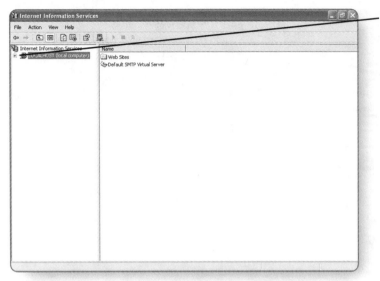

5. Click on the + sign next to the name of the server. The Web, FTP, and SMTP services currently running will appear.

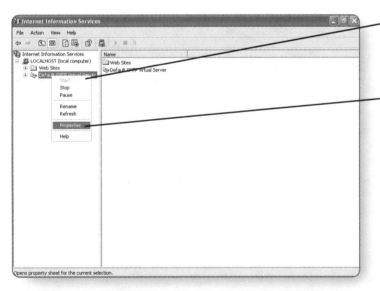

6. Right-click on Default SMTP Virtual Server. The submenu will appear.

7. Select Properties. The Default SMTP Server Properties dialog box will open.

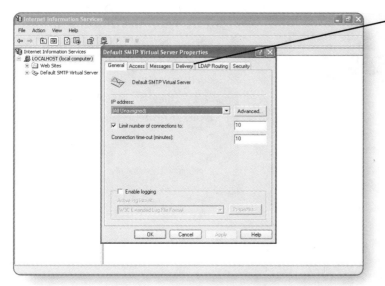

8. Click on the Delivery tab. The Delivery tab will come to the front.

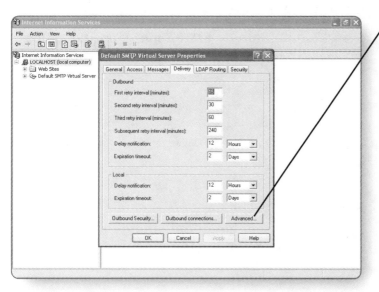

9. Click on Advanced. The Advanced Delivery dialog box will open.

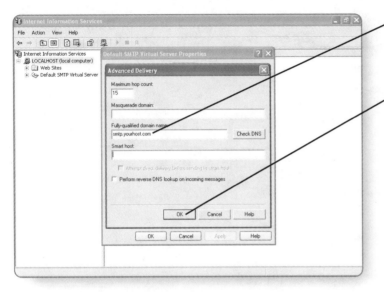

10. Enter the URL of your server in the Fully Qualified Domain Name text box.

11. Click on OK. The Advanced Delivery dialog box will close.

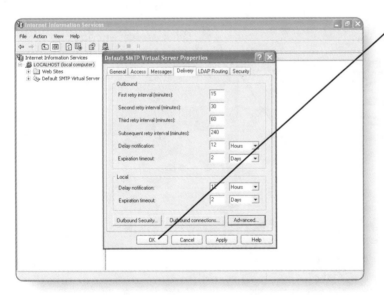

12. Click on OK. The Default SMTP Server Properties dialog box will close.

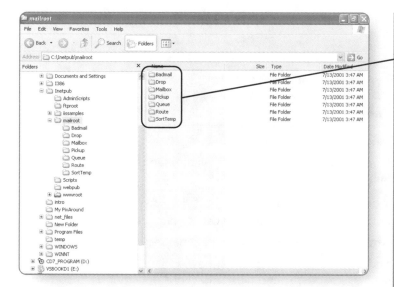

NOTE

There is a MailRoot folder within the InetPub folder. The MailRoot folder has seven subfolders that are used when the SMTP service processes the messages. Messages are placed in the Pickup folder before they are sent.

- The BadMail folder stores messages that can't be delivered.

- The Drop folder stores incoming messages.

- The Pickup folder stores outgoing messages.

- The Queue folder holds messages that can't be sent immediately.

- The SortTemp folder stores messages while they are sorted.

Using the SmtpMail Object

Sending email in ASP.NET is easy: You are no longer required to purchase expensive third-party components. The `SmtpMail` object, which is located in the `System.Web.Mail` namespace, incorporates all the functionality required to send email messages from an ASP.NET application. The `System.Web.Mail` namespace also contains other objects that allow you to model, encode, and format an email message before it is actually sent via the Simple Mail Transfer Protocol (SMTP).

Table 14.1 lists the classes contained in the `System.Web.Mail` namespace.

Table 14.1 The System.Web.Mail Namespace

Object	Purpose
SmtpMail	Models the messaging system.
MailMessage	Models the structure of an email message (To, From, Subject, and Body).
MailFormat	Sets the content type of the message to either text or HTML.
MailPriority enum	Sets the message priority. It can be high, low, or normal.
MailAttachment	Attaches a list of files to an email message.
MailEncoding	Encodes email messages that have binary file attachments, such as images, sound files, and Word documents. Encoding methods include MIME, BinHex, and UUEncode.

Table 14.2 Using the MailMessage Object to Model a Message

Property	Description
To	The email address of the receiver
From	The email address of the sender
Subject	The subject of the message
Body	The body of the message
Cc	Additional recipients of the message that can be viewed by the main recipient
Bcc	Additional recipients of the message that can't be viewed by the main recipient
Priority	The priority of the message (high, low, or normal)
BodyEncoding	The encoding of the body message and file attachments
BodyFormat	Format of the message (HTML or text)
Attachments	A list of `MailAttachment` objects that represent files that must be attached to the email message

Sending a Simple Email Message

It takes only a few simple lines of C# code to send an email message. You need to create a new instance of the `MailMessage` object and specify the sender's email address, the recipient's email address, the subject, and the actual message. To post the email message, you need to call the `Send` method of the `SmtpMail` object.

NOTE

This code is easy to customize. You only need to change the email addresses and SMTP server details.

---

1. Use the `page` directive to set the `language` to C#.

2. Import the `System.Web.Mail` namespace. This namespace includes the classes used to send email.

3. Insert opening and closing `<script>` tags. Set the `language` attribute to C# and the `runat` attribute to `server`.

```
<% @ Page language="C#" %>
<% @ Import Namespace="System.Web.Mail" %>
<script language="C#" runat="server">
void Page_Load(Object src, EventArgs E) {
    try {
        MailMessage emailMsg = new MailMessage();
        emailMsg.To = "someone@somewhere.com";
        emailMsg.From = "someone@somewhere.com";
        emailMsg.Subject = "An important message";
        emailMsg.Body = "Hi!\nHow are you?\nASP.NET is very powerful.\nAneesha";
        SmtpMail.Send(emailMsg);
        msg.Text = "The E-mail message has been sent.";
    }
    catch {
        msg.Text = "An error occurred while sending the e-mail message";
    }
}
</script>
<html>
    <body>
        <form runat="server">
            <asp:Label id="msg" runat="server" />
        </form>
    </body>
</html>
```

4. Insert a `Page_Load` method. This method will send the email message after the page has loaded.

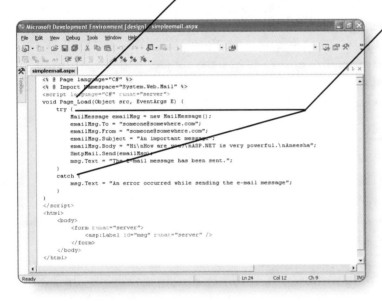

5. Use the `try-catch` exception-handling mechanism to deal with any unexpected conditions that might occur, such as the Email server being temporarily unavailable. It is important that you handle exceptions in an elegant manner. Refer to Chapter 8, "Handling Exceptions and Tracing," for more information about handling exceptions.

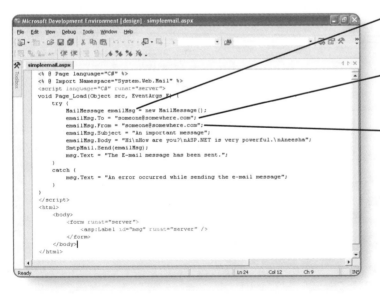

6. Create an instance of the `MailMessage` object.

7. Assign the recipient's email address to the `To` property.

8. Assign the sender's email address to the `From` property.

TIP

You can send the same message to multiple recipients by separating the email address of each recipient with a semicolon (as in "email1@xyz.com; email2@xyz.com; email3@xyz.com").

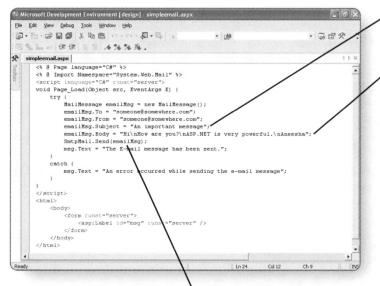

9. Assign the message subject to the `Subject` property.

10. Assign the message body to the `Body` property.

TIP

You can insert a line break by typing **\n** in the message body. Insert a paragraph break by typing **\r** in the message body.

---

11. Pass the instance of the `MailMessage` object to the `Send` method of the `SmtpMail` object. Calling the `Send` method will post the email.

Sending Carbon and Blind Copies of an Email Message

You can also send copies of an email message to additional recipients. When you specify additional recipients using the carbon-copy attribute, the main recipient is aware that other users have also received the message. All email clients such as Microsoft Outlook or Eudora display these addresses. Sending blind carbon copies (BCC), on the other hand, keeps the identity of other recipients a secret.

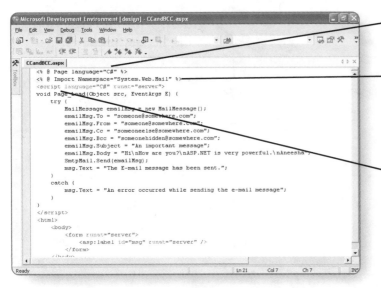

1. Use the page directive to set the language to C#.

2. Import the System.Web.Mail namespace. This namespace includes the classes used to send email.

3. Insert opening and closing <script> tags. Set the language attribute to C# and the runat attribute to server.

4. Insert a Page_Load method. This method will send the email message after the page has loaded.

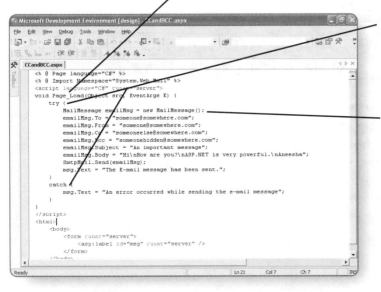

5. Use the try-catch exception-handling mechanism to deal with any unexpected conditions that might occur.

6. Create an instance of the MailMessage object.

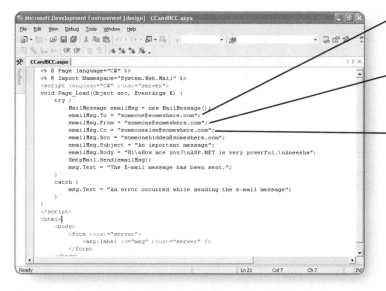

```
Microsoft Development Environment [design] - CCandBCC.aspx
File  Edit  View  Debug  Tools  Window  Help

CCandBCC.aspx

<% @ Page language="C#" %>
<% @ Import Namespace="System.Web.Mail" %>
<script language="C#" runat="server">
void Page_Load(Object src, EventArgs E) {
    try {
        MailMessage emailMsg = new MailMessage();
        emailMsg.To = "someone@somewhere.com";
        emailMsg.From = "someone@somewhere.com";
        emailMsg.Cc = "someoneelse@somewhere.com";
        emailMsg.Bcc = "someonehidden@somewhere.com";
        emailMsg.Subject = "An important message";
        emailMsg.Body = "Hi\nHow are you?\nASP.NET is very powerful.\nAneesha";
        SmtpMail.Send(emailMsg);
        msg.Text = "The E-mail message has been sent.";
    }
    catch (
        msg.Text = "An error occurred while sending the e-mail message";
    )
}
</script>
<html>
    <body>
        <form runat="server">
            <asp:label id="msg" runat="server" />
        </form>
    </body>
</html>
```

7. Assign the recipient's email address to the To property.

8. Assign the sender's email address to the From property.

9. Assign additional recipients that the main recipient can know about to the Cc property.

```
Microsoft Development Environment [design] - CCandBCC.aspx
File  Edit  View  Debug  Tools  Window  Help

CCandBCC.aspx

<script language="C#" runat="server">
void Page_Load(Object src, EventArgs E) {
    try {
        MailMessage emailMsg = new MailMessage();
        emailMsg.To = "someone@somewhere.com";
        emailMsg.From = "someone@somewhere.com";
        emailMsg.Cc = "someoneelse@somewhere.com";
        emailMsg.Bcc = "someonehidden@somewhere.com";
        emailMsg.Subject = "An important message";
        emailMsg.Body = "Hi\nHow are you?\nASP.NET is very powerful.\nAneesha";
        SmtpMail.Send(emailMsg);
        msg.Text = "The E-mail message has been sent.";
    }
    catch (
        msg.Text = "An error occurred while sending the e-mail message";
    )
}
</script>
<html>
    <body>
        <form runat="server">
            <asp:label id="msg" runat="server" />
        </form>
    </body>
</html>
```

10. Assign additional recipients that the main recipient can't know about to the Bcc property.

TIP

You can set multiple cc and bcc recipients by separating the email address of each recipient with a semicolon (as in "email1@xyz.com; email2@xyz.com; email3@xyz.com").

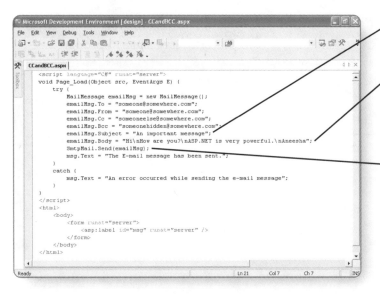

11. Assign the message subject to the `Subject` property.

12. Assign the message body to the `Body` property.

13. Pass the instance of the `MailMessage` object to the `Send` method of the `SmtpMail` object. Calling the `Send` method will post the email.

Setting the Priority of an Email Message

Some messages are more important than others and require immediate attention. A recipient will immediately notice a high-priority message in her inbox. You set the priority of a message using the `MailPriority` property. You can set the priority of a message to high, normal, or low:

1. Use the `page` directive to set the `language` to C#.

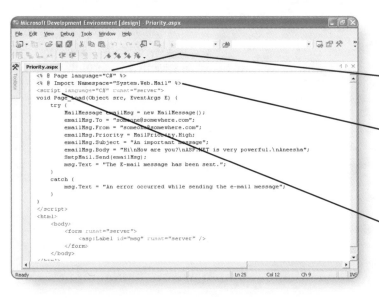

2. Import the `System.Web.Mail` namespace. This namespace includes the classes used to send email.

3. Insert opening and closing `<script>` tags. Set the `language` attribute to C# and the `runat` attribute to `server`.

4. Insert a `Page_Load` method. This method will send the email message after the page has loaded.

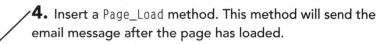

5. Use the `try-catch` exception-handling mechanism to deal with any unexpected conditions that might occur.

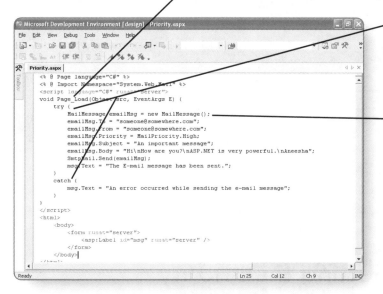

6. Create an instance of the `MailMessage` object.

7. Assign the recipient's email address to the `To` property.

8. Assign the sender's email address to the `From` property.

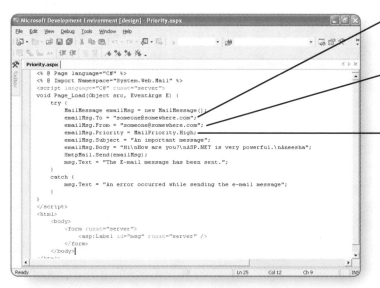

9. Set the `priority` property to either `High` or `Low`. The default priority for a message is `Normal`.

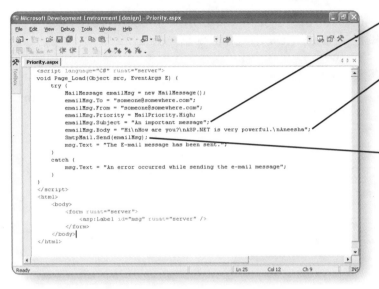

10. Assign the message subject to the `Subject` property.

11. Assign the message body to the `Body` property.

12. Pass the instance of the `MailMessage` object to the `Send` method of the `SmtpMail` object. Calling the `Send` method will post the email.

Attaching Files to an Email Message

You can use email to transfer files such as images, Word documents, Excel spreadsheets, and WinZip archives. In fact, you can attach all kinds of files to an email message. The recipient can then open these attachments. You use the `MailAttachment` object to attach files to an email message.

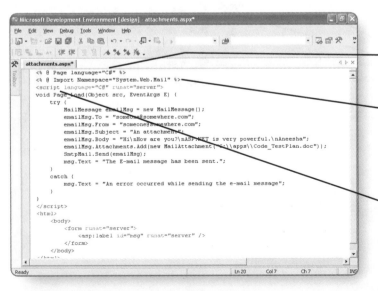

1. Use the `page` directive to set the `language` to `C#`.

2. Import the `System.Web.Mail` namespace. This namespace includes the classes used to send email.

3. Insert opening and closing `<script>` tags. Set the `language` attribute to `C#` and the `runat` attribute to `server`.

4. Insert a `Page_Load` method. This method will send the email message after the page has loaded.

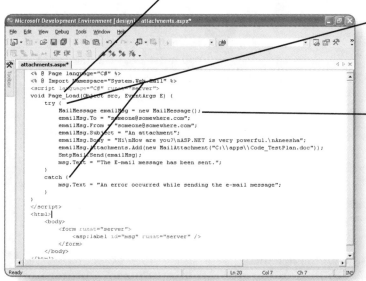

5. Use the `try-catch` exception-handling mechanism to deal with any unexpected conditions that might occur.

6. Create an instance of the `MailMessage` object.

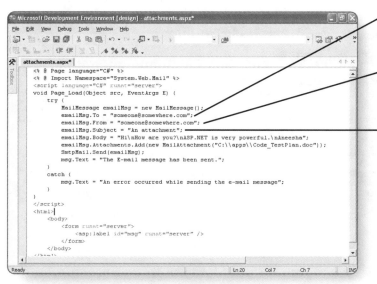

7. Assign the recipient's email address to the `To` property.

8. Assign the sender's email address to the `From` property.

9. Assign the message subject to the `Subject` property.

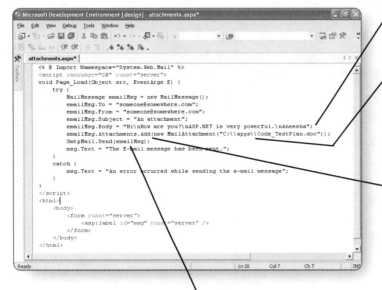

```
Microsoft Development Environment [design] - attachments.aspx*
File  Edit  View  Debug  Tools  Window  Help

attachments.aspx*

<%@ Import Namespace="System.Web.Mail" %>
<script language="C#" runat="server">
void Page_Load(Object src, EventArgs E) {
    try {
        MailMessage emailMsg = new MailMessage();
        emailMsg.To = "someone@somewhere.com";
        emailMsg.From = "someone@somewhere.com";
        emailMsg.Subject = "An attachment";
        emailMsg.Body = "Hi\nHow are you?\nASP.NET is very powerful.\nAneesha";
        emailMsg.Attachments.Add(new MailAttachment("C:\\apps\\Code_TestPlan.doc"));
        SmtpMail.Send(emailMsg);
        msg.Text = "The E-mail message has been sent.";
    }
    catch {
        msg.Text = "An error occurred while sending the e-mail message";
    }
}
</script>
<html>
    <body>
        <form runat="server">
            <asp:label id="msg" runat="server" />
        </form>
    </body>
</html>

Ready                                              Ln 20    Col 7    Ch 7    INS
```

10. Assign the message body to the Body property.

11. Create a new instance of the MailAttachment object. You must pass the file name and path to the MailAttachment constructor.

12. Use the Add method to include the MailAttachment objects.

13. Pass the instance of the MailMessage object to the Send method of the SmtpMail object. Calling the Send method will post the email.

Processing an Email Form

The contents of an email message will most likely be entered by a Web site visitor. The ability to retrieve the information entered by a user and send it as an email message is important. You use this functionality to gather comments, feedback, and enquiries from your Web site visitors.

1. Create the email form. You will need to insert the following Web form controls:

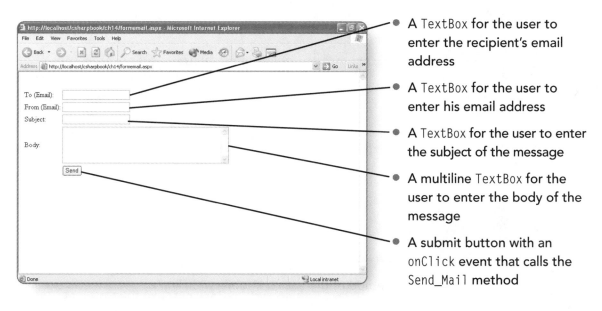

- A TextBox for the user to enter the recipient's email address

- A TextBox for the user to enter his email address

- A TextBox for the user to enter the subject of the message

- A multiline TextBox for the user to enter the body of the message

- A submit button with an onClick event that calls the Send_Mail method

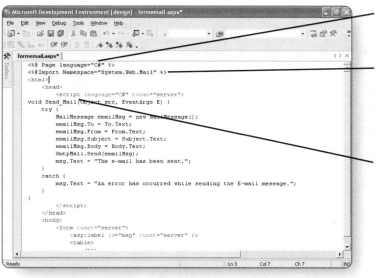

2. Use the page directive to set the language to C#.

3. Import the System.Web.Mail namespace. This namespace includes the classes used to send email.

4. Insert opening and closing <script> tags. Set the language attribute to C# and the runat attribute to server.

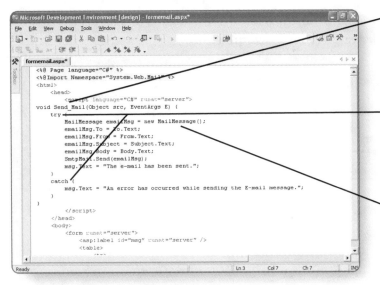

5. Insert a `Send_Mail` method. The `Send_Mail` method will execute on the server when the user clicks the submit button.

6. Use the `try-catch` exception-handling mechanism to deal with any unexpected conditions that might occur.

7. Create an instance of the `MailMessage` object.

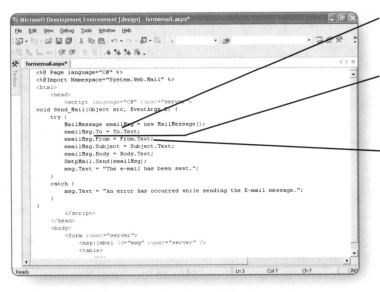

8. Retrieve the recipient's email address from the form.

9. Assign the recipient's email address to the `To` property of the `MailMessage` object instance.

10. Retrieve the sender's email address from the form. The `Text` property of the `TextBox` stores the data entered by the user.

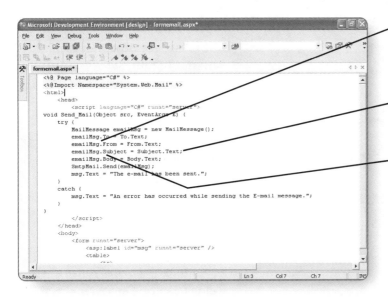

11. Assign the sender's email address to the `From` property of the `MailMessage` object instance.

12. Retrieve the message subject from the form.

13. Assign the message subject to the `Subject` property of the `MailMessage` object instance.

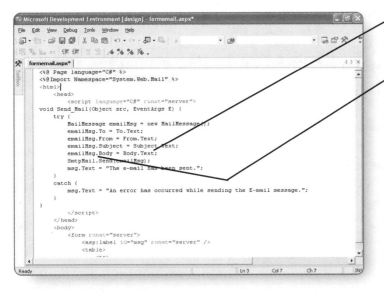

14. Retrieve the message body from the form.

15. Assign the message body to the `Body` property of the `MailMessage` object instance.

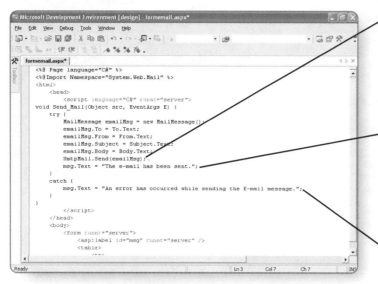

16. Pass the instance of the `MailMessage` object to the `Send` method of the `SmtpMail` object. Calling the `Send` method will post the email.

17. Acknowledge that the email has been sent successfully. You can use the `text` property in a label control to display the message.

18. Specify the error message that must be displayed if the email can't be sent. You must place this message within the `catch` statement block.

Sending HTML-Formatted Email Messages

Email messages are usually sent in plain text, which provides no flexibility in layout and design. Many email clients such as Netscape Communicator and Microsoft Outlook can display HTML-formatted messages. Adding images, links, and tables can increase the impact of promotional email. Many popular email newsletters already take advantage of this feature. Sending HTML-formatted email messages is simple: You set the `BodyFormat` property of the `MailMessage` object to `HTML`.

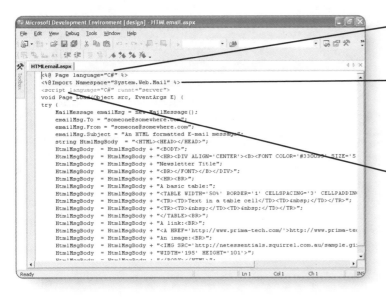

1. Use the `page` directive to set the `language` to `C#`.

2. Import the `System.Web.Mail` namespace. This namespace includes the classes used to send email.

3. Insert opening and closing `<script>` tags. Set the `language` attribute to `C#` and the `runat` attribute to `server`.

4. Insert a `Page_Load` method. This method will send the email message after the page has loaded.

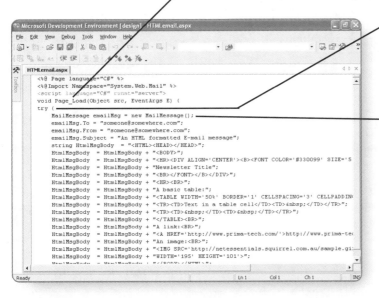

5. Use the `try-catch` exception-handling mechanism to deal with any unexpected conditions that might occur.

6. Create an instance of the `MailMessage` object.

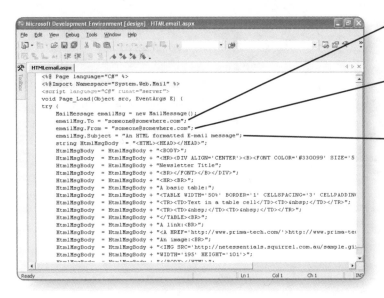

7. Assign the recipient's email address to the To property.

8. Assign the sender's email address to the From property.

9. Assign the message subject to the Subject property.

10. Use a variable to store the HTML-formatted email message and assign the message body to the Body property.

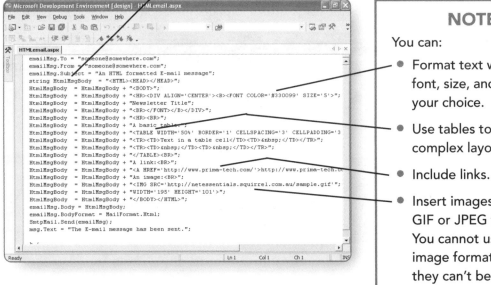

NOTE

You can:

- Format text with the font, size, and color of your choice.

- Use tables to create complex layouts.

- Include links.

- Insert images in either GIF or JPEG format. You cannot use other image formats because they can't be displayed in HTML. Be sure to use absolute URLs when referencing images that reside on a Web server. For a more thorough lesson on HTML, please refer to *Hands On HTML* (Premier Press, Inc.).

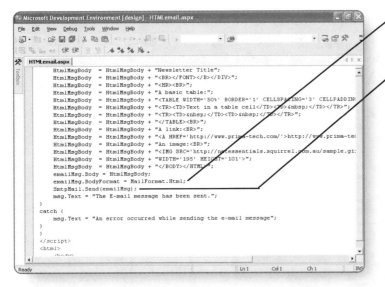

```
Microsoft Development Environment [design] - HTMLemail.aspx
File  Edit  View  Debug  Tools  Window  Help

HTMLemail.aspx

      HtmlMsgBody   = HtmlMsgBody + "Newsletter Title";
      HtmlMsgBody   = HtmlMsgBody + "<BR></FONT></B></DIV>";
      HtmlMsgBody   = HtmlMsgBody + "<HR><BR>";
      HtmlMsgBody   = HtmlMsgBody + "A basic table:";
      HtmlMsgBody   = HtmlMsgBody + "<TABLE WIDTH='50%' BORDER='1' CELLSPACING='3' CELLPADDIN(
      HtmlMsgBody   = HtmlMsgBody + "<TR><TD>Text in a table cell</TD><TD> </TD></TR>";
      HtmlMsgBody   = HtmlMsgBody + "<TR><TD> </TD><TD> </TD></TR>";
      HtmlMsgBody   = HtmlMsgBody + "</TABLE><BR>";
      HtmlMsgBody   = HtmlMsgBody + "A link:<BR>";
      HtmlMsgBody   = HtmlMsgBody + "<A HREF='http://www.prima-tech.com/'>http://www.prima-tec
      HtmlMsgBody   = HtmlMsgBody + "An image:<BR>";
      HtmlMsgBody   = HtmlMsgBody + "<IMG SRC='http://notessentials.squirrel.com.au/sample.gi:
      HtmlMsgBody   = HtmlMsgBody + "WIDTH='195' HEIGHT='101'>";
      HtmlMsgBody   = HtmlMsgBody + "</BODY></HTML>";
      emailMsg.Body = HtmlMsgBody;
      emailMsg.BodyFormat = MailFormat.Html;
      SmtpMail.Send(emailMsg);
      msg.Text = "The E-mail message has been sent.";
  )
  catch (
      msg.Text = "An error occurred while sending the e-mail message";
  )
  )
  )
  </script>
  <html>
```

11. Set the `BodyFormat` property to `MailFormat.Html`.

12. Pass the instance of the `MailMessage` object to the `Send` method of the `SmtpMail` object. Calling the `Send` method will post the email.

Sending Electronic Postcards

Using HTML to format email messages certainly opens up a few more opportunities. I am sure you have either received or sent an electronic postcard. As you will remember, you had to click on a link within an email message to launch a browser and retrieve your card. You can now extend the concept by creating a Web application that actually sends the card in an email message. The ability to embed HTML in an email messages makes this possible. The card will contain images, tables, and links:

1. Create the email form. This form must allow the user to select the image to be displayed on the postcard. You need to insert the following Web form controls:

- A TextBox for the user to enter the recipient's email address

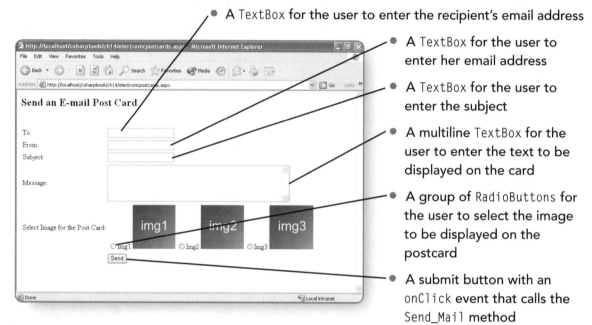

- A TextBox for the user to enter her email address

- A TextBox for the user to enter the subject

- A multiline TextBox for the user to enter the text to be displayed on the card

- A group of RadioButtons for the user to select the image to be displayed on the postcard

- A submit button with an onClick event that calls the Send_Mail method

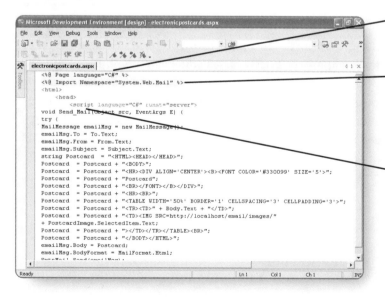

2. Use the page directive to set the language to C#.

3. Import the System.Web.Mail namespace. This namespace includes the classes used to send email.

4. Insert opening and closing <script> tags. Set the language attribute to C# and the runat attribute to server.

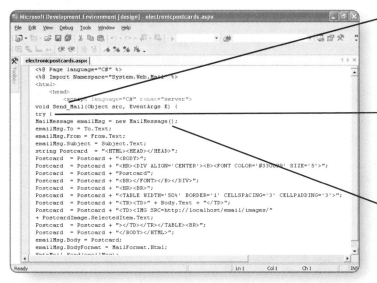

5. Insert a `Send_Mail` method. The `Send_Mail` method will execute on the server when the user clicks the submit button.

6. Use the `try-catch` exception-handling mechanism to deal with any unexpected conditions that might occur.

7. Create an instance of the `MailMessage` object.

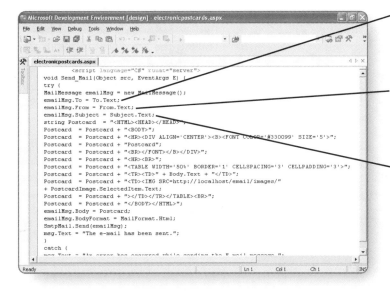

8. Assign the recipient's email address to the `To` property of the `MailMessage` object instance.

9. Assign the sender's email address to the `From` property of the `MailMessage` object instance.

10. Assign the subject that the user has entered to the `Subject` property.

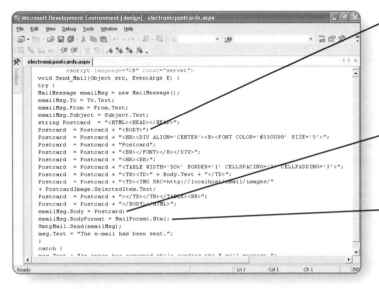

11. Construct the HTML for the postcard and insert the appropriate image. The HTML is stored in a variable and assigned to the Body property.

12. Assign the message body to the Body property of the MailMessage object instance.

13. Set the BodyFormat property to MailFormat.Html.

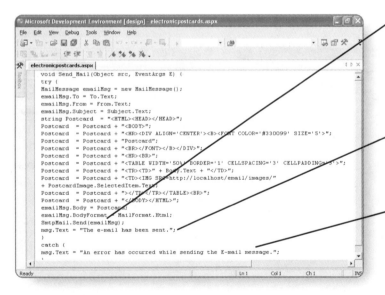

14. Pass the instance of the MailMessage object to the Send method of the SmtpMail object. Calling the Send method will post the email.

15. Acknowledge that the postcard has been sent successfully.

16. Specify the error message that must appear if the postcard can't be sent. You must place this message within the catch statement block.

15

Working with Cookies and Sessions

The Hypertext Transfer Protocol (HTTP), which handles communication between a Web browser and server, is a *stateless protocol*. This means that each transaction is treated as unique. HTTP does not track or store user-specific data. The ability to retain state is essential for Web applications that implement shopping carts and varying forms of personalization. Cookies and sessions are two key technologies used to store data between successive requests to a Web server. Both of these technologies, although in widespread use, have disadvantages, but ASP.NET goes a long way to address them and implements a method of state maintenance that is easy to use, scalable, and robust. In this chapter, you'll learn to:

- Store and retrieve cookies.
- Store and retrieve session variables.
- Enable cookieless sessions.
- Use State Server and SQL Server to store session state.
- Store and retrieve application variables.

Creating Cookies

A cookie is a small amount of information stored on a user's computer until a specified expiry data. Many users view cookies as a major security risk because they believe the sensitive data stored in a cookie is freely accessible to other Web sites. However, only the server that sets the cookie can retrieve it. Many popular browsers also allow users to disable cookies:

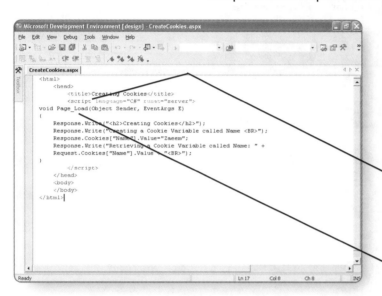

1. Insert opening and closing `<script>` tags. Set the `language` attribute to `C#` and the `runat` attribute to `server`.

2. Insert a `Page_Load` method. This method will execute when the page loads.

3. Type the name of the cookie within quotation marks between square brackets of the `Cookie` property of the `Response` object. You use square brackets to access indexed properties of the `Response.Cookies` object in C#.

4. Use the equal sign (=) to store data in the `Value` property of the cookie.

5. Type the name of the cookie within quotation marks between square brackets of the `Cookie` property of the `Response` object to retrieve the data stored in the session variable.

Retrieving Multiple Cookies

You can use the Cookie object to store multiple values for a single key. Use the foreach loop to retrieve all cookie variables stored for a particular user:

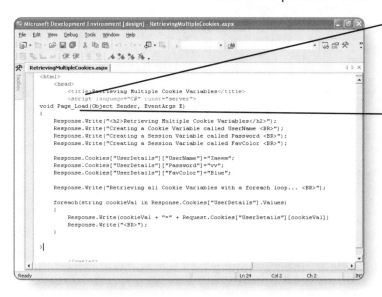

1. Insert opening and closing <script> tags. Set the language attribute to C# and the runat attribute to server.

2. Insert a Page_Load method. This method will execute when the page loads.

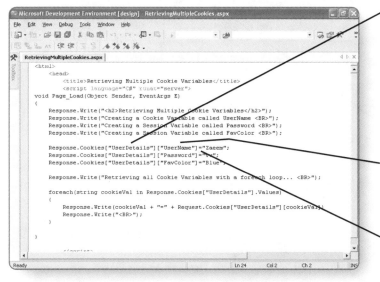

3. Type the name of the key within quotation marks between square brackets of the Cookie property of the Response object. You use square brackets to access indexed properties of the Response.Cookies object in C#.

4. Type the name of the key within quotation marks between square brackets.

5. Use the equal sign (=) to store data in the cookie.

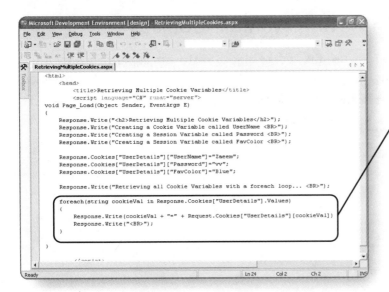

NOTE

You can store more cookies in the same key.

6. Use a `foreach` loop to iterate through the `Response.Cookies` collection for a particular key.

Deleting Cookies

You delete a cookie by setting the `Expiry` property to the current date and time. When the browser is closed, the cookie is deleted. This automatically occurs when no expiry date is set:

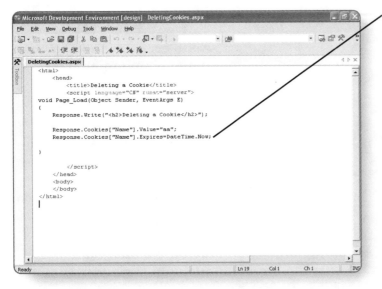

1. Set the `Expires` property to the current date and time. The `Now` property of the `DateTime` object will return the current date and time.

NOTE

You can also store cookies for longer periods of time. The following code stores the cookie for an hour:

```
Response.Cookies["Name"].
Expires = DateTime.Now.
AddHours(1);
```

Creating a Session

The Session object stores data for individual Web site visitors while they have an active connection to the server. A session can start at any time while the user accesses pages from the site but ends when she has been inactive for specified amount of time (20 minutes by default). Each user is assigned a unique ID known as the SessionID. The ID is stored as a cookie on the user's computer. All the session data is stored in memory, but ASP.NET allows you to change this, as you will learn later in this chapter:

```
<html>
    <head>
        <title>Creating a Session</title>
        <script language="C#" runat="server">
void Page_Load(Object Sender, EventArgs E)
{
    Response.Write("<h2>Creating a Session</h2>");
    Response.Write("Creating a Session Variable called Name (Session[\"Name\"]) <BR>");

    Session["Name"] = "Celine";

    Response.Write("Retrieving a Session Variable called Name (Session[\"Name\"]): " +
    Session["Name"] + "<BR>");
    Response.Write("Retrieving the unique SessionID (Session.SessionID): " +
    Session.SessionID);

}
        </script>
    </head>
    <body>
    </body>
</html>
```

1. Insert opening and closing \<script\> tags. Set the language attribute to C# and the runat attribute to server.

2. Insert a Page_Load method. This method will execute when the page loads.

3. Type the name of the session variable within quotation marks between square brackets of the Session object. You use square brackets to access indexed properties of the Session object in C#.

4. Use the equal sign (=) to store data in the session variable.

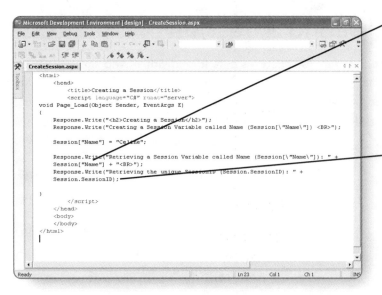

5. Type the name of the session variable within quotation marks between square brackets of the `Session` object to retrieve the data stored in the session variable.

6. Type `Session.SessionID` to retrieve the unique ID assigned to the user.

Retrieving Multiple Session Variables

You can create numerous session variables, but keep in mind that session data by default is stored in memory. The `Session` object has a `count` property that returns the number of session variables stored. You can also iterate over the `Session.Contents` collection, to return all the session data currently being stored:

1. Create and store data in at least three session variables.

2. Retrieve the `Count` property of the `Session` object. This will return the number of session variables stored for a particular user.

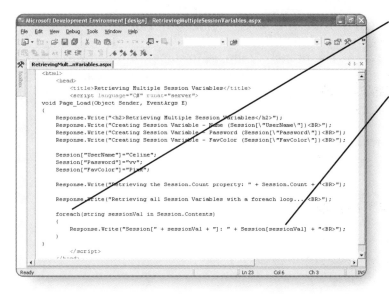

3. Use a `foreach` loop to iterate through the `Session.Contents` collection.

4. Use the `Response.Write` method to print the contents of each session variable to the page.

Abandoning a Session

A session will terminate if the user has not requested a page for 20 minutes. You can use the `Timeout` property of the session object to change the default time limit. When a session is terminated, all session variables are deleted. You can use the `Abandon` method, which terminates a session, on a logout page:

1. Set the `Timeout` property. You must set the `Timeout` property in terms of minutes.

2. Call the `Abandon` method to delete a session.

Configuring Session State with the web.config File

You use the <sessionState> tag in the web.config file to configure the way ASP.NET handles sessions. The mode attribute specifies where session state is stored. InProc is a default setting and stores session data in memory. Later in this chapter, you'll learn about the StateServer and SQLServer modes.

Here is the complete syntax for a <sessionState> tag:

```
<sessionState
  mode = "InProc" | "SQLServer" | "StateServer" | "off"
  cookieLess = "true" | "false"
  timeout = 40
/>
```

NOTE

The timeout attribute specifies the amount of time a user can remain inactive before his session data is deleted.

Creating Cookieless Sessions

Sessions use cookies to store the SessionID on a user's computer. The SessionID associates a user with the data stored on a server. A user can choose not to accept cookies from a Web site or disable the use of cookies altogether. In ASP.NET, you can store session variables without using cookies, which is a major improvement. You don't even need to make any changes to your code. You enable cookieless sessions in the web.config file. Once you enable a cookieless session, the unique ID is appended to all URLs:

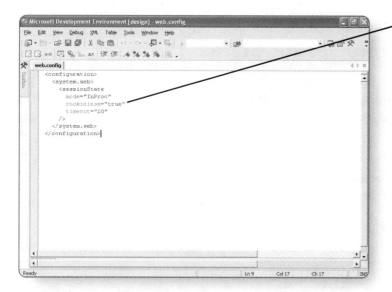

1. Set the `cookieless` attribute to `True`.

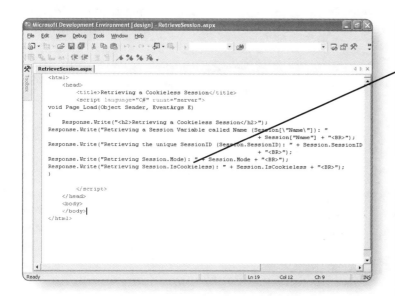

NOTE

You can use the `IsCookieless` property to determine whether cookieless sessions are enabled.

NOTE

The Session ID is added to the `QueryString` when the `cookieless` attribute is set to `True`.

Using State Server to Store Session State

By default, session state is stored in memory, which limits the scalability of an ASP.NET application. This is also not practical when you use multiple servers to handle browser requests in a Web farm in which multiple servers can handle browser requests. You must store session state in a location that is accessible to all servers. The whole process should be transparent the user. In ASP.NET, you can set up a special server that just processes user sessions. State Server is a Windows service that must be started from the Computer Management Console (CMC). It also stores session data in memory but has the advantage of being accessible by other servers in a Web farm. You don't need to make any changes to your code; you change only the web.config file:

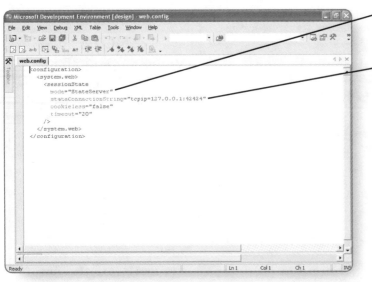

1. Set the `mode` attribute in the web.config file to `StateServer`.

2. Insert a `stateConnectionString` attribute within the `<sessionState>` tag.

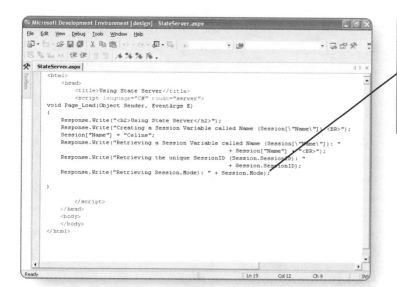

```
Microsoft Development Environment [design] - StateServer.aspx
File  Edit  View  Debug  Tools  Window  Help

StateServer.aspx
<html>
    <head>
        <title>Using State Server</title>
        <script language="C#" runat="server">
void Page_Load(Object Sender, EventArgs E)
{
    Response.Write("<h2>Using State Server</h2>");
    Response.Write("Creating a Session Variable called Name (Session[\"Name\"]) <BR>");
    Session["Name"] = "Celine";
    Response.Write("Retrieving a Session Variable called Name (Session[\"Name\"]): "
                            + Session["Name"] + "<BR>");
    Response.Write("Retrieving the unique SessionID (Session.SessionID): "
                            + Session.SessionID);
    Response.Write("Retrieving Session.Mode): " + Session.Mode);


}

        </script>
    </head>
    <body>
    </body>
</html>
```

NOTE

You can use the `Mode` property to determine where user sessions are stored.

Using SQL Server to Store Session State

You can also store session variables in an SQL Server database that can be accessed by other servers in a Web farm. The major advantage of using a database is that data won't be lost if the server crashes. This method is scalable because it is not dependant upon memory. It is slightly slower than using State Server. You must configure the web.config file before session data is stored in a SQL Server database:

1. Create a database using the InstallSqlState.sql file located in C:\Program Files\ASP.NET\Premium\V1.0Beta2 folder. This file contains SQL to create a database called ASPState, which consists of two tables and stored procedures.

2. Type the following:

```
osql servername username password C:\Program Files\
ASP.NET\Premium\

V1.0Beta2\ InstallSqlState.sql
```

servername is the name and port of SQL Server at the command prompt.

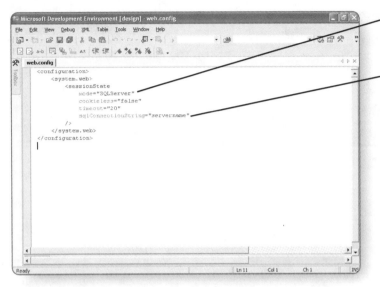

3. Set the mode attribute in the web.config file to `SQLServer`.

4. Insert an `SqlConnectionString` **attribute** within the `<sessionState>` **tag.**

5. Assign the database connection string to the `SqlConnectionString` **attribute.**

Managing Session State

The performance of ASP.NET applications can be improved by either disabling session state or making it read-only.

Disabling session state at a page level:

```
<%@ Page enableSessionState="false" %>
```

Making session state read-only:

```
<%@ Page enableSessionState="ReadOnly" %>
```

Creating Application Variables

Although sessions and cookies store data for individual users, application variables store data that all users can access. You must lock application variables before you update them to prevent multiple pages from accessing variables at the same time. The following example implements a page counter:

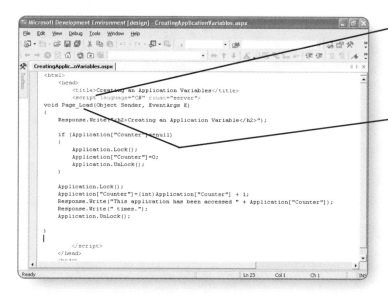

1. Insert opening and closing `<script>` tags. Set the `language` attribute to `C#` and the `runat` attribute to `server`.

2. Insert a `Page_Load` method. This method will execute when the page loads.

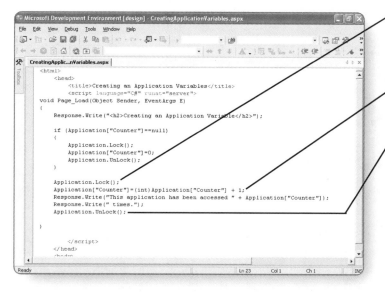

3. Call the `Lock` method. Only the current page will have access to application variables.

4. Assign a value to an application variable.

5. Call the `UnLock` method. The application variables will be available to all other pages.

16

Configuring and Deploying Web Applications

In ASP.NET, each Web application can have its own settings. The web.config file stores the settings in an XML format that you can easily edit. You can also define event handlers in C# for application-specific events. You must place the event handlers in the global.asax file, which gets compiled when the first page in an application is accessed. You deploy ASP.NET applications by simply copying a virtual directory to another server. In this chapter, you'll learn to:

- Create a global.asax file.
- Create a web.config file.
- Store application-specific data in a web.config file.
- Deploy an ASP.NET application.

Creating a global.asax File

Each virtual folder on your Web server is considered an ASP.NET application. An application is initialized when a user requests the first page contained in a virtual folder. You can use the global.asax file to code event handlers for application-specific events such as Application_Start and Application_End. The global.asax file gets compiled into a .NET Framework class when a user requests the first page.

> **NOTE**
>
> An HttpApplication object actually gets created when a user accesses the first page within an application.

The following global.asax file defines handlers for the Application_Start, Application_End, Application_BeginRequest, Application_EndRequest, Session_Start, and Session_End events:

1. Insert opening and closing <script> tags. Set the language attribute to C# and the runat attribute to server.

> **TIP**
>
> You can also import namespaces in a global.asax file.

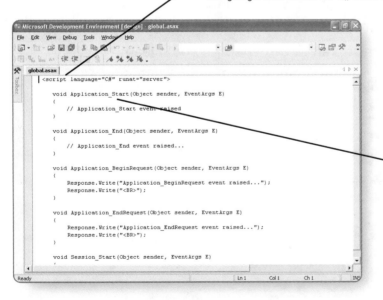

2. Insert a method called Application_Start. Place the code that must execute when the event is fired within the opening and closing braces.

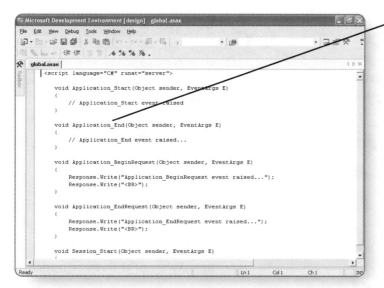

3. Insert a method called `Application_End`. Place the code that must execute when the event is fired within the opening and closing braces.

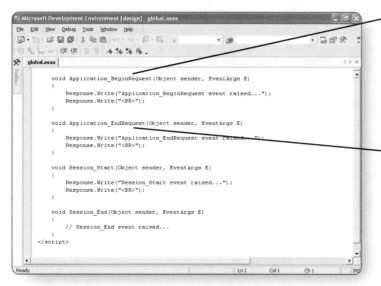

4. Insert a method called `Application_BeginRequest`. Place the code that must execute when the event is fired within the opening and closing braces.

5. Insert a method called `Application_EndRequest`. Place the code that must execute when the event is fired within the opening and closing braces.

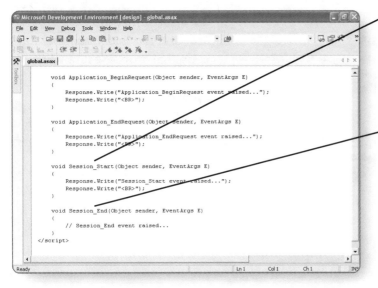

6. Insert a method called Session_Start. Place the code that must execute when the event is fired within the opening and closing braces.

7. Insert a method called Session_End. Place the code that must execute when the event is fired within the opening and closing braces.

8. Save the file as global.asax in the root of the virtual folder.

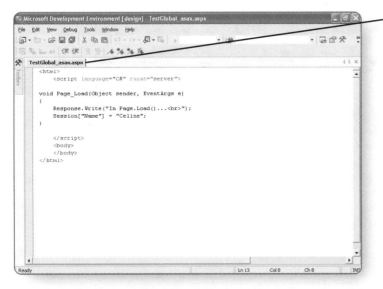

9. Create a simple .aspx page. This page will test the event handlers in the global.asax file.

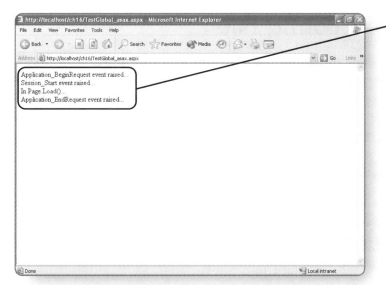

10. Preview the page in a Web browser. The event handler within the global.asax file will execute as the appropriate events are fired.

NOTE

The example executes the following events:

```
Application_BeginRequest
Application_EndRequest
Session_Start
```

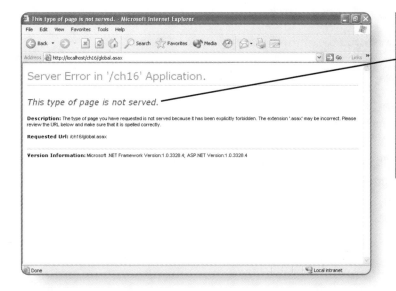

NOTE

You cannot display the global.asax file in a Web browser. This error message gets displayed when you try to view a global.asax file in a Web browser.

Using the web.config File

The web.config file is an XML document that stores custom settings for an ASP.NET application. You have already used the web.config file to enable tracing (Chapter 8), specify custom error pages (Chapter 8), and change the way ASP.NET stores session data (Chapter 15). You can edit the web.config file with any text editor. You can even change it programmatically. Changes made to the web.config file take immediate effect. You don't need to restart the Web server. You can place the web.config file in any folder; all subfolders inherit the settings.

The machine.config file stores the default settings for the whole Web server. The machine.config file is located in WinNT\Microsoft.NET\Framework\<version>\ config. Any changes you make in the web.config file overwrite these settings for the current folder.

The structure of a web.config file follows:

- The `<configuration>` tag must be the root element of the XML document.
- The `<configSections>` tag defines handlers.
- The `<system.web>` tag stores the ASP.NET configuration settings.
- The `<system.net>` tag stores .NET runtime settings.

NOTE

The machine.config file already sets the default for the `<configSections>` and `<system.net>` sections, so you only need to be concerned with the `<system.web>` section.

Here is an example of a web.config file that uses the `sessionState`, `trace`, and `customErrors` tags to configure an application:

1. Create a new web.config file and save it to the root directory of your web application.

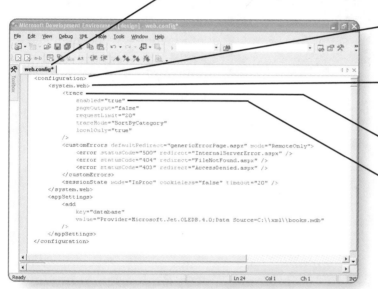

2. Insert opening and closing `<configuration>` tags.

3. Insert opening and closing `<system.web>` tags.

4. Insert a `trace` tag.

5. Set the `enabled` attribute to `True`. This will turn on tracing for all the pages placed in the same folder as the web.config file.

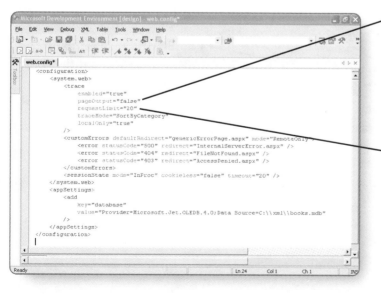

6. Set the mode `pageOutput` to `False`. This means that trace information will not appear at the end of each page. You will access the trace information using the trace.axd utility.

7. Set the `requestLimit` to 20. The `requestLimit` specifies the number of times to collect page-tracing information. The default value is 10.

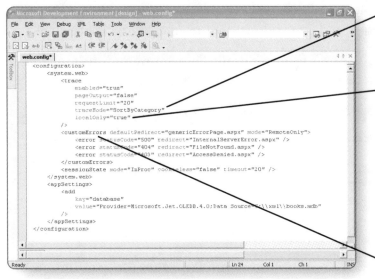

8. Set the `traceMode` to `SortByCategory`. `SortByTime` is the default.

9. Set the `localOnly` attribute to `True`. This means that trace information will only be available to localhost users. You will be able to display tracing information even while your application is being accessed by external users.

10. Insert a `customErrors` tag.

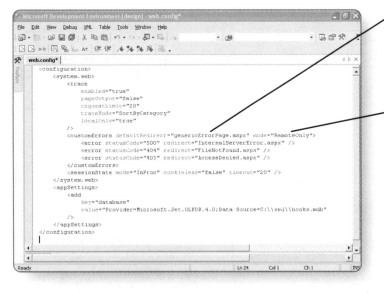

11. Set the `defaultRedirect` attribute to the page that must appear when an exception is thrown.

12. Set the `mode` attribute to `On`. You could also set the `mode` attribute to `Off` or `RemoteOnly`.

13. Insert an `<error>` tag and set the status code to 500. Set the `redirect` attribute to the file that will handle internal server errors.

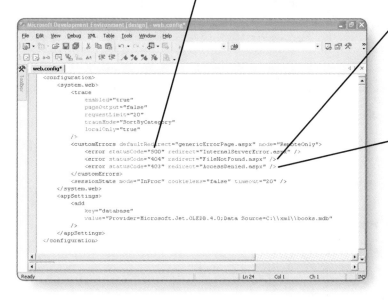

14. Insert an `<error>` tag and set the status code to 404. Set the `redirect` attribute to the file that must display when the requested file can't be found.

15. Insert an `<error>` tag and set the status code to 403. Set the `redirect` attribute to the file that must display when the user does not have the appropriate access privileges to view the requested page.

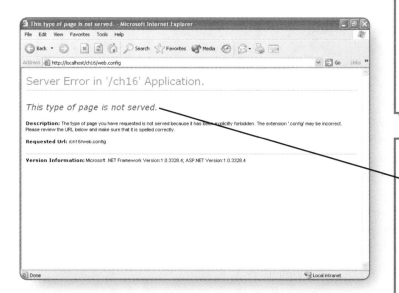

TIP
The web.config file is case sensitive. You must adhere to the capitalization used in tag names and properties or you will produce errors.

NOTE
You cannot display the web.config file in a Web browser. This error message gets displayed when you try to view a web.config file in a Web browser.

> **TIP**
> A web.config file placed in the wwwroot folder of your Web server will apply to all Web applications.

Storing Custom Settings in the web.config File

You can also use the web.config file as a centralized storage area for your Web application. You should store in one location the data used by many pages so you can easily update it. A database connection string is an ideal candidate, as you will see in the following example:

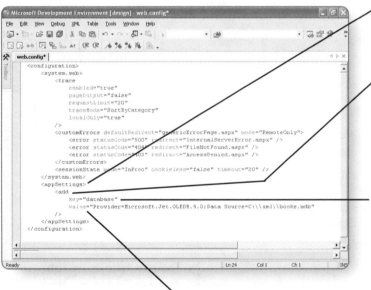

1. Insert an `<appSettings>` tag within the `<system.web>` tag in the web.config file.

2. Insert an `add` tag.

3. Set the `key` attribute. You are creating a constant named `database`.

4. Set the `value` attribute. You are storing the connection string that connects to the database.

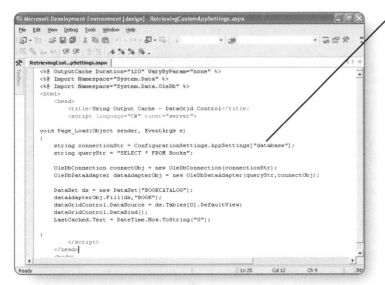

5. You can retrieve the data by passing the key within square brackets to the `ConfigurationSettings.AppSettings` **object.**

Deploying an ASP.NET Application

Deploying Web applications has never been easier. All you need to do is copy a virtual folder to another server. Both the global.asax and the web.config files will be contained within the folder, and ASP.NET will configure the application accordingly. There is no need to restart or reboot the server.

You can put a special /bin subdirectory in each virtual folder. The folder stores compiled DLLs that could include the business objects or custom controls your application uses. You can run multiple versions of the same application that uses different versions of the same DLL. This feature provides a handy solution to what was once known as DLL hell, whereby applications "broke" when a DLL was upgraded.

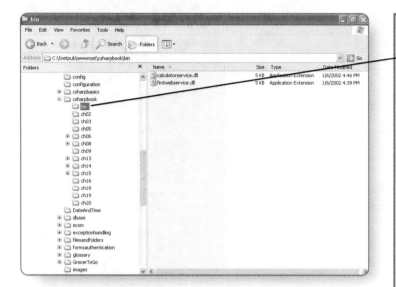

NOTE

An assembly is a class file that has been deployed. The Common Language Runtime (CLR) has both global and local assemblies. The global assembly is available to all applications. The local assembly is specific to a particular application. The \bin directory creates a local assembly. Each web application can execute in a local assembly and therefore use different versions of the same DLL.

You can also upgrade library files (that is, DLLs) without rebooting or restarting the server. The CLR uses the copy of the assembly that is stored in memory. You can modify a library file at any time because it does not get locked. The CLR will detect any changes and load the updated DLL library into memory. The copy of the library file that is stored in memory by the CLR is known as a "shadow assembly."

17

Password Protection

Not everything on the Web is freely accessible. Sometimes you need to register or pay a fee before you are allowed to view content. In ASP.NET, you can restrict areas of your Web site to users with the appropriate credentials. ASP.NET offers three modes of authentication: Windows, forms, and a service called Passport. Forms authentication, which provides the most flexibility, is the focus of this chapter. In this chapter, you'll learn to:

- Use Windows authentication.
- Configure the web.config file to handle Forms Authentication.
- Create a login form.
- Password protect pages in your Web site.
- Log a user out.

Windows Authentication

Windows authentication, as its name suggests, is based upon the security settings within the Windows operating system. When you request a page from an IIS Web site, you are automatically given anonymous access. Windows authentication is easy to set up and requires little or no coding on your part. However, it does not provide a lot of flexibility.

Windows XP uses a role-based security model. Each user is assigned to a group with predefined privileges. The Administrator group, for example, would have permission to install new software and change configuration settings. The Guest group, on the other hand, may only be able to browse files.

The IUSR_MachineName user is the default role assigned. No password is required because the IUSR_MachineName is allowed anonymous access.

You will create a new user assigned to the Guest group. You will also password-protect a virtual folder. When a user tries to access any page in this folder, a login dialog box will appear:

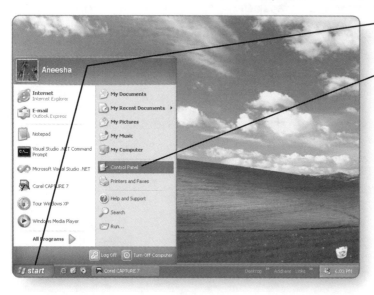

1. Click on Start. The Start Menu will appear.

2. Click on Control Panel. The Control Panel window will open.

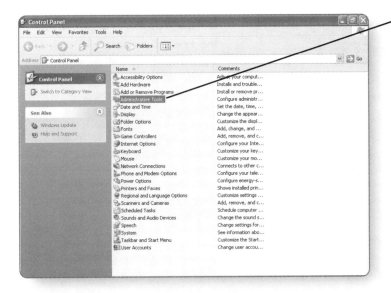

3. Double-click on the Administrative Tools icon. The Administrative Tools window will open.

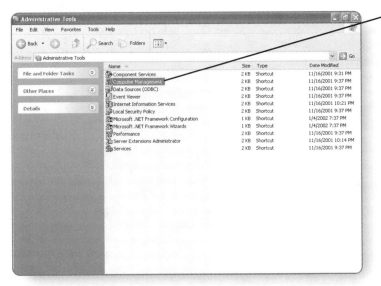

4. Double-click on the Computer Management icon. The Computer Management window will open.

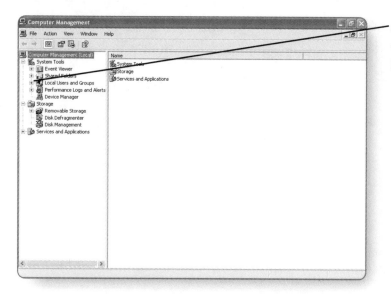

5. Click on the + sign next to the Local Users and Groups icon. The node will expand.

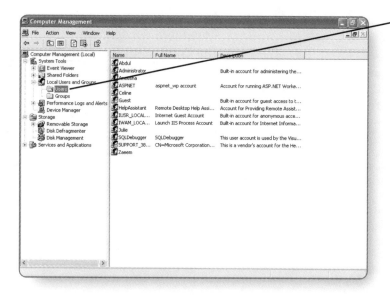

6. Click on the Users folder. A list of users will appear.

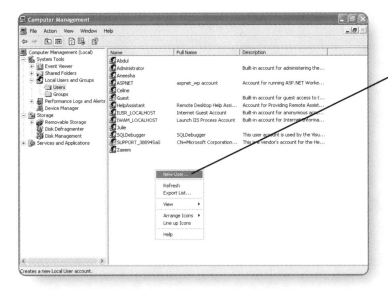

7. Right-click on the left pane. A submenu will appear.

8. Click on New User. The New User window will open.

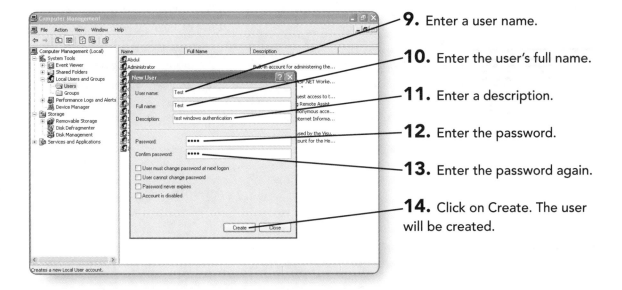

9. Enter a user name.

10. Enter the user's full name.

11. Enter a description.

12. Enter the password.

13. Enter the password again.

14. Click on Create. The user will be created.

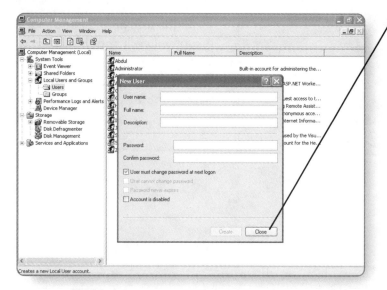

15. Click on Close. The New User window will close.

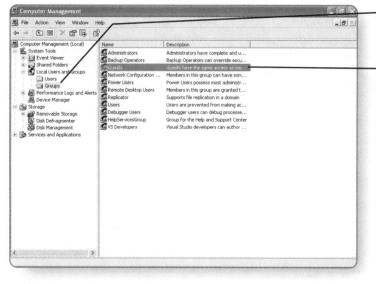

16. Click on the Groups folder. A list of Groups will appear.

17. Double-click on Guests. The Guests Properties window will open.

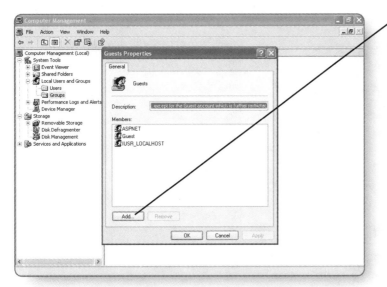

18. Click on Add. The Select Users or Groups window will open and display a list of users.

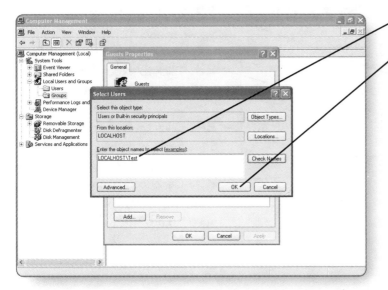

19. Enter the Username.

20. Click on OK. The user will be added to the group.

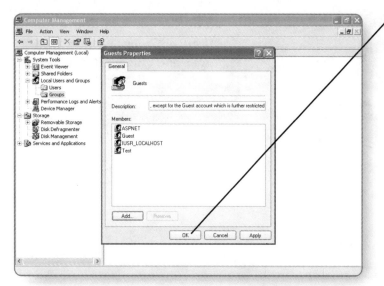

21. Click on OK. The Guest Properties window will close.

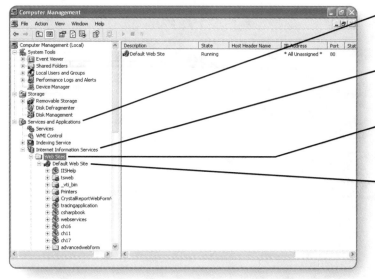

22. Click to expand the Services and Applications node.

23. Click to expand the Internet Information Services node.

24. Click to expand the Web Sites node.

25. Click to expand the Default Web Site node. The list of folders in your Web site will appear.

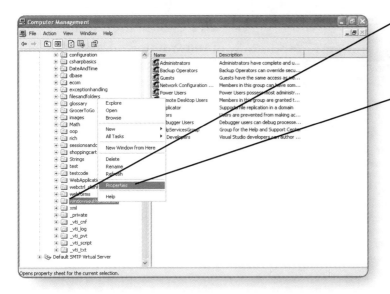

26. Right-click on the folder you want to password-protect. A submenu will appear.

27. Click on Properties. The Properties window will open.

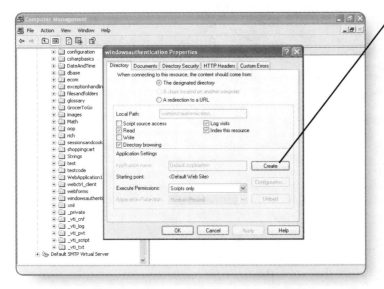

28. Click on Create. The folder will be converted to an ASP.NET application.

29. Click on the Directory Security tab. The Directory Security tab will be displayed.

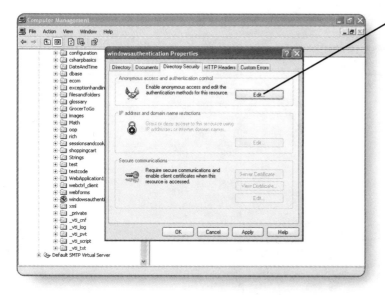

30. Click on Edit. The Authentication Methods dialog box will open.

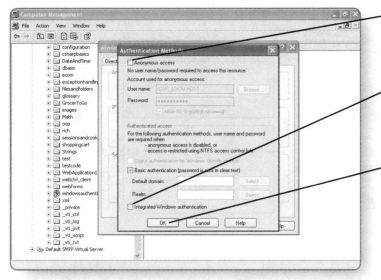

31. Click on the Anonymous Access checkbox. The checkbox will be unchecked.

32. Click on the Integrated Windows checkbox. The checkbox will be unchecked.

33. Click on OK. The Authentication Methods dialog box will close.

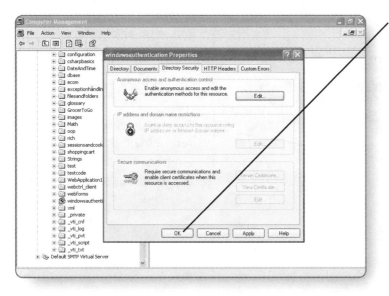

34. Click on OK. The Properties dialog box will close.

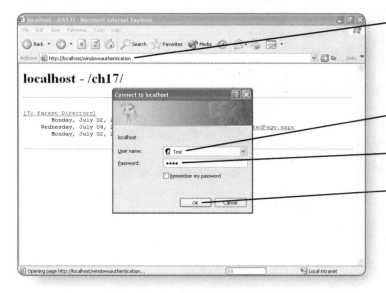

35. Access a page that resides in the password-protected Web application. A login dialog box will open.

36. Enter the user name.

37. Enter the password.

38. Click on OK. The page will load if the details are correct.

CAUTION

Basic Windows authentication transfers the user name and password as regular text. It uses no encryption.

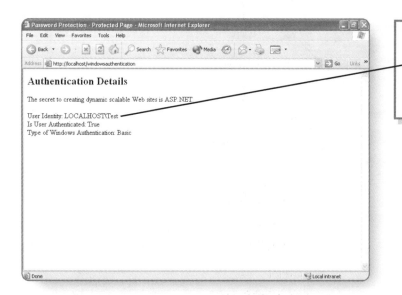

NOTE

You can programmatically determine the identity of a user.

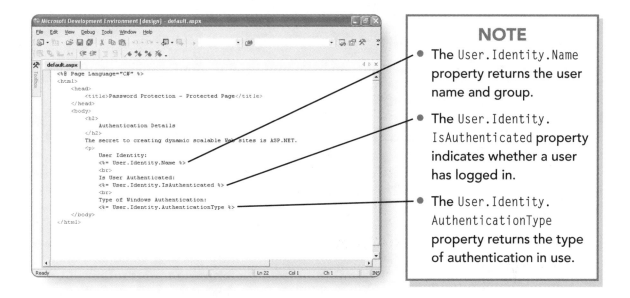

NOTE

- The `User.Identity.Name` property returns the user name and group.

- The `User.Identity.IsAuthenticated` property indicates whether a user has logged in.

- The `User.Identity.AuthenticationType` property returns the type of authentication in use.

NOTE

The browser will store your login details until it is closed.

Forms Authentication

Forms authentication is more flexible and lets you implement custom security solutions. You can store user credentials in the web.config file, an XML document, or a database. You are also free to design your own login form. Face it: The gray login dialog box the Windows authentication security model uses might not match the visual appearance of your site.

Setting the web.config File

The web.config file plays an important role in authentication. You use it to specify the authentication model used by ASP.NET. You can also store credentials (user name and password) for users with access to the protected folder.

The web.config file provides a central location where you can change the type of authentication at any time:

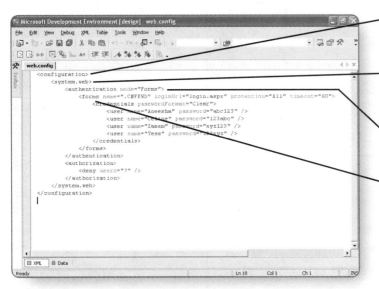

1. Insert opening and closing `<configuration>` tags.

2. Insert opening and closing `<system.web>` tags.

3. Insert opening and closing `<authentication>` tags.

4. Insert opening and closing `<forms>` tags. Set the mode attribute to `Forms`. This will enable Forms Authentication.

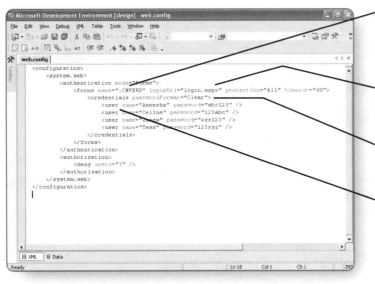

5. Set the `name` attribute. This is the name of the cookie that gets stored on the user's computer.

6. Set the `loginUrl` attribute. This must specify the login form.

7. Insert opening and closing `<credentials>` tags.

8. Insert a `<user>` tag for each user that can access the site.

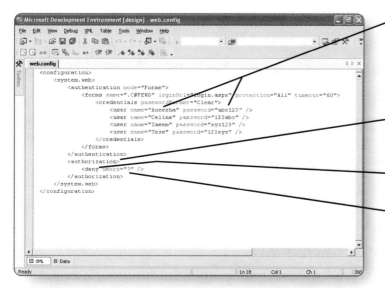

9. Set the `name` and `password` attributes for each user.

10. Insert opening and closing `<authorization>` tags.

11. Insert a `<deny>` tag.

12. Set the `users` attribute to ?. This will force all anonymous users to log in before they can access any files on the site.

Creating a Login Form

The login form allows the user to enter her user name and password. The `FormsAuthentication.Authenticate` method will validate her details against the credentials stored in the web.config file. The `FormsAuthentication.` `RedirectFromLoginPage` will redirect the user back to the password protected page that she was trying to access:

1. Insert opening and closing `<form>` tags. Set the `runat` attribute to `server`.

2. Insert a `textbox` control. The user name will be entered into this control.

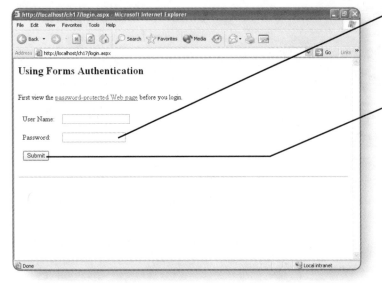

3. Insert a textbox control with the mode attribute set to password. The password will be entered into this control.

4. Insert a button control. The OnClick event will execute the Login method.

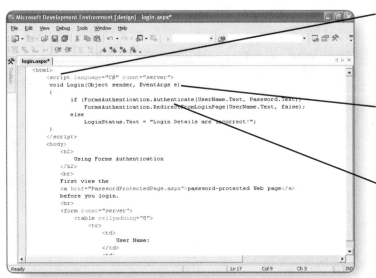

5. Insert opening and closing script tags. Set the language attribute to C# and the runat attribute to server.

6. Insert a Login method. This method will execute when the user clicks the Login button.

7. Use the FormsAuthentication. Authenticate method to determine whether the user name and password are valid. Pass the user name and password that the user enters to the FormsAuthentication. Authenticate method.

NOTE

The FormsAuthentication.Authenticate method validates users against the data that is stored in the <credentials> tag in the web.config file. You can also write your own method that validates users against a database or an XML file.

8. Execute the FormsAuthentication.RedirectFromLoginPage method if the FormsAuthentication.Authenticate method returns True.

9. Inform the user whether his login details are incorrect.

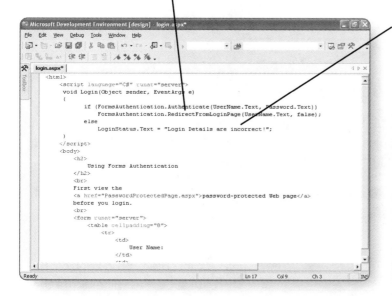

NOTE

The URL of the password-protected page is stored in the query string. The FormsAuthentication.RedirectFromLoginPage uses this information to redirect the user back to the page he was requesting.

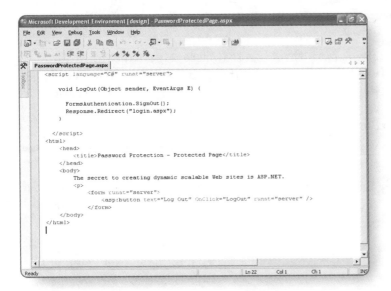

Creating a Password-Protection Page

You don't need to insert any code to password-protect a page. You just need to place it in a folder that has a web.config file with the appropriate settings.

Logging Out a User

Logging out is also easy, thanks to the FormsAuthentication. SignOut method. All the pages in your site can have a logout button that will log out the user:

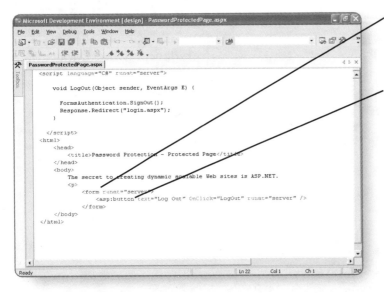

1. Insert opening and closing form tags. Set the runat attribute to server.

2. Insert a button control. The OnClick event will execute the Logout method.

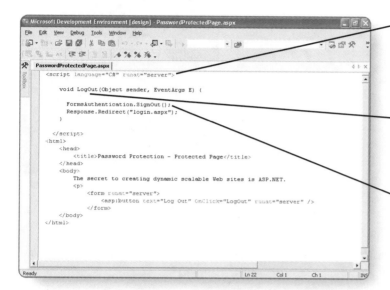

```
Microsoft Development Environment [design] - PasswordProtectedPage.aspx
File  Edit  View  Debug  Tools  Window  Help

PasswordProtectedPage.aspx

<script language="C#" runat="server">

    void LogOut(Object sender, EventArgs E) {

    FormsAuthentication.SignOut();
    Response.Redirect("login.aspx");
    }

</script>
<html>
    <head>
        <title>Password Protection - Protected Page</title>
    </head>
    <body>
        The secret to creating dynamic scalable Web sites is ASP.NET.
        <p>
            <form runat="server">
                <asp:button text="Log Out" OnClick="LogOut" runat="server" />
            </form>
    </body>
</html>
```

3. Insert opening and closing `<script>` tags. Set the `language` attribute to `C#` and the `runat` attribute to `server`.

4. Insert a `LogOut` method. This method will execute when the user clicks the LogOut button.

5. Call the `FormsAuthentication.SignOut` method.

Passport Authentication

Passport authentication is the third type of authentication that ASP.NET offers. Passport authentication is actually a service that Microsoft provides. A user can obtain a passport account for free. Once a user authenticates to the passport service, she can access all sites that implement passport authentication. Many of Microsoft's sites already use Passport; Hotmail is one popular site that comes to mind. To implement Passport authentication on your Web site you must be a member of the service, which involves paying a fee.

NOTE

You can visit the Passport Web site at **http://www.passport.com**. There you can download the SDK to implement Passport authentication.

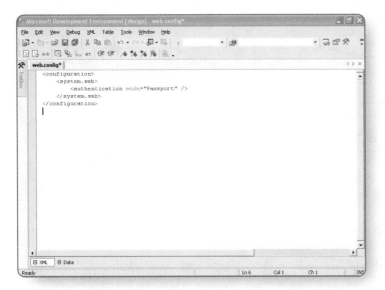

NOTE

You must set the mode attribute to Passport to implement Passport authentication.

18

Processing XML in C#

The Extensible Markup Language (XML) is a universally supported format for data storage and exchange. XML is integral to the success of core .NET initiatives such as Web Services. As a result, the `System.Xml` namespace includes classes that simplify XML processing. In this chapter, you'll learn to:

- Create an XML document.

- Send XML to a browser.

- Use XSL to format XML.

- Use the `XmlWriter` class to generate XML documents.

- Use the `XmlReader` class to read an XML document.

- Generate XML from a database.

- Bind XML to a `DataGrid` control.

- Insert data into an XML document.

Understanding XML

XML is a standard way to tag and represent data. Before XML was adopted as the de-facto data exchange format, data was usually stored in proprietary formats. Common formats such as comma- or tab-delimited files have numerous problems. For example, you can't specify what each field in a comma-delimited file stores, and data can span only a single line. XML was designed to address all these issues. It uses tags to store data in a structured format that is easily processed. XML is platform-neutral and ideally suited for data exchange over the Internet.

Creating XML Documents

An XML document is a text file that uses tags to structure and store data in a hierarchical format. XML looks just like HTML, which is also a tag-based markup language. The major difference is that XML is only used to store data. It does not format data for display in a browser. XML is extensible in the sense that you can define the tags to represent your information. The XML document that follows stores a book catalog with tags that describe the title, author, publisher, and price of each book:

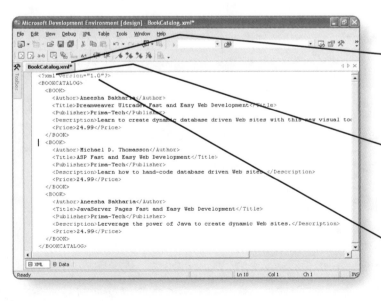

1. Create a new text file and save the file with an .xml extension. All XML documents must have .xml as an extension.

2. Use the `<?xml ?>` tag to define the XML document. This is the declaration tag for an XML document.

3. Set the `version` attribute of the `<?xml ?>` tag to `1.0`. This specifies the version that your XML complies to.

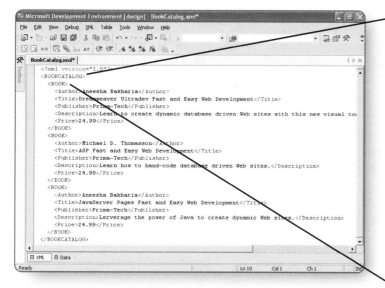

4. Insert an opening tag for the root element (BOOKCATALOG, in this example).

NOTE

All XML documents must have a root node to be valid. All tags must be placed within a root tag. The root tag describes the data set.

5. Insert an opening tag for the child node (BOOK, in this example).

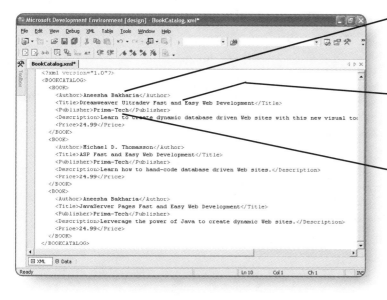

6. Type the name of the author between the opening and closing <AUTHOR> tags.

7. Type the title between the opening and closing <TITLE> tags.

8. Type the name of the publisher between the opening and closing <PUBLISHER> tags.

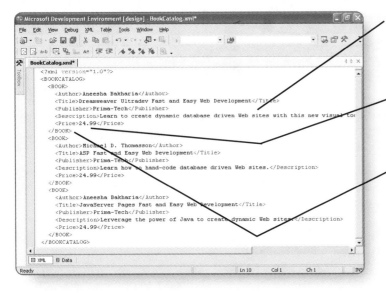

9. Type the description between the opening and closing <DESCRIPTION> tags.

10. Type the price between the opening and closing <PRICE> tags.

11. Insert a closing tag for the <BOOK> child tag.

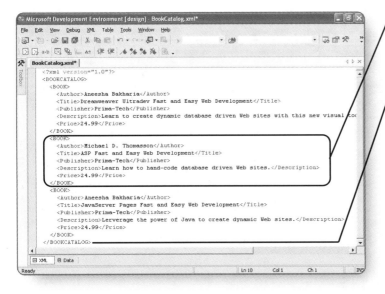

12. Repeat steps 5 through 11 for each book you want to include.

13. Insert a closing tag for the <BOOKCATALOG> root node.

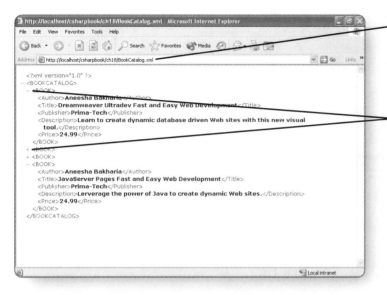

14. Preview the XML document in Microsoft Internet Explorer. A tree structure will represent the XML document.

15. You can click on the + sign next to expand the node, or you can click on the – sign next to a node to collapse the node.

Sending XML to a Browser

It is easy to dynamically render XML and send it to a Web browser in ASP.NET. All you need to do is change the content type of the page to `"text/xml"`:

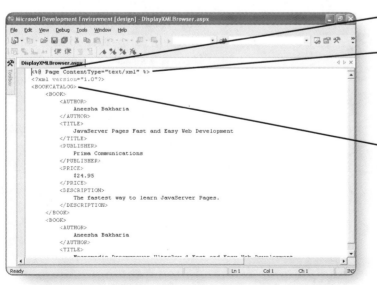

1. Insert the page directive.

2. Set the `ContentType` attribute to `"text/xml"`. This will inform the browser that data is being sent in an XML format.

3. Insert the tagged XML data in the .aspx page. It could be static data or dynamically generated.

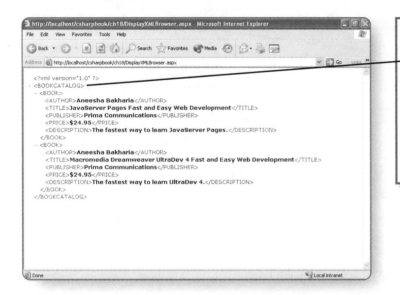

NOTE

Internet Explorer will display a tree structure that represents the data hierarchy in the XML document. You can click on the nodes to expand or collapse them.

Using XSL to Format XML

How do you output the XML data in a user-friendly manner? The Extensible Stylesheet Language (XSL) is the answer. XSL is a transformation language that extracts and formats the data from an XML document. XSL translates XML into different formats such as HTML. Here is a simple example that displays XML in an HTML table:

1. Create a new text file and save the file with an .xsl extension.

2. Use the `<?xml ?>` tag to define the XML document.

3. Set the version attribute of the `<?xml ?>` tag to 1.0.

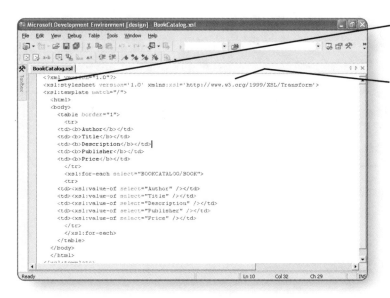

4. Insert an opening `<xsl:stylesheet>` tag.

5. Set the `<xmlns:xsl tag>` attribute to `http://www.w3.org/1999/XSL/Transform`.

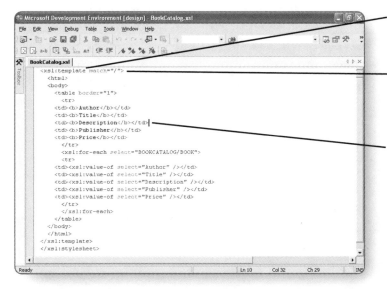

6. Insert an opening `<xsl:template>` tag.

7. Set the match attribute to /. This applies the template to the root of the XML document.

8. Insert the template HTML code to display a table.

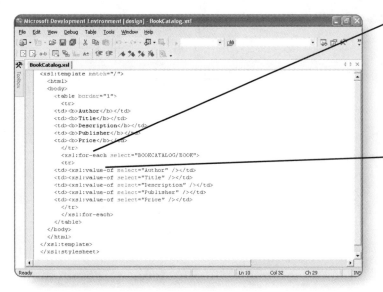

9. Insert the `<xsl:for-each>` tag to loop through all the BOOK child nodes that are found in the XML document. You must set the `select` attribute to BOOKCATALOG/BOOK.

10. Insert `<xsl:value-of>` to retrieve the tagged data from the XML document. The `select` attribute must specify the tag name.

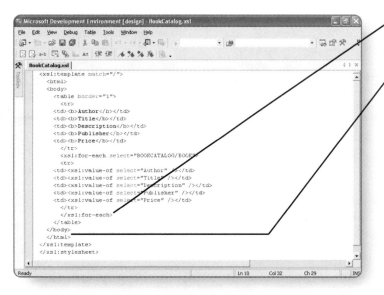

11. Insert a closing `<xsl:for-each>` tag.

12. Insert the closing HTML tags.

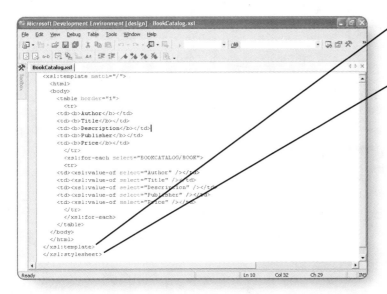

13. Insert a closing `<xsl:template>` tag.

14. Insert a closing `<xsl:stylesheet>` tag.

NOTE

XSL has many powerful features. You can use it to filter, manipulate, and sort XML data. Visit **http://www.w3schools.com/xsl** for a comprehensive introduction to XSL.

Using the XML Control

The XML server control applies an XSL stylesheet to an XML document and renders the resulting HTML output to a browser:

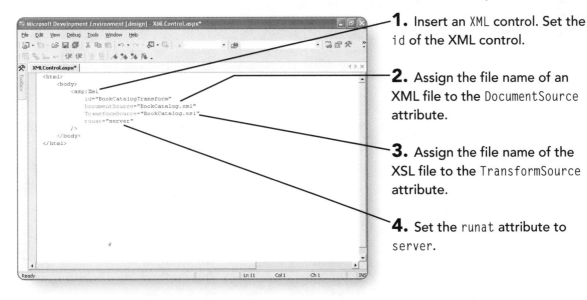

1. Insert an XML control. Set the id of the XML control.

2. Assign the file name of an XML file to the DocumentSource attribute.

3. Assign the file name of the XSL file to the TransformSource attribute.

4. Set the runat attribute to server.

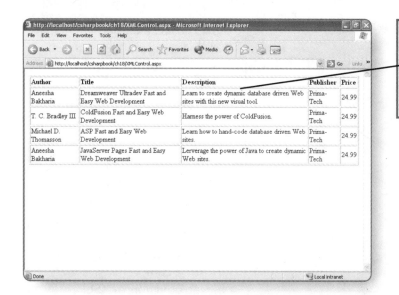

NOTE
You use XSL to generate the XML data as an HTML table.

Generating XML Documents

You use the XmlWriter class to generate well-formed XML that is fully compliant with the W3C's XML 1.0 specification. The XmlWriter class has methods that print data within opening and closing tags. The XmlWriter constructor will create a new file if the specified file does not exist:

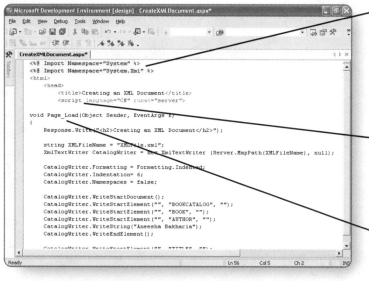

1. Import the System and System.Xml namespaces. The System.Xml namespace contains the XmlTextWriter class that you will use to create the XML document programmatically.

2. Insert opening and closing <script> tags. Set the language attribute to C# and the runat attribute to server.

3. Insert a Page_Load method. This method will execute when the page loads.

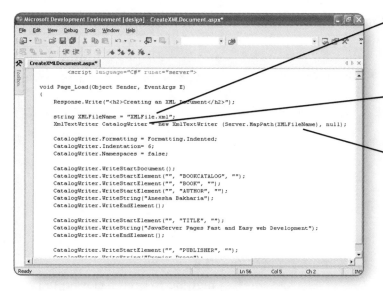

4. Declare a string variable and store the name of the XML file that must be created.

5. Create an instance of the `XmlTextWriter` class.

6. Pass the file name of the XML document to the `XmlTextWriter` constructor.

7. Set the `Formatting` property of the `XmlTextWriter` object to `Indented`. This will indent the XML tags according to their position in the document hierarchy.

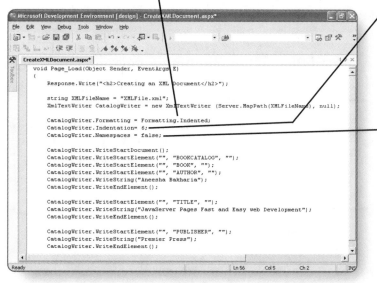

8. Set the `Indentation` property of the `XmlTextWriter` object to the number of spaces that must be used when indenting the tags.

9. Set the `Namespace` property of the `XmlTextWriter` object to `False`. The resulting XML document will not appear within a namespace.

10. Call the `WriteStartDocument` method. This will insert the `<?xml ?>` tag.

11. Use the `WriteStartElement` method to print an opening tag. You must pass the name of the tag as the second parameter.

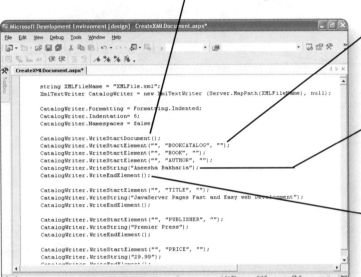

```
string XMLFileName = "XMLFile.xml";
XmlTextWriter CatalogWriter = new XmlTextWriter (Server.MapPath(XMLFileName), null);

CatalogWriter.Formatting = Formatting.Indented;
CatalogWriter.Indentation= 6;
CatalogWriter.Namespaces = false;

CatalogWriter.WriteStartDocument();
CatalogWriter.WriteStartElement("", "BOOKCATALOG", "");
CatalogWriter.WriteStartElement("", "BOOK", "");
CatalogWriter.WriteStartElement("", "AUTHOR", "");
CatalogWriter.WriteString("Aneesha Bakharia");
CatalogWriter.WriteEndElement();

CatalogWriter.WriteStartElement("", "TITLE", "");
CatalogWriter.WriteString("JavaServer Pages Fast and Easy web Development");
CatalogWriter.WriteEndElement();

CatalogWriter.WriteStartElement("", "PUBLISHER", "");
CatalogWriter.WriteString("Premier Press");
CatalogWriter.WriteEndElement();

CatalogWriter.WriteStartElement("", "PRICE", "");
CatalogWriter.WriteString("29.99");
CatalogWriter.WriteEndElement();
```

12. Use the `WriteString` method to print the tag data. The data appears after the opening tag.

13. Use the `WriteEndElement` method to print a closing tag. You must pass the name of the tag as the second parameter.

14. Repeat steps 11 through 13 for each tag that you want to insert.

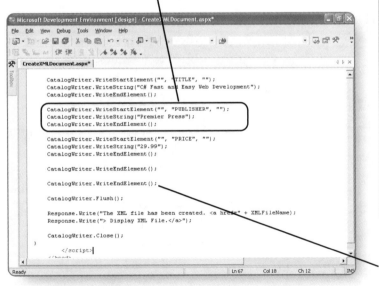

```
CatalogWriter.WriteStartElement("", "TITLE", "");
CatalogWriter.WriteString("C# Fast and Easy Web Development");
CatalogWriter.WriteEndElement();

CatalogWriter.WriteStartElement("", "PUBLISHER", "");
CatalogWriter.WriteString("Premier Press");
CatalogWriter.WriteEndElement();

CatalogWriter.WriteStartElement("", "PRICE", "");
CatalogWriter.WriteString("29.99");
CatalogWriter.WriteEndElement();

CatalogWriter.WriteEndElement();

CatalogWriter.WriteEndElement();

CatalogWriter.Flush();

Response.Write("The XML file has been created. <a href=" + XMLFileName);
Response.Write("> Display XML File.</a>");

CatalogWriter.Close();
}
    </script>
```

NOTE

You can nest the `WriteStartElement` and `WriteEndElement` methods. Here, the `Author`, `Title`, `publisher`, and `price` tags appear within the `Book` tag. All the `Book` tags appear within the `BookCatalog` root element.

15. Call the `WriteEndElement` method.

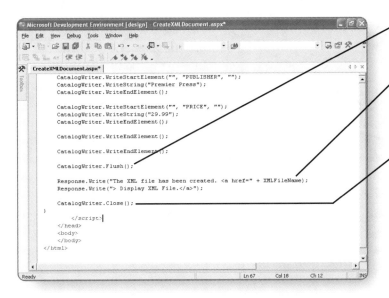

16. Call the Flush method. This will save the file.

17. Create a link to the generated file so that the user can view it from a Web browser.

18. Call the Close method.

Reading XML Documents

The XmlReader class, which appears in the System.Xml namespace, retrieves the nodes within an XML document in a fast-forward-only manner. The XmlReader uses a read-only cursor and can't be used to add nodes or update the data:

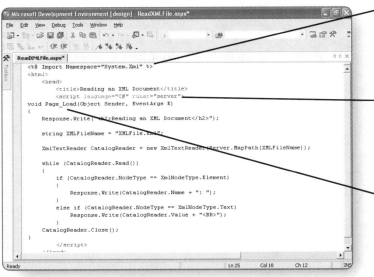

1. Import the System.Xml namespace. The System.Xml namespace contains the XmlTextReader class.

2. Insert opening and closing <script> tags. Set the language attribute to C# and the runat attribute to server.

3. Insert a Page_Load method. This method will execute when the page loads.

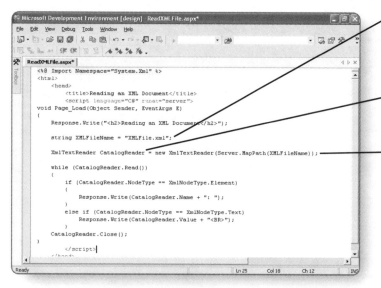

4. Declare a string variable and store the name of the XML file that must be read.

5. Create an instance of the `XmlTextReader` class.

6. Pass the file name of the XML document to the `XmlTextReader` constructor.

7. Use a `while` loop to iterate though each node in the XML document tree. The loop will end when the `Read` method of the `XmlTextReader` object returns `False`.

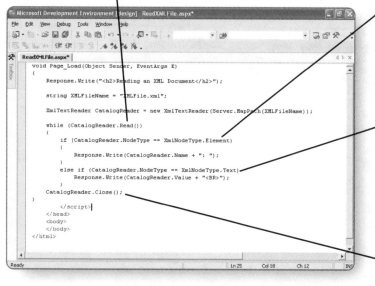

8. If the `NodeType` property of the `XmlReader` object is an `XmlNodeType.Element`, print the `Name` property to the page. This will print the name of the tag.

9. If the `NodeType` property of the `XmlReader` object is an `XmlNodeType.Text`, print the `Value` property to the page. This will print the data stored in the tag.

10. Call the `Close` method.

Using a Database to Generate XML

Proprietary data is usually stored in a database. This data must be converted to XML so others can understand and use it. This is easily achieved with the `WriteXml` method of the `DataSet` object. You first need to query the database and store the returned result in a `DataSet` object. This illustrates the power and flexibility that the `DataSet` object brings to XML processing:

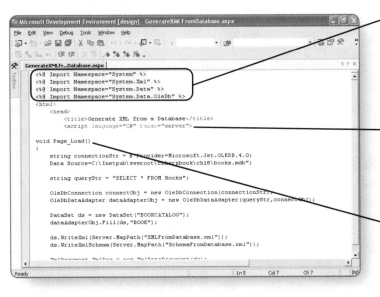

1. Import the `System`, `System.Xml`, `System.Data`, `System.Data.OleDB`, and the `System.Data.Common` namespaces.

2. Insert opening and closing `<script>` tags. Set the `language` attribute to `C#` and the `runat` attribute to `server`.

3. Insert a `Page_Load` method. This method will execute when the page loads.

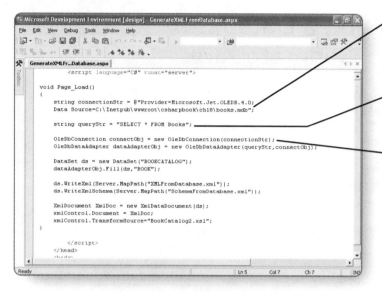

4. Declare a string variable and store the database connection details.

5. Declare a string variable and store the SQL query.

6. Create an instance of the `OleDbConnection` class. Pass the database connection string to the `OleDbConnection` constructor.

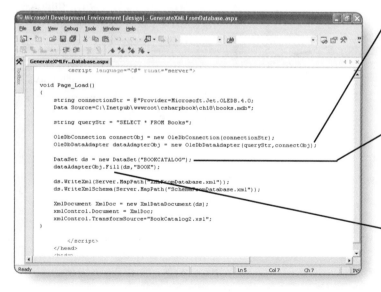

7. Create an instance of the `OleDbDataAdapter` class. Pass the SQL query and `OleDbConnection` object to the `OleDbDataAdapter` constructor.

8. Create a `DataSet` object. Pass the name of the root element in the XML document to the `DataSet` constructor.

9. Call the `Fill` method of the `OleDbDataAdapter` object to load each record that the query returns into the `DataSet` object.

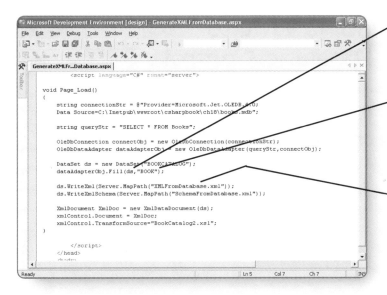

10. Pass the `DataSet` object as the first parameter to the `Fill` method.

11. Pass the name of the tag that must be used to represent each row returned from the database.

12. Call the `WriteXml` method of the `DataSet` object. This will save the XML file.

You will use the XML control to transform the data into HTML and display it in a browser.

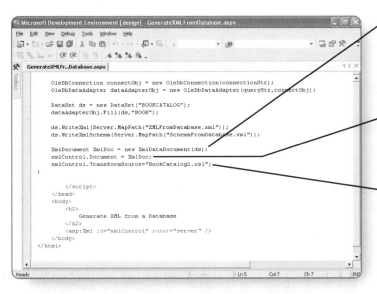

13. Create an `XmlDocument` object. You must pass the `DataSet` object to the `XmlDocument` constructor.

14. Set the `Document` property of the XML control to the `XmlDocument` object.

15. Set the `TransformSource` property to the XSL file. This file must transform XML to HTML.

Binding XML to a DataGrid Control

The `DataGrid` control can display XML data. Basically, you can load XML into a `DataSet` object, which can then be bound to a `DataGrid` control. The `ReadXml` method retrieves that data from an XML document and stores it in a `DataSet` object. This provides a practical solution for displaying XML data in a table:

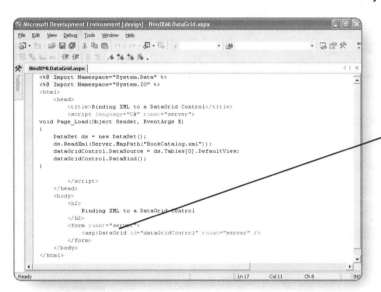

1. Insert a `DataGrid` control. Set the `id` attribute. Set the `runat` attribute to `server`. XML will be bound to this control.

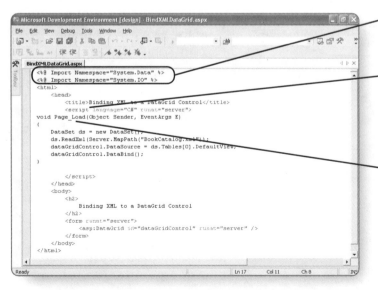

2. Import the `System.Xml` and `System.Data` namespaces.

3. Insert opening and closing `<script>` tags. Set the `language` attribute to `C#` and the `runat` attribute to `server`.

4. Insert a `Page_Load` method. This method will execute when the page loads.

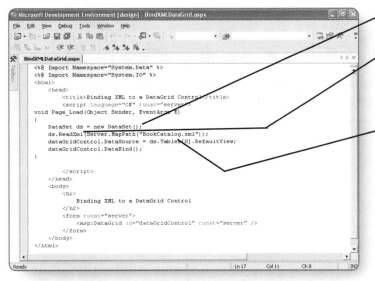

5. Create a `DataSet` object.

6. Call the `ReadXml` method. This method will load an XML file into a `DataSet` object.

7. Pass the XML file name to the `ReadXml` method.

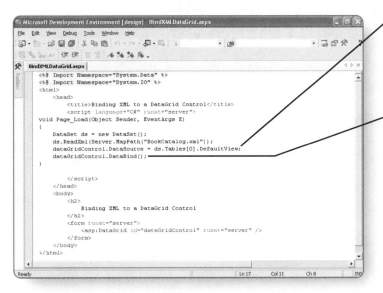

8. Assign the `DefaultView` property of the `DataSet` object to the `DataSource` property of the `DataGrid` control.

9. Call the `DataBind` method of the `DataGrid` control. The XML data will be bound to the control.

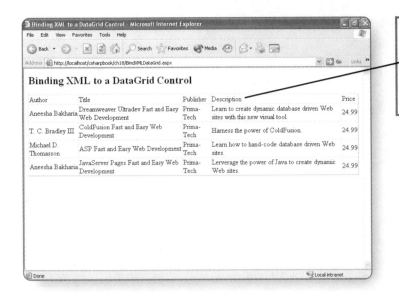

NOTE

The DataGrid control displays the XML data in a tabular form.

Inserting Data into an XML Document

The DataSet object contains methods to read, write, and insert new data into an XML document. The DataSet object is modeled with DataTable, DataColumn, and DataRow objects. You use the DataRow object to add new data to the DataSet object. This enables you to retrieve the XML data from a file, store it in a DataSet object, insert new data, and then save the data back to an XML file:

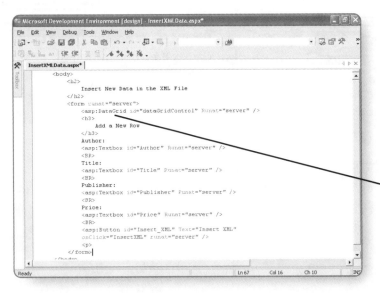

1. Insert a DataGrid control. Set the id attribute. Set the runat attribute to server. This control will display the data stored in the XML file.

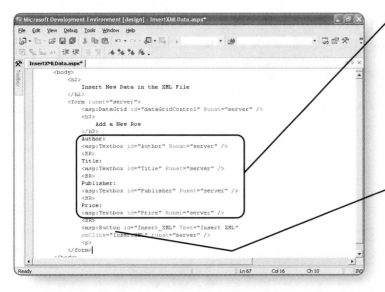

2. Insert a `TextBox` control for each attribute that makes up a new record in the XML document. In this example, each record has an `Author`, `Title`, `Publisher`, and `Price` field, so you insert a `TextBox` control for each.

3. Insert a `Button` control. Set the `OnClick` event to `InsertXML`. This method will insert the new data in the XML file.

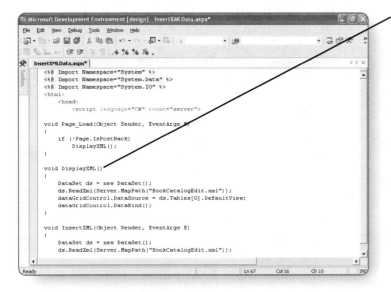

4. Insert a `DisplayXML` method. This method binds the XML data to the `DataGrid` control.

5. Insert an `InsertXML` method. This method will execute when the user clicks the `Insert_XML` button.

6. Create a `DataSet` object.

7. Call the `ReadXml` method. Pass the XML file name to the `ReadXml` method. This method will load an XML file into a `DataSet` object.

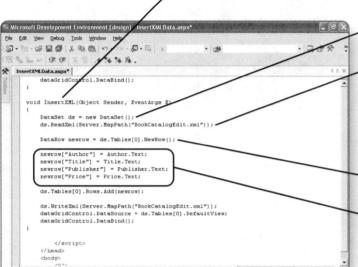

8. Create a new `DataRow` object.

9. Retrieve the data entered by the user and store it in the appropriate fields within the `DataRow` object. The field names must match the tag names in the XML document.

10. Call the `Add` method to add the row of data. You must pass the `DataRow` object to the `Add` method.

11. Call the `WriteXml` method. This method will save the XML file.

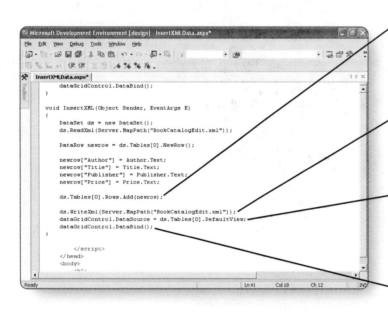

12. Assign the `DefaultView` property of the `DataSet` object to the `DataSource` property of the `DataGrid` control.

13. Call the `DataBind` method of the `DataGrid` control. The XML data will be bound to the control.

19

Creating Web Services

A *Web service* exposes application functionality on the Internet. You can offer your existing applications as a service for others to access over the Internet without worrying about compatibility issues. The true power of a Web service, however, stems from the fact that you can use Web services that other companies make available. If you want to validate a user's credit-card number, you just access the appropriate Web service from a credit-card company. Web services have the potential to revolutionize the way the Web is programmed. The hype that surrounds this innovative new technology is certainly founded. In this chapter, you'll learn to:

- Create a simple Web service.
- Generate a `Proxy` class.
- Consume Web services.
- Locate Web services offered by other companies.

What Is a Web Service?

A Web service creates a programmable interface for applications that reside on a Web server. In other words, a Web service exposes methods within an application and allows any client with access to the Web (the ability to communicate via HTTP) to call them. A Web service provides a new model for distributed computing that is platform and programming language independent. Web services make Microsoft's vision of delivering software as service come to life.

Although many companies have already Web-enabled their core business applications, these applications don't facilitate data exchange. Companies want to exchange business-critical data with their business partners in the most cost-effective manner. Web-enabling an application only provides an end-user interface that is rendered in HTML. Although it is not impossible to extract data from HTML, the code is specific and would have to change to suit the HTML you parse. You would also have to rewrite the code whenever the layout of a page got redesigned. XML provides only a partial solution because even though it is a self-describing data exchange format, you still need to parse it.

A Web service, on the other hand, provides seamless integration between disparate platforms. Web services use standard Internet protocols and are accessible via a URL. You can call methods in your application through HTTP requests and data is returned. This data exchange uses the Simple Object Access Protocol (SOAP), which stores complex data types in XML for transfer over the Internet.

In the next few sections, you'll discover just how easy it is to offer and use a Web service. I'm sure that the simplicity will amaze you.

Creating a Simple Web Service

You can implement any application as a Web service. You need to make only a couple of changes to an existing class to automatically generate a programmable interface. In fact, you can turn an application into a Web service without writing any HTML or ASP.NET code.

It's time to just jump right in and create a Web service. The Web service itself will be trivial, but remember that at this stage, the underlying concepts are what's important.

Here is the class that you will convert to a Web service. It contains a single method that returns some text:

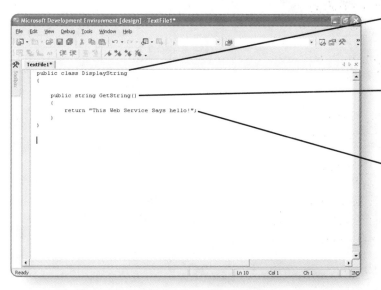

1. Create a public class. Type the name of the class after the `class` keyword.

2. Insert a public method called `GetString` that returns a string value.

3. Use the `return` keyword to return the string to the calling method. You must place the string in quotation marks and after the `return` keyword.

This code will form the basis of the Web service.

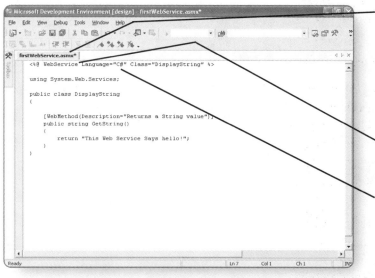

4. Create a new page and save it with an .asmx extension. You must save every Web service you create with an .asmx extension, and you must save the file to a virtual directory.

5. Insert a `WebService` directive as the first line in the .asmx file.

6. Set the `language` attribute to `C#`.

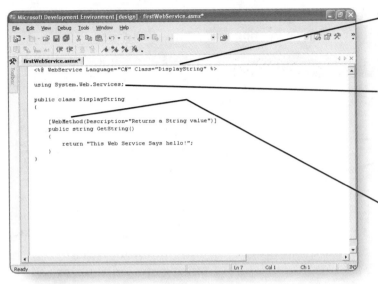

7. Set the `class` attribute to the name of the class contained in the file.

8. Import the `System.Web.Services` namespace. Use the `using` keyword to import a namespace.

9. Insert a `[WebMethod]` directive above the method that can be accessed through the Web service programmatically.

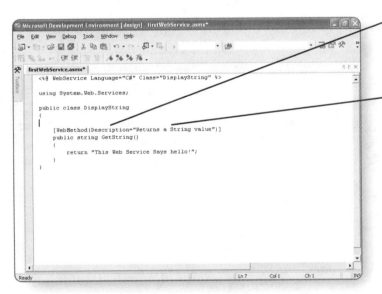

10. Enter a description for the method within the braces that follow the `WebMethod` keyword.

11. Assign a description to the `Description` attribute.

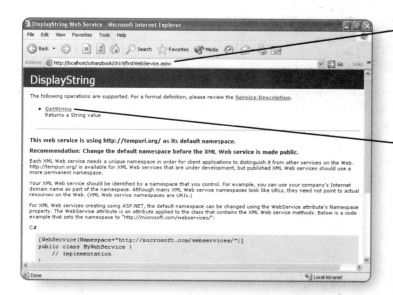

12. View the page in a Web browser. The .asmx file will be compiled when the initial request is made. You will see an interface for the Web service.

13. Click on the GetString link. A description of the method appears below the link. You will see a page that allows you to test the method.

NOTE

The interface lists all of the methods the Web service exposes. Any programmer who wants to use the Web service can access this documentation. You do not have to write any code to document the Web service; it happened automatically when the .asmx page was called.

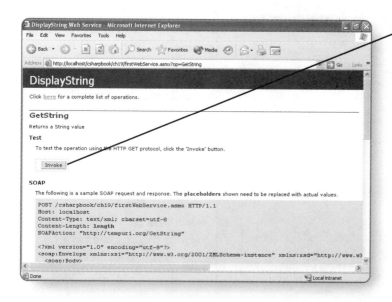

14. Click on Invoke. The GetString method will execute and return the resulting data in XML.

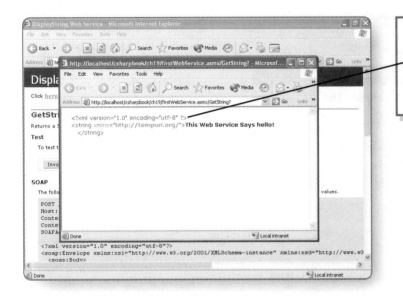

NOTE
The string that the
GetString method returns
is transferred as XML.

Viewing the WSDL Contract

The Web Service Description Language (WSDL) is an XML
document that describes methods exposed by the Web
service. The application accessing the Web service uses a
WSDL contract. The WSDL
documents methods, their
parameters, and return values.

1. Type **?wsdl** after the name
of the .asmx file in the URL.
The WSDL contract will appear.
It describes the methods and
the data types they return.

NOTE

Don't be concerned
about the complexity of
the WSDL contract
because you won't need
to use it directly.

Generating a Proxy Class

A Proxy class does all the hard work. It sends your method calls to a Web service and receives the SOAP-encoded WSDL response. The WSDL command-line tool (WSDL.exe) generates the source for the Proxy class. You must compile it as a library (.DLL) file:

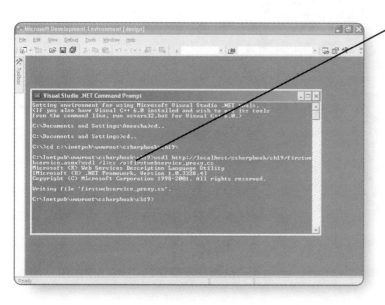

1. Type **WSDL** at the command prompt.

2. Type the URL to access the WSDL contract the Web service produces. Remember to type **?WSDL** after the .asmx file name.

3. Type **/l:cs** to set the language of the generated C# source code.

4. Type **/o:** followed by a file name for the source code. The file must have a .cs extension.

5. Press the Enter key. The Proxy class will be generated.

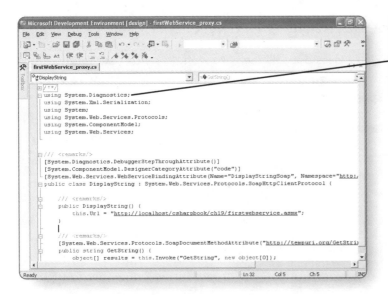

6. Create a bin directory within the virtual directory. You must place the compiled Proxy class in this folder.

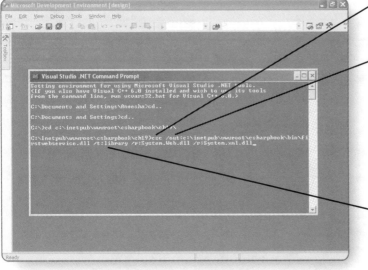

7. Type **CSC** at the command prompt.

8. Type **/out:** followed by the path and name of the generated DLL.

9. Type **/t:library** to compile the Proxy class to a library (that is, create a .DLL file).

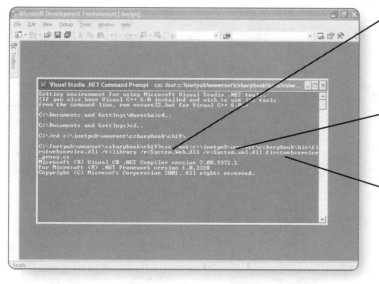

10. Type **/r:** followed by **System.Web.dll**. The Proxy class uses the System.Web.dll assembly.

11. Type **/r:** followed by **System.xml.dll**. The Proxy class uses the System.xml.dll assembly.

12. Type the name and path of the Proxy class generated by the WSDL tool.

13. Press the Enter key. The library will be created and saved in the /bin subfolder.

Consuming a Web Service

You can now access the methods exposed by the Web service as if the class were installed locally. Each method call, however, is accessing the Web service, but this occurs behind the scenes. You only need to create an object of the class and call the appropriate methods from your code. The data transfer that occurs is transparent:

1. Insert opening and closing <script> tags. Set the language attribute to C# and the runat attribute to server.

2. Insert a Page_Load method.

3. Create a DisplayString object. The class name of the Web service is DisplayString.

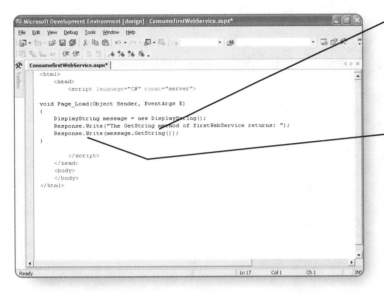

4. Call the GetString method of the DisplayString object. The method will execute on the server that offers the Web service and a value will return.

5. Use the Response.Write method to print the string that was returned by the GetString method to the page.

Creating a Calculator Web Service

Following is a slightly more advanced example of a Web service where you can pass parameters to callable methods. The Calculator class has methods that perform addition and subtraction. Both of the methods take two parameters:

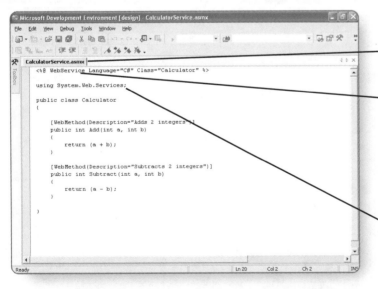

1. Create a new page and save it with an .asmx extension.

2. Insert a WebService directive as the first line in the .asmx file. Set the language attribute to C#. Set the class attribute to the name of the class contained in the file.

3. Import the System.Web. Services namespace. Use the using keyword to import a namespace.

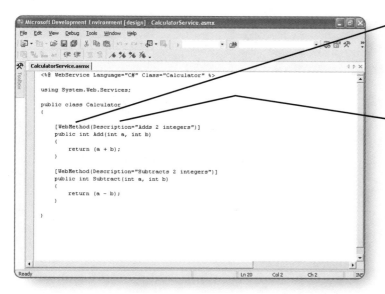

4. Insert a [WebMethod] directive above the Add method. This will make the method available through the Web service.

5. Enter a description for the Add method.

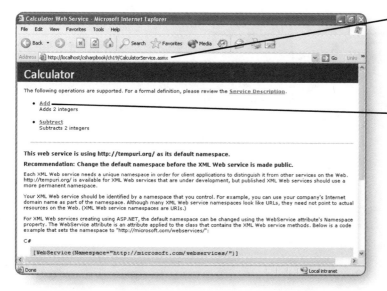

6. View the page in a Web browser. The Web service will be documented. You will see links to the exposed methods.

7. Click on the Add link. A test page for the add page will appear.

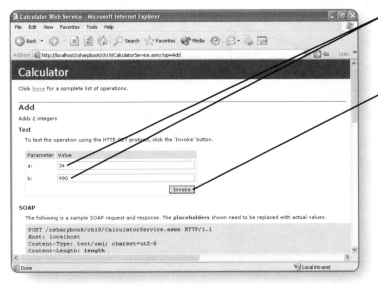

8. Enter the two numbers that you want to add in the text entry fields.

9. Click on Invoke. The Add method will execute and the sum of the two numbers will return in an XML format.

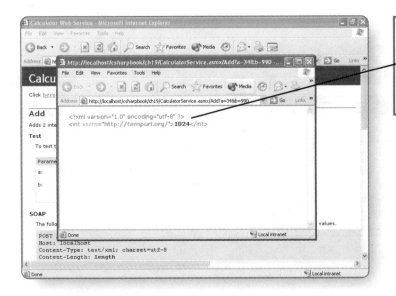

NOTE

The XML that gets returned contains the sum of the two numbers.

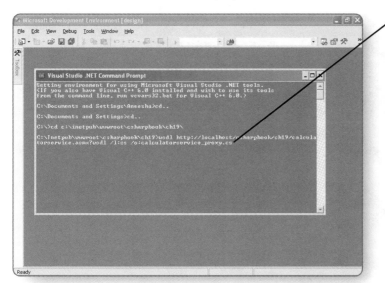

10. Use the WSDL tool to generate a Proxy class. The source code for the Proxy class will be generated.

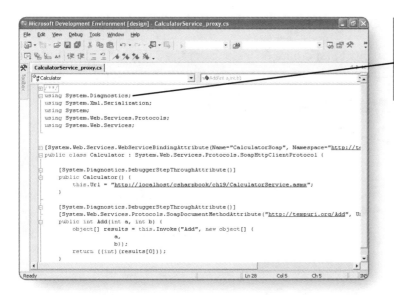

NOTE

Here is the source code for the Proxy class.

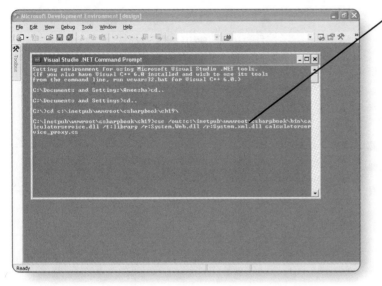

11. Compile the Proxy class into a library (a .DLL file).

Consuming the Calculator Web Service

You must first create an instance of the Calculator class before you can pass parameters to the Add and Subtract methods:

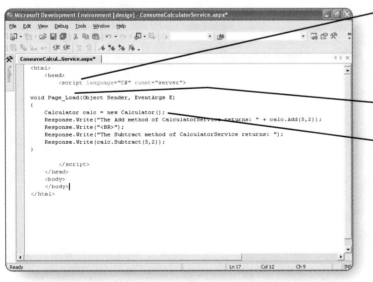

1. Insert opening and closing `<script>` tags. Set the language attribute to C# and the runat attribute to server.

2. Insert a Page_Load method.

3. Create a Calculator object. The class name of the Web service is Calculator.

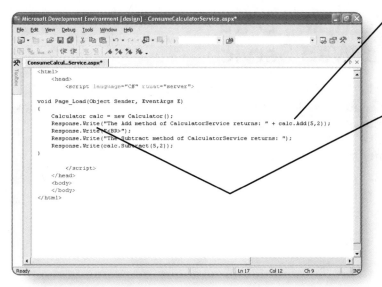

4. Call the Add method and pass two numbers as parameters. The method will execute and return the sum of the two numbers.

5. Use the Response.Write method to print the sum to the page.

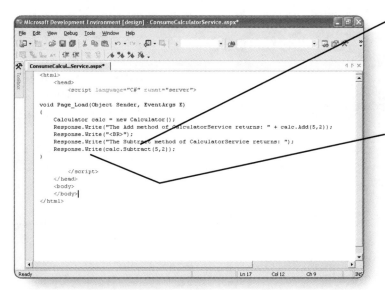

6. Call the Subtract method and pass two numbers as parameters. The method will execute and return the difference between the numbers.

7. Use the Response.Write method to print the difference to the page.

Returning Complex Data Types from a Web Service

Web services are not limited to primitive data types. Web services rely upon SOAP, which serializes complex data types into XML. You can transfer arrays, enumerations, structs, classes, and data sets to and from a Web service method.

The following sample method returns an array:

```
[WebMethod]
public int[] GetArray()
{
    int[] TestScores = new int[3];
    TestScores[0] = 5;
    TestScores[1] = 3;
    TestScores[3] = 1;
    return TestScores;
}
```

Discovering Web Services

You use a disco file to publish the URLs of the Web services you offer. A disco file is just an XML file that allows you to specify the .asmx pages which reside on your Web server. If you need to use a Web service, you have to view a default.disco file.

NOTE

Insert a new `<scl:contractRef>` tag for each Web service you offer and assign the path to each .asmx path to the `ref` attribute.

20

Caching Data

You can improve the performance and scalability of a Web application by caching the output of frequently accessed pages. There is no need to regenerate a page for each request if the content has not changed. Caching a page involves storing the generated content for a certain amount of time. Each subsequent request is then served from memory. With ASP.NET, you can easily implement practical caching solutions. The flexibility that ASP.NET brings to caching is not matched by any competing technology. In this chapter, you'll learn to:

- Cache the output of a dynamic page.
- Cache sections of a page.
- Cache objects.

Using the OutputCache Directive

The OutputCache mechanism caches all the content generated (that is, the whole page). Insert the OutputCache directive in all pages you want to cache. You must also specify the amount of time in seconds that the page should be cached. When the time period elapses, the cached version of the page is deleted. When a user makes a new request for the page, it is cached again:

1. Insert the OutputCache directive in the page to cache.

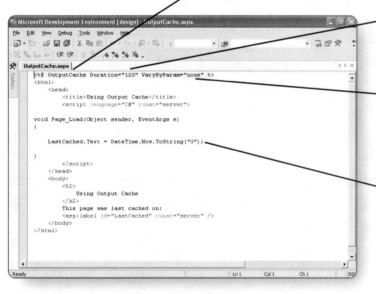

2. Specify the amount of time in seconds to store the cached version of the file.

3. Set the VaryByParam attribute to None. I explain the purpose of this attribute later in the chapter.

4. This simple page uses a label control to display the time the page gets stored.

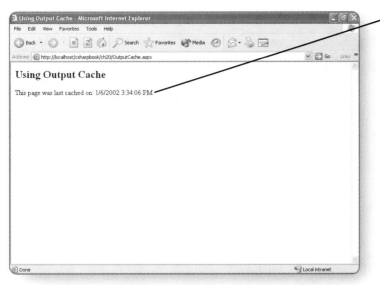

5. Preview the page in a Web browser. The time indicates when the page was generated dynamically.

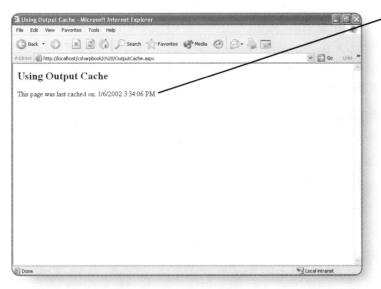

6. Reload the page. The time will not change because the page is retrieved from cache.

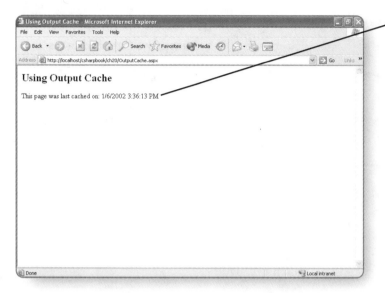

7. Reload the page after the specified timeframe has elapsed. The time will change because the file will be generated again, and a new version of the file will be stored in cache.

Caching the Data Retrieved from a Database

Although the previous example illustrated the use of the OutputCache directive, it was not a good example because it is highly unlikely you would cache a page that displays the current date and time. You should not cache data that is constantly updated. A page that delivers stock quotes should never be cached. The following example caches content retrieved from a database:

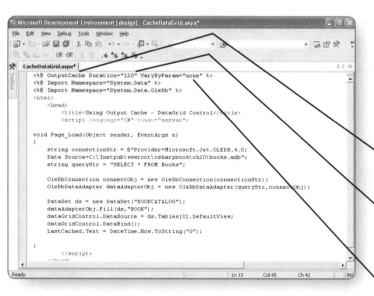

1. Insert the OutputCache directive in the page to cache.

2. Specify the amount of time in seconds to store the cached version of the file.

3. Set the VaryByParam attribute to None.

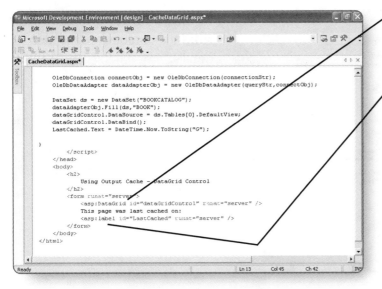

4. Insert a `DataGrid` control. Set the `id` attribute. Set the `runat` attribute to `server`.

5. Insert a `Label` control. The label will display the time the page is cached.

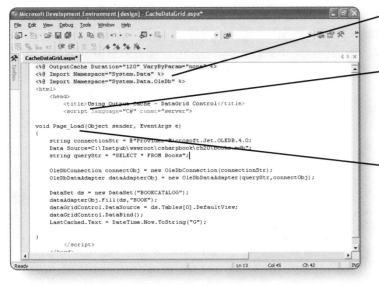

6. Import the `System.Data` and `System.Data.OleDB` namespaces.

7. Insert opening and closing `<script>` tags. Set the `language` attribute to `C#` and the `runat` attribute to `server`.

8. Insert a `Page_Load` method. This method will execute when the page loads.

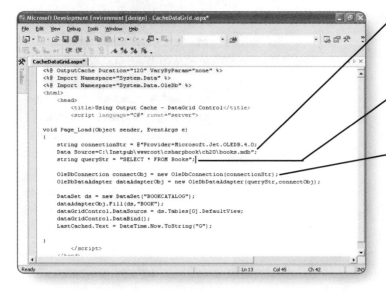

9. Declare a string variable and store the database connection details.

10. Declare a string variable and store the SQL query.

11. Create an instance of the `OleDbConnection` class. Pass the database connection string to the `OleDbConnection` constructor.

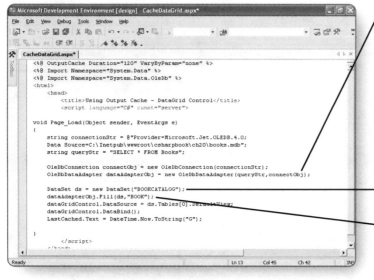

12. Create an instance of the `OleDbDataAdapter` class. Pass the SQL query and `OleDbConnection` object to the `OleDbDataAdapter` constructor.

13. Create a `DataSet` object.

14. Call the `Fill` method of the `OleDbDataAdapter` object to load each record that the query returns into the `DataSet` object.

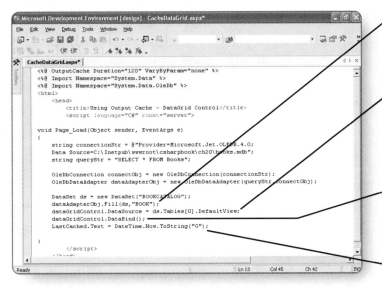

15. Pass the DataSet object as the first parameter to the Fill method.

16. Assign the DefaultView property of the DataSet object to the DataSource property of the DataGrid control.

17. Call the DataBind method of the DataGrid control. The data will be bound to the control.

18. Assign the current date and time to the label control.

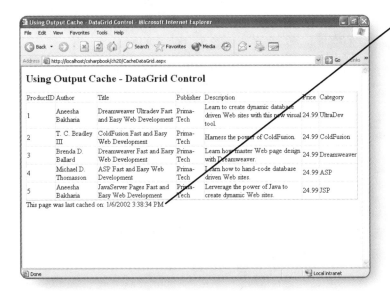

19. Preview the page in a Web browser. The time indicates when the page was generated dynamically.

NOTE

The DataGrid control displays the data in a tabular form.

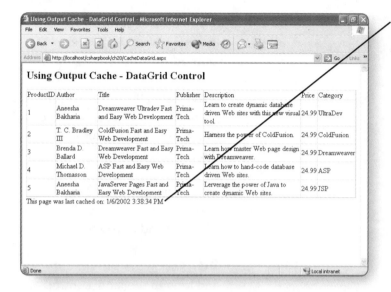

20. Reload the page. The time will not change because the page is retrieved from cache.

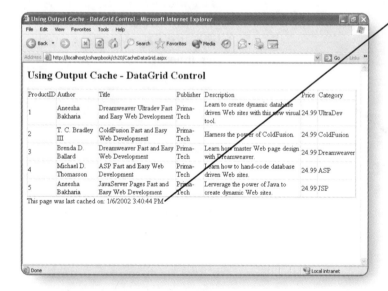

21. Reload the page after the specified time frame has elapsed. The time will change because the file will be generated again, and a new version of the file will be stored in cache.

Using the VaryByParam Attribute of the OutputCache Directive

The VaryByParam attribute of the OutputCache directive allows you to cache versions of a page based upon the name-value pairs contained within the query string. You can cache pages that use the query string to dynamically generate content. This is a powerful feature:

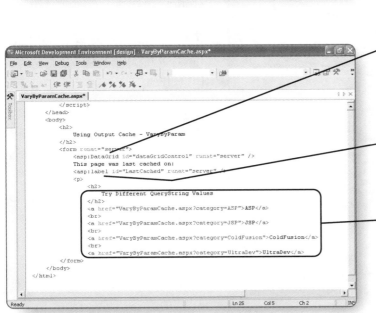

1. Insert the OutputCache directive in the page to cache.

2. Specify the amount of time in seconds to store the cached version of the file.

3. Set the VaryByParam attribute to the name of the value passed in the query string.

4. Insert a DataGrid control. Set the id attribute. Set the runat attribute to server. XML will be bound to this control.

5. Insert a Label control. The label will display the time the page is cached.

6. Insert links to the page that have different key-value pairs appended to the query string.

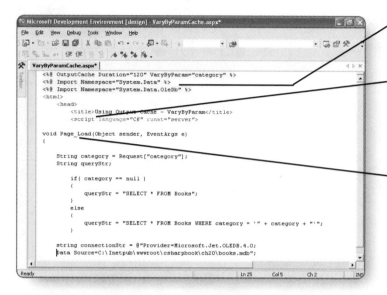

7. Import the System.Data and System.Data.OleDB namespaces.

8. Insert opening and closing <script> tags. Set the language attribute to C# and the runat attribute to server.

9. Insert a Page_Load method. This method will execute when the page loads.

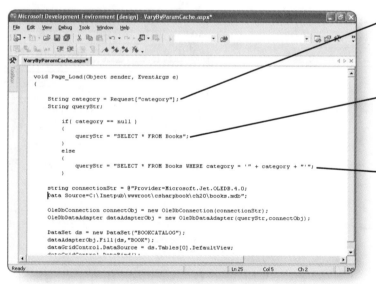

10. Use the Request object to retrieve the data from the query string.

11. Create a simple select query if no query string is present.

12. Include a where clause in the query if a key-value pair is present in the query string.

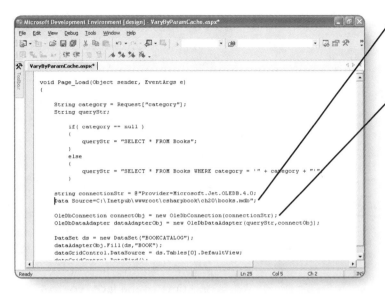

13. Declare a string variable and store the database connection details.

14. Create an instance of the `OleDbConnection` class. Pass the database connection string to the `OleDbConnection` constructor.

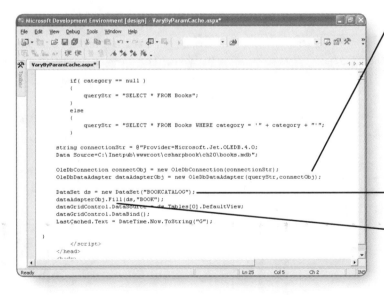

15. Create an instance of the `OleDbDataAdapter` class. Pass the SQL query and `OleDbConnection` object to the `OleDbDataAdapter` constructor.

16. Create a `DataSet` object.

17. Call the `Fill` method of the `OleDbDataAdapter` object to load each record that the query returns into the `DataSet` object.

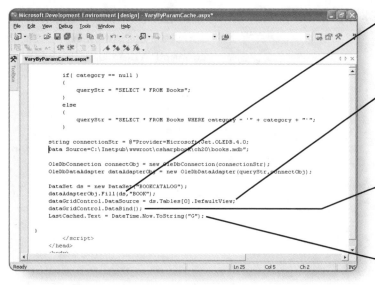

18. Pass the `DataSet` object as the first parameter to the `Fill` method.

19. Assign the `DefaultView` property of the `DataSet` object to the `DataSource` property of the `DataGrid` control.

20. Call the `DataBind` method of the `DataGrid` control. The data will be bound to the control.

21. Assign the current date and time to the label control.

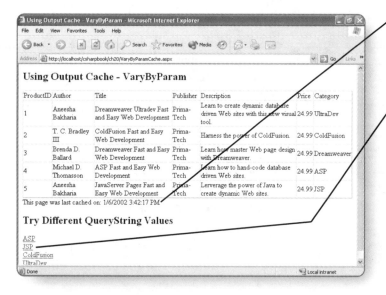

22. Preview the page in a Web browser. The time indicates when the page was generated dynamically.

23. Click on a link. A key-value pair will be appended to the query string. The new page will be cached.

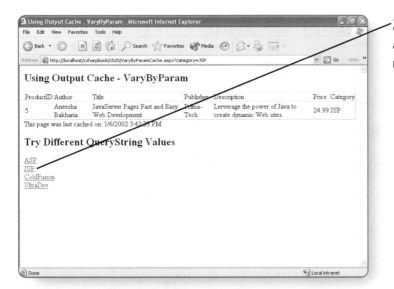

24. Click on the same link again. The page will be retrieved from cache.

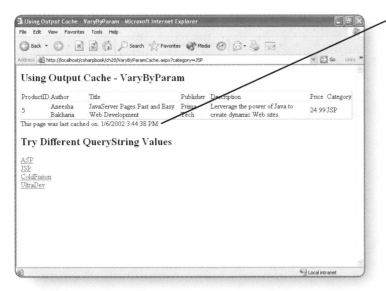

25. Reload the page after the specified timeframe has elapsed. The time will change because the file will be generated again, and a new version of the file will be stored in cache.

Using Fragment Caching

You can also cache sections of a page, a process known as fragment caching. You implement this feature by placing the OutputCache directive in a user control:

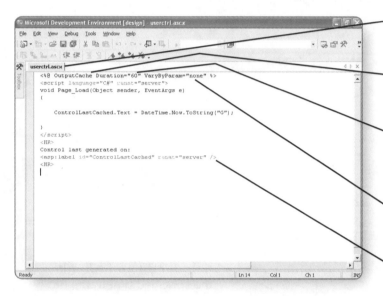

1. Create an .ascx page. This extension defines a user control.

2. Insert the OutputCache directive in the page to cache.

3. Specify the amount of time in seconds to store the cached version of the file.

4. Set the VaryByParam attribute to None.

5. Use a Label control to display the time the user control gets stored in cache.

6. Insert a Register directive in the page that will use the control.

7. Set the TagPrefix.

8. Set the TagName.

9. Assign the file that contains the user control to the src attribute.

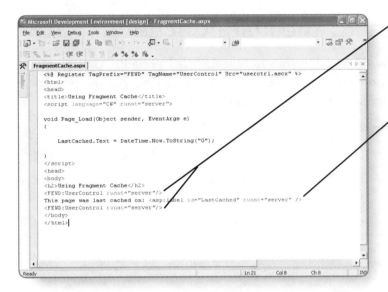

10. Insert the user control twice. You want to display the time the user control gets cached.

11. Display the time when the page is cached.

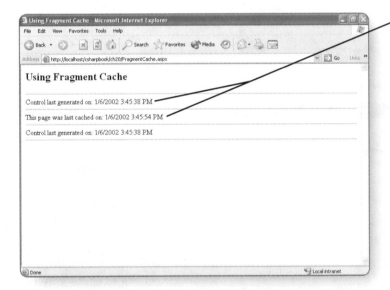

12. Preview the page in a Web browser. The page and the user control will get cached at different times.

NOTE

The time displayed will be the same for both places where the user control is inserted. The second user control is retrieved from cache.

CAUTION

You can't manipulate a cached control programmatically.

Using the Data Cache

The third caching model that ASP.NET provides, data caching, is perhaps the most powerful. Data caching lets you store in memory an object, such as a `DataSet`. Data caching is resource intensive, but objects are removed from cache when memory becomes scarce:

1. Insert a `DataGrid` control. Set the `id` attribute. Set the `runat` attribute to `server`.

2. Insert a `Label` control. The label will display the time the page is cached.

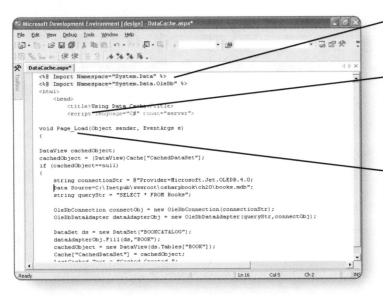

3. Import the `System.Data` and `System.Data.OleDB` namespaces.

4. Insert opening and closing `<script>` tags. Set the `language` attribute to `C#` and the `runat` attribute to `server`.

5. Insert a `Page_Load` method. This method will execute when the page loads.

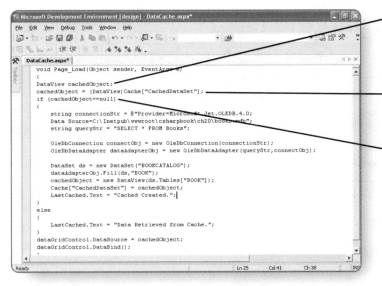

6. Create a `DataView` object. This object will hold the `DataSet` to cache.

7. Retrieve the `DataView` object from cache.

8. If the `DataView` object is empty (that is, it is not cached), retrieve the data from the data source. Follow steps 9 through 18.

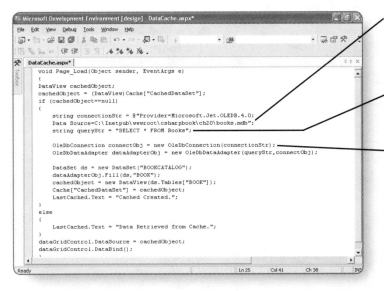

9. Declare a string variable and store the database connection details.

10. Declare a string variable and store the SQL query.

11. Create an instance of the `OleDbConnection` class. Pass the database connection string to the `OleDbConnection` constructor.

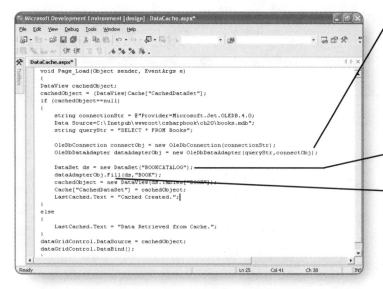

12. Create an instance of the `OleDbDataAdapter` class. Pass the SQL query and `OleDbConnection` object to the `OleDbDataAdapter` constructor.

13. Create a `DataSet` object.

14. Call the `Fill` method of the `OleDbDataAdapter` object to load each record that the query returns into the `DataSet` object.

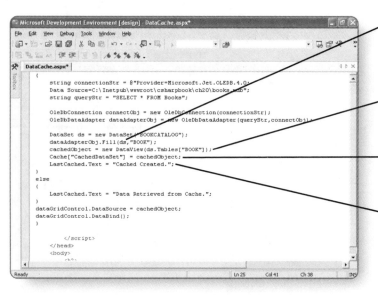

15. Pass the `DataSet` object as the first parameter to the `Fill` method.

16. Pass the `DataSet` table to the `DataView` constructor.

17. Store the `DataView` object in cache.

18. Inform the user that the data has been cached.

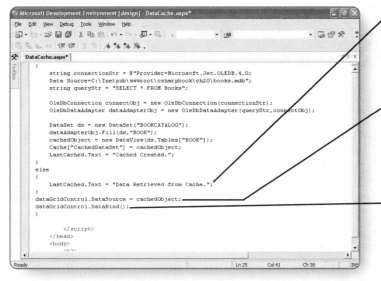

```
            {
            string connectionStr = @"Provider=Microsoft.Jet.OLEDB.4.0;
            Data Source=C:\Inetpub\wwwroot\csharpbook\ch20\books.mdb";
            string queryStr = "SELECT * FROM Books";

            OleDbConnection connectObj = new OleDbConnection(connectionStr);
            OleDbDataAdapter dataAdapterObj = new OleDbDataAdapter(queryStr,connectObj);

            DataSet ds = new DataSet("BOOKCATALOG");
            dataAdapterObj.Fill(ds,"BOOK");
            cachedObject = new DataView(ds.Tables["BOOK"]);
            Cache["CachedDataSet"] = cachedObject;
            LastCached.Text = "Cached Created.";
            }
            else
            {
            LastCached.Text = "Data Retrieved from Cache.";
            }
            dataGridControl.DataSource = cachedObject;
            dataGridControl.DataBind();
            }

                </script>
            </head>
            <body>
```

19. If the cached object already exists, inform the user that the data has been retrieved from cache.

20. Call the `DataBind` method of the `DataGrid` control. The data will be bound to the control.

21. Assign the `cachedObject` to the `DataSource` property of the `DataGrid` control.

Creating a Data Cache Dependency

What happens when a data source gets updated? The cached version won't reflect the changes unless you set a dependency. This means that you can remove an object from cache when the data source is updated. You use the `Cache.Insert` method to set a dependency. You also need to make a `CacheDependency` object for the data source. The data source can be an XML document or a database.

Modify the previous example to make the cached version expire when the database gets updated:

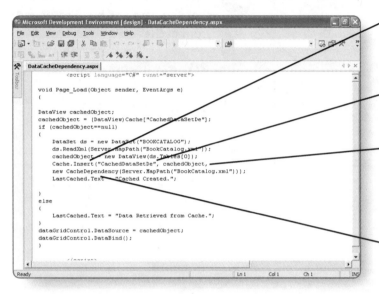

1. Call the `Cache.Insert` method to add the object to the cache.

2. Pass the name of the cached object as the first parameter.

3. Pass the object to cache as the second parameter. In this case, the object is a `DataView` object.

4. Pass the `CacheDependency` object as the third parameter. You must pass the database file or an XML document to the `CacheDependency` constructor.

NOTE

The cached version will be deleted when the database or XML file gets updated.

TIP

You can also delete an object from cache by calling the `Remove` method, as in `cache.Remove["cachedObject"]`.

21

Creating an Online Store

Stores that sell goods and services via the Web are everywhere. You can order anything from groceries to books just by visiting a few Web sites. This is convenient for the end user as well as the company that runs the store. As a Web developer, you might often be asked to build an online store. C# in many respects is the perfect language to use for building scalable and robust ecommerce applications. In this chapter, you'll learn to:

- Build a product catalog.
- Build a shopping cart.
- Display the contents of a shopping cart.

The GrocerToGo Quickstart Application

Microsoft has already written a simple yet well-designed online store. This application uses the DataList control to create an intuitive interface. Instead of reinventing the wheel, I am going to analyze this application in terms of user interface, database design, and code structure. Let's first take a look at how a shopper would use the application to purchase a few products:

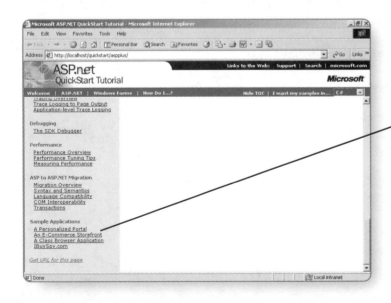

1. Open the ASP.NET Quickstart Web site. Enter **http://localhost/quickstart/aspplus** as the URL. If your server is not called localhost, please substitute localhost with the name of your computer/server.

2. Scroll to the bottom of the page. A list of sample applications will appear.

3. Click on An E-Commerce Storefront. A description of the application will appear.

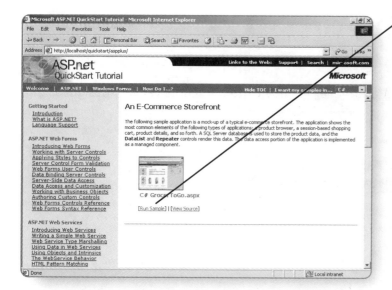

4. Click on Run Sample. The GrocerToGo application will open in a new browser window.

NOTE

The Milk category will display by default. Information about the first product in the category automatically appears. The Add To Cart button applies to the currently selected product. The contents of the shopping cart appear in the right pane. The cart is initially empty.

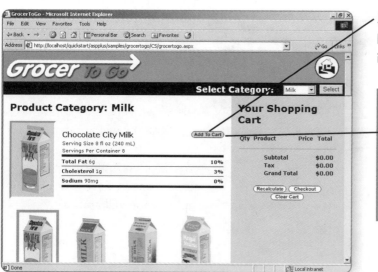

5. Click on the Add To Cart button. The product will appear in the shopping-cart pane.

NOTE

The product details appear in the right pane. The quantity, amount, and sales tax are also calculated.

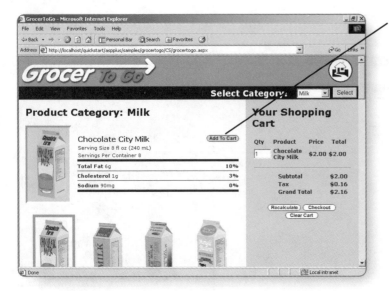

6. Click on the Add To Cart button again. The product quantity will increase.

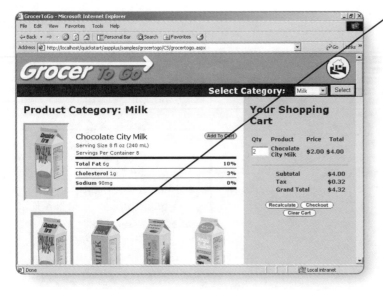

7. Click on the picture of another product. The product will be selected. More details about the product will appear.

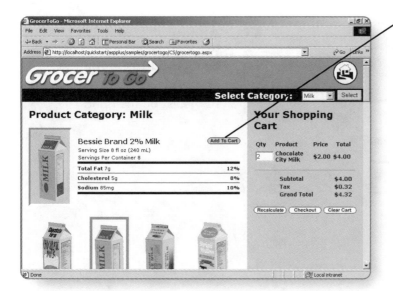

8. Click on the Add To Cart button. The product will appear in the shopping-cart pane.

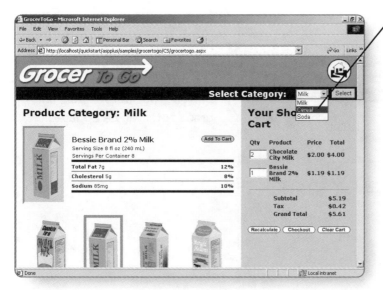

9. Select a new category from the drop-down list. The products within this category will appear.

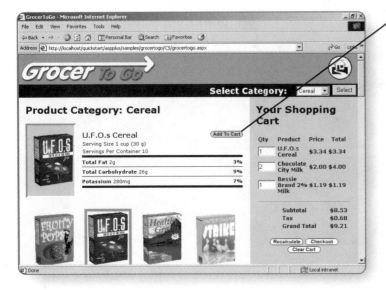

10. Add more products to the shopping cart by clicking on the Add To Cart button. The products will be added to the list on the right.

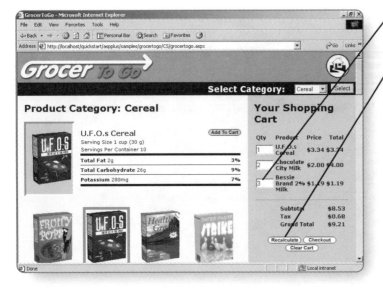

11. Change the quantity of a product.

12. Click the Recalculate button. The subtotal, tax, and grand total will be updated.

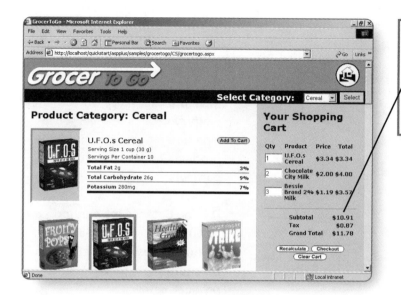

NOTE

The total cost of a product is the product's single-quantity price multiplied by the quantity.

The Market Namespace

The Market namespace is in the Market.cs file. The InventoryDB, OrderItem, and OrderList classes appear within the Market namespace. The InventoryDB class has three methods that query the GrocerToGo database and return either a DataTable or DataRow object. The OrderItem class models a product, but the OrderList class models the entire shopping cart, which contains multiple OrderItem objects:

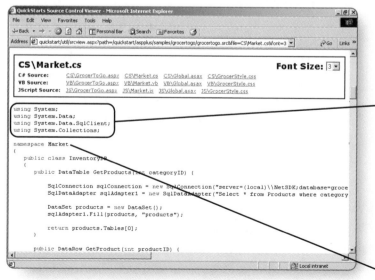

1. The code imports the System, System.Data, System.SqlClient, and System.Collections namespaces. You need the System.SqlClient namespace because you are using an SQL Server database.

2. All classes appear in the Market namespace.

3. The `InventoryDB` class has methods that query and return data to the GrocerToGo database.

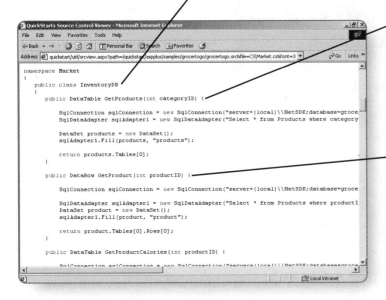

4. The `GetProducts` method returns a `DataTable` object. The method takes a `categoryID` as a parameter and returns all the products that belong to a particular category.

5. The `GetProduct` method returns a `DataRow` object. The method takes a `productID` as a parameter and returns the product details.

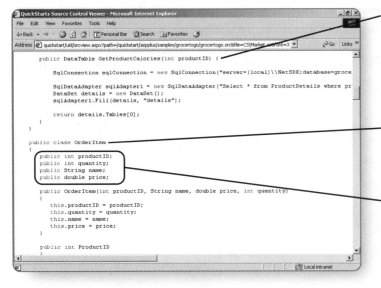

6. The `GetProductCalories` method returns a `DataTable` object. The method takes the `productID` as a parameter and returns calorie details.

7. The `OrderItem` class models a product. The `OrderItem` object gets stored in the shopping cart.

8. The `productID`, `quantity`, `name`, and `price` properties model a product.

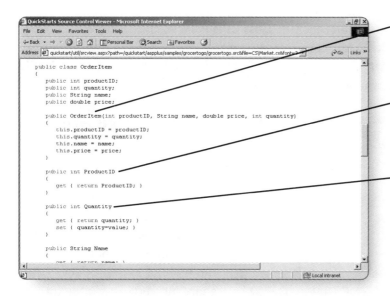

9. The `OrderItem` constructor creates an `OrderItem` object and sets the properties.

10. The `ProductID` property is read-only because it has only a `get` accessor method.

11. The `Quantity` property can be both read from and written to because it has `get` and `set` accessor methods.

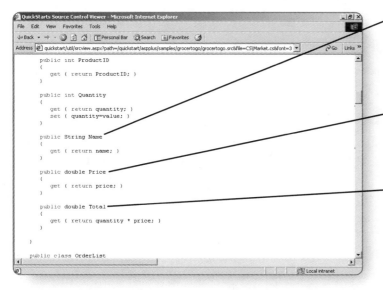

12. The `Name` property is revealed in a read-only method because it has only a `get` accessor method.

13. The `Price` property is read-only because it has only a `get` accessor method.

14. The `Total` property is read-only because it has only a `get` accessor method.

15. The `OrderList` class uses a `Hashtable` to store each item in the shopping cart. A `Hashtable` provides the data structure for the storage of `OrderItem` objects. Each `OrderItem` object is a product in the shopping cart.

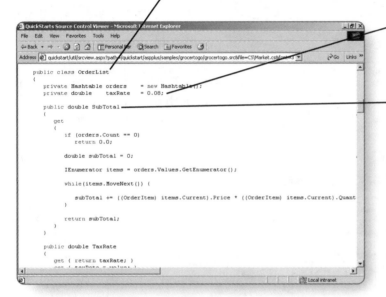

16. The `taxRate` is set to 8 percent. You can adjust this as required.

17. The `SubTotal` property is read-only. It has only a `get` accessor method. Code within the `get` accessor method adds the price of each product in the shopping cart. The `Price` for each item must be multiplied by the amount of products ordered (the quantity).

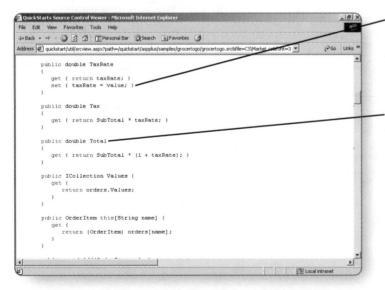

18. The `taxRate` property can be both read from and written to because it has `get` and `set` accessor methods.

19. The `Total` property returns the total cost, including tax.

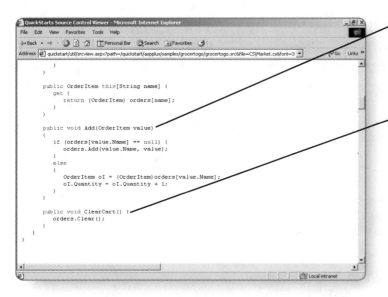

20. The Add method adds an item to the shopping cart. If the item is already in the cart, its quantity gets increased by 1.

21. The ClearCart method deletes the contents of a shopping cart.

The Global.asax File

The Global.asax file creates an OrderList object when a user session begins:

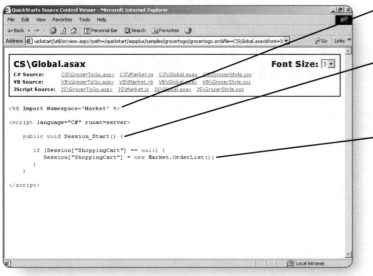

1. The code imports the Market namespace.

2. The Session_Start method will be invoked when a user session begins.

3. If the ShoppingCart session variable is empty, the code assigns an OrderList object to it.

The GrocerStyle.css File

The GrocerStyle.css style sheet defines the colors and fonts used by the GrocerToGo application. This provides a central location where you can change the format of the application.

The GrocerToGo.aspx Page

The GrocerToGo.aspx file displays the product and the contents of the shopping cart. The code that adds and removes items from the cart appears within a script declaration block. Users can also change the category that is displayed:

- The shopper uses a drop-down list to select a category.

- A `DataList` control displays the shopping cart contents.

- A `Repeater` control displays the product details.

- A `DataList` control displays the products in the currently selected category.

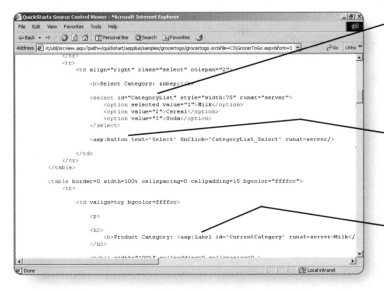

1. The `CategoryList` drop-down list displays the available product categories. This list is hard-coded, but you could easily extract a list from a database.

2. The user must click a button after selecting a new category. The `CategoryList_Select` method will execute.

3. The `CurrentCategory` label displays the currently selected product category.

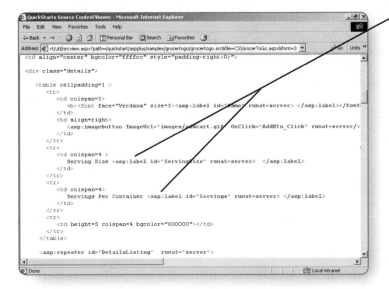

4. `Label` controls display the product details.

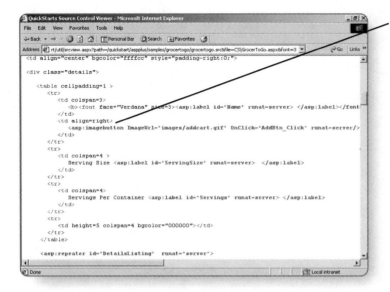

5. An `ImageButton` control executes the `AddBtn_Click` method. This method adds the product to the shopping cart.

6. The `DetailsListing` repeater control displays the calories details for a product.

7. The `DataBinderEval` method displays the `Name`, `Grams`, and `Percent` fields.

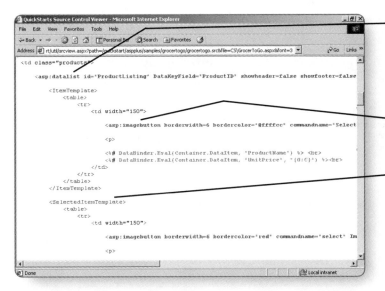

8. The ProductListing datalist control displays all of the products in the currently selected category.

9. An image displays for each item in the category.

10. A separate template specifies the item that is selected.

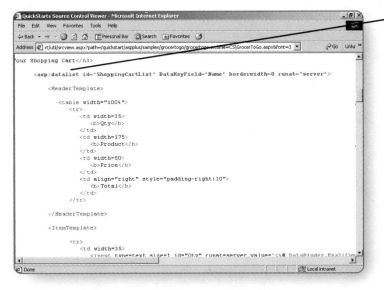

11. The ShoppingCartList datalist control displays all of the products in the shopping cart.

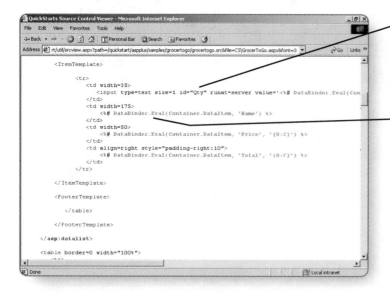

12. The product quantity displays in an editable input box. The user can change the quantity of a product.

13. The `DataBinderEval` method displays the `Name`, `Price`, and `Total`.

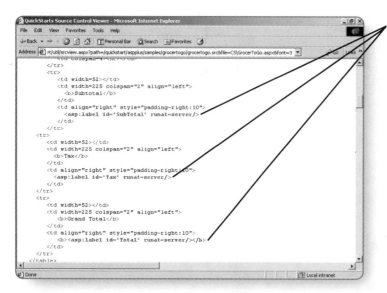

14. `Label` controls display the `SubTotal`, `Tax`, and `Total` value of all the products in the shopping cart.

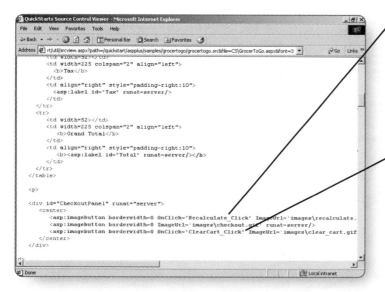

15. An imagebutton control executes the Recalculate_Click method. This method will update the price of a product when the quantity of a product changes.

16. An imagebutton also executes the ClearCart_Click method, which removes all of the items from the shopping cart.

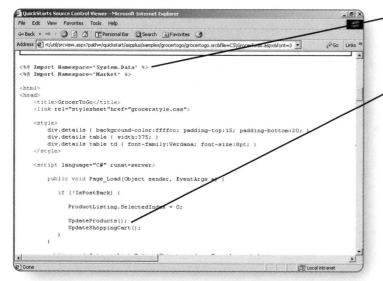

17. The code imports the System.Data and the Market namespaces.

18. The first time the page gets loaded, the UpdateProducts and UpdateShoppingCart methods are invoked.

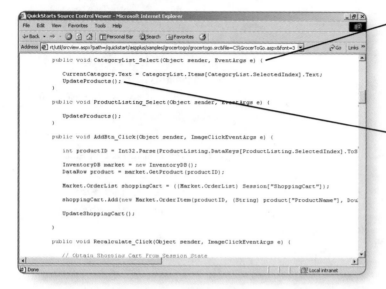

19. The `CategoryList_Select` executes when a category changes. The `CurrentCategory` label displays the name of the category.

20. The `UpdateProducts` method displays the products in the currently selected category.

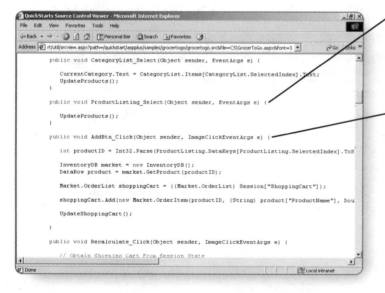

21. The `ProductListing_Select` method simply calls the `UpdateProducts` method.

22. The `AddBtn_Click` method adds a product to the shopping cart. If the product already exists, its quantity gets increased.

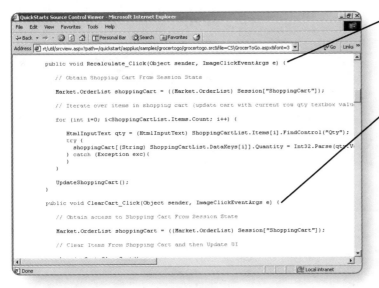

23. The `Recalculate_Click` method calculates the price for a product when the quantity changes.

24. The `ClearCart_Click` method removes all products from the shopping cart.

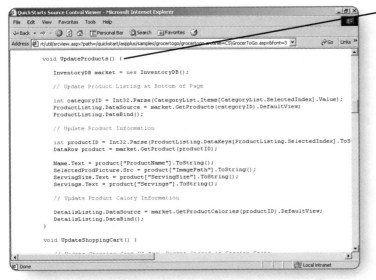

25. The `UpdateProducts` method creates an `InventoryDB` object. The `GetProducts` method returns all the products in a category. The returned data is bound to the `ProductListing` control.

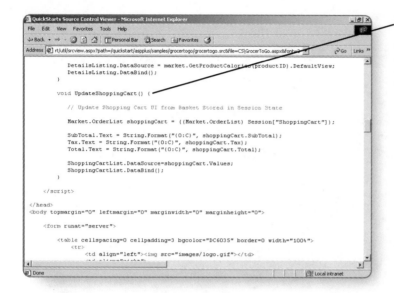

26. The `UpdateShoppingCart` method updates the `SubTotal`, `Tax`, and `Total` for the shopping cart.

ASP.NET
WebForms
Quick Reference

A detailed reference for Web Server controls can be found at
**http://msdn.microsoft.com/library/default.asp?url=/library/
en-us/cpgenref/html/cpconaspsyntaxforwebcontrols.asp**.

To Insert This Control	Use This Tag
TextBox	`<asp:Textbox id="Name" MaxLength="20" Columns="10" runat="server" />`
Password TextBox	`<asp:Textbox id="Password" TextMode ="Password" runat="server" />`
Multiline TextBox	`<asp:Textbox id="Address" TextMode ="Multiline" runat="server" />`
Label	`<asp:Label id="LabelName" runat="server" />`
Checkbox	`<asp:CheckBox id="CheckboxName" Text ="Option" Checked="True|False" runat="server" />`
RadioButton	`<asp:RadioButton d="RadioButtonName" GroupName = "GroupName" Text ="Option" Checked="True|False" runat="server" />`

ListBox	`<asp:ListBox id="ListBoxName" runat="server">`
	`        <asp:ListItem id="ItemName1" />`
	`            <asp:ListItem id="ItemName2"  Selected="True|False">`
	`</asp:ListBox>`

DropDownList Image	`<asp:Image ImageURL="Http://www.yourserver.com/image.gif" AlterNate="Text description" runat="server"/>`
Panel	`<asp:Panel id="PanelName" runat="server" />`

Table	`<asp:Table id="TableName" runat="server">`
	`        <asp:TableRow>`
	`                <asp:TableCell>Row 1 Cell 1</ASP:TableCell>`
	`                <asp:TableCell>Row 1 Cell 2</ASP:TableCell>`
	`        </asp:TableRow>`
	`        <asp:TableRow>`
	`                <asp:TableCell>Row 2 Cell 1</ASP:TableCell>`
	`                <asp:TableCell>Row 2 Cell 2</ASP:TableCell>`
	`        </asp:TableRow>`
	`</asp:Table>`

Button	`<asp:Button Text="ButtonLabel" onClick"MethodName" runat="server" />`
LinkButton	`<asp:LinkButton Text="LinkText" onClick"MethodName" runat="server" />`
ImageButton	`<asp:ImageButton ImageURL="http://www.yourserver.com/image.gif" onClick"MethodName" />`
Hyperlink	`<asp:ImageButton NavigateURL="http://www.yourserver.com/page.aspx" Text="LinkText" />`

B

C# Quick Reference

This appendix provides a syntax summary for the C# programming constructs that were introduced throughout this book. I illustrate simple tasks in C# with practical and easy-to-follow examples. I also include a full list of C# reserved words.

C# Reserved Words

Reserved words are keywords used in C# programming constructs. They are defined as part of the language and must be used in a particular manner. You can't use reserved words to name variables, methods, or classes.

abstract	for	sbyte
as	foreach	sealed
base	get	set
bool	goto	short
break	if	sizeof
byte	implicit	stackalloc
case	in	static
catch	int	string
char	interface	struct
checked	internal	switch
class	is	this
const	lock	throw
continue	long	true
decimal	namespace	try
default	new	typeof
delegate	null	uint
do	object	ulong
double	operator	unchecked
else	out	unsafe
enum	override	ushort
event	params	using
explicit	private	value
extern	protected	virtual
false	public	void
finally	readonly	while
fixed	ref	
float	return	

Common C# Programming Tasks

Table B.1 lists common programming tasks in C#.

Table B.1 Programming in C#

To	Do This

Declare a `string` variable.
Declare an `integer` variable.
Create an `if...elseif` statement.
	```string name="Celine";```
	```int Age=3;```
	```if(condition)```
	```{```
	``` // Execute this code```
	```}```
	```else if (condition)```
	```{```
	``` // Execute this code```
	```}```
	```else```
	```{```
	``` // Execute if no other conditions are met```
	```}```

Create a `for` loop.	```for(i=0;i<maxloopvalue;i++)```
	```{```
	``` // Insert code that must be executed```
	``` // until MaxLoopValue is met```
	```}```

Create a `while` loop.	```while (condition)```
	```{```
	``` // Insert code that must be```
	``` // executed repeatedly until the condition```
	``` is met```
	```}```

Mathematical Operators

Addition	+
Subtraction	-
Multiplication	*
Division	/
Division remainder	%

Relational Operators

Less than	<
Greater than	>
Less than or equal to	<=
Greater than or equal to	>=
Type equality	is
Equal to	==
Not equal to	!=

Boolean Operators

And	&&
Or	||
Not	!

C# and ASP.NET Resources

Reaching the end of this book is really the start of your adventure as a C# programmer. You need to continually update and enhance your knowledge of C#. This appendix contains a list of Web sites that offer up-to-date C#, ASP.NET, and ADO.NET information.

C#

These Web sites focus on C# and .NET related technologies:

C# Corner	**http://www.c-sharpcorner.com/**
C# Today	**http://www.csharptoday.com/**
Bipin Joshi	**http://www.bipinjoshi.com/**
C# Help	**http://www.csharphelp.com**
C# Index	**http://www.csharpindex.com**
C# Station	**http://www.csharp-station.com**

ASP.NET

Here are some popular ASP.NET articles and tutorial Web sites that you should regularly visit:

ASP.NET	**http://www.asp.net/**
GotDotNet	**http://www.gotdotnet.com**
123ASPX	**http://www.123aspx.com/**
.NET Extreme	**http://www.dotnetextreme.com/**
411 ASP.NET	**http://www.411asp.net/**
4 Guys from Rolla	**http://www.4guysfromrolla.com/webtech/LearnMore/ASPPlus.asp**
ASP Free	**http://aspfree.com/aspnet/Default.aspx**
ASP Next Generation	**http://www.ASPNG.com**
Dot Net 101	**http://www.dotnet101.com/**

ADO.NET

The following Web sites have a strong focus on database access:

DotNetJunkies	**http://www.dotnetjunkies.com/**
ADO Guy	**http://www.adoguy.com/net.aspx**

What's on the Web Site

The companion Web site for this book can be found at **http://www.premierpressbooks.com/downloads.asp**.

The Web site contains the following:

- Source code for all examples in the book

- Links to server controls: SoftwareArtisans Pop 3 and TreeView

- Links to C# and ASP.NET Web sites

- Links to C# and ASP.NET Editors: SharpDevelop, ASPEdit 2001, and Antechinus C# Editor

- A bonus tutorial for generating graphics in ASP.NET

Index